The Problem of Evil
Selected Readings

EDITED BY

Michael L. Peterson

ad hominem = appealing
to feelings / prejudices
rather than
intellect

epistemic = relating to
or involving knowledge

theodicy: defense
of God's goodness
+ omnipotence in
view of existence
of evil

omnipotent = having
unlimited power

a posteriori = relating
to what can be known
by observation

ontological =

University of Notre Dame Press
Notre Dame, Indiana

Manufactured in the United States of America

Reprinted in 1994, 1996, 2003, 2005, 2006, 2009

Library of Congress Cataloging-in-Publication Data

The Problem of evil : selected readings / edited by Michael L.
Peterson.
    p.   cm.—(Library of religious philosophy : v. 8)
    Includes bibliographical references.
    ISBN 0-268-01514-7 (cloth)
    ISBN 13: 978-0-268-01515-2 (pbk.)
    ISBN 10: 0-268-01515-5 (pbk.)
    1. Good and evil.   I. Peterson, Michael L., 1950– .
II. Series.
BJ1401.P77   1992
231'.8—dc20   91-50576
                                                 CIP

∞ *This book is printed on acid-free paper.*

For Edward H. Madden,
TEACHER AND FRIEND

Contents

Preface

This book is designed as an introduction to the problem of evil as it has occurred for Western theistic traditions generally and the Christian tradition specifically. As all significant intellectual problems, the problem of evil has a development and a structure. The problem evolves through myriad arguments and debates, moves and counter-moves, on a variety of important points. Philosophers and theologians sometimes agree on what points are relatively settled and what ones need further consideration, thus giving shape to the continuing discussion. I have tried to present the selected readings in a way that clearly exhibits the main contours of the overall problem and the outlines of the ongoing controversy.

My hope is that this anthology is helpful to serious, thoughtful readers who are interested in the study of the issues surrounding God and evil. In order to enhance the value of the book as a text, or even as a resource for more advanced scholarly work, I have included a comprehensive introduction, which leads the reader into the dynamics of the problem, and an extensive bibliography, which offers a listing of relevant scholarly literature.

I am grateful to Thomas Morris, General Editor of the Library of Religious Philosophy series, for perceptive comments on the formation of this text. I cannot adequately express my gratitude to Edward Madden, teacher and friend, for his deep insights into the problem of evil. Over many years, I have enjoyed and profited from our philosophical conversations on this perennial problem. Though it is too small a token of my appreciation, I dedicate this book to him.

Introduction

THE PROBLEM OF EVIL

The problem of evil is a serious and enduring challenge to religious faith; it strikes at the heart of traditional belief in God. Many thoughtful people contend that evil makes theistic belief in an omnipotent, omniscient, and perfectly good God problematic in the extreme. According to theologian Hans Küng, the problem is so severe that it has become "the rock of atheism." Through the centuries, many great thinkers have wrestled with this intellectual difficulty which arises equally for the three major theistic religions—Judaism, Christianity, and Islam.

Many Anglo-American philosophers have discussed the problem of evil in terms of the core of beliefs common to all these major theistic religious traditions. However, some have discussed it in terms of more specifically Christian beliefs as well, thus allowing doctrinal concepts of creation, sin, grace, incarnation, redemption, afterlife, and so forth to add color and texture to their treatments of the problem. This expanded set of beliefs has provided a larger and perhaps more interesting target for critics. Of course, if critics can show that general theistic belief is somehow rationally unacceptable, then they thereby will have shown that specifically Christian theistic belief is rationally unacceptable.

To be sure, the problem of evil may also be discussed in terms of the other theistic religious traditions of Judaism and Islam. In such discussions, specifically Jewish and Islamic doctrines—beyond basic theistic commitments—would enter the dialectical situation between religious believer and critic. While it is certainly legitimate to consider the problem of evil in light of specific doctrinal commitments, such commitments are themselves subject to philosophical debate on other grounds. Thus, certain religious doctrines may augment one's response to the problem of evil beyond that which is available on generally theistic terms, but at the same time make the whole controversy more complex.

1

Close examination reveals that the problem of evil is really not just one problem but a cluster of interrelated arguments and issues. The interplay of these arguments and issues gives the ongoing debate over evil a certain structure and flow. The readings included here are arranged in a manner which exhibits some of the main contours of the continuing discussion of the problem. Thus, this book provides an overview of the vast and complex literature on the problem of evil as it has been raised against both general theism and Christian theism.

CLASSIC STATEMENTS OF THE PROBLEM

Readings in the first section, drawn from both traditional and modern writers, are representative of a number of classic treatments of the problem. They have come to be considered masterpieces in their own right. From the lament of the ancient patriarch, Job, to Albert Camus's disturbing tale about a bubonic plague epidemic in the French town of Oran, we see the horrors of natural evil. Each piece raises in its own way the question of how the God of theism—a being who is thought to be omnipotent, omniscient, and perfectly good—could allow undeserved physical suffering. Then, in the exchange between Ivan and Alyosha Karamozov given to us by Fyodor Dostoevsky, and in the chilling account of the Holocaust by Elie Wiesel, we sense the terrible and haunting human capacity for moral evil. These two pieces accent the troubling question of why God, if he exists, allows human beings to be so inhuman to each other.

Philosophers who attempt to think logically and systematically are particularly skillful at clarifying the logic of important issues. Thus we include traditional statements from two famous philosophers. The Angelic Doctor, Thomas Aquinas, argues that all evil is the result of essentially good creatures gone wrong. David Hume, eloquent skeptical philosopher of the eighteenth century, begins with a catalogue of quite terrible physical maladies and concludes that such evils pose an almost insurmountable obstacle for theistic belief.

Many other works could be cited to do justice to the very large body of classic philosophic statements of the problem in Western theistic thought. These additional statements might include Leibniz's case that this is the best of all possible worlds, Kant's attack on theodicy, and Mill's rejection of a higher divine morality. Of course, outside the pale of professional philosophy, past and present, many profound expressions of the theistic problem of evil occur in the great literature of the Western world. Among the literary works that could be added to the pieces included in this anthology are Milton's *Paradise Lost,* Voltaire's "Poem on the Lisbon Earthquake," Blake's "The Tiger," and even Mark Twain's *Huckleberry Finn.* Such works manifest persistent attempts on the part of morally sensitive writers to come to grips with evil in human experience. In a sense, the vast body of literary treatments of the problem forms one common basis for the more technical discussions among professional philosophers.

VERSIONS OF THE PROBLEM OF EVIL

The second section of this anthology presents several somewhat technical discussions revolving around the very nature of the problem of evil. Important differences among philosophers over the problem's precise structure and strategy lead to distinctions among its different formulations. Perhaps the broadest division is between what we may call the theoretical and existential dimensions of the problem. In its theoretical dimension, the problem of evil concerns the logical and epistemic relations which hold among certain propositions about God and evil. In its existential dimension, the problem of evil pertains not simply to the abstract analysis of propositions but to one's subjective experience, including a total sense of life or conscious attitude toward God. A large proportion of the literature on the nature of the problem can be classified helpfully by using this broad taxonomy.

The theoretical dimension of the problem of evil may itself be divided into logical and evidential versions—two important versions which must now be defined in some detail. The logical version of the problem (also called the *a priori* problem and the deductive problem) arises on the basis of an alleged inconsistency between certain claims about God and certain claims about evil. There are actually different renditions of the logical problem of evil, depending on exactly which propositions about God and evil are selected. The variant that has received most attention states that there is an inconsistency between the proposition that an omnipotent, omniscient, and wholly good God exists and the proposition that evil exists. Critics of theism—such as J. L. Mackie, H. J. McCloskey, and Richard LaCroix— have declared that this rendition of the logical argument from evil successfully reveals a fatal inconsistency in traditional theistic beliefs.

There are other presentations of the logical version of the problem of evil which are less widely discussed. A second rendition asks whether the existence of particular kinds, amounts, and distributions of evil—as opposed to the sheer existence of evil—are logically compatible with the existence of God. A third and somewhat rare rendition of the logical problem concerns itself with the question of whether the existence of God is logically compatible with the existence of pointless or gratuitous evil.

In discussions of all versions of the logical argument from evil, the alleged inconsistency is typically implicit and not explicit. That is, the purported contradiction does not arise just on the basis of the initial theistic propositions about God and evil, but only when some additional propositions are introduced. The nontheist, then, must specify these supplementary propositions in order to make the inconsistency explicit. Nontheists typically propose supplementary propositions which define key concepts, such as how a morally good being would act toward evil. Plantinga has stipulated conditions which these additional propositions must meet: "to make good his claim the atheologian must provide some proposition which is either necessarily true, essential to theism, or a logical consequence of such propositions." It appears that, on the whole, theists have been very successful in pointing out that critics fail to meet these conditions. Indeed it appears that critics typically commit one or both of two fallacies: either begging the question by designating propositions to which theists are not committed, or lifting out of context propositions to which theists are committed but imputing new and unacceptable meanings to them.

In a famous exchange of views included in this volume, Mackie and Plantinga focus on the first version of the logical problem. Mackie contends that theistic beliefs can be plainly shown to be inconsistent. He analyzes many attempts to remove the alleged inconsistency which he considers inadequate: that evil is a necessary counterpart or contrast to good, that evil is a necessary means to good, that the universe is better with some evil than with no evil in it, and that evil is due to human free will. He argues that, in a great many cases, theists who offer such solutions frequently misunderstand the logic of the concept of omnipotence. According to Mackie, it is not possible both that God is omnipotent and that he was unable to create a universe containing moral good but no moral evil.

Plantinga's free will defense is aimed precisely at refuting Mackie's basic claim. After explaining certain technical points of logic, he develops a brief scenario of human freedom in relation to divine omnipotence: God creates a universe which contains free creatures who sometimes choose good and sometimes evil. He argues that God cannot control the actions of significantly free human beings and thus that, contrary to Mackie, it is indeed possible both that God is omnipotent and that it was not within his power to create a universe containing moral good without creating one containing moral evil. This is the heart of his reply.

The evidential version of the problem (also called the *a posteriori* problem, the inductive problem, and the empirical problem) is a theoretical difficulty concerning whether theism is plausible given the facts of evil. Thus certain propositions about evil in the world are taken to function as evidence against theism; these propositions are said to make theism unlikely or improbable. Several permutations of the evidential problem have appeared in the literature. Like the renditions of the logical problem, variants of the evidential problem may be distinguished in terms of which facts of evil they take as putative evidence against theistic belief: the existence of any evil whatsoever; the existence of particular kinds, amounts, and distributions of evil; or the existence of pointless evil. Further distinctions among the different renditions of the evidential problem can be made according to how the evidential relation between propositions about evil and propositions about God is conceived.

Some writers who discuss the evidential problem have understood the concepts of evidence and probability at work here in quasi-scientific or formalistic ways. George Schlesinger has argued that we can indeed talk about the confirmation or disconfirmation of theism in exactly the same way that we can talk about the confirmation or disconfirmation of scientific hypotheses, and thus seems to align himself with this kind of thinking. In his conception of the evidential problem, Wesley Salmon employed a frequentist theory of probability. Plantinga has responded to Salmon's frequentist argument from evil and to all probabilistic arguments from evil which rest upon personalistic and logical theories of probability as well, and has shown how no such approaches succeed. In particular, Plantinga has provided a lengthy and sophisticated argument to show that none of the extant interpretations of probability provides sufficient resources for mounting a coherent and plausible objection to theism that is based on evil. That is, he destroys support for the claim that the probability of God's existence, given the evidence of evil, is low. Of course, some of the difficulties which surface in attempted probabilistic arguments from evil simply reflect inherent troubles in probability theory studies in general.

In contrast to those who conceive of the evidential relation as either quasi-scientific or probabilistic, Edward Madden and Peter Hare have argued that the evidential problem is best construed in another broadly inductive way. They explicitly indicate that they are not raising the problem of the sheer consistency or coherence of theism, but are raising one of its likely truth or reasonableness. Madden and Hare ask the theist to provide good, credible reasons for evil that are both philosophically acceptable and theologically compatible with orthodox theistic commitments. According to Madden and Hare, it is apparently gratuitous or meaningless evil—evil for which there seems to be no acceptable theistic explanation—that counts against the rational credibility of theism. Thus, evil is relevant to theistic belief in the broad sense in which all theoretical commitments must be squared with the main features of the world. As proposed explanations break down in the light of full-scale philosophical argument and counter-argument, evil for which there is no good theistic explanation counts as evidence against theism.

If the process of reasoning involved here must be characterized as inductive, then it is the inductive reasoning employed in philosophical dialectic generally. Over a period of years, William Rowe has carefully crafted and refined his own manner of expressing the evidential problem of evil along these lines. Others making contributions to the discussion of the evidential problem include Robert Adams, Harold Moore, Robert Pargetter, Bruce Reichenbach, Mary Trau, Edward Wierenga, Stephen Wykstra, and Keith Yandell.

In a piece included in this text, Michael Martin has attempted to clarify the precise nature of the inductive reasoning involved in the evidential argument. He maintains that (what he takes to be) the absence of a morally sufficient reason for God's permission of evil conjoined with (what he takes to be) the absence of independent positive reasons to think that God exists provide the basis of a strong inductive argument against theistic belief. Martin's objective is not to show that God does not exist but that on rational grounds we ought not to believe that God exists. In the succeeding paper, David Basinger offers a reply, contending that many more points must be established before we accept Martin's case. Among the points that Basinger identifies for further debate are the following: whether we fully know how to compare and evaluate world systems which God might have created, whether we possess definitions of "rationality" and "good reasons" that are independent of our respective world views, and whether it has really been shown that the traditional arguments for God's existence are bankrupt.

Although the theoretical dimension of the problem of evil, comprised of both the logical and evidential versions, has received a great deal of attention in the scholarly literature, some work has also been done on what might be called the existential dimension of the problem. Essentially, the existential problem of evil has been conceived to have a kind of "real life" dimension in addition to its abstract or conceptual dimension. For present purposes, the existential problem involves how the experience of evil conditions one's attitude toward God and perhaps toward the world. This problem cannot simply be reduced to an emotional or psychological one or divorced from the structure of one's beliefs and values. Rather it arises when the experience of evil creates a crisis for religious faith. For some people, the experience of evil, which is conditioned by moral convictions as well as a variety of theoretical commitments, can make it impossible to embrace religious faith. Ivan Karamozov is a paradigm case of the existential rejection of theistic religion. For others, the experience of evil, while terrible and disturbing, can somehow be reconciled with faith. In the tradition of C. S. Lewis's *A Grief Observed*, Nicholas Wolterstorff's very moving recent book, *Lament for a Son*, explores this aspect of the problem for believers.

Literature on the existential problem which involves more explicit analytical rigor is also available. Independent articles by Robert Adams and William Hasker argue that happy people who do not regret their own individual existence cannot meaningfully raise a problem of evil, since their existence and identity are causally dependent upon certain past evil events. Thus, insofar as the problem of evil is raised as a personal and moral complaint against God and the world he has created, the answers to it by Adams and Hasker work only for individuals who meet the conditions of relative happiness or non-regret. Also, both Eleonore Stump and Marilyn Adams have offered pieces related to the redemptive or salvific nature of human suffering, providing what we might consider to be a forthrightly spiritual solution to the existential problem of evil. Papers by William Hasker and Marilyn Adams are included here as a representative sampling of how the current philosophical literature is addressing the existential problem.

It is worth observing that the existential response to evil is inevitably shaped by one's precise theological, philosophical, and moral commitments. That is, the existential dimension of the problem of evil is intimately bound up with the theoretical understandings one has, i.e., by the categories one employs and the beliefs one holds. This means, at the very least, that various theoretical considerations related to evil are partially constitutive of the existential problem and may ultimately figure into its further analysis.

In addition to a taxonomy of the different formulations of the problem of evil, we can provide a classification of the different types of response to the problem. To a large extent, distinct responses to the problem can be

categorized in ways which relate them to particular versions of the problem. In the contemporary scholarship on the problem of evil, two fundamentally different types of response have been clearly identified: _defense_
and _theodicy_. Whereas the aim of defense is just to show that anti-theistic
arguments from evil—either logical or evidential—are not successful on
their own terms, the aim of theodicy is to give positive, plausible reasons
for the existence of evil in a theistic universe. Much controversy has arisen
over the relative need for defense or for theodicy and, as we shall see, has
created something of a crucial breach between philosophers who address
the problem of evil.

As we have seen, the logical argument—which purports to show
that is is not logically possible for the propositions "God exists" and "evil
exists" both to be true—has been met with strong defensive maneuvers on
the part of theists. Plantinga, Pike, Yandell, Ahern, and others have argued that is is logically possible that both of these propositions be true. In
this context, Plantinga's free will defense—formulated in terms of all of
the machinery afforded by a quantified modal logic—has now become
classic. In a sense, this is a kind of minimalist response, although such a
response is all that the purely logical problem of evil really requires: accusations that theism is inconsistent can be met with vindications showing
that it is not.

Adams, Plantinga, Wolterstorff, and some others have also treated
the various evidential arguments from evil more or less as though they
require a kind of defense similar to that given for the logical arguments
from evil. In reaction to the basic charge that theism is rendered implausible, improbable, or unlikely, such theistic philosophers have crafted defenses to the effect that the arguments produced to support this charge
have not succeeded in showing that it is implausible, improbable, or unlikely. Again, this is to provide a minimalist defense against the evidential
problems of evil. Using their insights concerning certain formal features
and interpretations of the probability calculus, then, many theists have
simply erected another purely defensive shield. Of course, several important points have emerged from essentially defensive reactions to the evidential problem. For example, one point emerging from discussions of the
probabilistic version of the evidential argument is that the final probability assigned to theism on the basis of the facts of evil depends in large part
on the initial probabilities of various propositions, and that these initial
probabilities will almost assuredly be different for the theist and the
nontheist.

A number of thinkers have become increasingly dissatisfied with a
purely defensive posture in regard to the problem of evil. They admit that

defense has its appropriate functions: against the logical problem it must be shown that theism is not inconsistent and against the evidential problem it must be shown that theism is not implausible. Yet all that defense against the logical problem establishes is that there is at least one *possible* world in which the propositions "God exists" and "evil exists" are both true, but it does not establish that it is reasonable to think that God exists despite the evil in *our* world. This is the point at which the evidential problem, properly conceived, faces the theist with the question of the reasonableness of belief in God and thus prompts the need for theodicy. Only a theodicy will address directly the question of how it can be plausible to think that all the evil in the world is allowed by a God who is both perfectly powerful and perfectly good. Only a theodicy will attempt to help us understand the nature of the goodness that could allow this.

It is understandable, then, why some thinkers say that pure defense in response to well-formulated versions of the evidential problem is even less satisfying and less appropriate than defense in response to versions of the logical problem. They see theodicy to be related to believing in God with full rational integrity. Such thinkers would be content to do without a theodicy only if they had grounds to believe that a theodicy would not be available to us, even if there *is* a God. That is to say, if they cannot have a satisfying theodicy, they at least want a satisfying meta-theodicy explaining why the former is not available. Defense alone does not address these kinds of concerns.

However, some philosophers, such as Plantinga and Wolterstorff, can be interpreted as advocating a purely defensive posture against the evidential problem as well as the logical problem of evil. In advocating their version of "Reformed epistemology" against foundationalism and evidentialism, these thinkers have argued that a person can be rationally entitled to embrace belief in God as "basic." In other words, belief in God need not be the conclusion of a process of reasoning, but may be held directly. Reformed epistemologists have argued both for the rational legitimacy of embracing belief in God without being able to give discursive reasons to support it and for being rationally obligated only to defend against any objection to one's theistic belief, including the objection from evil. According to this way of thinking about the matter, then, the role of anything resembling theodicy is a limited and primarily negative one.

In rejoinder, the way is open for philosophers advocating a more positive role for theodicy to point out that belief in God is never really the acceptance of one or even a few isolated propositions, but is the acceptance, at least tacitly, of a whole set of logically interrelated propositions that define the nature and purposes of God. Upon reflection, this set of theistic propositions can be seen to constitute an interpretation of many important features of human life and the world at large. Hence, to believe that God exists is already to possess a rudimentary understanding of evil which may be articulated and systematized as a theodicy. In this light, theodicy is not only appropriate in the dialectic between theist and critic but is also appropriate as the theistic believer seeks to understand his own faith more deeply.

Contemporary philosophers—both theistic and nontheistic—who endorse the enterprise of theodicy see it as linked to the rational integrity of religious belief. They do not simply desire explanations of evil that are logically *possible* (which is the most a mere defense to the evidential problem could even provide), but rather explanations for why God might allow evil that are *plausible* or likely *true*. Proposing and analyzing explanations for evil is an ancient and important venture in philosophy of religion, a venture to which we now turn.

PERSPECTIVES IN THEODICY

While the enterprise of theodicy has had a venerable status throughout most of the history of philosophy, interest in theodicy in the latter part of the twentieth century has been uneven. The names of Augustine, Aquinas, and Leibniz only begin the list of historic theodicists. Theodicies from the more recent past include Jacques Maritain's application of Thomism to the modern discussion and John Hick's "soul-making" theodicy which is still influential in debates over the problem of evil. Yet, in the decades of the 1960s and 1970s, the attempt to provide a theodicy was not a flourishing endeavor. Ostensibly, there were two main reasons for this. First, there was widespread preoccupation with the logical argument from evil and the construction of a defense against it. Second, doubt was cast both on the need for and the viability of constructing a theodicy.

Interestingly, as the evidential argument from evil became more prominent during the decade of the 1980s, more philosophers began to display their dissatisfaction with mere defense. Robert Adams, for example, has suggested the need for a more "aggressive defense" against the evidential problem, indicating that theists should try to develop a defense which proposes believable claims about some of the reasons that God might indeed have for permitting evil. Adams is clearly gesturing in the direction of at least some sort of minimalist theodicy, and some other philosophers are even more ambitious concerning what they think theodicy might accomplish.

Responding to the evidential problem, Stephen T. Davis, James Ross, Richard Swinburne, Eleonore Stump, and others in recent years have articulated interesting and important theodicies. It seems that, as long as the purely logical problem and the relatively small set of beliefs that are basic to general theism were at the fore of the debate, neither the motivation nor the conceptual resources were present for generating much theodicy. However, the increasing interest in the evidential problem in general does seem to be prompting more aggressive attempts to suggest explanations of evil, explanations which, in full form, move in the direction of theodicy. Additionally, many philosophers are now willing to draw from specifically Christian theological themes in creating their theodicies. The expanded set of specifically Christian theistic beliefs is thus providing once again more fruitful and promising conceptual resources for developing a theodicy than those supplied by general theism alone.

There is some advantage in considering first those theodicies that have been articulated and amplified by many thinkers, and thus form cohesive, ongoing traditions. Several major traditions in theodicy have claimed the allegiance of philosophers over long periods of time. One example would be the highly rationalistic Leibnizian tradition which maintains that all existing evil is a component of the best of all possible worlds; and another would be the tradition of personal idealism which claims that evil is explicable in terms of God's being finite and including within himself an irrational, surd element. In this anthology, three major traditions that continue to be of serious interest to philosophers of religion are presented: Augustinian theodicy, Irenaean theodicy, and process theodicy. These systematic theodicies may be viewed as providing answers to the evidential argument from evil.

The rich and complex theodicy of the Augustinian tradition focuses on the causal genesis of evil in the world in order to accomplish two basic objectives: to exonerate God and to maintain the guilt of creatures. Augustine held that God brought an originally good and innocent creation into existence. Since all of creation comes from the hand of a perfectly good and sovereign Creator, all creatures are inherently good. Thus, according to Augustine's metaphysics, evil has no positive reality; evil is instead *privatio boni,* the "privation of good." One central theme in Augustinian theodicy is that evil is produced by good human creatures misusing their own free choice, falling into sin. In effect, Augustine augments the same basic intuition that underlies the contemporary free will defense and turns it into a fundamental part of his theodicy. Another theme in Augustine's thinking is that the created world, even with its evil, is beautiful and fitting when seen from God's perspective. Many such Augustinian ideas recur in the works of later Christian thinkers, such as St. Thomas and subsequent Thomistic philosophers, and in the work of John Calvin along with subsequent Calvinistic philosophers.

One very important response to the Augustinian tradition in theodicy was offered by David Ray Griffin, a process philosopher. Griffin argues that the overall orientation of Augustine's theology, which emphasizes the absolute power and goodness of God, unwittingly entails that there is no genuine evil in the universe. A perfectly good deity controls everything, and no evil can be ascribed to him. Griffin then discusses reasons for thinking that this denial of genuine evil is faithful neither to the facts of human experience nor to the Christian faith itself.

In developing what he calls "soul-making" theodicy, John Hick has associated his position with the thought of Bishop Irenaeus of the early Eastern Orthodox church. Without debating here the degree of similarity between the ideas of Irenaeus and Hick, we can note that their basic orientation in theodicy is markedly different from that of the Augustinian tradition. Instead of focusing on the causal genesis of evil, the Irenaean tradition in theodicy emphasizes the evolving resolution of evil. According to Hick, an Irenaean theodicy does not view evil in the world as a fall from a once perfect state, but rather as a necessary stage in the development of a relatively immature creation into a more mature state. The divine plan, on the Irenaean account, is for the gradual improvement of the human race, a process that will ultimately culminate in the afterlife. God seeks to bring forth mature moral and spiritual beings who are capable of exercising faith in him and love toward their fellows. The conditions for accomplishing the divine goal of soul-making include "epistemic distance" between finite minds and the Creator (so that the world can appear as if there is no God and thus protect humans from being overwhelmed by the presence of the Creator), an assortment of genuine challenges and risks (so that free creatures may respond and grow), and the existence of moral and natural evils (so that a number of important virtues may have occasion to flourish).

Reactions to Hick's version of a soul-making theodicy have been many and varied. Among those who have criticized his views are Edward Madden and Peter Hare, Dom Illtyd Trethowan, Keith Ward, and John Rist. In a particularly incisive critique of Hick's theodicy, Roland Puccetti, a nontheist, has focused in on what he takes to be the dubious status of the claim that God has a morally sufficient reason for allowing instances of innocent suffering.

G. Stanley Kane, a theist, also has argued against Hick's theodicy. One particularly interesting point that Kane makes is that Hick's notion of epistemic distance seems to encounter a damaging dilemma: On the one hand, the soul-making theodicy places a high premium on human freedom and autonomy; on the other hand, the eschatological component of Hick's theodicy assures us that God will bring about the universal salvation of the human race. Yet it appears that universal salvation can be effected for free creatures only if there is an alteration in the degree of epistemic distance which presently allows many to continue to reject God. Now, either this alteration in epistemic distance still provides the requisite freedom for soul-making or it does not. If the requisite freedom remains, then Hick must admit that less epistemic distance than we presently have would suffice for soul-making. If the requisite freedom is lost, then Hick must admit that God will violate his program of soul-making in order to accomplish the universal salvation of all persons.

Arising out of the general position of process philosophy, process theodicy provides another distinctive response to the problem of evil. Process thinkers adopt a quasi-theistic position in that they modify certain traditional divine attributes in order to retain what they consider to be the most important or desirable characteristics of the classical theistic concept of God (e.g., worshipability) while avoiding the undesirable ones (e.g., the tension they see between omnipotence and creaturely free will). Process theodicy emerges logically from the metaphysical commitments of Alfred North Whitehead and has been articulated in various contexts by his intellectual descendants, such as Charles Hartshorne, John Cobb, David Griffin, Shubert Ogden, and Lewis Ford.

According to process thinkers, God's chief goal is the realization and maximization of value within the experiences of creatures. However, by virtue of being actual, every creature possesses some degree of self-determination or free choice. Since God does not have a monopoly on power, creatures can genuinely resist the divine plan; in other words, they have the power to do evil. God thus attempts to influence ("persuade" or "lure") creatures into fulfilling good possibilities and avoiding evil ones. He then continually interacts with their choices, weaving together all events, both good and bad, into a fitting pattern within his own experience. Of course, no finite being ever attains a complete perspective on the whole world in order to see how all events fit together for God. Yet, according to Whitehead, God in his "consequent nature" conserves everything that happens and "loses nothing that can be saved."

For years, many religious philosophers ignored process metaphysics in general, along with its religious and theological ramifications, on grounds that it abandons certain essentials of the theistic tradition. However, in the past few decades, process theodicy has been increasingly recognized both for advancing trenchant critiques of classical concepts of God and for propounding intrinsically important philosophical theses of its own. As process thought as a whole has become more widely discussed, process theodicy has gained proportionately more attention. One persistent criticism against it, however, has been that the basically aesthetic values of challenge, diversity, and the like which connote the focal point of process theodicy are not worth the moral price in human pain and suffering. Another major criticism has been that a deity who is not omnipotent, whose aims are fundamentally aesthetic, and who is an impersonal metaphysical principle is not after all worthy of religious devotion and worship. Process thinkers have been active in responding to such charges and in keeping process theodicy a live option for a number of serious philosophers.

Edward Madden and Peter Hare have argued against the process concept of divine persuasive power. Madden and Hare take issue with process thinkers who say that "the only power capable of any worthwhile result is the power of persuasion." They argue that there are conditions under which the exercise of coercive power on the part of God is morally required to avoid or remove evil. Furthermore, they insist that there is no empirical evidence that the unlimited persuasive power of the process deity is at work in the world.

On behalf of the process tradition, Lewis Ford has replied to these criticisms. In a piece included in this anthology, he maintains on metaphysical grounds that God's power cannot be coercive, and on moral grounds that it ought not to be; moreover, he has argued that persuasive power alone enhances creaturely freedom. Ford also expresses the firm hope that good will triumph in the world as creatures come to cooperate more completely with God. Madden and Hare in turn have issued a rejoinder to Ford, also included here. They make a number of important points, among them a challenge to process thinkers to explain why so many people seem to remain unpersuaded by such a great degree of divine persuasive power.

ISSUES IN THE PROBLEM OF EVIL

In the analysis and discussion of any formulation of the argument from evil, as well as any defense or theodicy offered in response, many subsidiary issues arise. For each move and counter-move in the debate, there are key concepts to be clarified, hidden assumptions to be made explicit, and logical implications to be traced out. Taking care of this level of philosophical work is often crucial to settling one's larger position on the problem of evil. Among the numerous issues nested within the overall problem, four important ones deserve comment at this juncture and have corresponding pieces in this volume. These issues pertain to the nature of any moral obligations or other necessities that might rest upon God to create the best possible world, the idea of a natural order to which appeal is made by theodicists, the relative roles of defense and theodicy, and the challenge that theoretical theodicy is morally insensitive.

The first issue pertains to whether an omnipotent, omniscient, morally perfect deity is obligated to create the best possible world. Great thinkers such as Plato and Leibniz have believed that God must indeed create the best. In his essay, "Must God Create the Best?" Robert Adams argues to the contrary that God is not obligated to do so. Although some thinkers attempt to show that God has no obligation to create the best possible world by maintaining that the concept of a best possible world, like the concept of the highest possible integer, is logically incoherent, Adams builds his case along somewhat different lines. He maintains that moral obligation does not attach to the Creator's choice among possible worlds, since, prior to the action of creation, there are no moral obligations God would have to merely possible beings. Adams also appeals to the theme of divine grace, holding that God does not choose creatures because of their own desirable characteristics, and thus might select less excellent creatures than he could have selected.

Responses to Adams have been forthcoming from Jerome Weinstock and Philip Quinn. In the paper, "God, Moral Perfection, and Possible Worlds," Quinn explores issues regarding how we determine the moral goodness of possible worlds and of moral agents. He provides an argument for twin conclusions: that it is not wrong for God not to actualize a world less morally good than some other one he could have actualized instead, but that his not doing so would imply that he is not the superlatively good moral agent which theists normally take him to be. Quinn thereby believes he has shown, contrary to Adams, that theists are committed to believing that God must do his best in creation.

Another controversy incorporated into the overall debate over evil regards natural law explanations for natural evils. Responding to H. J. McCloskey's rejection of theism on the grounds that it does not adequately account for natural evils, Bruce Reichenbach and Richard Swinburne have advanced their own variations on a natural law theme. Both Reichenbach

and Swinburne grant that McCloskey has indeed cited many weak and unacceptable explanations of natural evil: that it is deserved punishment for
sin, that it is a necessary contrast to the good, and that it is a warning for
people to repent. However, Reichenbach has replied that we must take
seriously the possibility of natural evil within a world order operating by
natural laws. The stability of a natural order diminishes expectations for
frequent divine intervention to prevent or eliminate many natural evils,
but this is consistent with an intelligent version of theism. Moreover, the
regular natural order provides a framework within which rational delib-
eration and action can occur, thus supporting a very valuable state of
affairs.

Swinburne's discussion of natural evil is perhaps more venturesome
than Reichenbach's. Instead of arguing that the possibility of natural evil
is inherent in a natural system, Swinburne contends that the actual existence of natural evil is necessary in a natural system which accommodates
meaningful moral freedom. Swinburne assumes that some kind of free will
theodicy shows how moral evil is compatible with the existence of God and
then builds an argument that people must acquire knowledge of how to
bring about good and evil in order to be significantly free. He claims that
people can only acquire this knowledge from experience of and inference
from actual natural evils. Like Reichenbach, then, Swinburne links the
explanation for natural evils in an interesting way to the explanation for
moral evils.

Eleonore Stump responded to Swinburne's theodicy for natural evils
by arguing that the existence of natural evils is *not* necessary for acquiring
the knowledge which provides for the exercise of free will. She agrees with
Swinburne that free will is very valuable and that the relevant knowledge
is therefore instrumentally valuable. However, she maintains that such
knowledge is available through other avenues than induction from actual
natural evils, such as divine revelation or scientific means. Stump attempts to block any recourse Swinburne might have by further considering whether it is perhaps *better* to attain the knowledge which allows
significant moral freedom by induction from actual natural evils, even if
we grant that it is not *necessary* to do so. The exchange between Swinburne
and Stump typifies some of the contemporary thinking on the very important subject of natural evils.

The third issue treated here regards a peculiar relationship between
Plantinga's free will defense and free will theodicy. Plantinga has gone to
great pains to insist that one need not believe that libertarian (incompatibilist) freedom is the case in order to construct a successful free will de-

fense. He merely affirms that libertarian freedom is *possible* in order to complete the defense. This allows Plantinga to draw the well-known conclusion that it is *possible* that it was not within God's power to create a world containing moral good but no moral evil. Yet Jerry Walls argues that God could properly eliminate all moral evil if persons were free only in the compatibilist sense. Thus, he maintains that Plantinga's free will defense commits him to libertarian freedom, and thus moves him from pure defense into the project of theodicy. Plantinga responds by arguing that a key premise which Walls takes to be necessarily true—that God could properly eliminate moral evil in a compatibilist world—is not obviously true and may be false. The exchange between Walls and Plantinga deserves to be read in detail.

The fourth issue is exemplified in an exchange between Kenneth   4
Surin and James Wetzel. Surin, a contemporary theologian, has argued in *Theology and the Problem of Evil* that the theoretical problem of evil, centering on the problematic deity created by the philosophical theism of the Enlightenment, has been the major preoccupation of professional philosophers such as Plantinga, Hick, Swinburne, and process theologians. Suggesting that theoretical attempts to address the problem of evil are morally   why?
insensitive, Surin opts for theodicies with "practical" (victim-oriented) emphasis, such as those offered by Dorothee Soelle, Jürgen Moltmann, and P. T. Forsyth. Surin calls for developing an adequate "grammar" of salvation, namely a way of communicating that God justifies himself by justifying sinners on the cross. The piece included here explores how we might root our attempts at "practical" theodicy in the concrete realities of human suffering by developing solidarity with the victims of suffering. In reply to Surin, James Wetzel claims that the charge of moral insensitivity commits a kind of *ad hominem* fallacy against theoretical theodicists and that the enterprise of theoretical theodicy cannot be completely avoided anyway. Wetzel explores the distinction between what he calls "minimalist theodicy" (which philosophers typically label "defense") and "speculative theodicy," maintaining that the attempt to speculate about the general explanations for evil is a fundamental and legitimate human endeavor.

Beyond the four issues in the problem of evil featured in this anthology, additional issues abound. Some of these complex and intertwined difficulties have not commanded as much attention from philosophers as others, but will surely attract more attention as the debate continues. The following issues can be reasonably forecast to appear in future discussions: more penetrating analyses of the evidential argument from apparently gratuitous evil; continued debate over the relation of defense and theodicy; evaluations of how the problem of evil is treated by contemporary theologians; studies of how the theological doctrine of hell relates to the problem of evil; examinations of the problem of evil as it appears in great literature; and discussions of the problems of evil that occur for Eastern religions. Let us look briefly at each of these areas of potential debate and discussion.

First, myriad important issues arise as philosophers feel the force of the increasingly important evidential argument from gratuitous evil. On the one hand, there needs to be further careful analysis of the principle held by many, but not all, theists that God allows no gratuitous evil. This analysis will likely generate questions about whether any form of greater good theodicy is viable and whether either general theism or Christian theism can countenance genuine tragedy in the world. On the other hand, there should be more discussion of the status of the purportedly factual claim that there is gratuitous evil. Here questions arise regarding the weight of our ordinary moral judgments as well as the overall method for evaluating goods and evils.

Second, various issues arise regarding the functions of and prospects for defense and theodicy. While there is a fair amount of agreement that the free will defense seriously damages the critic's chances of formulating a successful logical argument from evil, and while there is also a readily detectable shift of interest toward theodicy of late, many matters remain to be clarified and debated. For example, some thinkers maintain that a fully plausible theodicy, by the very nature of the situation, is either going to be extremely difficult or impossible to attain. Of course, this estimation is based in part on certain debatable conceptions of the project of theodicy. How aggressive or ambitious is theodicy to be? Is theodicy meant to give merely partial suggestions about theistic explanations for evil, or rather is it committed to coming up with good, rationally plausible explanations for evil? Does the theodicist have to be able to provide God's reasons for individual cases or merely sketch a relevant theistic explanation for large classes of evils?

A third topic that also deserves more attention in the future relates to the way the problem of evil is treated by theologians. The exchange between Surin and Wetzel reveals the need for philosophers to bring their analytical skills to bear on theological approaches to the problem. As theologians are led, by the very content of their discipline, to deal with the problem of evil, they stand to benefit from the technical precision of philosophers in formulating arguments and counter-arguments in the debate. By the same token, philosophers can benefit from more complete and accurate information about significant theological traditions and biblical themes which theologians can offer. We are already seeing more and more philosophers, somewhat in the vein and spirit of John Hick, employing specifically Christian theological themes in constructing theodicies.

Fourth, the theological doctrine of hell supplies philosophers with another topic that can be reasonably predicted to gain increasing prominence in future discussions of the problem of evil. After all, when construed in certain ways, the concept of hell constitutes an almost intractable difficulty for thinkers seeking to defend the moral goodness of God. For example, notions regarding the eternal damnation of those who have not had a fair chance to repent are morally repugnant.

A fifth interesting study for those serious about the problem of evil is an analysis of the problem as it occurs in great pieces of world literature. Great literature not only makes the problem more concrete, but also exposes us to particular conceptions of its depth and many dimensions — thus providing the basis of an intrinsically valuable study. A forthcoming book by Daniel Clendenin entitled *Evil: A Bibliography* promises to be an extremely helpful resource for the study of the problem in literary as well as philosophical and theological circles.

Sixth and finally, the problem evil presents for the construction of a reasonable worldview takes a different form in each nontheistic religion. Increasing intellectual interest in the many issues surrounding our world's religious diversity improves the prospect that theistic philosophers will become ever more aware of Eastern religious traditions and then seek to derive from them whatever philosophical benefits are available through studying the similarities and differences in the way they formulate and answer their own problems of evil.

In both quality and quantity, the past and present philosophical literature discussing the problem of evil witnesses to the tremendous importance of the problem itself. Of all the issues in the philosophy of religion, the problem of evil arguably commands more attention than any other and will very likely continue to do so. At their own levels, both the highly specialized philosopher and the thoughtful layperson puzzle over how certain theological concepts fit together, how to evaluate various explanations of why God allows evil, and what personal stance to adopt toward a world such as ours which includes so much evil. Progress in dealing with the problem of evil is made as reflective persons, theists and nontheists, engage in honest, disciplined discussion and debate. It is my hope that this collection of readings will contribute to that progress.

PART ONE

Classic Statements of the Problem

Traditional Treatments
Modern Treatments

Job's Complaint
and the Whirlwind's Answer

FROM THE BOOK OF JOB

One assumption underlying Old Testament writings is that we live in a moral universe which is created and sustained by God. The prevailing orthodoxy held that God has structured the world so that the righteous and the wicked are rewarded or punished according to their just deserts. The Book of Proverbs, despite its occasional flashes of cynicism, essentially reflects this view. The Book of Job, on the other hand, struggles with the accepted religious opinion, for it begins by insisting that the justice of God is not confirmed by the facts of human experience. It thus calls into question the popular interpretation of what it means to live in a divinely governed moral universe.

In a manner of speaking, this book is a philosophical forum put in the format of an old folk tale. It addresses the most perplexing of human problems: Why do the innocent suffer? According to the story, Job was a morally virtuous and religiously devout patriarch. As the book indicates, "There was a man in the land of Uz, whose name was Job; and that man was blameless and upright, one who feared God, and turned away from evil" (Job 1:1). Nevertheless all sorts of evil befell this good man, devastating his once prosperous and flourishing life. His seven sons and three daughters were killed, all of his flocks were destroyed, all of his slaves were slaughtered, and he himself was smitten with leprosy. The unfolding drama of this ancient book displays the exquisite intermingling of theological ideas with psychological anguish.

Scripture quotations are from the Revised Standard Version Bible, copyright 1946, 1952, 1971 by the Division of Christian Education of the National Council of the Churches of Christ in the U.S.A. Used by permission.

Job's first reaction is to suffer in silence. Unable to bear the misery, Job's wife urges him to "curse God and die," whereupon he answers:

> "You speak as one of the foolish women would speak. Shall we receive good at the hand of God, and shall we not receive evil?"
>
> 2:10

Eventually, three of Job's friends come to comfort him as he sits on an ash-heap and scrapes his sores. They are "Eliphaz the Temanite, Bildad the Shuhite, and Zophar the Naamathite" (2:11). At first, the three seem unable to find words to express their sympathy, sitting with him without speaking for seven days and seven nights. Apparently, Job knew them to embrace the conventional orthodoxy that misfortune is punishment for sin. As the strain of silence among the group proves too much for Job, he bursts forth bitterly:

> "Why did I not die at birth, come forth from the womb and expire?
> Why did the knees receive me? Or why the breasts, that I should suck?
> For then I should have lain down and been quiet; I should have slept, then I should have been at rest. . . .
> Why is light given to him that is in misery, and life to the bitter in soul,
> Who long for death, but it comes not, and dig for it more than for hid treasures;
> Who rejoice exceedingly, and are glad, when they find the grave?"
>
> 3:11–13, 20–22

Job's outburst shocks the comforters, and they begin to argue with him. The first, Eliphaz, insists that God is probably disciplining Job for his own good:

> "Behold, happy is the man whom God reproves; therefore despise not the chastening of the Almighty.
> For he wounds, but he binds up; he smites, but his hands heal.
> He will deliver you from six troubles; in seven there shall no evil touch you."
>
> 5:17–19

Job, however, answers that he does not stand in need of any such disciplining. He cries out directly to God:

> "If I sin, what do I do to thee, thou watcher of men?
> Why hast thou made me thy mark? Why have I become a burden to thee?"
>
> 7:20

Soon Bildad, the second comforter, begins to rebuke Job, saying:

> "How long will you say these things, and the words of your mouth
>   be a great wind?
> Does God pervert justice? Or does the Almighty pervert the
>   right? . . .
> If you are pure and upright, surely then he will rouse himself for you
>   and reward you with a rightful habitation."
>
> 8:2–3, 6

To which Job replies:

> "I loathe my life; I will give free utterance to my complaint; I will
>   speak in the bitterness of my soul.
> I will say to God, 'Do not condemn me; let me know why thou dost
>   contend against me.
> Does it seem good to thee to oppress, to despise the work of thy
>   hands and favor the designs of the wicked?
> Hast thou eyes of flesh? Dost thou see as man sees?
> Are thy days as the days of man, or thy years as man's years,
> That thou dost seek out my iniquity and search for my sin,
> Although thou knowest that I am not guilty, and there is none to
>   deliver out of thy hand?' "
>
> 10:1–7

Then, the third comforter, Zophar, is so outraged that he cries:

> "Should your babble silence men, and when you mock, shall no one
>   shame you?
> For you say, 'My doctrine is pure, and I am clean in God's eyes.'
> But oh, that God would speak, and open his lips to you,
> And that he would tell you the secrets of wisdom! For he is manifold
>   in understanding. Know then that God
> Exacts of you less than your guilt deserves."
>
> 11:3–6

Thus the argument continues. Job readily admits that God is omniscient
and omnipotent, but questions his justice and goodness. Says Job:

> "I am blameless; I regard not myself; I loathe my life.
> It is all one; therefore I say, he destroys both the blameless and the
>   wicked.
> When disaster brings sudden death, he mocks at the calamity of the
>   innocent.

The earth is given into the hand of the wicked; he covers the faces of
    its judges—if it is not he, who then is it?"

                                                            9:21–24

God, it would seem, is deliberately seeking to put Job in the wrong:

"Though I am innocent, I cannot answer him; I must appeal for
    mercy to my accuser.
If I summoned him and he answered me, I would not believe that he
    was listening to my voice.
For he crushes me with a tempest, and multiplies my wounds with-
    out cause;
He will not let me get my breath, but fills me with bitterness.
If it is a contest of strength, behold him! If it is a matter of justice,
    who can summon him?
Though I am innocent, my own mouth would condemn me; though
    I am blameless, he would prove me perverse. . . .
I become afraid of all my suffering, for I know thou wilt not hold me
    innocent.
I shall be condemned; why then do I labor in vain? If I wash myself
    with snow, and cleanse my hands with lye,
Yet thou wilt plunge me into a pit, and my own clothes will
    abhor me.
For he is not a man, as I am, that I might answer him, that we
    should come to trial together.
There is no umpire between us, who might lay his hand upon
    us both.
Let him take his rod away from me, and let not dread of him ter-
    rify me.
Then I would speak without fear of him, for I am not so in myself."

                                                        9:15–20, 28–35

In spite of all that his friends say to the contrary, Job insists that God deals
unfairly with human beings:

"When I think of it I am dismayed, and shuddering seizes my flesh.
Why do the wicked live, reach old age, and grow mighty in power?
Their children are established in their presence, and their offspring
    before their eyes.
Their houses are safe from fear, and no rod of God is upon them.
Their bull breeds without fail; their cow calves, and does not cast
    her calf.

They send forth their little ones like a flock, and their children
    dance.
They sing to the tambourine and the lyre, and rejoice to the sound
    of the pipe.
They spend their days in prosperity, and in peace they go down
    to Sheol.
They say to God, 'Depart from us! We do not desire the knowledge
    of thy ways.
What is the Almighty, that we should serve him? And what profit
    do we get if we pray to him?' "

21:6–15

So the debate goes, point and counterpoint, Job against his friends. Near-
ing the end of the discussion, a fourth comforter, the young Elihu, comes
forward to refute Job:

"God thunders wondrously with his voice; he does great things
    which we cannot comprehend. . . .
The Almighty—we cannot find him; he is great in power and jus-
    tice, and abundant righteousness he will not violate."

37:5, 23

Finally, God himself enters the debate. He speaks out of a whirlwind,
hurling one question after another at Job:

"Who is this that darkens counsel by words without knowledge?
Gird up your loins like a man, I will question you, and you shall
    declare to me.
Where were you when I laid the foundation of the earth? Tell me, if
    you have understanding.
Who determined its measurements—surely you know! Or who
    stretched the line upon it?
On what were its bases sunk, or who laid its cornerstone,
When the morning stars sang together, and all the sons of God
    shouted for joy?
Or who shut in the sea with doors, when it burst forth from the
    womb;
When I made clouds its garment, and thick darkness its swaddling
    band,
And prescribed bounds for it, and set bars and doors, and said,
    'Thus far shall you come, and no farther, and here shall your
    proud waves be stayed'?

Have you commanded the morning since your days began, and
caused the dawn to know its place,

That it might take hold of the skirts of the earth, and the wicked be
shaken out of it?

It is changed like clay under the seal, and it is dyed like a garment.

From the wicked their light is withheld, and their uplifted arm is
broken.

Have you entered into the springs of the sea, or walked in the re-
cesses of the deep?

Have the gates of death been revealed to you, or have you seen the
gates of deep darkness?

Have you comprehended the expanse of the earth? Declare, if you
know all this.

Where is the way to the dwelling of light, and where is the place of
darkness,

That you may take it to its territory and that you may discern the
paths to its home? . . .

Gird up you loins like a man; I will question you, and you declare
to me.

Will you even put me in the wrong? Will you condemn me that you
may be justified?

Have you an arm like God, and can you thunder with a voice
like his?

Deck yourself with majesty and dignity; clothe yourself with glory
and splendor.

Pour forth the overflowings of your anger, and look on every one
that is proud, and abase him.

Look on every one that is proud, and bring him low; and tread down
the wicked where they stand.

Hide them all in the dust together; bind their faces in the world
below.

Then will I also acknowledge to you, that your own right hand can
give you victory."

38:2–20; 40:6–14

Job is overwhelmed and answers:

"Behold, I am of small account; what shall I answer thee? I lay my
hand on my mouth. . . .

I know that thou canst do all things, and that no purpose of thine
can be thwarted.

'Who is this that hides counsel without knowledge?' Therefore I
have uttered what I did not understand, things too wonderful
for me, which I did not know.
'Hear, and I will speak; I will question you, and you declare to me.'
I had heard of thee by hearing of the ear, but now my eye sees thee;
Therefore I despise myself, and repent in dust and ashes."

40:4; 42:2–6

He knows and anticipates the objections to his way of thinking.

No Evil Comes from God

ST. THOMAS AQUINAS

A form of argument common in his time "Disputacco" → 5 parts

sed contra

We next inquire into the cause of evil. Concerning this there are three points of inquiry: (1) Whether good can be the cause of evil? (2) Whether the supreme good, God, is the cause of evil? (3) Whether there be any supreme evil, which is the first cause of all evils?

*1
2
3
=
in favor of his position*

① A question is raised ↓

FIRST ARTICLE
WHETHER GOOD CAN BE THE CAUSE OF EVIL?

We proceed thus to the First Article:—

Arguments against ("auc toritates")

Objection 1. It would seem that good cannot be the cause of evil. For it is said (Matth. vii 18): *A good tree cannot bring forth evil fruit.*

Obj. 2. Further, one contrary cannot be the cause of another. But evil is the contrary to good. Therefore good cannot be the cause of evil.

Obj. 3. Further, a deficient effect can proceed only from a deficient cause. But evil is a deficient effect. Therefore its cause, if it has one, is deficient. But everything deficient is an evil. Therefore the cause of evil can only be evil.

Obj. 4. Further, Dionysius says (*Div. Nom.* iv) that evil has no cause. Therefore good is not the cause of evil.

② *On the contrary,* Augustine says (*Contra Julian.* i. 9): *There is no possible source of evil except good.*   *agrees w/ Augustine*

③ General statement in favor of his position

I answer that, It must be said that every evil in some way has a cause. For evil is the absence of the good, which is natural and due to a thing. But that anything fail from its natural and due disposition, can come only from some cause drawing it out of its proper disposition. For a heavy thing

④ *his own opinion in corpus of argument*

From *Summa Theologica*, Part I, Question 49, articles 1–3. Translated by Fathers of the English Dominican Province, available through Christian Classics, Westminster, Md.

31

is not moved upwards except by some impelling force; nor does an agent fail in its action except from some impediment. But only good can be a cause; because nothing can be a cause except inasmuch as it is a being, and every being, as such, is good.

And if we consider the special kinds of causes, we see that the agent, the form, and the end, import some kind of perfection which belongs to the notion of good. Even matter, as a potentiality to good, has the nature of good. Now that good is the cause of evil by way of the material cause was shown above (Q. 48, A. 3). For it was shown that good is the subject of evil. But evil has no formal cause, rather it is a privation of form; likewise, neither has it a final cause, but rather it is a privation of order to the proper end; since not only the end has the nature of good, but also the useful, which is ordered to the end. Evil, however, has a cause by way of an agent, not directly, but accidentally.

In proof of this, we must know that evil is caused in the action otherwise than in the effect. In the action evil is caused by reason of the defect of some principle of action, either of the principal or the instrumental agent; thus the defect in the movement of an animal may happen by reason of the weakness of the motive power, as in the case of children, or by reason only of the ineptitude of the instrument, as in the lame. On the other hand, evil is caused in a thing, but not in the proper effect of the agent, sometimes by the power of the agent, sometimes by reason of a defect, either of the agent or of the matter. It is caused by reason of the power or perfection of the agent when there necessarily follows on the form intended by the agent the privation of another form; as, for instance, when on the form of fire there follows the privation of the form of air or of water. Therefore, as the more perfect the fire is in strength, so much the more perfectly does it impress its own form, so also the more perfectly does it corrupt the contrary. Hence that evil and corruption befall air and water comes from the perfection of the fire: but this is accidental; because fire does not aim at the privation of the form of water, but at the bringing in of its own form, though by doing this it also accidentally causes the other. But if there is a defect in the proper effect of the fire—as, for instance, that it fails to heat—this comes either by defect of the action, which implies the defect of some principle, as was said above, or by the indisposition of the matter, which does not receive the action of fire, the agent. But this very fact that it is a deficient being is accidental to good to which of itself it belongs to act. Hence it is true that evil in no way has any but an accidental cause: and thus is good the cause of evil.

Reply Obj. 1. As Augustine says (*Contra Julian.* i): *The Lord calls an evil will the evil tree, and a good will a good tree.* Now, a good will does not produce a morally bad act, since it is from the good will itself that a moral act is judged to be good. Nevertheless the movement itself of an evil will is caused by the rational creature, which is good; and thus good is the cause of evil.

Reply Obj. 2. Good does not cause that evil which is contrary to itself, but some other evil: thus the goodness of the fire causes evil to the water, and man, good as to his nature, causes an act morally evil. And, as explained above (Q. 19, A. 9), this is by accident. Moreover it does happen sometimes that one contrary causes another by accident: for instance, the exterior surrounding cold heats (the body) through the concentration of the inward heat.

Reply Obj. 3. Evil has a deficient cause in voluntary things otherwise than in natural things. For the natural agent produces the same kind of effect as it is itself, unless it is impeded by some exterior thing, and this amounts to some defect belonging to it. Hence evil never follows in the effect, unless some other evil pre-exists in the agent or in the matter, as was said above. But in voluntary things the defect of the action comes from the will actually deficient, inasmuch as it does not actually subject itself to its proper rule. This defect, however, is not a fault, but fault follows upon it from the fact that the will acts with this defect.

Reply Obj. 4. Evil has no direct cause, but only an accidental cause, as was said above.

SECOND ARTICLE
WHETHER THE SUPREME GOOD, GOD, IS THE CAUSE OF EVIL?

We proceed thus to the Second Article:—

Objection 1. It would seem that the supreme good, God, is the cause of evil. For it is said (Isa. xlv. 5, 7): *I am the Lord, and there is no other God, forming the light, and creating darkness, making peace, and creating evil.* And (Amos iii. 6), *Shall there be evil in a city, which the Lord hath not done?*

Obj. 2. Further, the effect of the secondary cause is reduced to the first cause. But good is the cause of evil, as was said above (A. 1). Therefore, since God is the cause of every good, as was shown above (Q. 2, A. 3; Q. 6, AA. 1, 4), it follows that also every evil is from God.

Obj. 3. Further, as is said by the Philosopher (*Phys.* ii, text. 30), the cause of both safety and danger of the ship is the same. But God is the cause of the safety of all things. Therefore He is the cause of all perdition and of all evil.

On the contrary, Augustine says (QQ. 83, *qu.* 21), that, *God is not the author of evil because He is not the cause of tending to not-being.*

I answer that, As appears from what was said (A. 1), the evil which consists in the defect of action is always caused by the defect of the agent. But in God there is no defect, but the highest perfection, as was shown above (Q. 4, A. 1). Hence, the evil which consists in defect of action, or which is caused by defect of the agent, is not reduced to God as to its cause.

But the evil which consists in the corruption of some things is re-duced to God as the cause. And this appears as regards both natural things and voluntary things. For it was said (A. 1) that some agent inasmuch as it produces by its power a form to which follows corruption and defect, causes by its power that corruption and defect. But it is manifest that the form which God chiefly intends in things created is the good of the order of the universe. Now, the order of the universe requires, as was said above (Q. 22, A. 2 *ad* 2; Q. 48, A. 2), that there should be some things that can, and do sometimes, fail. And thus God, by causing in things the good of the order of the universe, consequently and as it were by accident, causes the corruptions of things, according to 1 Kings ii. 6: *The Lord kill-eth and maketh alive.* But when we read that *God hath not made death* (Wis. i. 13), the sense is that God does not will death for its own sake. Never-theless the order of justice belongs to the order of the universe; and this requires that penalty should be dealt out to sinners. And so God is the author of the evil which is penalty, but not of the evil which is fault, by reason of what is said above.

Reply Obj. 1. These passages refer to the evil of penalty, and not to the evil of fault.

Reply Obj. 2. The effect of the deficient secondary cause is reduced to the first non-deficient cause as regards what it has of being and per-fection, but not as regards what it has of defect; just as whatever there is of motion in the act of limping is caused by the motive power, whereas what there is of obliqueness in it does not come from the motive power, but from the curvature of the leg. And, likewise, whatever there is of be-ing and action in a bad action, is reduced to God as the cause; whereas whatever defect is in it is not caused by God, but by the deficient sec-ondary cause.

Reply Obj. 3. The sinking of a ship is attributed to the sailor as the cause, from the fact that he does not fulfil what the safety of the ship requires; but God does not fail in doing what is necessary for the safety of all. Hence there is no parity.

THIRD ARTICLE
WHETHER THERE BE ONE SUPREME EVIL WHICH IS THE CAUSE OF EVERY EVIL?

We proceed thus to the Third Article:—

Objection 1. It would seem that there is one supreme evil which is the cause of every evil. For contrary effects have contrary causes. But contrariety is found in things, according to Ecclus. xxxiii. 15: *Good is set against evil, and life against death; so also is the sinner against a just man.* Therefore there are many contrary principles, one of good, the other of evil.

Obj. 2. Further, if one contrary is in nature, so is the other. But the supreme good is in nature, and is the cause of every good, as was shown above (Q. 2, A. 3; Q. 6, AA. 2, 4). Therefore, also, there is a supreme evil opposed to it as the cause of every evil.

Obj. 3. Further, as we find good and better things, so we find evil and worse. But good and better are so considered in relation to what is best. Therefore evil and worse are so considered in relation to some supreme evil.

Obj. 4. Further, everything participated is reduced to what is essential. But things which are evil among us are evil not essentially, but by participation. Therefore we must seek for some supreme essential evil, which is the cause of every evil.

Obj. 5. Further, whatever is accidental is reduced to that which is *per se.* But good is the accidental cause of evil. Therefore, we must suppose some supreme evil which is the *per se* cause of evils. Nor can it be said that evil has no *per se* cause, but only an accidental cause; for it would then follow that evil would not exist in the many, but only in the few.

Obj. 6. Further, the evil of the effect is reduced to the evil of the cause; because the deficient effect comes from the deficient cause, as was said above (AA. 1, 2). But we cannot proceed to infinity in this matter. Therefore, we must suppose one first evil as the cause of every evil.

On the contrary, The supreme good is the cause of every being, as was shown above (Q. 2, A. 3; Q. 6, A. 4). Therefore there cannot be any principle opposed to it as the cause of evils.

I answer that, It appears from what precedes that there is no one first principle of evil, as there is one first principle of good.

First, indeed, because the first principle of good is essentially good, as was shown above (Q. 6, AA. 3, 4). But nothing can be essentially bad. For it was shown above that every being, as such, is good (Q. 5, A. 3); and that evil can exist only in good as in its subject (Q. 48; A. 3).

Secondly, because the first principle of good is the highest and perfect good which pre-contains in itself all goodness, as shown above (Q. 6, A. 2). But there cannot be a supreme evil; because, as was shown above (Q. 48, A. 4), although evil always lessens good, yet it never wholly consumes it; and thus, while good ever remains, nothing can be wholly and perfectly bad. Therefore, the Philosopher says (*Ethic.* iv. 5) that *if the wholly evil could be, it would destroy itself;* because all good being destroyed (which it need be for something to be wholly evil), evil itself would be taken away, since its subject is good.

Thirdly, because the very nature of evil is against the idea of a first principle; both because every evil is caused by good, as was shown above (A. 1), and because evil can be only an accidental cause, and thus it cannot be the first cause, for the accidental cause is subsequent to the direct cause.

Those, however, who upheld two first principles, one good and the other evil, fell into this error from the same cause, whence also arose other strange notions of the ancients; namely, because they failed to consider the universal cause of all being, and considered only the particular causes of particular effects. For on that account, if they found a thing hurtful to something by the power of its own nature, they thought that the very nature of that thing was evil; as, for instance, if one should say that the nature of fire was evil because it burnt the house of a poor man. The judgment, however, of the goodness of anything does not depend upon its order to any particular thing, but rather upon what it is in itself, and on its order to the whole universe, wherein every part has its own perfectly ordered place, as was said above (Q. 47, A. 2 *ad* 1).

Likewise, because they found two contrary particular causes of two contrary particular effects, they did not know how to reduce these contrary particular causes to the universal common cause; and therefore they extended the contrariety of causes even to the first principles. But since all contrarieties agree in something common, it is necessary to search for one common cause for them above their own contrary proper causes; as above the contrary qualities of the elements exists the power of a heavenly body;

and above all things that exist, no matter how, there exists one first principle of being, as was shown above (Q. 2, A. 3).

Reply Obj. 1. Contraries agree in one genus, and they also agree in the nature of being; and therefore, although they have contrary particular causes, nevertheless we must come at last to one first common cause.

Reply Obj. 2. Privation and habit belong naturally to the same subject. Now the subject of privation is a being in potentiality, as was said above (Q. 48, A. 3). Hence, since evil is privation of good, as appears from what was said above (*ibid.*, AA. 1, 2, 3), it is opposed to that good which has some potentiality, but not to the supreme good, who is pure act.

Reply Obj. 3. Increase in intensity is in proportion to the nature of a thing. And as the form is a perfection, so privation removes a perfection. Hence every form, perfection, and good is intensified by approach to the perfect term; but privation and evil by receding from that term. Hence a thing is not said to be evil and worse, by reason of access to the supreme evil, in the same way as it is said to be good and better, by reason of access to the supreme good.

Reply Obj. 4. No being is called evil by participation, but by privation of participation. Hence it is not necessary to reduce it to any essential evil.

Reply Obj. 5. Evil can only have an accidental cause, as was shown above (A. 1). Hence reduction to any *per se* cause of evil is impossible. And to say that evil is in the greater number is simply false. For things which are generated and corrupted, in which alone can there be natural evil, are the smaller part of the whole universe. And again, in every species the defect of nature is in the smaller number. In man alone does evil appear as in the greater number; because the good of man as regards the senses is not the good of man as man—that is, in regard to reason; and more men seek good in regard to the senses than good according to reason.

Reply Obj. 6. In the causes of evil we do not proceed to infinity, but reduce all evils to some good cause, whence evil follows accidentally.

Cleanthes =
naïve believer

Imaginary
characters

Evil and the God of Religion

DAVID HUME

Scottish 1711 – 1776 *of colon cancer*

a sceptic

"The Dialogues" about rationality of religious belief

PART X

It is my opinion, I own, replied Demea, that each man feels, in a manner, the truth of religion within his own breast, and, from a consciousness of his imbecility and misery rather than from any reasoning, is led to seek protection from that Being on whom he and all nature is dependent. So anxious or so tedious are even the best scenes of life that futurity is still the object of all our hopes and fears. We incessantly look forward and endeavor, by prayers, adoration, and sacrifice, to appease those unknown powers whom we find, by experience, so able to afflict and oppress us. Wretched creatures that we are! What resource for us amidst the innumerable ills of life did not religion suggest some methods of atonement, and appease those terrors with which we are incessantly agitated and tormented?

I am indeed persuaded, said Philo, that the best and indeed the only method of bringing everyone to a due sense of religion is by just representations of the misery and wickedness of men. And for that purpose a talent of eloquence and strong imagery is more requisite than that of reasoning and argument. For is it necessary to prove what everyone feels within himself? It is only necessary to make us feel it, if possible, more intimately and sensibly.

The people, indeed, replied Demea, are sufficiently convinced of this great and melancholy truth. The miseries of life, the unhappiness of man, the general corruptions of our nature, the unsatisfactory enjoyment of pleasures, riches, honors—these phrases have become almost proverbial in all languages. And who can doubt of what all men declare from their own immediate feeling and experience?

From *Dialogues Concerning Natural Religion*, Parts X and XI.

In this point, said Philo, the learned are perfectly agreed with the vulgar; and in all letters, *sacred* and *profane,* the topic of human misery has been insisted on with the most pathetic eloquence that sorrow and melancholy could inspire. The poets, who speak from sentiment, without a system, and whose testimony has therefore the more authority, abound in images of this nature. From Homer down to Dr. Young, the whole inspired tribe have ever been sensible that no other representation of things would suit the feeling and observation of each individual.

As to authorities, replied Demea, you need not seek them. Look round this library of Cleanthes. I shall venture to affirm that, except authors of particular sciences, such as chemistry or botany, who have no occasion to treat of human life, there is scarce one of those innumerable writers from whom the sense of human misery has not, in some passage or other, extorted a complaint and confession of it. At least, the chance is entirely on that side; and no one author has ever, so far as I can recollect, been so extravagant as to deny it.

There you must excuse me, said Philo: Leibniz has denied it, and is perhaps the first who ventured upon so bold and paradoxical an opinion; at least, the first who made it essential to his philosophical system.

And by being the first, replied Demea, might he not have been sensible of his error? For is this a subject in which philosophers can propose to make discoveries especially in so late an age? And can any man hope by a simple denial (for the subject scarcely admits of reasoning) to bear down the united testimony of mankind, founded on sense and consciousness?

And why should man, added he, pretend to an exemption from the lot of all other animals? The whole earth, believe me, Philo, is cursed and polluted. A perpetual war is kindled amongst all living creatures. Necessity, hunger, want stimulate the strong and courageous; fear, anxiety, terror agitate the weak and infirm. The first entrance into life gives anguish to the newborn infant and to its wretched parent; weakness, impotence, distress attend each stage of that life, and it is, at last, finished in agony and horror.

Observe, too, says Philo, the curious artifices of nature in order to embitter the life of every living being. The stronger prey upon the weaker and keep them in perpetual terror and anxiety. The weaker, too, in their turn, often prey upon the stronger, and vex and molest them without relaxation. Consider that innumerable race of insects, which either are bred on the body of each animal or, flying about, infix their stings in him. These insects have others still less than themselves which torment them.

And thus on each hand, before and behind, above and below, every animal is surrounded with enemies which incessantly seek his misery and destruction.

Man alone, said Demea, seems to be, in part, an exception to this rule. For by combination in society he can easily master lions, tigers, and bears, whose greater strength and agility naturally enable them to prey upon him.

On the contrary, it is here chiefly, cried Philo, that the uniform and equal maxims of nature are most apparent. Man, it is true, can, by combination, surmount all his *real* enemies and become master of the whole animal creation; but does he not immediately raise up to himself *imaginary* enemies, the demons of his fancy, who haunt him with superstitious terrors and blast every enjoyment of life? His pleasure, as he imagines, becomes in their eyes a crime; his food and repose give them umbrage and offense; his very sleep and dreams furnish new materials to anxious fear; and even death, his refuge from every other ill, presents only the dread of endless and innumerable woes. Nor does the wolf molest more the timid flock than superstition does the anxious breast of wretched mortals.

Besides, consider, Demea: This very society by which we surmount those wild beasts, our natural enemies, what new enemies does it not raise to us? What woe and misery does it not occasion? Man is the greatest enemy of man. Oppression, injustice, contempt, contumely, violence, sedition, war, calumny, treachery, fraud—by these they mutually torment each other, and they would soon dissolve that society which they had formed were it not for the dread of still greater ills which must attend their separation.

But though these external insults, said Demea, from animals, from men, from all the elements, which assault us form a frightful catalog of woes, they are nothing in comparison of those which arise within ourselves, from the distempered condition of our mind and body. How many lie under the lingering torment of diseases? Hear the pathetic enumeration of the great poet.

> Intestine stone and ulcer, colic-pangs,
> Demoniac frenzy, moping melancholy,
> And moon-struck madness, pining atrophy,
> Marasmus, and wide-wasting pestilence.
> Dire was the tossing, deep the groans: *Despair*
> Tended the sick, busiest from couch to couch.
> And over them triumphant *Death* his dart

Shook: but delay'd to strike, though oft invok'd
With vows, as their chief good and final hope.

The disorders of the mind, continued Demea, though more secret,
are not perhaps less dismal and vexatious. Remorse, shame, anguish,
rage, disappointment, anxiety, fear, dejection, despair—who has ever
passed through life without cruel inroads from these tormentors? How
many have scarcely ever felt any better sensations? Labor and poverty, so
abhorred by everyone, are the certain lot of the far greater number; and
those few privileged persons who enjoy ease and opulence never reach contentment or true felicity. All the goods of life united would not make a
very happy man, but all the ills united would make a wretch indeed; and
any one of them almost (and who can be free from every one?), nay, often
the absence of one good (and who can possess all?) is sufficient to render
life ineligible.

Were a stranger to drop on a sudden into this world, I would show
him, as a specimen of its ills, a hospital full of diseases, a prison crowded
with malefactors and debtors, a field of battle strewed with carcases, a
fleet foundering in the ocean, a nation languishing under tyranny, famine, or pestilence. To turn the gay side of life to him and give him a notion
of its pleasures—whither should I conduct him? To a ball, to an opera, to
court? He might justly think that I was only showing him a diversity of
distress and sorrow.

There is no evading such striking instances, said Philo, but by
apologies which still further aggravate the charge. Why have all men, I
ask, in all ages, complained incessantly of the miseries of life? . . . They
have no just reason, says one: these complaints proceed only from their
discontented, repining, anxious disposition. . . . And can there possibly,
I reply, be a more certain foundation of misery than such a wretched
temper?

But if they were really as unhappy as they pretend, says my antagonist, why do they remain in life? . . . Not satisfied with life, afraid of
death—this is the secret chain, say I, that holds us. We are terrified, not
bribed to the continuance of our existence.

It is only a false delicacy, he may insist, which a few refined spirits
indulge, and which has spread these complaints among the whole race of
mankind. . . . And what is this delicacy, I ask, which you blame? Is it
anything but a greater sensibility to all the pleasures and pains of life?
And if the man of a delicate, refined temper, by being so much more alive
than the rest of the world, is only so much more unhappy, what judgment
must we form in general of human life?

Let men remain at rest, says our adversary, and they will be easy. They are willing artificers of their own misery. . . . No! reply I: an anxious languor follows their repose; disappointment, vexation, trouble, their activity and ambition.

I can observe something like what you mention in some others, replied Cleanthes, but I confess I feel little or nothing of it in myself, and hope that it is not so common as you represent it.

If you feel not human misery yourself, cried Demea, I congratulate you on so happy a singularity. Others, seemingly the most prosperous, have not been ashamed to vent their complaints in the most melancholy strains. Let us attend to the great, the fortunate emperor, Charles V, when, tired with human grandeur, he resigned all his extensive dominions into the hands of his son. In the last harangue which he made on that memorable occasion, he publicly avowed *that the greatest prosperities which he had ever enjoyed had been mixed with so many adversities that he might truly say he had never enjoyed any satisfaction or contentment.* But did the retired life in which he sought for shelter afford him any greater happiness? If we may credit his son's account, his repentance commenced the very day of his resignation.

Cicero's fortune, from small beginnings, rose to the greatest luster and renown; yet what pathetic complaints of the ills of life do his familiar letters, as well as philosophical discourses, contain? And suitably to his own experience, he introduces Cato, the great, the fortunate Cato protesting in his old age that had he a new life in his offer he would reject the present.

Ask yourself, ask any of your acquaintance, whether they would live over again the last ten or twenty years of their life. No! but the next twenty, they say, will be better:

> And from the dregs of life, hope to receive
> What the first sprightly running could not give.

Thus, at last, they find (such is the greatness of human misery, it reconciles even contradictions) that they complain at once of the shortness of life and of its vanity and sorrow.

And is it possible, Cleanthes, said Philo, that after all these reflections, and infinitely more which might be suggested, you can still persevere in your anthropomorphism, and assert the moral attributes of the Deity, his justice, benevolence, mercy, and rectitude, to be of the same nature with these virtues in human creatures? His power, we allow, is infinite; whatever he wills is executed; but neither man nor any other animal is happy; therefore, he does not will their happiness. His wisdom is infinite; he is never mistaken in choosing the means to any end; but the course of nature tends not to human or animal felicity; therefore, it is not established for that purpose. Through the whole compass of human knowledge there are no inferences more certain and infallible than these. In what respect, then, do his benevolence and mercy resemble the benevolence and mercy of men?

Epicurus' old questions are yet unanswered.

Is he willing to prevent evil, but not able? then he is impotent. Is he able, but not willing? then is he malevolent. Is he both able and willing? whence then is evil?

You ascribe, Cleanthes, (and I believe justly) a purpose and intention to nature. But what, I beseech you, is the object of that curious artifice and machinery which she has displayed in all animals—the preservation alone of individuals, and propagation of the species? It seems enough for her purpose, if such a rank be barely upheld in the universe, without any care or concern for the happiness of the members that compose it. No resource for this purpose: no machinery in order merely to give pleasure or ease; no fund of pure joy and contentment; no indulgence without some want or necessity accompanying it. At least, the few phenomena of this nature are overbalanced by opposite phenomena of still greater importance.

Our sense of music, harmony, and indeed beauty of all kinds, gives satisfaction, without being absolutely necessary to the preservation and propagation of the species. But what racking pains, on the other hand, arise from gouts, gravels, megrims, toothaches, rheumatisms, where the injury to the animal machinery is either small or incurable? Mirth, laughter, play, frolic seem gratuitous satisfactions which have no further tendency; spleen, melancholy, discontent, superstition are pains of the same nature. How then does the Divine benevolence display itself, in the sense of you anthropomorphites? None but we mystics, as you were pleased to call us, can account for this strange mixture of phenomena, by deriving it from attributes infinitely perfect but incomprehensible.

And have you, at last, said Cleanthes smiling, betrayed your intentions, Philo? Your long agreement with Demea did indeed a little surprise me, but I find you were all the while erecting a concealed battery against me. And I must confess that you have now fallen upon a subject worthy of your noble spirit of opposition and controversy. If you can make out the present point, and prove mankind to be unhappy or corrupted, there is an end at once of all religion. For to what purpose establish the natural attributes of the Deity, while the moral are still doubtful and uncertain?

You take umbrage very easily, replied Demea, at opinions the most innocent and the most generally received, even amongst the religious and devout themselves; and nothing can be more surprising than to find a topic like this—concerning the wickedness and misery of man—charged with no less than atheism and profaneness. Have not all pious divines and preachers who have indulged their rhetoric on so fertile a subject, have they not easily, I say, given a solution of any difficulties which may attend it? This world is but a point in comparison of the universe; this life but a moment in comparison of eternity. The present evil phenomena, therefore, are rectified in other regions, and in some future period of existence. And the eyes of men, being then opened to larger views of things, see the whole connection of general laws, and trace, with adoration, the benevolence, and rectitude of the Deity through all the mazes and intricacies of his providence.

No! replied Cleanthes, no! These arbitrary suppositions can never be admitted, contrary to matter of fact, visible and uncontroverted. Whence can any cause be known but from its known effects? Whence can any hypothesis be proved but from the apparent phenomena? To establish one hypothesis upon another is building entirely in the air; and the utmost we ever attain by these conjectures and fictions is to ascertain the bare possibility of our opinion, but never can we, upon such terms, establish its reality.

The only method of supporting Divine benevolence—and it is what I willingly embrace—is to deny absolutely the misery and wickedness of man. Your representations are exaggerated; your melancholy views mostly fictitious; your inferences contrary to fact and experience. Health is more common than sickness; pleasure than pain; happiness than misery. And for one vexation which we meet with, we attain, upon computation, a hundred enjoyments.

Admitting your position, replied Philo, which yet is extremely doubtful, you must at the same time allow that, if pain be less frequent than pleasure, it is infinitely more violent and durable. One hour of it is often able to outweigh a day, a week, a month of our common insipid enjoyments; and how many days, weeks, and months are passed by several in the most acute torments? Pleasure, scarcely in one instance, is ever able to reach ecstasy and rapture; and in no one instance can it continue for any time at its highest pitch and altitude. The spirits evaporate, the nerves relax, the fabric is disordered, and the enjoyment quickly degenerates into fatigue and uneasiness. But pain often, good God, how often! rises to torture and agony; and the longer it continues, it becomes still more genuine agony and torture. Patience is exhausted, courage languishes, melancholy seizes us, and nothing terminates our misery but the removal of its cause or another event which is the sole cure of all evil, but which, from our natural folly, we regard with still greater horror and consternation. *Death!* *But who knows??*

But not to insist upon these topics, continued Philo, though most obvious, certain, and important, I must use the freedom to admonish you, Cleanthes, that you have put the controversy upon a most dangerous issue, and are unawares introducing a total skepticism into the most essential articles of natural and revealed theology. What! no method of fixing a just foundation for religion unless we allow the happiness of human life, and maintain a continued existence even in this world, with all our present pains, infirmities, vexations, and follies, to be eligible and desirable! But this is contrary to everyone's feeling and experience; it is contrary to an authority so established as nothing can subvert. No decisive proofs can ever be produced against this authority; nor is it possible for you to compute, estimate, and compare all the pains and all the pleasures in the lives of all men and of all animals; and thus, by your resting the whole system of religion on a point which, from its very nature, must forever be uncertain, you tacitly confess that that system is equally uncertain. *FAITH*

But allowing you what never will be believed, at least, what you never possibly can prove, that animal or, at least, human happiness in this life exceeds its misery, you have yet done nothing; for this is not, by any means, what we expect from infinite power, infinite wisdom, and infinite goodness. Why is there any misery at all in the world? Not by chance, surely. From some cause then. Is it from the intention of the Deity? But he is perfectly benevolent. Is it contrary to his intention? But he is almighty. Nothing can shake the solidity of this reasoning, so short, so clear, so decisive, except we assert that these subjects exceed all human capacity, and that our common measures of truth and falsehood are not applicable to them—a topic which I have all along insisted on, but which you have, from the beginning, rejected with scorn and indignation.

But I will be contented to retire still from this entrenchment, for I deny that you can ever force me in it. I will allow that pain or misery in man is *compatible* with infinite power and goodness in the Deity, even in your sense of these attributes: what are you advanced by all these concessions? A mere possible compatibility is not sufficient. You must *prove* these pure, unmixed, and uncontrollable attributes from the present mixed and confused phenomena, and from these alone. A hopeful undertaking! Were the phenomena ever so pure and unmixed, yet, being finite, they would be

Demea: god's mercy / benevolence are not what we conceive as such.

insufficient for that purpose. How much more, where they are also so jarring and discordant!

Here, Cleanthes, I find myself at ease in my argument. Here I triumph. Formerly, when we argued concerning the natural attributes of intelligence and design, I needed all my skeptical and metaphysical subtlety to elude your grasp. In many views of the universe and of its parts, particularly the latter, the beauty and fitness of final causes strike us with such irresistible force that all objections appear (what I believe they really are) mere cavils and sophisms; nor can we then imagine how it was ever possible for us to repose any weight on them. But there is no view of human life or of the condition of mankind from which, without the greatest violence, we can infer the moral attributes or learn that infinite benevolence, conjoined with infinite power and infinite wisdom, which we must discover by the eyes of faith alone. It is your turn now to tug the laboring oar, and to support your philosophical subtleties against the dictates of plain reason and experience.

Philo to C.

cavil = petty objection
sophism = statement to deceive in debate

PART XI

I scruple not to allow, said Cleanthes, that I have been apt to suspect the frequent repetition of the word *infinite,* which we meet with in all theological writers, to savor more of panegyric than of philosophy, and that any purposes of reasoning, and even of religion, would be better served were we to rest contented with more accurate and more moderate expressions. The terms *admirable, excellent, superlatively great, wise,* and *holy*—these sufficiently fill the imaginations of men, and anything beyond, besides that it leads into absurdities, has no influence on the affections or sentiments. Thus, in the present subject, if we abandon all human analogy, as seems your intention, Demea, I am afraid we abandon all religion and retain no conception of the great object of our adoration. If we preserve human analogy, we must forever find it impossible to reconcile any mixture of evil in the universe with infinite attributes; much less can we ever prove the latter from the former. But supposing the Author of nature to be finitely perfect, though far exceeding mankind, a satisfactory account may then be given of natural and moral evil, and every untoward phenomenon be explained and adjusted. A less evil may then be chosen in order to avoid a greater; inconveniences be submitted to in order to reach a desirable end; and, in a word, benevolence, regulated by wisdom and limited by necessity, may produce just such a world as the present. You, Philo, who are so prompt at starting views and reflections and analogies,

text of praise

I would gladly hear, at length, without interruption, your opinion of this new theory; and if it deserve our attention, we may afterwards, at more leisure, reduce it into form.

My sentiments, replied Philo, are not worth being made a mystery of; and, therefore, without any ceremony, I shall deliver what occurs to me with regard to the present subject. It must, I think, be allowed that, if a very limited intelligence whom we shall suppose utterly unacquainted with the universe were assured that it were the production of a very good, wise, and powerful Being, however finite, he would, from his conjectures, form *beforehand* a different notion of it from what we find it to be by experience; nor would he ever imagine, merely from these attributes of the cause of which he is informed, that the effect could be so full of vice and misery and disorder, as it appears in this life. Supposing now that this person were brought into the world, still assured that it was the workmanship of such a sublime and benevolent Being, he might, perhaps, be surprised at the disappointment, but would never retract his former belief if founded on any very solid argument, since such a limited intelligence must be sensible of his own blandness and ignorance, and must allow that there may be many solutions of those phenomena which will forever escape his comprehension. But supposing, which is the real case with regard to man, that this creature is not antecedently convinced of a supreme intelligence, benevolent, and powerful, but is left to gather such a belief from the appearances of things—this entirely alters the case, nor will he ever find any reason for such a conclusion. He may be fully convinced of the narrow limits of his understanding, but this will not help him in forming an inference concerning the goodness of superior powers, since he must form that inference from what he knows, not from what he is ignorant of. The more you exaggerate his weakness and ignorance, the more diffident you render him, and give him the greater suspicion that such subjects are beyond the reach of his faculties. You are obliged, therefore, to reason with him merely from the known phenomena, and to drop every arbitrary supposition or conjecture.

Did I show you a house or palace where there was not one apartment convenient or agreeable, where the windows, doors, fires, passages, stairs, and the whole economy of the building were the source of noise, confusion, fatigue, darkness, and the extremes of heat and cold, you would certainly blame the contrivance, without any further examination. The architect would in vain display his subtlety, and prove to you that, if this door or that window were altered, greater ills would ensue. What he says may be strictly true: the alteration of one particular, while the other parts of the building remain, may only augment the inconveniences. But still you would assert in general that, if the architect had had skill and good intentions, he might have formed such a plan of the whole, and might have adjusted the parts in such a manner as would have remedied all or most of these inconveniences. His ignorance, or even your own ignorance of such a plan, will never convince you of the impossibility of it. If you find any inconveniences and deformities in the building, you will always, without entering into any detail, condemn the architect.

In short, I repeat the question: Is the world, considered in general and as it appears to us in this life, different from what a man or such a limited being would, *beforehand,* expect from a very powerful, wise, and benevolent Deity? It must be strange prejudice to assert the contrary. And from thence I conclude that, however consistent the world may be, allowing certain suppositions and conjectures with the idea of such a Deity, it can never afford us an inference concerning his existence. The consistency is not absolutely denied, only the inference. Conjectures, especially where infinity is excluded from the Divine attributes, may perhaps be sufficient to prove a consistency, but can never be foundations for any inference.

There seem to be *four* circumstances on which depend all or the greatest part of the ills that molest sensible creatures; and it is not impossible but all these circumstances may be necessary and unavoidable. We know so little beyond common life, or even of common life, that, with regard to the economy of a universe, there is no conjecture, however wild, which may not be just, nor any one, however plausible, which may not be erroneous. All that belongs to human understanding, in this deep ignorance and obscurity, is to be skeptical or at least cautious, and not to admit of any hypothesis whatever, much less of any which is supported by no appearance of probability. Now this I assert to be the case with regard to all the causes of evil and the circumstances on which it depends. None of them appear to human reason in the least degree necessary or unavoidable, nor can we suppose them such, without the utmost license of imagination.

The *first* circumstance which introduces evil is that contrivance or economy of the animal creation by which pains, as well as pleasures, are employed to excite all creatures to action, and make them vigilant in the great work of self-preservation. Now pleasure alone, in its various degrees, seem to human understanding sufficient for this purpose. All animals might be constantly in a state of enjoyment; but when urged by any of the necessities of nature, such as thirst, hunger, weariness, instead of pain, they might feel a diminution of pleasure by which they might be prompted to seek that object which is necessary to their subsistence. Men pursue pleasure as eagerly as they avoid pain; at least, they might have been so constituted. It seems, therefore, plainly possible to carry on the business of life without any pain. Why then is any animal ever rendered susceptible of such a sensation? If animals can be free from it an hour, they might enjoy a perpetual exemption from it, and it required as particular a contrivance of their organs to produce that feeling as to endow them with sight, hearing, or any of the senses. Shall we conjecture that such a contrivance was necessary, without any appearance of reason, and shall we build on that conjecture as on the most certain truth?

But a capacity of pain would not alone produce pain were it not for the *second* circumstance, viz., the conducting of the world by general laws; and this seems nowise necessary to a very perfect Being. It is true, if everything were conducted by particular volitions, the course of nature would be perpetually broken, and no man could employ his reason in the conduct of life. But might not other particular volitions remedy this inconvenience? In short, might not the Deity exterminate all ill, wherever it were to be found, and produce all good, without any preparation or long progress of causes and effects?

Besides, we must consider that, according to the present economy of the world, the course of nature, though supposed exactly regular, yet to us appears not so, and many events are uncertain, and many disappoint our expectations. Health and sickness, calm and tempest, with an infinite number of other accidents whose causes are unknown and variable, have a great influence both on the fortunes of particular persons and on the prosperity of public societies; and indeed all human life, in a manner, depends on such accidents. A being, therefore, who knows the secret springs of the universe might easily, by particular volitions, turn all these accidents to the good of mankind and render the whole world happy, without discovering himself in any operation. A fleet whose purposes were salutary to society might always meet with a fair wind. Good princes enjoy sound health and long life. Persons born to power and authority be framed with good tempers and virtuous dispositions. A few such events as these, regularly and wisely conducted, would change the face of the world, and yet would no more seem to disturb the course of nature or confound human conduct than the present economy of things where the causes are secret and variable and compounded. Some small touches given to Caligula's brain in his infancy might have converted him into a Trajan. One wave, a little higher than the rest, by burying Caesar and his fortune in the bottom of the ocean, might have restored liberty to a considerable part of mankind. There may, for aught we know, be good reasons why Providence interposes not in this manner, but they are unknown to us; and, though the mere supposition that such reasons exist may be sufficient to *save* the conclusion concerning the Divine attributes, yet surely it can never be sufficient to *establish* that conclusion.

If everything in the universe be conducted by general laws, and if animals be rendered susceptible of pain, it scarcely seems possible but some ill must arise in the various shocks of matter and the various concurrence and opposition of general laws; but this ill would be very rare were it not for the *third* circumstance which I proposed to mention, viz., the great frugality with which all powers and faculties are distributed to every particular being. So well adjusted are the organs and capacities of all animals, and so well fitted to their preservation, that, as far as history or tradition reaches, there appears not to be any single species which has yet been extinguished in the universe. Every animal has the requisite endowments, but these endowments are bestowed with so scrupulous an economy that any considerable diminution must entirely destroy the creature. Wherever one power is increased, there is a proportional abatement in the others. Animals which excel in swiftness are commonly defective in force. Those which possess both are either imperfect in some of their senses or are oppressed with the most craving wants. The human species, whose chief excellence is reason and sagacity, is of all others the most necessitous, and the most deficient in bodily advantages, without clothes, without arms, without food, without lodging, without any convenience of life, except what they owe to their own skill and industry. In short, nature seems to have formed an exact calculation of the necessities of her creatures, and, like a *rigid master*, has afforded them little more powers or endowments than what are strictly sufficient to supply those necessities. An *indulgent parent* would have bestowed a large stock in order to guard against accidents, and secure the happiness and welfare of the creature in the most unfortunate concurrence of circumstances. Every course of life would not have been so surrounded with precipices that the least departure from the true path, by mistake or necessity, must involve us in misery and ruin. Some reserve, some fund, would have been provided to ensure happiness, nor would the powers and the necessities have been adjusted with so rigid an economy. The Author of nature is inconceivably powerful; his force is supposed great, if not altogether inexhaustible, nor is there any reason, as far as we can judge, to make him observe this strict frugality in his dealings with his creatures. It would have been better, were his power extremely limited, to have created fewer animals, and to have endowed these with more faculties for their happiness and preservation. A builder is never esteemed prudent who undertakes a plan beyond what his stock will enable him to finish.

In order to cure most of the ills of human life, I require not that man should have the wings of the eagle, the swiftness of the stag, the force of the ox, the arms of the lion, the scales of the crocodile or rhinoceros; much less do I demand the sagacity of an angel or cherubim. I am contented to take an increase in one single power or faculty of his soul. Let him be endowed with a greater propensity to industry and labor, a more vigorous spring and activity of mind, a more constant bent to business and application. Let the whole species possess naturally an equal diligence with that which many individuals are able to attain by habit and reflection, and the most beneficial consequences, without any allay of ill, is the immediate and necessary result of this endowment. Almost all the moral as well as natural evils of human life arise from idleness; and were our species, by the original constitution of their frame, exempt from this vice or infirmity, the perfect cultivation of land, the improvement of arts and manufactures, the exact execution of every office and duty, immediately follow; and men at once may fully reach that state of society which is so imperfectly attained by the best-regulated government. But as industry is a power, and the most valuable of any, nature seems determined, suitably to her usual maxims, to bestow it on men with a very sparing hand, and rather to punish him severely for his deficiency in it than to reward him for his attainments. She has so contrived his frame that nothing but the most violent necessity can oblige him to labor; and she employs all his other wants to overcome, at least in part, the want of diligence, and to endow him with some share of a faculty of which she has thought fit naturally to bereave him. Here our demands may be allowed very humble, and therefore the more reasonable. If we required the endowments of superior penetration and judgment, of a more delicate taste of beauty, of a nicer sensibility to benevolence and friendship, we might be told that we impiously pretend to break the order of nature, that we want to exalt ourselves into a higher rank of being, that the presents which we require, not being suitable to our state and condition, would only be pernicious to us. But it is hard, I dare to repeat it, it is hard that, being placed in a world so full of wants and necessities, where almost every being and element is either our foe or refuses its assistance . . . we should also have our own temper to struggle with, and should be deprived of that faculty which can alone fence against these multiplied evils.

The *fourth* circumstance whence arises the misery and ill of the uni- (4)
verse is the inaccurate workmanship of all the springs and principles of the
great machine of nature. It must be acknowledged that there are few
parts of the universe which seem not to serve some purpose, and whose
removal would not produce a visible defect and disorder in the whole. The
parts hang all together, nor can one be touched without affecting the rest,
in a greater or less degree. But at the same time, it must be observed that
none of these parts or principles, however useful, are so accurately adjusted as to keep precisely within those bounds in which their utility consists; but they are, all of them, apt, on every occasion, to run into the one
extreme or the other. One would imagine that this grand production had
not received the last hand of the maker—so little finished is every part,
and so coarse are the strokes with which it is executed. Thus the winds are
requisite to convey the vapors along the surface of the globe, and to assist
men in navigation; but how often, rising up to tempests and hurricanes,
do they become pernicious? Rains are necessary to nourish all the plants
and animals of the earth; but how often are they defective? how often excessive? Heat is requisite to all life and vegetation, but is not always found
in the due proportion. On the mixture and secretion of the humors and
juices of the body depend the health and prosperity of the animal; but the
parts perform not regularly their proper function. What more useful than
all the passions of the mind, ambition, vanity, love, anger? But how often
do they break their bounds and cause the greatest convulsions in society?
There is nothing so advantageous in the universe but what frequently becomes pernicious, by its excess or defect; nor has nature guarded, with the
requisite accuracy, against all disorder or confusion. The irregularity is
never perhaps so great as to destroy any species, but is often sufficient to
involve the individuals in ruin and misery.

On the concurrence, then, of these *four* circumstances does all or the
greatest part of natural evil depend. Were all living creatures incapable of
pain, or were the world administered by particular volitions, evil never
could have found access into the universe; and were animals endowed with
a large stock of powers and faculties, beyond what strict necessity requires, or were the several springs and principles of the universe so accurately framed as to preserve always the just temperament and medium,
there must have been very little ill in comparison with what we feel at
present. What then shall we pronounce on this occasion? Shall we say that
these circumstances are not necessary, and they might easily have been altered in the contrivance of the universe? This decision seems too presump-
tuous for creatures so blind and ignorant. Let us be more modest in our

conclusions. Let us allow that, if the goodness of the Deity (I mean a goodness like the human) could be established on any tolerable reasons a priori, these phenomena however untoward, would not be sufficient to subvert that principle, but might easily, in some unknown manner, be reconcilable to it. But let us still assert that, as this goodness is not antecedently established but must be inferred from the phenomena, there can be no grounds for such an inference while there are so many ills in the universe, and while these ills might so easily have been remedied, as far as human understanding can be allowed to judge on such a subject. I am skeptic enough to allow that the bad appearances, notwithstanding all my reasonings, may be compatible with such attributes as you suppose, but surely they can never prove these attributes. Such a conclusion cannot result from skepticism, but must arise from the phenomena, and from our confidence in the reasonings which we deduce from these phenomena.

Look round this universe. What an immense profusion of beings, animated and organized, sensible and active! You admire this prodigious variety and fecundity. But inspect a little more narrowly these living existences, the only beings worth regarding. How hostile and destructive to each other! How insufficient all of them for their own happiness! How contemptible or odious to the spectator! The whole presents nothing but the idea of a blind nature, impregnated by a great vivifying principle, and pouring forth from her lap, without discernment or parental care, her maimed and abortive children!

Here the Manichean system occurs as a proper hypothesis to solve the difficulty; and, no doubt, in some respects it is very specious and has more probability than the common hypothesis, by giving a plausible account of the strange mixture of good and ill which appears in life. But if we consider, on the other hand, the perfect uniformity and agreement of the parts of the universe, we shall not discover in it any marks of the combat of a malevolent with a benevolent being. There is indeed an opposition of pains and pleasures in the feelings of sensible creatures; but are not all the operations of nature carried on by an opposition of principles, of hot and cold, moist and dry, light and heavy? The true conclusion is that the original Source of all things is entirely indifferent to all these principles, and has no more regard to good above ill than to heat above cold, or to drought above moisture, or to light above heavy.

There may *four* hypotheses be framed concerning the first causes of the universe: that they are endowed with perfect goodness; that they have perfect malice; that they are opposite and have both goodness and malice; that they have neither goodness nor malice. Mixed phenomena can never prove the two former unmixed principles; and the uniformity and steadiness of general laws seem to oppose the third. The fourth, therefore, seems by far the most probable.

What I have said concerning natural evil will apply to moral [evil] with little or no variation; and we have no more reason to infer that the rectitude of the Supreme Being resembles human rectitude than that his benevolence resembles the human. Nay, it will be thought that we have still greater cause to exclude from him moral sentiments, such as we feel them, since moral evil, in the opinion of many, is much more predominant above moral good than natural evil above natural good.

But even though this should not be allowed, and though the virtue which is in mankind should be acknowledged much superior to the vice, yet, so long as there is any vice at all in the universe, it will very much puzzle you anthropomorphites how to account for it. You must assign a cause for it, without having recourse to the first cause. But as every effect must have a cause, and that cause another, you must either carry on the progression *in infinitum* or rest on that original principle, who is the ultimate cause of all things. . . .

Hold! hold! cried Demea: Whither does your imagination hurry you? I joined in alliance with you in order to prove the incomprehensible nature of the Divine Being, and refute the principles of Cleanthes, who would measure everything by human rule and standard. But I now find you running into all the topics of the greatest libertines and infidels, and betraying that holy cause which you seemingly espoused. Are you secretly, then, a more dangerous enemy than Cleanthes himself?

And are you so late in perceiving it? replied Cleanthes. Believe me, Demea, your friend Philo, from the beginning, has been amusing himself at both our expense; and it must be confessed that the injudicious reasoning of our vulgar theology has given him but too just a handle of ridicule. The total infirmity of human reason, the absolute incomprehensibility of the Divine Nature, the great and universal misery, and still greater wickedness of men—these are strange topics, surely, to be so fondly cherished by orthodox divines and doctors. In ages of stupidity and ignorance, indeed, these principles may safely be espoused; and perhaps no views of things are more proper to promote superstition than such as encourage the blind amazement, the diffidence, and melancholy of mankind. But at present . . .

Blame not so much, interposed Philo, the ignorance of these reverend gentlemen. They know how to change their style with the times. Formerly, it was a most popular theological topic to maintain that human life was vanity and misery, and to exaggerate all the ills and pains which are incident to men. But of late years, divines, we find, begin to retract this position and maintain, though still with some hesitation, that there are more goods than evils, more pleasures than pains, even in this life. When religion stood entirely upon temper and education, it was thought proper to encourage melancholy, as, indeed, mankind never have recourse to superior powers so readily as in that disposition. But as men have now learned to form principles and to draw consequences, it is necessary to change the batteries, and to make use of such arguments as will endure at least some scrutiny and examination. This variation is the same (and from the same causes) with that which I formerly remarked with regard to skepticism.

Thus Philo continued to the last his spirit of opposition, and his censure of established opinions. But I could observe that Demea did not at all relish the latter part of the discourse; and he took occasion soon after, on some pretense or other, to leave the company.

Sparknotes:

Philo : God may be morally corrupt

Demea: God beyond our understanding

Cleanthes: learn about God by observing nature.

Rebellion

FYODOR DOSTOEVSKY

"I must admit one thing to you," Ivan began. "I could never understand how one can love one's neighbors. It's just one's neighbors, to my mind, that one can't love, though one might love those at a distance. I once read somewhere of 'John the Merciful,'[1] a saint, that when a hungry, frozen beggar came to him, and asked him to warm him up, he took him into his bed, held him in his arms, and began breathing into his mouth, which was putrid and loathsome from some awful disease. I am convinced that he did that from the laceration of falsity, for the sake of the love imposed by duty, as a penance laid on him. For anyone to love a man, he must be hidden, for as soon as he shows his face, love is gone."

"Father Zosima has talked of that more than once," observed Alyosha; "he, too, said that the face of a man often hinders many people not practised in love, from loving him. But yet there's a great deal of love in mankind, and almost Christ-like love. I know that myself, Ivan."

"Well, I know nothing of it so far, and can't understand it, and the innumerable mass of mankind are with me there. The question is, whether that's due to men's bad qualities or whether it's inherent in their nature. To my thinking, Christ-like love for men is a miracle impossible on earth. He was God. But we are not gods. Suppose I, for instance, suffer intensely. Another can never know how much I suffer, because he is another and not I. And what's more, a man is rarely ready to admit another's suffering (as though it were a distinction). Why won't he admit it, do you think? Because I smell unpleasant, because I have a stupid face, because I once trod on his foot. Besides there is suffering and suffering; degrading,

Reprinted from THE BROTHERS KARAMAZOV by Fyodor Dostoevsky, A Norton Critical Edition, The Constance Garnett Translation revised by Ralph E. Matlaw, edited by Ralph E. Matlaw, by permission of W. W. Norton and Company, Inc. Copyright © 1976 by W. W. Norton and Company, Inc.

humiliating suffering such as humbles me—hunger, for instance—my benefactor will perhaps allow me; but when you come to higher suffering—for an idea, for instance—he will very rarely admit that, perhaps because my face strikes him not at all as what he fancies a man should have who suffers for an idea. And so he deprives me instantly of his favor, and not at all from badness of heart. Beggars, especially genteel beggars, ought never to show themselves, but to ask for charity through the newspapers. One can love one's neighbors in the abstract, or even at a distance, but at close quarters it's almost impossible. If it were as on the stage, in the ballet, where if beggars come in, they wear silken rags and tattered lace and beg for alms dancing gracefully, then one might like looking at them. But even then we would not love them. But enough of that. I simply wanted to show you my point of view. I meant to speak of the suffering of mankind generally, but we had better confine ourselves to the sufferings of the children. That reduces the scope of my argument to a tenth of what it would be. Still we'd better keep to the children, though it does weaken my case. But, in the first place, children can be loved even at close quarters, even when they are dirty, even when they are ugly (I fancy, though, children never are ugly). The second reason why I won't speak of grown-up people is that, besides being disgusting and unworthy of love, they have retribution—they've eaten the apple and know good and evil, and they have become 'like God.' They go on eating it still. But the children haven't eaten anything, and are so far innocent. Are you fond of children, Alyosha? I know you are, and you will understand why I prefer to speak of them. If they, too, suffer horribly on earth, they must suffer for their fathers, they must be punished for their fathers, who have eaten the apple; but that reasoning is of the other world and is incomprehensible for the heart of man here on earth. The innocent must not suffer for another's sins, and especially such innocents! You may be surprised at me, Alyosha, but I am awfully fond of children, too. And observe, cruel people, the violent, the rapacious, the Karamazovs are sometimes very fond of children. Children while they are quite little—up to seven, for instance— are so remote from grown-up people; they are different creatures, as it were, of a different species. I knew a criminal in prison who had, in the course of his career as a burglar, murdered whole families, including several children.[2] But when he was in prison, he had a strange affection for them. He spent all his time at his window, watching the children playing in the prison yard. He trained one little boy to come up to his window and made great friends with him. . . . You don't know why I am telling you all this, Alyosha? My head aches and I am sad."

"You speak with a strange air," observed Alyosha uneasily, "as though you were not quite yourself."

"By the way, a Bulgarian I met lately in Moscow," Ivan went on, seeming not to hear his brother's words, "told me about the crimes committed by Turks and Circassians in all parts of Bulgaria through fear of a general rising of the Slavs. They burn villages, murder, rape women and children, they nail their prisoners to the fences by the ears, leave them so till morning, and in the morning they hang them—all sorts of things you can't imagine. People talk sometimes of bestial cruelty, but that's a great injustice and insult to the beast; a beast can never be so cruel as a man, so artistically cruel. The tiger only tears and gnaws, that's all he can do. He would never think of nailing people by the ears, even if he were able to do it. These Turks took a pleasure in torturing children, too; cutting the unborn child from the mother's womb, and tossing babies up in the air and catching them on the points of their bayonets before their mother's eyes. Doing it before the mother's eyes was what gave zest to the amusement. Here is another scene that I thought very interesting. Imagine a trembling mother with her baby in her arms, a circle of invading Turks around her. They've planned a diversion; they pet the baby, laugh to make it laugh. They succeed, the baby laughs. At that moment a Turk points a pistol four inches from the baby's face. The baby laughs with glee, holds out its little hands to the pistol, and he pulls the trigger in the baby's face and blows out its brains. Artistic, wasn't it? By the way, Turks are particularly fond of sweet things, they say."

"Brother, what are you driving at?" asked Alyosha.

"I think if the devil doesn't exist, but man has created him, he has created him in his own image and likeness."

"Just as he did God, then?" observed Alyosha.

"It's wonderful how you can turn words, as Polonius says in *Hamlet*," laughed Ivan. "You turn my words against me. Well, I am glad. Yours must be a fine God, if man created Him in His image and likeness. You asked just now what I was driving at. You see, I am fond of collecting certain little facts, and, would you believe, I even copy anecdotes of a certain sort from newspapers and stories, and I've already got a fine collection. The Turks, of course, have gone into it, but they are foreigners. I have specimens from home that are even better than the Turks. You know we prefer beating—rods and scourges—that's our national institution. Nailing ears is unthinkable for us, for we are, after all, Europeans. But the rod and the scourge we have always with us and they cannot be taken from us. Abroad now they scarcely do any beating. Perhaps manners

are more humane, or laws have been passed, so that they don't dare to flog
men now. But they make up for it in another way just as national as ours.
And so national that it would be practically impossible among us, though
I believe we are being inoculated with it, since the religious movement
began in our aristocracy. I have a charming pamphlet, translated from the
French, describing how, quite recently, five years ago, a murderer, Richard, was executed—a young man, of twenty-three, I believe, who repented and was converted to the Christian faith at the very scaffold. This
Richard was an illegitimate child who was *given* as a child of six by his
parents to some shepherds on the Swiss mountains. They brought him up
to work for them. He grew up like a little wild beast among them. The
shepherds taught him nothing, and scarcely fed or clothed him, but sent
him out at age seven to herd the flock in cold and wet, and no one hes-
itated or scrupled to treat him so. Quite the contrary, they thought they
had every right, for Richard had been given to them as a chattel, and they
did not even see the necessity of feeding him. Richard himself describes
how in those years, like the Prodigal Son in the Gospel, he longed to eat
of the mash given to the pigs, which were fattened for sale. But they
wouldn't even give him that, and beat him when he stole from the pigs.
And that was how he spent all his childhood and his youth, till he grew
up and was strong enough to go away and be a thief. The savage began to
earn his living as a day laborer in Geneva. He drank what he earned, he
lived like a monster, and finished by killing and robbing an old man. He
was caught, tried, and condemned to death. They are not sentimentalists
there. And in prison he was immediately surrounded by pastors, members
of Christian brotherhoods, philanthropic ladies, and the like. They taught
him to read and write in prison, and expounded the Gospel to him. They
exhorted him, worked upon him, drummed at him incessantly, till at last
he solemnly confessed his crime. He was converted. He wrote to the court
himself that he was a monster, but that in the end God had vouchsafed
him light and shown grace. All Geneva was in excitement about him—all
philanthropic and religious Geneva. All the aristocratic and well-bred society of the town rushed to the prison, kissed Richard and embraced him;
'You are our brother, you have found grace.' And Richard does nothing
but weep with emotion, 'Yes, I've found grace! All my youth and childhood I was glad of pigs' food, but now even I have found grace. I am
dying in the Lord.' 'Yes, Richard, die in the Lord; you have shed blood
and must die in the Lord. Though it's not your fault that you knew not the
Lord, when you coveted the pig's food and were beaten for stealing it
(which was very wrong of you, for stealing is forbidden); but you've shed

blood and you must die.' And on the last day, Richard, perfectly limp, did nothing but cry and repeat every minute 'This is my happiest day. I am going to the Lord.' 'Yes,' cry the pastors and the judges and philanthropic ladies. 'This is the happiest day of your life, for you are going to the Lord!' They all walk or drive to the scaffold in procession behind the prison van. At the scaffold they call to Richard: 'Die, brother, die in the Lord, for even thou hast found grace!' And so, covered with his brothers' kisses, Richard is dragged on to the scaffold, and led to the guillotine. And they chopped off his head in brotherly fashion, because he had found grace. Yes, that's characteristic. That pamphlet is translated into Russian by some Russian philanthropists of aristocratic rank and evangelical aspirations, and has been distributed gratis for the enlightenment of the people. The case of Richard is interesting because it's national. Though to us it's absurd to cut off a man's head, because he has become our brother and has found grace, yet we have our own speciality, which is all but worse. Our historical pastime is the direct satisfaction of inflicting pain. There are lines in Nekrasov describing how a peasant lashes a horse on the eyes, 'on its meek eyes,' everyone must have seen it.[3] It's peculiarly Russian. He describes how a feeble little nag had foundered under too heavy a load and cannot move. The peasant beats it, beats it savagely, beats it at last not knowing what he is doing in the intoxication of cruelty, thrashes it mercilessly over and over again. 'However weak you are, you must pull, if you die for it.' The nag strains, and then he begins lashing the poor defenseless creature on its weeping, on its 'meek eyes.' The frantic beast tugs and draws the load, trembling all over, gasping for breath, moving sideways, with a sort of unnatural spasmodic action—it's awful in Nekrasov. But that's only a horse, and God has given horses to be beaten. So the Tatars have taught us, and they left us the knout as a remembrance of it. But men, too, can be beaten. A well-educated, cultured gentleman and his wife beat their own child with a birch rod; a girl of seven. I have an exact account of it. The papa was glad that the birch was covered with twigs. 'It stings more,' said he, and so he began stinging his daughter. I know for a fact there are people who at every blow are worked up to sensuality, to literal sensuality, which increases progressively at every blow they inflict. They beat for a minute, for five minutes, for ten minutes, more often and more savagely. The child screams. At last the child cannot scream, it gasps, 'Daddy! daddy!' By some diabolical unseemly chance the case was brought into court. A lawyer is engaged. The Russian people have long called a lawyer 'a conscience for hire.' The lawyer protests in his client's defense. 'It's such a simple thing,' he says, 'an everyday domestic event. A father corrects his child. To our shame be it said, it is brought into court.' The jury, convinced by him, gives a favorable verdict.[4] The public roars with delight that the torturer is acquitted. Ah, pity I wasn't there! I would have proposed to raise a subscription in his honor! . . . Charming pictures.

"But I've still better things about children. I've collected a great, great deal about Russian children, Alyosha. There was a little girl of five who was hated by her father and mother, 'most worthy and respectable people, of good education and breeding.' You see, I must repeat again, it is a peculiar characteristic of many people, this love of torturing children, and children only. To all other types of humanity these torturers behave mildly and benevolently, like cultivated and humane Europeans; but they are very fond of tormenting children, even fond of children themselves in that sense. It's just their defenselessness that tempts the tormentor, just the angelic confidence of the child who has no refuge and no appeal, that sets his vile blood on fire. In every man, of course, a beast lies hidden— the beast of rage, the beast of lustful heat at the screams of the tortured victim, the beast of lawlessness let off the chain, the beast of diseases that follow on vice, gout, kidney disease, and so on.

"This poor girl of five was subjected to every possible torture by those cultivated parents. They beat her, thrashed her, kicked her for no reason till her body was one bruise. Then, they went to greater refinements of cruelty—shut her up all night in the cold and frost in a privy, and because she didn't ask to be taken up at night (as though a child of five sleeping its angelic, sound sleep could be trained to wake and ask), they smeared her face and made her eat that excrement, and it was her mother, her mother did this. And that mother could sleep, hearing the poor child's groans locked up in that vile place! Can you understand why a little creature, who can't even understand what's done to her, should beat her little aching heart with her tiny fist in that vile place, in the dark and the cold, and weep her sanguine meek, unresentful tears to dear, kind God to protect her? Do you understand that infamy, my friend and my brother, my pious and humble novice? Do you understand why this rigmarole must be and is permitted? Without it, I am told, man could not have existed on earth, for he could not have known good and evil. Why should he know that diabolical good and evil when it costs so much? Why, the whole world of knowledge is not worth that child's prayer to 'dear, kind God'! I say nothing of the sufferings of grown-up people, they have eaten the apple, damn them, and the devil take them all! But these little ones! I am making you suffer, Alyoshka, you are not yourself. I'll leave off if you like."

"Never mind, I want to suffer too," muttered Alyosha.

"One picture, only one more, because it's so curious, so character-istic, and I have only just read it in some collection of Russian antiquities in the *Archive*, or the *Past*. I've forgotten the name. I must look it up. It was in the darkest days of serfdom at the beginning of the century, and long live the Liberator of the People! There was in those days a general of aristocratic connections, the owner of great estates, one of those men—somewhat exceptional, I believe, even then—who, retiring from the ser-vice into a life of leisure, are convinced that they've earned the power of life and death over their subjects. There were such men then. So our gen-eral, settled on his property of two thousand souls, lives in pomp, and domineers over his poor neighbors as though they were dependents and buffoons. He has kennels of hundreds of hounds and nearly a hundred dog-boys—all mounted, and in uniform. One day a serf boy, a little child of eight, threw a stone in play and hurt the paw of the general's favorite hound. 'Why is my favorite dog lame?' He is told that the boy threw a stone that hurt the dog's paw. 'So you did it.' The general looked the child up and down. 'Take him.' He was taken—taken from his mother and kept shut up all night. Early that morning the general comes out in full pomp, mounts his horse with the hounds, his dependents, dog-boys, and the huntsmen, all mounted around him. The servants are summoned for their edification, and in front of them all stands the mother of the child. The child is brought from the lockup. It's a gloomy cold, foggy autumn day, a capital day for hunting. The general orders the child to be undressed; the child is stripped naked. He shivers, numb with terror, not daring to cry. . . . 'Make him run,' commands the general. 'Run! run!' shout the dog-boys. The boy runs. . . . 'At him!' yells the general, and he sets the whole pack of hounds on the child. The hounds catch him, and tear him to pieces before his mother's eyes! . . . I believe the general was after-wards declared incapable of administering his estates. Well—what did he deserve? To be shot? To be shot for the satisfaction of our moral feelings? Speak, Alyoshka!"

"To be shot," murmured Alyosha, lifting his eyes to Ivan with a pale, twisted smile.

"Bravo!" shouted Ivan delighted. "If even you say so, it means . . . You're a pretty monk! So there is a little devil sitting in your heart, Aly-oshka Karamazov!"

"What I said was absurd, but—"

"That's just the point, that 'but'!" cried Ivan. "Let me tell you, nov-ice, that the absurd is only too necessary on earth. The world stands on absurdities, and perhaps nothing would have come to pass in it without them. We know what we know!"

"What do you know?"

"I understand nothing," Ivan went on, as though in delirium. "I don't want to understand anything now. I want to stick to the fact. I made up my mind long ago not to understand. If I try to understand anything, I shall be false to the fact and I have determined to stick to the fact."

"Why are you trying me?" Alyosha cried out with a bitter outburst. "Will you say what you mean at last?"

"Of course, I will; that's what I've been leading up to. You are dear to me, I don't want to let you go, and I won't give you up to your Zosima."

Ivan for a minute was silent, his face became all at once very sad.

"Listen! I took the case of children only to make my case clearer. Of the other tears of humanity with which the earth is soaked from its crust to its center, I will say nothing. I have narrowed my subject on purpose. I am a bug, and I recognize in all humility that I cannot understand why the world is arranged as it is. Men are themselves to blame, I suppose; they were given paradise, they wanted freedom, and stole fire from heaven, though they knew they would become unhappy, so there is no need to pity them. With my pitiful, earthly, Euclidean understanding, all I know is that there is suffering and that there are none guilty; that cause follows effect, simply and directly; that everything flows and finds its level—but that's only Euclidean nonsense, I know that, and I can't consent to live by it! What comfort is it to me that there are none guilty and that cause follows effect simply and directly, and that I know it—I must have retribution, or I will destroy myself. And not retribution in some remote infinite time and space, but here on earth, and that I could see myself. I have believed in it. I want to see it, and if I am dead by then, let me rise again, for if it all happens without me, it will be too unfair. Surely I haven't suffered, simply that I, my crimes and my sufferings, may manure the soil of the future harmony for somebody else. I want to see with my own eyes the hind lie down with the lion and the victim rise up and embrace his murderer. I want to be there when everyone suddenly understands what it has all been for. All the religions of the world are built on this longing, and I am a believer. But then there are the children, and what am I to do about them? That's a question I can't answer. For the hundredth time I repeat, there are numbers of questions, but I've only taken the children, because in their case what I mean is so unanswerably clear. Listen! If all must suffer to pay for the eternal harmony, what have children to do with it, tell me, please? It's beyond all comprehension why they should suffer, and why they should pay for the harmony. Why should they, too, furnish material to enrich the soil for the harmony of the future? I understand solidarity in sin among men. I understand solidarity in retribution, too; but there can be no such solidarity in sin with children. And if it is really true that they must share responsibility for all their fathers' crimes, such a truth is not of this world and is beyond my comprehension. Some jester will say, perhaps, that the child would have grown up and have sinned, but you see he didn't grow up, he was torn to pieces by the dogs, at eight years old. Oh, Alyosha, I am not blaspheming! I understand, of course, what an upheaval of the universe it will be, when everything in heaven and earth blends in one hymn of praise and everything that lives and has lived cries aloud: 'Thou art just, O Lord, for Thy ways are revealed.' When the mother embraces the fiend who threw her child to the dogs, and all three cry aloud with tears, 'Thou art just, O Lord!' then, of course, the crown of knowledge will be reached and all will be made clear. But what pulls me up here is that I can't accept that harmony. And while I am on earth, I make haste to take my own measures. You see, Alyosha, perhaps it really may happen that if I live to that moment, or rise again to see it, I, too, perhaps, may cry aloud with the rest, looking at the mother embracing the child's torturer, 'Thou art just, O Lord!' but I don't want to cry aloud then. While there is still time, I hasten to protect myself and so I renounce the higher harmony altogether. It's not worth the tears of that one tortured child who beat itself on the breast with its little fist and prayed in its stinking outhouse, with its unexpiated tears to 'dear, kind God'! It's not worth it, because those tears are unatoned for. They must be atoned for, or there can be no harmony. But how? How are you going to atone for them? Is it possible? By their being avenged? But what do I care for avenging them? What do I care for a hell for oppressors? What good can hell do, since those children have already been tortured? And what becomes of harmony, if there is hell? I want to forgive. I want to embrace. I don't want more suffering. And if the sufferings of children go to swell the sum of sufferings which was necessary to pay for truth, then I protest that the truth is not worth such a price. I don't want the mother to embrace the oppressor who threw her son to the dogs! She dare not forgive him! Let her forgive him for herself, if she will, let her forgive the torturer for the immeasurable suffering of her mother's heart. But the sufferings of her tortured child she has no right to forgive; she dare not forgive the torturer, even if the child were to forgive him! And if that is so, if they dare not forgive, what becomes of harmony? Is there in the whole world a being who would have the right to forgive and could forgive? I don't want harmony. From love for humanity I don't want it. I would rather be left with the unavenged suffering. I would rather remain with my unavenged suffering and unsatisfied indignation, *even if I were wrong.* Besides, too high a price is asked for harmony; it's beyond our means to pay so much to enter on it. And so I hasten to give back my entrance ticket,[5] and if I am an honest man I am bound to give it back as soon as possible. And that I am doing. It's not God that I don't accept, Alyosha, only I most respectfully return Him the ticket."

"That's rebellion," murmured Alyosha, looking down.

"Rebellion? I am sorry you call it that," said Ivan earnestly. "One can hardly live in rebellion, and I want to live. Tell me yourself, I challenge you—answer. Imagine that you are creating a fabric of human destiny with the object of making men happy in the end, giving them peace and rest at last, but that it was essential and inevitable to torture to death only one tiny creature—that little child beating it breast with its fist, for instance—and to found that edifice on its unavenged tears, would you consent to be the architect on those conditions? Tell me, and tell the truth."

"No, I wouldn't consent," said Alyosha softly. . . .

NOTES

1. Flaubert's *The Legend of St. Julian the Hospitaler* was published in a translation by Turgenev in 1877, a dozen years after the purported time of the novel. Ivan changes the name to Ioann—that is, John (Ivan).

2. Dostoevsky relates such things in his fictionalized autobiography *Notes from a Dead House.* Ivan was never in prison.

3. In *Till Twilight* (1859). Dostoevsky had earlier used the scene in *Crime and Punishment* (1866).

4. See Dostoevsky's *The Writer's Diary*, February 1876. Published as *Dnevnik Pisatelya* trans. by R. E. Matlaw (Paris, YMCA Press, 1951), II 66–101.

5. A reference to Schiller's poem "Resignation."

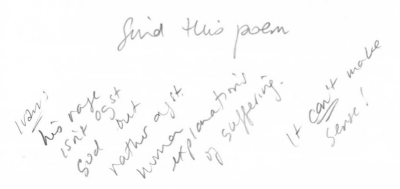

Physical Suffering and the Justice of God

ALBERT CAMUS

But where some saw abstraction others saw the truth. The first month of the plague ended gloomily, with a violent recrudescence of the epidemic and a dramatic sermon preached by Father Paneloux, the Jesuit priest who had given an arm to old Michel when he was tottering home at the start of his illness. Father Paneloux had already made his mark with frequent contributions to the Oran Geographical Society; these dealt chiefly with ancient inscriptions, on which he was an authority. But he had also reached a wider, non-specialist public with a series of lectures on present-day individualism. In these he had shown himself a stalwart champion of Christian doctrine at its most precise and purest, equally remote from modern laxity and the obscurantism of the past. On these occasions he had not shrunk from trouncing his hearers with some vigorous home-truths. Hence his local celebrity.

Toward the end of the month the ecclesiastical authorities in our town resolved to do battle against the plague with the weapons appropriate to them, and organized a Week of Prayer. These manifestations of public piety were to be concluded on Sunday by a High Mass celebrated under the auspices of St. Roch, the plague-stricken saint, and Father Paneloux was asked to preach the sermon. For a fortnight he desisted from the research work on St. Augustine and the African Church that had won for him a high place in his Order. A man of a passionate, fiery temperament, he flung himself wholeheartedly into the task assigned him. The sermon was a topic of conversation long before it was delivered and, in its way, it marks an important date in the history of the period.

There were large attendances at the services of the Week of Prayer. It must not, however, be assumed that in normal times the townsfolk of Oran are particularly devout. On Sunday mornings, for instance, sea-bathing competes seriously with churchgoing. Nor must it be thought that they had seen a great light and had a sudden change of heart. But, for one thing, now that the town was closed and the harbor out of bounds, there was no question of bathing; moreover, they were in a quite exceptional frame of mind and, though in their heart of hearts they were far from recognizing the enormity of what had come on them, they couldn't help feeling, for obvious reasons, that decidedly something had changed. Nevertheless, many continued hoping that the epidemic would soon die out and they and their families be spared. Thus they felt under no obligation to make any change in their habits as yet. Plague was for them an unwelcome visitant, bound to take its leave one day as unexpectedly as it had come. Alarmed, but far from desperate, they hadn't yet reached the phase when plague would seem to them the very tissue of their existence; when they forgot the lives that until now it had been given them to lead. In short, they were waiting for the turn of events. With regard to religion—as to many other problems—plague had induced in them a curious frame of mind, as remote from indifference as from fervor; the best name to give it, perhaps, might be "objectivity." Most of those who took part in the Week of Prayer would have echoed a remark made by one of the churchgoers in Dr. Rieux's hearing: "Anyhow, it can't do any harm." Even Tarrou, after recording in his notebook that in such cases the Chinese fall to playing tambourines before the Genius of Plague, observed that there was no means of telling whether, in practice, tambourines proved more efficacious than prophylactic measures. He merely added that, to decide the point, we should need first to ascertain if a Genius of Plague actually existed, and our ignorance on this point nullified any opinions we might form.

In any case the Cathedral was practically always full of worshippers throughout the Week of Prayer. For the first two or three days many stayed outside, under the palms and pomegranate trees in the garden in front of the porch, and listened from a distance to the swelling tide of prayers and invocations whose backwash filled the neighboring streets. But once an example had been given, they began to enter the Cathedral and join timidly in the responses. And on the Sunday of the sermon a huge congregation filled the nave, overflowing onto the steps and precincts. The sky had clouded up on the previous day, and now it was raining heavily. Those in the open unfurled umbrellas. The air inside the Cathedral was heavy with fumes of incense and the smell of wet clothes when Father Paneloux stepped into the pulpit.

He was a stockily built man, of medium height. When he leaned on the edge of the pulpit, grasping the woodwork with his big hands, all one saw was a black, massive torso and, above it, two rosy cheeks overhung by steel-rimmed spectacles. He had a powerful, rather emotional delivery, which carried to a great distance, and when he launched at the congregation his opening phrase in clear, emphatic tones: "Calamity has come on you, my brethren, and, my brethren, you deserved it," there was a flutter that extended to the crowd massed in the rain outside the porch.

In strict logic what came next did not seem to follow from this dramatic opening. Only as the sermon proceeded did it become apparent to the congregation that, by a skillful oratorical device, Father Paneloux had launched at them, like a fisticuff, the gist of his whole discourse. After launching it he went on at once to quote a text from Exodus relating to the plague of Egypt, and said: "The first time this scourge appears in history, it was wielded to strike down the enemies of God. Pharaoh set himself up against the divine will, and the plague beat him to his knees. Thus from the dawn of recorded history the scourge of God has humbled the proud of heart and laid low those who hardened themselves against Him. Ponder this well, my friends, and fall on your knees."

The downpour had increased in violence, and these words, striking through a silence intensified by the drumming of raindrops on the chancel windows, carried such conviction that, after a momentary hesitation, some of the worshippers slipped forward from their seats on to their knees. Others felt it right to follow their example, and the movement gradually spread until presently everyone was kneeling, from end to end of the cathedral. No sound, except an occasional creak of chairs, accompanied the movement. Then Paneloux drew himself up to his full height, took a deep breath, and continued his sermon in a voice that gathered strength as it proceeded.

"If today the plague is in your midst, that is because the hour has struck for taking thought. The just man need have no fear, but the evil-doer has good cause to tremble. For plague is the flail of God and the world His threshing-floor, and implacably He will thresh out His harvest until the wheat is separated from the chaff. There will be more chaff than wheat, few chosen of the many called. Yet this calamity was not willed by God. Too long this world of ours has connived at evil, too long has it counted on the divine mercy, on God's forgiveness. Repentance was enough, men thought; nothing was forbidden. Everyone felt comfortably

assured; when the day came, he would surely turn from his sins and repent. Pending that day, the easiest course was to surrender all along the
line; divine compassion would do the rest. For a long while God gazed
down on this town with eyes of compassion; but He grew weary of waiting, His eternal hope was too long deferred, and now He has turned His
face away from us. And so, God's light withdrawn, we walk in darkness,
in the thick darkness of this plague."

Someone in the congregation gave a little snort, like that of a restive
horse. After a short silence the preacher continued in a lower tone.

"We read in the *Golden Legend* that in the time of King Umberto
Italy was swept by plague and its greatest ravages took place in Rome and
Pavia. So dreadful were these that the living hardly sufficed to bury the
dead. And a good angel was made visible to human eyes, giving his orders
to an evil angel who bore a great hunting-spear, and bidding him strike
the houses; and as many strokes as he dealt a house, so many dead were
carried out of it."

Here Paneloux stretched forth his two short arms toward the open
porch, as if pointing to something behind the tumbling curtain of
the rain.

"My brothers," he cried, "that fatal hunt is up, and harrying our
streets today. See him there, that angel of the pestilence, comely as Lu-
cifer, shining like Evil's very self! He is hovering above your roofs with his
great spear in his right hand, poised to strike, while his left hand is
stretched toward one or other of your houses. Maybe at this very moment
his finger is pointing to your door, the red spear crashing on its panels,
and even now the plague is entering your home and settling down in your
bedroom to await your return. Patient and watchful, ineluctable as the
order of the scheme of things, it bides its time. No earthly power, nay, not
even—mark me well—the vaunted might of human science can avail you
to avert that hand once it is stretched toward you. And winnowed like
corn on the blood-stained threshing-floor of suffering, you will be cast
away with the chaff."

At this point the Father reverted with heightened eloquence to the
symbol of the flail. He bade his hearers picture a huge wooden bar whirl-
ing above the town, striking at random, swinging up again in a shower of
drops of blood, and spreading carnage and suffering on earth, "for the
seedtime that shall prepare the harvest of the truth."

At the end of his long phrase Father Paneloux paused; his hair was
straggling over his forehead, his body shaken by tremors that his hands
communicated to the pulpit. When he spoke again, his voice was lower,
but vibrant with accusation.

"Yes, the hour has come for serious thought. You fondly imagined it was enough to visit God on Sundays, and thus you could make free of your weekdays. You believed some brief formalities, some bendings of the knee, would recompense Him well enough for your criminal indifference. But God is not mocked. These brief encounters could not sate the fierce hunger of His love. He wished to see you longer and more often; that is His manner of loving and, indeed, it is the only manner of loving. And this is why, wearied of waiting for you to come to Him, He loosed on you this visitation; as He has visited all the cities that offended against Him since the dawn of history. Now you are learning your lesson, the lesson that was learned by Cain and his offspring, by the people of Sodom and Gomorrah, by Job and Pharaoh, by all that hardened their hearts against Him. And like them you have been beholding mankind and all creation with new eyes, since the gates of this city closed on you and on the pestilence. Now, at last, you know the hour has struck to bend your thoughts to first and last things."

A wet wind was sweeping up the nave, making the candle-flames bend and flicker. The pungency of burning wax, coughs, a stifled sneeze, rose toward Father Paneloux, who, reverting to his exordium with a subtlety that was much appreciated, went on in a calm, almost matter-of-fact voice: "Many of you are wondering, I know, what I am leading up to. I wish to lead you to the truth and teach you to rejoice, yes, rejoice—in spite of all that I have been telling you. For the time is past when a helping hand or mere words of good advice could set you on the right path. Today the truth is a command. It is a red spear sternly pointing to the narrow path, the one way of salvation. And thus, my brothers, at last it is revealed to you, the divine compassion which has ordained good and evil in everything; wrath and pity; the plague and your salvation. This same pestilence which is slaying you works for your good and points your path.

"Many centuries ago the Christians of Abyssinia saw in the plague a sure and God-sent means of winning eternal life. Those who were not yet stricken wrapped round them sheets in which men had died of plague, so as to make sure of their death. I grant you such a frenzied quest of salvation was not to be commended. It shows an overhaste—indeed, a presumptuousness, which we can but deplore. No man should seek to force God's hand or to hurry on the appointed hour, and from a practice that aims at speeding up the order of events which God has ordained unalterably from all time, it is but a step to heresy. Yet we can learn a salutary lesson from the zeal, excessive though it was, of those Abyssinian Christians. Much of it is alien to our more enlightened spirits, and yet it gives us a glimpse of that radiant eternal light which glows, a small still flame, in the dark core of human suffering. And this light, too, illuminates the shadowed paths that lead towards deliverance. It reveals the will of God in action, unfailingly transforming evil into good. And once again today it is leading us through the dark valley of fears and groans towards the holy silence, the well-spring of all life. This, my friends, is the vast consolation I would hold out to you, so that when you leave this house of God you will carry away with you not only words of wrath, but a message, too, of comfort for your hearts."

Everyone supposed that the sermon had ended. Outside, the rain had ceased and watery sunshine was yellowing the Cathedral square. Vague sounds of voices came from the streets, and a low hum of traffic, the speech of an awakening town. Discreetly, with a subdued rustling, the congregation gathered together their belongings. However, the Father had a few more words to say. He told them that after having made it clear that this plague came from God for the punishment of their sins, he would not have recourse, in concluding, to an eloquence that, considering the tragic nature of the occasion, would be out of keeping. He hoped and believed that all of them now saw their position in its true light. But, before leaving the pulpit, he would like to tell them of something he had been reading in an old chronicle of the Black Death at Marseille. In it Mathieu Marais, the chronicler, laments his lot; he says he has been cast into hell to languish without succor and without hope. Well, Mathieu Marais was blind! Never more intensely than today had he, Father Paneloux, felt the immanence of divine succor and Christian hope granted to all alike. He hoped against hope that, despite all the horrors of these dark days, despite the groans of men and women in agony, our fellow citizens would offer up to heaven that one prayer which is truly Christian, a prayer of love. And God would see to the rest.

Toward the close of October Castel's anti-plague serum was tried for the first time. Practically speaking, it was Rieux's last card. If it failed, the doctor was convinced the whole town would be at the mercy of the epidemic, which would either continue its ravages for an unpredictable period or perhaps die out abruptly of its own accord.

The day before Castel called on Rieux, M. Othon's son had fallen ill and all the family had to go into quarantine. Thus the mother, who had only recently come out of it, found herself isolated once again. In deference to the official regulations the magistrate had promptly sent for Dr. Rieux the moment he saw symptoms of the disease in his little boy.

Mother and father were standing at the bedside when Rieux entered the room. The boy was in the phase of extreme prostration and submitted without a whimper to the doctor's examination. When Rieux raised his eyes he saw the magistrate's gaze intent on him, and, behind, the mother's pale face. She was holding a handkerchief to her mouth, and her big, dilated eyes followed each of the doctor's movements.

"He has it, I suppose?" the magistrate asked in a toneless voice.

"Yes." Rieux gazed down at the child again.

The mother's eyes widened yet more, but she still said nothing. M. Othon, too, kept silent for a while before saying in an even lower tone:

"Well, Doctor, we must do as we are told to do."

Rieux avoided looking at Mme. Othon, who was still holding her handkerchief to her mouth.

"It needn't take long," he said rather awkwardly, "if you'll let me use your phone."

The magistrate said he would take him to the telephone. But before going, the doctor turned toward Mme. Othon.

"I regret very much indeed, but I'm afraid you'll have to get your things ready. You know how it is."

Mme. Othon seemed disconcerted. She was staring at the floor.

Then, "I understand," she murmured, slowly nodding her head. "I'll set about it at once."

Before leaving, Rieux on a sudden impulse asked the Othons if there wasn't anything they'd like him to do for them. The mother gazed at him in silence. And now the magistrate averted his eyes.

"No," he said, then swallowed hard. "But—save my son."

In the early days a mere formality, quarantine had now been reorganized by Rieux and Rambert on very strict lines. In particular they insisted on having members of the family of a patient kept apart. If, unawares, one of them had been infected, the risks of an extension of the infection must not be multiplied. Rieux explained this to the magistrate, who signified his approval of the procedure. Nevertheless, he and his wife exchanged a glance that made it clear to Rieux how keenly they both felt the separation thus imposed on them. Mme. Othon and her little girl could be given rooms in the quarantine hospital under Rambert's charge. For the magistrate, however, no accommodation was available except in an isolation camp the authorities were now installing in the municipal stadium, using tents supplied by the highway department. When Rieux apologized for the poor accommodation, M. Othon replied that there was one rule for all alike, and it was only proper to abide by it.

The boy was taken to the auxiliary hospital and put in a ward of ten beds which had formerly been a classroom. After some twenty hours Rieux became convinced that the case was hopeless. The infection was steadily spreading, and the boy's body was putting up no resistance. Tiny, half-formed, but acutely painful buboes were clogging the joints of the child's puny limbs. Obviously it was a losing fight.

Under the circumstances Rieux had no qualms about testing Castel's serum on the boy. That night, after dinner, they performed the inoculation, a lengthy process, without getting the slightest reaction. At daybreak on the following day they gathered round the bed to observe the effects of this test inoculation on which so much hung.

The child had come out of his extreme prostration and was tossing about convulsively on the bed. From four in the morning Dr. Castel and Tarrou had been keeping watch and noting, stage by stage, the progress and remissions of the malady. Tarrou's bulky form was slightly drooping at the head of the bed, while at its foot, with Rieux standing beside him, Castel was seated, reading, with every appearance of calm, an old leather-bound book. One by one, as the light increased in the former classroom, the others arrived. Paneloux, the first to come, leaned against the wall on the opposite side of the bed to Tarrou. His face was drawn with grief, and the accumulated weariness of many weeks, during which he had never spared himself, had deeply seamed his somewhat prominent forehead. Grand came next. It was seven o'clock, and he apologized for being out of breath; he could only stay a moment, but wanted to know if any definite results had been observed. Without speaking, Rieux pointed to the child. His eyes shut, his teeth clenched, his features frozen in an agonized grimace, he was rolling his head from side to side on the bolster. When there was just light enough to make out the half-obliterated figures of an equation chalked on a blackboard that still hung on the wall at the far end of the room, Rambert entered. Posting himself at the foot of the next bed, he took a package of cigarettes from his pocket. But after his first glance at the child's face he put it back.

From his chair Castel looked at Rieux over his spectacles.

"Any news of his father?"

"No," said Rieux. "He's in the isolation camp."

The doctor's hands were gripping the rail of the bed, his eyes fixed on the small tortured body. Suddenly it stiffened, and seemed to give a little at the waist, as slowly the arms and legs spread out X-wise. From the body, naked under an army blanket, rose a smell of damp wool and stale sweat. The boy had gritted his teeth again. Then very gradually he

relaxed, bringing his arms and legs back toward the center of the bed, still
without speaking or opening his eyes, and his breathing seemed to
quicken. Rieux looked at Tarrou, who hastily lowered his eyes.

They had already seen children die—for many months now death
had shown no favoritism—but they had never yet watched a child's agony
minute by minute, as they had now been doing since daybreak. Needless
to say, the pain inflicted on these innocent victims had always seemed to
them to be what in fact it was: an abominable thing. But hitherto they
had felt its abomination in, so to speak, an abstract way; they had never
had to witness over so long a period the death-throes of an innocent child.

And just then the boy had a sudden spasm, as if something had bit-
ten him in the stomach, and uttered a long, shrill wail. For moments that
seemed endless he stayed in a queer, contorted position, his body racked
by convulsive tremors; it was as if his frail frame were bending before the
fierce breath of the plague, breaking under the reiterated gusts of fever.
Then the storm-wind passed, there came a lull, and he relaxed a little; the
fever seemed to recede, leaving him gasping for breath on a dank, pesti-
lential shore, lost in a languor that already looked like death. When for
the third time the fiery wave broke on him, lifting him a little, the child
curled himself up and shrank away to the edge of the bed, as if in terror
of the flames advancing on him, licking his limbs. A moment later, after
tossing his head wildly to and fro, he flung off the blanket. From between
the inflamed eyelids big tears welled up and trickled down the sunken,
leaden-hued cheeks. When the spasm had passed, utterly exhausted, tens-
ing his thin legs and arms, on which, within forty-eight hours, the flesh
had wasted to the bone, the child lay flat, racked on the tumbled bed, in
a grotesque parody of crucifixion.   one of the docs

Bending, Tarrou gently stroked with his big paw the small face
stained with tears and sweat. Castel had closed his book a few moments
before, and his eyes were now fixed on the child. He began to speak, but
had to give a cough before continuing, because his voice rang out so
harshly.

"There wasn't any remission this morning, was there, Rieux?"

Rieux shook his head, adding, however, that the child was putting
up more resistance than one would have expected. Paneloux, who was
slumped against the wall, said in a low voice: Jesuit

"So if he is to die, he will have suffered longer."

Light was increasing in the ward. The occupants of the other nine
beds were tossing about and groaning, but in tones that seemed deliberately subdued. Only one, at the far end of the ward, was screaming, or

rather uttering little exclamations at regular intervals, which seemed to convey surprise more than pain. Indeed, one had the impression that even for the sufferers the frantic terror of the early phase had passed, and there was a sort of mournful resignation in their present attitude toward the disease. Only the child went on fighting with all his little might. Now and then Rieux took his pulse—less because this served any purpose than as an escape from his utter helplessness—and when he closed his eyes, he seemed to feel its tumult mingling with the fever of his own blood. And then, at one with the tortured child, he struggled to sustain him with all the remaining strength of his own body. But, linked for a few moments, the rhythms of their heartbeats soon fell apart, the child escaped him, and again he knew his impotence. Then he released the small, thin wrist and moved back to his place.

The light on the whitewashed walls was changing from pink to yellow. The first waves of another day of heat were beating on the windows. They hardly heard Grand saying he would come back as he turned to go. All were waiting. The child, his eyes still closed, seemed to grow a little calmer. His clawlike fingers were feebly plucking at the sides of the bed. Then they rose, scratched at the blanket over his knees, and suddenly he doubled up his limbs, bringing his thighs above his stomach, and remained quite still. For the first time he opened his eyes and gazed at Rieux, who was standing immediately in front of him. In the small face, rigid as a mask of grayish clay, slowly the lips parted and from them rose a long, incessant scream, hardly varying with his respiration, and filling the ward with a fierce, indignant protest, so little childish that it seemed like a collective voice issuing from all the sufferers there. Rieux clenched his jaws, Tarrou looked away. Rambert went and stood beside Castel, who closed the book lying on his knees. Paneloux gazed down at the small mouth, fouled with the sordes of the plague and pouring out the angry death-cry that has sounded through the ages of mankind. He sank on his knees, and all present found it natural to hear him say in a voice hoarse but clearly audible across that nameless, never ending wail:

"My God, spare this child!"

But the wail continued without cease and the other sufferers began to grow restless. The patient at the far end of the ward, whose little broken cries had gone on without a break, now quickened their tempo so that they flowed together in one unbroken cry, while the others' groans grew louder. A gust of sobs swept through the room, drowning Paneloux's prayer, and Rieux, who was still tightly gripping the rail of the bed, shut his eyes, dazed with exhaustion and disgust.

When he opened them again, Tarrou was at his side.

"I must go," Rieux said, "I can't bear to hear them any longer."

But then, suddenly, the other sufferers fell silent. And now the doctor grew aware that the child's wail, after weakening more and more, had fluttered out into silence. Around him the groans began again, but more faintly, like a far echo of the fight that now was over. For it was over. Castel had moved round to the other side of the bed and said the end had come. His mouth still gaping, but silent now, the child was lying among the tumbled blankets, a small, shrunken form, with the tears still wet on his cheeks.

Paneloux went up to the bed and made the sign of benediction. Then gathering up his cassock, he walked out by the passage between the beds.

"Will you have to start it all over again?" Tarrou asked Castel.

The old doctor nodded slowly, with a twisted smile.

"Perhaps. After all, he put up a surprisingly long resistance."

Rieux was already on his way out, walking so quickly and with such a strange look on his face that Paneloux put out an arm to check him when he was about to pass him in the doorway.

"Come, Doctor," he began.

Rieux swung round on him fiercely.

"Ah! That child, anyhow, was innocent, and you know it as well as I do!"

He strode on, brushing past Paneloux, and walked across the school playground. Sitting on a wooden bench under the dingy, stunted trees, he wiped off the sweat that was beginning to run into his eyes. He felt like shouting imprecations—anything to loosen the stranglehold lashing his heart with steel. Heat was flooding down between the branches of the fig trees. A white haze, spreading rapidly over the blue of the morning sky, made the air yet more stifling. Rieux lay back wearily on the bench. Gazing up at the ragged branches, the shimmering sky, he slowly got back his breath and fought down his fatigue.

He heard a voice behind him. "Why was there that anger in your voice just now? What we'd been seeing was as unbearable to me as it was to you."

Rieux turned toward Paneloux.

"I know. I'm sorry. But weariness is a kind of madness. And there are times when the only feeling I have is one of mad revolt."

"I understand," Paneloux said in a low voice. "That sort of thing is revolting because it passes our human understanding. But perhaps we should love what we cannot understand."

Rieux straightened up slowly. He gazed at Paneloux, summoning to his gaze all the strength and fervor he could muster against his weariness. Then he shook his head.

"No, Father. I've a very different idea of love. And until my dying day I shall refuse to love a scheme of things in which children are put to torture."

A shade of disquietude crossed the priest's face. "Ah, Doctor," he said sadly, "I've just realized what is meant by 'grace.' "

Rieux had sunk back again on the bench. His lassitude had returned and from its depths he spoke, more gently:

"It's something I haven't got; that I know. But I'd rather not discuss that with you. We're working side by side for something that unites us— beyond blasphemy and prayers. And it's the only thing that matters."

Paneloux sat down beside Rieux. It was obvious that he was deeply moved.

"Yes, yes," he said, "you, too, are working for man's salvation."

Rieux tried to smile.

"Salvation's much too big a word for me. I don't aim so high. I'm concerned with man's health; and for me his health comes first."

Paneloux seemed to hesitate. "Doctor—" he began, then fell silent. Down his face, too, sweat was trickling. Murmuring: "Good-by for the present," he rose. His eyes were moist. When he turned to go, Rieux, who had seemed lost in thought, suddenly rose and took a step toward him.

"Again, please forgive me. I can promise there won't be another outburst of that kind."

Paneloux held out his hand, saying regretfully:

"And yet—I haven't convinced you!"

"What does it matter? What I hate is death and disease, as you well know. And whether you wish it or not, we're allies, facing them and fighting them together." Rieux was still holding Paneloux's hand. "So you see"—but he refrained from meeting the priest's eyes—"God Himself can't part us now."

Night

ELIE WIESEL

The cherished objects we had brought with us thus far were left behind in the train, and with them, at last, our illusions.

Every two yards or so an SS man held his tommy gun trained on us. Hand in hand we followed the crowd.

An SS noncommissioned officer came to meet us, a truncheon in his hand. He gave the order:

"Men to the left! Women to the right!"

Eight words spoken quietly, indifferently, without emotion. Eight short, simple words. Yet that was the moment when I parted from my mother. I had not had time to think, but already I felt the pressure of my father's hand: we were alone. For a part of a second I glimpsed my mother and my sisters moving away to the right. Tzipora held Mother's hand. I saw them disappear into the distance; my mother was stroking my sister's fair hair, as though to protect her, while I walked on with my father and the other men. And I did not know that in that place, at that moment, I was parting from my mother and Tzipora forever. I went on walking. My father held onto my hand.

Behind me, an old man fell to the ground. Near him was an SS man, putting his revolver back in its holster.

My hand shifted on my father's arm. I had one thought—not to lose him. Not to be left alone.

The SS officers gave the order:

"Form fives!"

Commotion. At all costs we must keep together.

"Here, kid, how old are you?"

Excerpts from NIGHT by Elie Wiesel. Translation copyright © 1960 by MacGibbon and Kee. Renewal copyright © 1988 by The Collins Publishing Group. Reprinted by permission of Hill and Wang, a division of Farrar, Straus, and Giroux, Inc.

It was one of the prisoners who asked me this. I could not see his face, but his voice was tense and weary.

"I'm not quite fifteen yet."

"No. Eighteen."

"But I'm not," I said. "Fifteen."

"Fool. Listen to what *I* say."

Then he questioned my father, who replied:

"Fifty."

The other grew more furious than ever.

"No, not fifty. Forty. Do you understand? Eighteen and forty."

He disappeared into the night shadows. A second man came up, spitting oaths at us.

"What have you come here for, you sons of bitches? What are you doing here, eh?"

Someone dared to answer him.

"What do you think? Do you suppose we've come here for our own pleasure? Do you think we asked to come?"

A little more, and the man would have killed him.

"You shut your trap, you filthy swine, or I'll squash you right now! You'd have done better to have hanged yourselves where you were than come here. Didn't you know what was in store for you at Auschwitz? Haven't you heard about it? In 1944?"

No, we had not heard. No one had told us. He could not believe his ears. His tone of voice became increasingly brutal.

"Do you see that chimney over there? See it? Do you see those flames? (Yes, we did see the flames.) Over there—that's where you're going to be taken. That's your grave, over there. Haven't you realized it yet? You dumb bastards, don't you understand anything? You're going to be burned. Frizzled away. Turned into ashes."

He was growing hysterical in his fury. We stayed motionless, petrified. Surely it was all a nightmare? An unimaginable nightmare?

I heard murmurs around me.

"We've got to do something. We can't let ourselves be killed. We can't go like beasts to the slaughter. We've got to revolt."

There were a few sturdy young fellows among us. They had knives on them, and they tried to incite the others to throw themselves on the armed guards.

One of the young men cried:

"Let the world learn of the existence of Auschwitz. Let everybody hear about it, while they can still escape. . . . "

But the older ones begged their children not to do anything foolish:

"You must never lose faith, even when the sword hangs over your head. That's the teaching of our sages. . . . "

The wind of revolt died down. We continued our march toward the square. In the middle stood the notorious Dr. Mengele (a typical SS officer: a cruel face, but not devoid of intelligence, and wearing a monocle); a conductor's baton in his hand, he was standing among the other officers. The baton moved unremittingly, sometimes to the right, sometimes to the left.

I was already in front of him:

"How old are you?" he asked, in an attempt at a paternal tone of voice.

"Eighteen." My voice was shaking.

"Are you in good health?"

"Yes."

"What's your occupation?"

Should I say that I was a student?

"Farmer," I heard myself say.

This conversation cannot have lasted more than a few seconds. It had seemed like an eternity to me.

The baton moved to the left. I took half a step forward. I wanted to see first where they were sending my father. If he went to the right, I would go after him.

The baton once again pointed to the left for him too. A weight was lifted from my heart.

We did not yet know which was the better side, right or left; which road led to prison and which to the crematory. But for the moment I was happy; I was near my father. Our procession continued to move slowly forward.

Another prisoner came up to us:

"Satisfied?"

"Yes," someone replied.

"Poor devils, you're going to the crematory."

He seemed to be telling the truth. Not far from us, flames were leaping up from a ditch, gigantic flames. They were burning something. A lorry drew up at the pit and delivered its load—little children. Babies! Yes, I saw it—saw it with my own eyes . . . those children in the flames. (Is it surprising that I could not sleep after that? Sleep had fled from my eyes.)

So this was where we were going. A little farther on was another and larger ditch for adults.

I pinched my face. Was I still alive? Was I awake? I could not believe it. How could it be possible for them to burn people, children, and for the world to keep silent? No, none of this could be true. It was a nightmare. . . . Soon I should wake with a start, my heart pounding, and find myself back in the bedroom of my childhood, among my books. . . .

My father's voice drew me from my thoughts:

"It's a shame . . . a shame that you couldn't have gone with your mother. . . . I saw several boys of your age going with their mothers. . . . "

His voice was terribly sad. I realized that he did not want to see what they were going to do to me. He did not want to see the burning of his only son.

My forehead was bathed in cold sweat. But I told him that I did not believe that they could burn people in our age, that humanity would never tolerate it. . . .

"Humanity? Humanity is not concerned with us. Today anything is allowed. Anything is possible, even these crematories. . . . "

His voice was choking.

"Father, " I said, "if that is so, I don't want to wait here. I'm going to run to the electric wire. That would be better than slow agony in the flames."

He did not answer. He was weeping. He body was shaken convulsively. Around us, everyone was weeping. Someone began to recite the Kaddish, the prayer for the dead. I do not know if it has ever happened before, in the long history of the Jews, that people have ever recited the prayer for the dead for themselves.

"*Yitgadal veyitkadach shmé raba.* . . . May His Name be blesssed and magnified. . . . " whispered my father.

For the first time, I felt revolt rise up in me. Why should I bless His name? The Eternal, Lord of the Universe, the All-Powerful and Terrible, was silent. What had I to thank Him for?

We continued our march. We were gradually drawing closer to the ditch, from which an infernal heat was rising. Still twenty steps to go. If I wanted to bring about my own death, this was the moment. Our line had now only fifteen paces to cover. I bit my lips so that my father would not hear my teeth chattering. Ten steps still. Eight. Seven. We marched slowly on, as though following a hearse at our own funeral. Four steps more. Three steps. There it was now, right in front of us, the pit and its flames. I gathered all that was left of my strength, so that I could break from the ranks and throw myself upon the barbed wire. In the depths of my heart, I bade farewell to my father, to the whole universe; and, in spite of myself, the words formed themselves and issued in a whisper from my lips: *Yitgadal veyitkadach shmé raba.* . . . May His name be blessed and magnified. . . . My heart was bursting. The moment had come. I was face to face with the Angel of Death. . . .

No. Two steps from the pit we were ordered to turn to the left and made to go into a barracks.

I pressed my father's hand. He said:

"Do you remember Madame Schächter, in the train?"

Never shall I forget that night, the first night in camp, which has turned my life into one long night, seven times cursed and seven times sealed. Never shall I forget that smoke. Never shall I forget the little faces of the children, whose bodies I saw turned into wreaths of smoke beneath a silent blue sky.

Never shall I forget those flames which consumed my faith forever.

Never shall I forget that nocturnal silence which deprived me, for all eternity, of the desire to live. Never shall I forget those moments which murdered my God and my soul and turned my dreams to dust. Never shall I forget these things, even if I am condemned to live as long as God Himself. Never.

A week later, on the way back from work, we noticed in the center of the camp, at the assembly place, a black gallows.

We were told that soup would not be distributed until after roll call. This took longer than usual. The orders were given in a sharper manner than on other days, and in the air there were strange undertones.

"Bare your heads!" yelled the head of the camp, suddenly.

Ten thousand caps were simultaneously removed,

"Cover your heads!"

Ten thousand caps went back onto their skulls, as quick as lightning.

The gate to the camp opened. As SS section appeared and surrounded us: one SS at every three paces. On the lookout towers the machine guns were trained on the assemby place.

"They fear trouble," whispered Juliek.

Two SS men had gone to the cells. They came back with the condemned man between them. He was a youth from Warsaw. He had three years of concentration camp life behind him. He was a strong, well-built boy, a giant in comparison with me.

His back to the gallows, his face turned toward his judge, who was the head of the camp, the boy was pale, but seemed more moved than afraid. His manacled hands did not tremble. His eyes gazed coldly at the hundreds of SS guards, the thousands of prisoners who surrounded him.

The head of the camp began to read his verdict, hammering out each phrase:

"In the name of Himmler . . . prisoner Number . . . stole during the alert. . . . According to the law . . . paragraph . . . prisoner Number . . . is condemned to death. May this be a warning and an example to all prisoners."

No one moved.

I could hear my heart beating. The thousands who had died daily at Auschwitz and at Birkenau in the crematory ovens no longer troubled me. But this one, leaning against his gallows—he overwhelmed me.

"Do you think this ceremony'll be over soon? I'm hungry. . . . " whispered Juliek.

At a sign from the head of the camp, the Lagerkapo advanced toward the condemned man. Two prisoners helped him in his task—for two plates of soup.

The Kapo wanted to bandage the victim's eyes, but he refused.

After a long moment of waiting, the executioner put the rope round his neck. He was on the point of motioning to his assistants to draw the chair away from the prisoner's feet, when the latter cried, in a calm, strong voice:

"Long live liberty! A curse upon Germany! A curse . . . ! A cur—"

The executioners had completed their task.

A command cleft the air like a sword.

"Bare your heads."

Ten thousand prisoners paid their last respects.

"Cover your heads!"

Then the whole camp, block after block, had to march past the hanged man and stare at the dimmed eyes, the lolling tongue of death. The Kapos and heads of each block forced everyone to look him full in the face.

After the march, we were given permission to return to the blocks for our meal.

I remember that I found the soup excellent that evening. . . .

I witnessed other hangings. I never saw a single one of the victims weep. For a long time those dried-up bodies had forgotten the bitter taste of tears.

Except once. The Oberkapo of the fifty-second cable unit was a Dutchman, a giant, well over six feet. Seven hundred prisoners worked under his orders, and they all loved him like a brother. No one had ever received a blow at his hands, nor an insult from his lips.

He had a young boy under him, a *pipel*, as they were called—a child with a refined and beautiful face, unheard of in this camp.

(At Buna, the *pipel* were loathed; they were often crueller than adults. I once saw one of thirteen beating his father because the latter had not made his bed properly. The old man was crying softly while the boy shouted: "If you don't stop crying at once I shan't bring you any more bread. Do you understand?" But the Dutchman's little servant was loved by all. He had the face of a sad angel.)

One day, the electric power station at Buna was blown up. The Gestapo, summoned to the spot, suspected sabotage. They found a trail. It eventually led to the Dutch Oberkapo. And there, after a search, they found an important stock of arms.

The Oberkapo was arrested immediately. He was tortured for a period of weeks, but in vain. He would not give a single name. He was transferred to Auschwitz. We never heard of him again.

But his little servant had been left behind in the camp in prison. Also put to torture, he too would not speak. Then the SS sentenced him to death, with two other prisoners who had been discovered with arms.

One day when we came back from work, we saw three gallows rearing up in the assembly place, three black crows. Roll call. SS all round us, machine guns trained: the traditional ceremony. Three victims in chains—and one of them, the little servant, the sad-eyed angel.

The SS seemed more preoccupied, more disturbed than usual. To hang a young boy in front of thousands of spectators was no light matter. The head of the camp read the verdict. All eyes were on the child. He was lividly pale, almost calm, biting his lips. The gallows threw its shadow over him.

This time the Lagerkapo refused to act as executioner. Three SS replaced him.

The three victims mounted together onto the chairs.

The three necks were placed at the same moment within the nooses.

"Long live liberty!" cried the two adults.

But the child was silent.

"Where is God? Where is He?" someone behind me asked.

At a sign from the head of the camp, the three chairs tipped over.

Total silence throughout the camp. On the horizon, the sun was setting.

"Bare your heads!" yelled the head of the camp. His voice was raucous. We were weeping.

"Cover your heads!"

Then the march past began. The two adults were no longer alive. Their tongues hung swollen, blue-tinged. But the third rope was still moving; being so light, the child was still alive. . . .

For more than half an hour he stayed there, struggling between life and death, dying in slow agony under our eyes. And we had to look him full in the face. He was still alive when I passed in front of him. His tongue was still red, his eyes were not yet glazed.

Behind me, I heard the same man asking:

"Where is God now?"

And I heard a voice within me answer him:

"Where is He? Here He is—He is hanging here on this gallows. . . ."

That night the soup tasted of corpses.

PART TWO

Versions of the Problem of Evil

The Logical Problem
The Evidential Problem
The Existential Problem

Evil and Omnipotence

J. L. MACKIE

The traditional arguments for the existence of God have been fairly thoroughly criticized by philosophers. But the theologian can, if he wishes, accept this criticism. He can admit that no rational proof of God's existence is possible. And he can still retain all that is essential to his position, by holding that God's existence is known in some other, nonrational way. I think, however, that a more telling criticism can be made by way of the traditional problem of evil. Here it can be shown, not that religious beliefs lack rational support, but that they are positively irrational, that the several parts of the essential theological doctrine are inconsistent with one another, so that the theologian can maintain his position as a whole only by a much more extreme rejection of reason than in the former case. He must now be prepared to believe, not merely what cannot be proved, but what can be *disproved* from other beliefs that he also holds. OUCH

The problem of evil, in the sense in which I shall be using the phrase, is problem only for someone who believes that there is a God who is both omnipotent and wholly good. And it is a logical problem, the problem of clarifying and reconciling a number of beliefs: it is not a scientific problem that might be solved by further observations, or a practical problem that might be solved by a decision or an action. These points are obvious; I mention them only because they are sometimes ignored by theologians, who sometimes parry a statement of the problem with such remarks as "Well, can you solve the problem yourself?" or "This is a mystery which may be revealed to us later" or "Evil is something to be faced and overcome, not to be merely discussed."

In its simplest form the problem is this: God is omnipotent; God is wholly good; and yet evil exists. There seems to be some contradiction between these three propositions, so that if any two of them were true the

From *Mind* 64 (1955), 200–12. Used by permission of the editor.

third would be false. But at the same time all three are essential parts of most theological positions: the theologian, it seems, at once *must* adhere and *cannot consistently* adhere to all three. (The problem does not arise only for theists, but I shall discuss it in the form in which it presents itself for ordinary theism.)

However, the contradiction does not arise immediately; to show it we need some additional premises, or perhaps some quasi-logical rules connecting the terms "good," "evil," and "omnipotent." These additional principles are that good is opposed to evil, in such a way that a good thing always eliminates evil as far as it can, and that there are no limits to what an omnipotent thing can do. From these it follows that a good omnipotent thing eliminates evil completely, and then the propositions that a good omnipotent thing exists, and that evil exists, are incompatible.

ADEQUATE SOLUTIONS

Now once the problem is fully stated it is clear that it can be solved, in the sense that the problem will not arise if one gives up at least one of the propositions that constitute it. If you are prepared to say that God is not wholly good, or not quite omnipotent, or that evil does not exist, or that good is not opposed to the kind of evil that exists, or that there are limits to what an omnipotent thing can do, then the problem of evil will not arise for you.

There are, then, quite a number of adequate solutions of the problem of evil, and some of these have been adopted, or almost adopted, by various thinkers. For example, a few have been prepared to deny God's omnipotence, and rather more have been prepared to keep the term "omnipotence" but severely to restrict its meaning, recording quite a number of things that an omnipotent being cannot do. Some have said that evil is an illusion, perhaps because they held that the whole world of temporal, changing things is an illusion, and that what we call evil belongs only to this world, or perhaps because they held that although temporal things *are* much as we see them, those that we call evil are not really evil. Some have said that what we call evil is merely the privation of good, that evil in a positive sense, evil that would really be opposed to good, does not exist. Many have agreed with Pope that disorder is harmony not understood, and that partial evil is universal good. Whether any of these views is *true* is, of course, another question. But each of them gives an adequate solution of the problems of evil in the sense that if you accept it this problem does not arise for you, though you may, of course, have *other* problems to face.

absence of good ?

But often enough these adequate solutions are only *almost* adopted. The thinkers who restrict God's power, but keep the term "omnipotence," may reasonably be suspected of thinking, in other contexts, that his power is really unlimited. Those who say that evil is an illusion may also be thinking, inconsistently, that this illusion is itself an evil. Those who say that "evil" is merely privation of good may also be thinking, inconsistently, that privation of good is an evil. (The fallacy here is akin to some forms of the "naturalistic fallacy" in ethics, where some think, for example, that "good" is just what contributes to evolutionary progress, and that evolutionary progress is itself good.) If Pope meant what he said in the first line of his couplet, that "disorder" is only harmony not understood, the "partial evil" of the second line must, for consistency, mean "that which, taken in isolation, falsely appears to be evil," but it would more naturally mean "that which, in isolation, really is evil." The second line, in fact, hesitates between two views, that "partial evil" isn't really evil, since only the universal quality is real, and that "partial evil" is really an evil, but only a little one.

In addition, therefore, to adequate solutions, we must recognize unsatisfactory inconsistent solutions, in which there is only a half-hearted or temporary rejection of one of the propositions which together constitute the problem. In these, one of the constituent propositions is explicitly rejected, but it is covertly reasserted or assumed elsewhere in the system.

where is Pope ?

FALLACIOUS SOLUTIONS

Besides these half-hearted solutions, which explicitly reject but implicitly assert one of the constituent propositions, there are definitely fallacious solutions which explicitly maintain all the constituent propositions, but implicitly reject at least one of them in the course of the argument that explains away the problem of evil.

There are, in fact, many so-called solutions which purport to remove the contradiction without abandoning any of its constituent propositions. These must be fallacious, as we can see from the very statement of the problem, but it is not so easy to see in each case precisely where the fallacy lies. I suggest that in all cases the fallacy has the general form suggested above: in order to solve the problem one (or perhaps more) of its constituent propositions is given up, but in such a way that it appears to have been retained, and can therefore be asserted without qualification in other contexts. Sometimes there is a further complication: the supposed solution moves to and fro between, say, two of the constituent propositions, at one point asserting the first of these but covertly abandoning the second, at another point asserting the second but covertly abandoning the first. These fallacious solutions often turn upon some equivocation with the words "good" and "evil," or upon some vagueness about the way in which good and evil are opposed to one another, or about how much is meant by "omnipotence." I propose to examine some of these so-called solutions, and to exhibit their fallacies in detail. Incidentally, I shall also be considering whether an adequate solution could be reached by a minor modification of one or more of the constituent propositions, which would, however, still satisfy all the essential requirements of ordinary theism.

1. *"Good cannot exist without evil" or "Evil is necessary as a counterpart to good."*

It is sometimes suggested that evil is necessary as a counterpart to good, that if there were no evil there could be no good either, and that this solves the problem of evil. It is true that it points to an answer to the question "Why should there be evil?" But it does so only by qualifying some of the propositions that constitute the problem.

First, it sets a limit to what God can do, saying that God *cannot* create good without simultaneously creating evil, and this means either that God is not omnipotent or that there are *some* limits to what an omnipotent thing can do. It may be replied that these limits are always presupposed, that omnipotence has never meant the power to do what is logically impossible, and on the present view the existence of good without evil would be a logical impossibility. This interpretation of omnipotence may, indeed, be accepted as a modification of our original account which does not reject anything that is essential to theism, and I shall in general assume it in the subsequent discussion. It is, perhaps, the most common theistic view, but I think that some theists at least have maintained that God can do what is logically impossible. Many theists, at any rate, have held that logic itself is created or laid down by God, that logic is the way in which God arbitrarily chooses to think. (This is, of course, parallel to the ethical view that morally right actions are those which God arbitrarily chooses to command, and the two views encounter similar difficulties.) And *this* account of logic is clearly inconsistent with the view that God is bound by logical necessities—unless it is possible for an omnipotent being to bind himself, an issue which we shall consider later, when we come to the Paradox of Omnipotence. This solution of the problem of evil cannot, therefore, be consistently adopted along with the view that logic is itself created by God.

But, secondly, this solution denies that evil is opposed to good in
our original sense. If good and evil are counterparts, a good thing will not
"eliminate evil as far as it can." Indeed, this view suggests that good and
evil are not strictly qualities of things at all. Perhaps the suggestion is that
good and evil are related in much the same way as great and small. Certainly, when the term "great" is used relatively as a condensation of
"greater than so-and-so," and "small" is used correspondingly, greatness
and smallness are counterparts and cannot exist without each other. But
in this sense greatness is not a quality, not an intrinsic feature of anything;
and it would be absurd to think of a movement in favor of greatness and
against smallness in this sense. Such a movement would be self-defeating,
since relative greatness can be promoted only by a simultaneous promotion
of relative smallness. I feel sure that no theists would be content to regard
God's goodness as analogous to this—as if what he supports were not the
good but the *better*, and as if he had the paradoxical aim that all things
should be better than other things.

This point is obscured by the fact that "great" and "small" seem to
have an absolute as well as a relative sense. I cannot discuss here whether
there is absolute magnitude or not, but if there is, there could be an absolute sense for "great," it could mean of at least a certain size, and it
would make sense to speak of all things getting bigger, of a universe that
was expanding all over, and therefore it would make sense to speak of pro-
moting greatness. But in *this* sense great and small are not logically necessary counterparts: either quality could exist without the other. There
would be no logical impossibility in everything's being small or in everything's being great.   *and small could become great—*

Neither in the absolute nor in the relative sense, then, of "great" and *contextual*
"small" do these terms provide an analogy of the sort that would be
needed to support this solution of the problem of evil. In neither case are
greatness and smallness *both* necessary counterparts *and* mutually opposed
forces or possible objects for support and attack.

It may be replied that good and evil are necessary counterparts in
the same way as any quality and its logical opposite: redness can occur, it
is suggested, only if nonredness also occurs. But unless evil is merely the
privation of good, they are not logical opposites, and some further argument would be needed to show that they are counterparts in the same way
as genuine logical opposites. Let us assume that this could be given. There
is still doubt of the correctness of the metaphysical principle that a quality
must have a real opposite: I suggest that it is not really impossible that
everything should be, say, red, that the truth is merely that if everything

were red we should not notice redness, and so we should have no word "red"; we observe and give names to qualities only if they have real opposites. If so, the principle that a term must have an opposite would belong only to our language or to our thought, and would not be an ontological principle, and, correspondingly, the rule that good cannot exist without evil would not state a logical necessity of a sort that God would just have to put up with. God might have made everything good, though *we* should not have noticed it if he had.

But, finally, even if we concede that this *is* an ontological principle, it will provide a solution for the problem of evil only if one is prepared to say, "Evil exists, but only just enough evil to serve as the counterpart of good." I doubt whether any theist will accept this. After all, the *ontological* requirement that nonredness should occur would be satisfied even if all the universe, except for a minute speck, were red, and, if there were a corresponding requirement for evil as a counterpart to good, a minute dose of evil would presumably do. But theists are not usually willing to say, in all contexts, that all the evil that occurs is a minute and necessary dose.

2. *"Evil is necessary as a means to good."*

It is sometimes suggested that evil is necessary for good not as a counterpart but as a means. In its simple form this has little plausibility as a solution of the problem of evil, since it obviously implies a severe restriction of God's power. It would be a *causal* law that you cannot have a certain end without a certain means, so that if God has to introduce evil as a means to good, he must be subject to at least some causal laws. This certainly conflicts with what a theist normally means by omnipotence. This view of God as limited by causal laws also conflicts with the view that causal laws are themselves made by God, which is more widely held than the corresponding view about the laws of logic. This conflict would, indeed, be resolved if it were possible for an omnipotent being to bind himself, and this possibility has still to be considered. Unless a favorable answer can be given to this question, the suggestion that evil is necessary as a means to good solves the problem of evil only by denying one of its constituent propositions, either that God is omnipotent or that "omnipotent" means what it says.

3. *"The universe is better with some evil in it than it could be if there were no evil."*

Much more important is a solution which at first seems to be a mere variant of the previous one, that evil may contribute to the goodness of a whole in which it is found, so that the universe as a whole is better as it is, with some evil in it, than it would be if there were no evil. This solution may be developed in either of two ways. It may be supported by an aesthetic analogy, by the fact that contrasts heighten beauty, that in a musical work, for example, there may occur discords which somehow add to the beauty of the work as a whole. Alternatively, it may be worked out in connection with the notion of progress, that the best possible organization of the universe will not be static, but progressive, that the gradual overcoming of evil by good is really a finer thing than would be the eternal unchallenged supremacy of good.

In either case, this solution usually starts from the assumption that the evil whose existence gives rise to the problem of evil is primarily what is called physical evil, that is to say, pain. In Hume's rather half-hearted presentation of the problem of evil, the evils that he stresses are pain and disease, and those who reply to him argue that the existence of pain and disease makes possible the existence of sympathy, benevolence, heroism, and the gradually successful struggle of doctors and reformers to overcome these evils. In fact, theists often seize the opportunity to accuse those who stress the problem of evil of taking a low, materialistic view of good and evil, equating these with pleasure and pain, and of ignoring the more spiritual goods which can arise in the struggle against evils.

But let us see exactly what is being done here. Let us call pain and misery "first order evil" or "evil (1)." What contrasts with this, namely, pleasure and happiness, will be called "first order good" or "good (1)." Distinct from this is "second order good" or "good (2)" which somehow emerges in a complex situation in which evil (1) is a necessary component—logically, not merely causally, necessary. (Exactly *how* it emerges does not matter: in the crudest version of this solution good [2] is simply the heightening of happiness by the contrast with misery, in other versions it includes sympathy with suffering, heroism in facing danger, and the gradual decrease of first order evil and increase of first order good.) It is also being assumed that second order good is more important than first order good or evil, in particular that it more than outweighs the first order evil it involves.

Now this is a particularly subtle attempt to solve the problem of evil. It defends God's goodness and omnipotence on the ground that (on a sufficiently long view) this is the best of all logically possible worlds, because it includes the important second order goods, and yet it admits that real evils, namely first order evils, exist. But does it still hold that good and evil are opposed? Not, clearly, in the sense that we set out originally: good does not tend to eliminate evil in general. Instead, we have a modified, a more complex pattern. First order good (e.g., happiness) *contrasts with* first order evil (e.g., misery): these two are opposed in a fairly mechanical way; some second order goods (e.g., benevolence) try to maximize first order good and minimize first order evil; but God's goodness is not this, it is rather the will to maximize *second* order good. We might, therefore, call God's goodness an example of a third order goodness, or good (3). While this account is different from our original one, it might well be held to be an improvement on it, to give a more accurate description of the way in which good is opposed to evil, and to be consistent with the essential theist position.

There might, however, be several objections to this solution.

First, some might argue that such qualities as benevolence—and a fortiori the third order goodness which promotes benevolence—have a merely derivative value, that they are not higher sorts of good, but merely means to good (1), that is, to happiness, so that it would be absurd for God to keep misery in existence in order to make possible the virtues of benevolence, heroism, etc. The theist who adopts the present solution must, of course, deny this, but he can do so with some plausibility, so I should not press this objection.

Secondly, it follows from this solution that God is not in our sense benevolent or sympathetic: he is not concerned to minimize evil (1), but only to promote good (2); and this might be a disturbing conclusion for some theists.

But, thirdly, the fatal objection is this. Our analysis shows clearly the possibility of the existence of a *second* order evil, an evil (2) contrasting with good (2) as evil (1) contrasts with good (1). This would include malevolence, cruelty, callousness, cowardice, and states in which good (1) is decreasing and evil (1) increasing. And just as good (2) is held to be the important kind of good, the kind that God is concerned to promote, so evil (2) will, by analogy, be the important kind of evil, the kind which God, if he were wholly good and omnipotent, would eliminate. And yet evil (2) plainly exists, and indeed most theists (in other contexts) stress its existence more than that of evil (1). We should, therefore, state the problem of evil in terms of second order evil, and against this form of the problem the present solution is useless.

An attempt might be made to use this solution again, at a higher level, to explain the occurrence of evil (2): indeed the next main solution that we shall examine does just this, with the help of some new notions. Without any fresh notions, such a solution would have little plausibility:

for example, we could hardly say that the really important good was a good (3), such as the increase of benevolence in proportion to cruelty, which logically required for its occurrence the occurrence of some second order evil. But even if evil (2) could be explained in this way, it is fairly clear that there would be third order evils contrasting with this third order good: and we should be well on the way to an infinite regress, where the solution of a problem of evil, stated in terms of evil (n), indicated the existence of an evil ($n + 1$), and a further problem to be solved.

oh brother!

4. "Evil is due to human free will."

Perhaps the most important proposed solution of the problem of evil is that evil is not to be ascribed to God at all, but to the independent actions of human beings, supposed to have been endowed by God with freedom of the will. This solution may be combined with the preceding one: first order evil (e.g., pain) may be justified as a logically necessary component in second order good (e.g., sympathy) while second order evil (e.g., cruelty) is not *justified*, but is so ascribed to human beings that God cannot be held responsible for it. This combination evades my third criticism of the preceding solution.

The free-will solution also involves the preceding solution at a higher level. To explain why a wholly good God gave men free will although it would lead to some important evils, it must be argued that it is better on the whole that men should act freely, and sometimes err, than that they should be innocent automata, acting rightly in a wholly determined way. Freedom, that is to say, is now treated as third order good, and as being more valuable than second order goods (such as sympathy and heroism) would be if they were deterministically produced, and it is being assumed that second order evils, such as cruelty, are logically necessary accompaniments of freedom, just as pain is a logically necessary precondition of sympathy.

I think that this solution is unsatisfactory primarily because of the incoherence of the notion of freedom of the will: but I cannot discuss this topic adequately here, although some of my criticisms will touch upon it.

First I should query the assumption that second order evils are logically necessary accompaniments of freedom. I should ask this: if God has made men such that in their free choices they sometimes prefer what is good and sometimes what is evil, why could he not have *made* men such that they always freely choose the good? If there is no logical impossibility in a man's freely choosing the good on one, or on several, occasions, there cannot be a logical impossibility in his freely choosing the good on every

occasion. God was not, then, faced with a choice between making innocent automata and making beings who, in acting freely, would sometimes
go wrong: there was open to him the obviously better possibility of making beings who would act freely but always go right. Clearly, his failure
to avail himself of this possibility is inconsistent with his being both omnipotent and wholly good.

If it is replied that this objection is absurd, that the making of some
wrong choices is logically necessary for freedom, it would seem that "freedom" must here mean complete randomness or indeterminacy, including
randomness with regard to the alternatives good and evil, in other words
that men's choices and consequent actions can be "free" only if they are
not determined by their characters. Only on this assumption can God escape the responsibility for men's actions; for if he made them as they are,
but did not determine their wrong choices, this can only be because the
wrong choices are not determined by men as they are. But then if freedom
is randomness, how can it be a characteristic of *will*? And, still more, how
can it be the most important good? What value or merit would there be
in free choices if these were random actions which were not determined by
the nature of the agent?

I conclude that to make this solution plausible two different senses
of "freedom" must be confused, one sense which will justify the view that
freedom is a third order good, more valuable than other goods would be
without it, and another sense, sheer randomness, to prevent us from as-
cribing to God a decision to make men such that they sometimes go
wrong when he might have made them such that they would always freely
go right.

This criticism is sufficient to dispose of this solution. But besides
this there is a fundamental difficulty in the notion of an omnipotent God
creating men with free will, for if men's wills are really free this must
mean that even God cannot control them, that is, that God is no longer
omnipotent. It may be objected that God's gift of freedom to men does not
mean that he *cannot* control their wills, but that he always *refrains* from
controlling their wills? But why, we may ask, should God refrain from
controlling evil wills? Why should he not leave men free to will rightly,
but intervene when he sees them beginning to will wrongly? If God could
do this, but does not, and if he is wholly good, the only explanation could
be that even a wrong free act of will is not really evil, that its freedom is
a value which outweighs its wrongness, so that there would be a loss of
value if God took away the wrongness and the freedom together. But this
is utterly opposed to what theists say about sin in other contexts. The

present solution of the problem of evil, then, can be maintained only in the form that God has made men so free that he *cannot* control their wills.

This leads us to what I call the "Paradox of Omnipotence": can an omnipotent being make things which he cannot subsequently control? Or, what is practically equivalent to this, can an omnipotent being make rules which then bind himself? (These are practically equivalent because any such rules could be regarded as setting certain things beyond his control, and vice versa.) The second of these formulations is relevant to the suggestions that we have already met, that an omnipotent God creates the rules of logic or causal laws, and is then bound by them.

It is clear that this is a paradox: the questions cannot be answered satisfactorily either in the affirmative or in the negative. If we answer "Yes," it follows that if God actually makes things which he cannot control, or makes rules which bind himself, he is not omnipotent once he had made them: there are *then* things which he cannot do. But if we answer "No," we are immediately asserting that there are things which he cannot do, that is to say that he is already not omnipotent.

It cannot be replied that the question which sets this paradox is not a proper question. It would make perfectly good sense to say that a human mechanic has made a machine which he cannot control: if there is any difficulty about the question it lies in the notion of omnipotence itself.

This, incidentally, shows that although we have approached this paradox from the free-will theory, it is equally a problem for a theological determinist. No one thinks that machines have free will, yet they may well be beyond the control of their makers. The determinist might reply that anyone who makes anything determines its ways of acting, and so determines its subsequent behavior: even the human mechanic does this by his *choice* of materials and structure for his machine, though he does not know all about either of these: the mechanic thus determines, though he may not foresee, his machine's actions. And since God is omniscient, and since his creation of things is total, he both determines and foresees the ways in which his creatures will act. We may grant this, but it is beside the point. The question is not whether God *originally* determined the future actions of his creatures, but whether he can *subsequently* control their actions, or whether he was able in his original creation to put things beyond his subsequent control. Even on determinist principles the answers "Yes" and "No" are equally irreconcilable with God's omnipotence.

Before suggesting a solution of this paradox, I would point out that there is a parallel Paradox of Sovereignty. Can a legal sovereign make a law restricting its own future legislative power? For example, could the

British parliament make a law forbidding any future parliament to social-
ize banking, and also forbidding the future repeal of this law itself? Or
could the British parliament, which was legally sovereign in Australia in,
say, 1899, pass a valid law, or series of laws, which made it no longer
sovereign in 1933? Again, neither the affirmative nor the negative answer
is really satisfactory. If we were to answer "Yes," we should be admitting
the validity of a law which, if it were actually made, would mean that
parliament was not longer sovereign. If we were to answer "No," we
should be admitting that there is a law, not logically absurd, which parliament cannot validly make, that is, that parliament is not now a legal
sovereign. This paradox can be solved in the following way. We should
distinguish between first order laws, that is laws governing the actions of
individuals and bodies other than the legislature, and second order laws,
that is laws about laws, laws governing the actions of the legislature itself.
Correspondingly, we should distinguish two orders of sovereignty, first order sovereignty (sovereignty [1]) which is unlimited authority to make
first order laws, and second order sovereignty (sovereignty [2]) which is
unlimited authority to make second order laws. If we say that parliament
is sovereign we might mean that any parliament at any time has sovereignty (1), or we might mean that parliament has both sovereignty (1) and
sovereignty (2) at present, but we cannot without contradiction mean both
that the present parliament has sovereignty (2) and that every parliament
at every time has sovereignty (1), for if the present parliament has sovereignty (2) it may use it to take away the sovereignty (1) of later parlia-
ments. What the paradox shows is that we cannot ascribe to any
continuing institution legal sovereignty in an inclusive sense.

The analogy between omnipotence and sovereignty shows that the
paradox of omnipotence can be solved in a similar way. We must distinguish between first order omnipotence (omnipotence [1]), that is unlimited power to act, and second order omnipotence (omnipotence [2]), that
is unlimited power to determine what powers to act things shall have.
Then we could consistently say that God all the time has omnipotence (1),
but if so no beings at any time have powers to act independently of God.
Or we could say that God at one time had omnipotence (2), and used it to
assign independent powers to act to certain things, so that God thereafter
did not have omnipotence (1). But what the paradox shows is that we cannot consistently ascribe to any continuing being omnipotence in an inclusive sense.

An alternative solution of this paradox would be simply to deny that
God is a continuing being, that any times can be assigned to his actions

at all. But on this assumption (which also has difficulties of its own) no meaning can be given to the assertion that God made men with wills so free that he could not control them. The paradox of omnipotence can be avoided by putting God outside time, but the free-will solution of the problem of evil cannot be saved in this way, and equally it remains impossible to hold that an omnipotent God *binds himself* by causal or logical laws.

CONCLUSION

Of the proposed solutions of the problem of evil which we have examined, none has stood up to criticism. There may be other solutions which require examination, but this study strongly suggests that there is no valid solution of the problem which does not modify at least one of the constituent propositions in a way which would seriously affect the essential core of the theistic position.

Quite apart form the problem of evil, the paradox of omnipotence has shown that God's omnipotence must in any case be restricted in one way or another, that unqualified omnipotence cannot be ascribed to any being that continues through time. And if God and his actions are not in time, can omnipotence, or power of any sort, be meaningfully ascribed to him?

The Free Will Defense

ALVIN PLANTINGA

In a widely discussed piece entitled "Evil and Omnipotence" John Mackie repeats this claim:

> I think, however, that a more telling criticism can be made by way of the traditional problem of evil. Here it can be shown, not that religious beliefs lack rational support, but that they are positively irrational, that the several parts of the essential theological doctrine are *inconsistent* with one another. . . . [1]

Is Mackie right? Does the theist contradict himself? But we must ask a prior question: just what is being claimed here? That theistic belief contains an inconsistency or contradiction, of course. But what, exactly, is an inconsistency or contradiction? There are several kinds. An *explicit* contradiction is a *proposition* of a certain sort—a conjunctive proposition, one conjunct of which is the denial or negation of the other conjunct. For example:

> Paul is a good tennis player, and it's false that Paul is a good tennis player.

(People seldom assert explicit contradictions). Is Mackie charging the theist with accepting such a contradiction? Presumably not; what he says is:

> In its simplest form the problem is this: God is omnipotent; God is wholly good; yet evil exists. There seems to be some contradiction between these three propositions, so that if any two of them were true the third would be false. But at the same time all three are essential parts of most theological positions; the theologian, it seems, at once *must* adhere and *cannot consistently* adhere to all three. [2]

From Alvin Plantinga, *God, Freedom, and Evil* (Grand Rapids, Mich., 1977), 12–49, by permission of the author and Wm. B. Eerdmans Publishing Co.

According to Mackie, then, the theist accepts a group or set of three propositions; this set is inconsistent. Its members, of course are,

(1) God is omnipotent

(2) God is wholly good

and

(3) Evil exists.

Call this set A; the claim is that A is an inconsistent set. But what is it for a *set* to be inconsistent or contradictory? Following our definition of an explicit contradiction, we might say that a set of propositions is explicitly contradictory if one of the members is the denial or negation of another member. But then, of course, it is evident that the set we are discussing is not explicitly contradictory; the denials of (1), (2), and (3), respectively, are

(1') God is not omnipotent (or it's false that God is omnipotent)

(2') God is not wholly good

and

(3') There is no evil

none of which is in set A.

Of course many sets are pretty clearly contradictory, in an important way, but not *explicitly* contradictory. For example, set B:

(4) If all men are mortal, then Socrates is mortal

(5) All men are mortal

(6) Socrates is not mortal.

This set is not explicitly contradictory; yet surely *some* significant sense of that term applies to it. What is important here is that by using only the rules of ordinary logic—the laws of propositional logic and quantification theory found in any introductory text on the subject—we can deduce an explicit contradiction from the set. Or to put it differently, we can use the laws of logic to deduce a proposition from the set, which proposition, when added to the set, yields a new set that is explicitly contradictory. For by using the law *modus ponens* (if *p,* then *q; p;* therefore *q*) we can deduce

(7) Socrates is mortal

from (4) and (5). The result of adding (7) to B is the set {(4), (5), (6), (7)}. This set, of course, is explicitly contradictory in that (6) is the denial of (7). We might say that any set which shares this characteristic with set B is *formally* contradictory. So a formally contradictory set is one from whose members an explicit contradiction can be deduced by the laws of logic. Is Mackie claiming that set A is formally contradictory?

If he is, he's wrong. No laws of logic permit us to deduce the denial of one of the propositions in A from the other members. Set A isn't formally contradictory either.

But there is still another way in which a set of propositions can be contradictory or inconsistent. Consider set C, whose members are

(8) George is older than Paul

(9) Paul is older than Nick

and

(10) George is not older than Nick.

This set is neither explicitly nor formally contradictory; we can't, just by using the laws of logic, deduce the denial of any of these propositions from the others. And yet there is a good sense in which it is consistent or contradictory. For clearly it is *not possible* that its three members all be true. It is *necessarily true* that

(11) If George is older than Paul, and Paul is older than Nick, then George is older than Nick.

And if we add (11) to set C, we get a set that is formally contradictory; (8), (9), and (11) yield, by the laws of ordinary logic, the denial of (10).

I said that (11) is *necessarily true;* but what does *that* mean? Of course we might say that a proposition is necessarily true if it is impossible that it be false, or if its negation is not possibly true. This would be to explain necessity in terms of possibility. Chances are, however, that anyone who does not know what necessity is will be equally at a loss about possibility; the explanation is not likely to be very successful. Perhaps all we can do by way of explanation is to give some examples and hope for the best. In the first place many propositions can be established by the laws of logic alone—for example,

(12) If all men are mortal and Socrates is a man, then Socrates is mortal.

Such propositions are truths of logic; and all of them are necessary in the sense of question. But truths of arithmetic and mathematics generally are also necessarily true. Still further, there is a host of propositions that are neither truths of logic nor truths of mathematics but are nonetheless necessarily true; (11) would be an example, as well as

(13) Nobody is taller than himself

(14) Red is a color

(15) No numbers are persons

(16) No prime number is a prime minister

and

(17) Bachelors are unmarried.

So here we have an important kind of necessity—let's call it "broadly logical necessity." Of course there is a correlative kind of *possibility:* a proposition *p* is possibly true (in the broadly logical sense) just in case its negation or denial is not necessarily true (in that same broadly logical sense). This sense of necessity and possibility must be distinguished from another that we may call *causal* or *natural* necessity and possibility. Consider

(18) Henry Kissinger has swum the Atlantic.

Although this proposition has an implausible ring, it is not necessarily false in the broadly logical sense (and its denial is not necessarily true in that sense). But there is a good sense in which it is impossible: it is *causally* or *naturally* impossible. Human beings, unlike dolphins, just don't have the physical equipment demanded for this feat. Unlike Superman, furthermore, the rest of us are incapable of leaping tall buildings at a single bound or (without auxiliary power of some kind) traveling faster than a speeding bullet. These things are *impossible* for us—but not *logically* impossible, even in the broad sense.

So there are several senses of necessity and possibility here. There are a number of propositions, furthermore, of which it's difficult to say whether they are or aren't possible in the broadly logical sense; some of these are subjects of philosophical controversy. Is it possible, for example, for a person never to be conscious during his entire existence? Is it possible for a (human) person to exist *disembodied?* If that's possible, is it possible that there be a person who *at no time at all* during his entire existence has a body? Is it possible to see without eyes? These are propositions about whose possibility in that broadly logical sense there is disagreement and dispute.

Now return to set C. What is characteristic of it is the fact that the conjunction of its members—the proposition expressed by the result of putting "and's" between (8), (9), and (10)—is necessarily false. Or we might put it like this: what characterizes set C is the fact that we can get a formally contradictory set by adding a necessarily true proposition—namely (11). Suppose we say that a set is *implicitly contradictory* if it resembles C in this respect. That is, a set *S* of propositions is implicitly contradictory if there is a necessary proposition *p* such that the result of adding *p* to *S* is a formally contradictory set. Another way to put it: *S* is implicitly contradictory if there is some necessarily true proposition *p* such that by using just the laws of ordinary logic, we can deduce an explicit contradiction from *p* together with the members of *S*. And when Mackie says that set A is contradictory, we may properly take him, I think, as holding that it is implicitly contradictory in the explained sense. As he puts it:

> However, the contradiction does not arise immediately; to show it we need some additional premises, or perhaps some quasi-logical rules connecting the terms "good" and "evil" and "omnipotent." These additional principles are that good is opposed to evil, in such a way that a good thing always eliminates evil as far as it can, and that there are no limits to what an omnipotent thing can do. From these it follows that a good omnipotent thing eliminates evil completely, and then the propositions that a good omnipotent thing exists, and that evil exists, are incompatible.[3]

Here Mackie refers to "additional premises"; he also calls them "additional principles" and "quasi-logical rules"; he says we need them to show the contradiction. What he means, I think, is that to get a formally contradictory set we must add some more propositions to set A; and if we aim to show that set A is implicitly contradictory, these propositions must be necessary truths—"quasi-logical rules" as Mackie calls them. The two additional principles he suggests are

(19) A good thing always eliminates evil as far as it can

and

(20) There are no limits to what an omnipotent being can do.

And, of course, if Mackie means to show that set A is implicitly contradictory, then he must hold that (19) and (20) are not merely *true* but *necessarily true*.

But, are they? What about (20) first? What does it mean to say that a being is omnipotent? That he is *all-powerful*, or *almighty*, presumably. But are there no limits *at all* to the power of such a being? Could he create square circles, for example, or married bachelors? Most theologians and theistic philosophers who hold that God is omnipotent, do not hold that He can create round squares or bring it about that He both exists and does not exist. These theologians and philosophers may hold that there are no *nonlogical* limits to what an omnipotent being can do, but they concede that not even an omnipotent being can bring about logically impossible states of affairs or cause necessarily false propositions to be true. Some theists, on the other hand—Martin Luther and Descartes, perhaps—have apparently thought that God's power is unlimited even by the laws of logic. For these theists the question whether set A is contradictory will not be of much interest. As theists they believe (1) and (2), and they also, presumably, believe (3). But they remain undisturbed by the claim that (1), (2), and (3) are jointly inconsistent—because, as they say, God can do what is logically impossible. Hence He can bring it about that the members of set A are all true, even if that set is contradictory (concentrating very intensely upon this suggestion is likely to make you dizzy). So the theist who thinks that the power of God isn't limited *at all,* not even by the laws of logic, will be unimpressed by Mackie's argument and won't find any difficulty in the contradiction set A is alleged to contain. This view is not very popular, however, and for good reason; it is quite incoherent. What the theist typically means when he says that God is omnipotent is not that there are *no* limits to God's power, but at most that there are no nonlogical limits to what He can do; and given this qualification, it is perhaps initially plausible to suppose that (20) is necessarily true.

But what about (19), the proposition that every good thing eliminates every evil state of affairs that it can eliminate? Is that necessarily true? Is it true at all? Suppose, first of all, that your friend Paul unwisely goes for a drive on a wintry day and runs out of gas on a deserted road. The temperature dips to -10°, and a miserably cold wind comes up. You are sitting comfortably at home (twenty-five miles from Paul) roasting chestnuts in a roaring blaze. Your car is in the garage; in the trunk there is the full five-gallon can of gasoline you always keep for emergencies. Paul's discomfort and danger are certainly an evil, and one which you could eliminate. You don't do so. But presumably you don't thereby forfeit your claim to being a "good thing"—you simply didn't know of Paul's plight. And so (19) does not appear to be necessary. It says that every good thing has a certain property—the property of eliminating every evil that it can. And if the case I described is possible—a good person's failing through ignorance to eliminate a certain evil he can eliminate—then (19) is by no means necessarily true.

But perhaps Mackie could sensibly claim that if you *didn't know* about Paul's plight, then in fact you were *not,* at the time in question, able to eliminate the evil in question; and perhaps he'd be right. In any event he could revise (19) to take into account the kind of case I mentioned:

(19a) Every good thing always eliminates every evil that *it knows about* and can eliminate.

{(1), (2), (3), (20), (19a)}, you'll notice is not a formally contradictory set—to get a formal contradiction we must add a proposition specifying that God *knows about* every evil state of affairs. But most theists do believe that God is omniscient or all-knowing; so if this new set—the set that results when we add to set A the proposition that God is omniscient—is implicitly contradictory then Mackie should be satisfied and the theist confounded. (And, henceforth, set A will be the old set A together with the proposition that God is omniscient.)

But is (19a) necessary? Hardly. Suppose you know that Paul is marooned as in the previous example, and you also know another friend is similarly marooned fifty miles in the opposite direction. Suppose, furthermore, that while you can rescue one or the other, you simply can't rescue both. Then each of the two evils is such that it is within your power to eliminate it; and you know about them both. But you can't eliminate *both;* and you don't forfeit your claim to being a good person by eliminating only one—it wasn't within your power to do more. So the fact that you don't doesn't mean that you are not a good person. Therefore (19a) is false; it is not a necessary truth or even a truth that every good thing eliminates every evil it knows about and can eliminate.

We can see the same thing another way. You've been rock climbing. Still something of a novice, you've acquired a few cuts and bruises by inelegantly using your knees rather than your feet. One of these bruises is fairly painful. You mention it to a physician friend, who predicts the pain will leave of its own accord in a day or two. Meanwhile, he says, there's nothing he can do, short of amputating your leg above the knee, to remove the pain. Now the pain in your knee is an evil state of affairs. All else being equal, it would be better if you had no such pain. And it is within the power of your friend to eliminate this evil state of affairs. Does his failure to do so mean that he is not a good person? Of course not; for he could eliminate this evil state of affairs only by bringing about another, much worse evil. And so it is once again evident that (19a) is false. It is entirely possible that a good person fail to eliminate an evil state of affairs that he knows about and can eliminate. This would take place, if, as in the present example, he couldn't eliminate the evil without bringing about a *greater* evil.   hmmm

A slightly different kind of case shows the same thing. A really impressive good state of affairs G will *outweigh* a trivial E—that is, the conjunctive state of affairs G *and* E is itself a good state of affairs. And surely a good person would not be obligated to eliminate a given evil if he could do so only by eliminating a good that outweighed it. Therefore (19a) is not necessarily true; it can't be used to show that set A is implicitly contradictory.

These difficulties might suggest another revision of (19); we might try

(19b) A good being eliminates every evil E that it knows about and that it can eliminate without either bringing about a greater evil or eliminating a good state of affairs that outweighs E.

Is this necessarily true? It takes care of the second of the two difficulties afflicting (19a) but leaves the first untouched. We can see this as follows. First, suppose we say that a being *properly eliminates* an evil state of affairs if it eliminates that evil without either eliminating an outweighing good or bringing about a greater evil. It is then obviously possible that a person find himself in a situation where he could properly eliminate an evil E and could also properly eliminate another evil E', but couldn't properly eliminate them *both*. You're rock climbing again, this time on the dreaded north face of the Grand Teton. You and your party come upon Curt and Bob, two mountaineers stranded 125 feet apart on the face. They untied to reach their cigarettes and then carelessly dropped the rope while lighting up. A violent, dangerous thunderstorm is approaching. You have time to rescue one of the stranded climbers and retreat before the storm hits; if you rescue both, however, you and your party and the two climbers will be caught on the face during the thunderstorm, which will very likely destroy your entire party. In this case you can eliminate one evil (Curt's being stranded on the face) without causing more evil or eliminating a greater good; and you are also able to properly eliminate the other evil (Bob's being thus stranded). But you can't properly eliminate them *both*. And so the fact that you don't rescue Curt, say, even though you could have, doesn't show that you aren't a good person. Here, then, each of the evils is such that you can properly eliminate it; but you can't properly eliminate them both, and hence can't be blamed for failing to eliminate one of them.

So neither (19a) nor (19b) is necessarily true. You may be tempted to reply that the sort of counterexamples offered—examples where someone is able to eliminate an evil A and also able to eliminate a different evil B, but unable to eliminate them both—are irrelevant to the case of a being who, like God, is both omnipotent and omniscient. That is, you may think that if an omnipotent and omniscient being is able to eliminate *each* of two evils, it follows that he can eliminate them *both*. Perhaps this is so; but it is not strictly to the point. The fact is the counterexamples show that (19a) and (19b) are not necessarily true and hence can't be used to show that set A is implicitly inconsistent. What the reply does suggest is that perhaps the atheologian will have more success if he works the properties of omniscience and omnipotence into (19). Perhaps he could say something like

> (19c) An omnipotent and omniscient good being eliminates every evil that it can properly eliminate.

And suppose, for purposes of argument, we concede the necessary truth of (19c). Will it serve Mackie's purposes? Not obviously. For we don't get a set that is formally contradictory by adding (20) and (19c) to set A. This set (call it A′) contains the following six members:

> (1)   God is omnipotent
> (2)   God is wholly good
> (2′)   God is omniscient
> (3)   Evil exists
> (19c) An omnipotent and omniscient good being eliminates every evil that it can properly eliminate

and

> (20) There are no nonlogical limits to what an omnipotent being can do.

Now if A′ were formally contradictory, then from any five of its members we could deduce the denial of the sixth by the laws of ordinary logic. That is, any five would *formally entail* the denial of the sixth. So if A′ were formally inconsistent, the denial of (3) would be formally entailed by the remaining five. That is, (1), (2), (2′), (19c), and (20) would formally entail

> (3′) There is no evil.

But they don't; what they formally entail is not that there is no evil *at all* but only that

> (3″) There is no evil that God can properly eliminate.

So (19c) doesn't really help either—not because it is not necessarily true but because its addition [with (20)] to set A does not yield a formally contradictory set.

Obviously, what the atheologian must add to get a formally contradictory set is

> (21) If God is omniscient and omnipotent, then he can properly eliminate every evil state of affairs.

Suppose we agree that the set consisting in A plus (19c), (20), and (21) is formally contradictory. So if (19c), (20), and (21) are all necessarily true, then set A is implicitly contradictory. We've already conceded that (19c)

qand (20) are indeed necessary. So we must take a look at (21). Is this proposition necessarily true?

No. To see this let us ask the following question. Under what conditions would an omnipotent being be unable to eliminate a certain evil E without eliminating an outweighing good? Well, suppose that E is *included in* some good state of affairs that outweighs it. That is, suppose there is some good state of affairs G so related to E that it is impossible that G obtain or be actual and E fail to obtain. (Another way to put this: a state of affairs S includes S' if the conjunctive state of affairs S *but not S'* is impossible, or if it is necessary that S' obtains if S does.) Now suppose that some good state of affairs G includes an evil state of affairs E that it outweighs. Then not even an omnipotent being could eliminate E without eliminating G. But *are* there any cases where a good state of affairs includes, in this sense, an evil that it outweighs?[4] Indeed there are such states of affairs. To take an artificial example, let's suppose that E is Paul's suffering from a minor abrasion and G is your being deliriously happy. The conjunctive state of affairs, G *and E*—the state of affairs that obtains if and only if both G and E obtain—is then a good state of affairs: it is better, all else being equal, that you be intensely happy and Paul suffer a mildly annoying abrasion than that this state of affairs not obtain. So G *and E* is a good state of affairs. And clearly G *and E* includes E: obviously it is necessarily true that if you are deliriously happy and Paul is suffering from an abrasion, then Paul is suffering from an abrasion.

But perhaps you think this example trivial, tricky, slippery, and irrelevant. If so, take heart; other examples abound. Certain kinds of values, certain familiar kinds of good states of affairs, can't exist apart from evil of some sort. For example, there are people who display a sort of creative moral heroism in the face of suffering and adversity—a heroism that inspires others and creates a good situation out of a bad one. In a situation like this the evil, of course, remains evil; but the total state of affairs—someone's bearing pain magnificently, for example—may be good. If it is, then the good present must outweigh the evil; otherwise the total situation would not be *good*. But, of course, it is not possible that such a good state of affairs obtain unless some evil also obtain. It is a necessary truth that if someone bears pain magnificently, then someone is in pain.

The conclusion to be drawn, therefore, is that (21) is not necessarily true. And our discussion thus far shows at the very least that it is no easy matter to find necessarily true propositions that yield a formally contradictory set when added to set A.[5] One wonders, therefore, why the many atheologians who confidently assert that this set is contradictory make no attempt whatever to *show* that it is. For the most part they are content just to *assert* that there is a contradiction here. Even Mackie, who sees that some "additional premises" or "quasi-logical rules" are needed, makes scarcely a beginning towards finding some additional premises that are necessarily true and that together with the members of set A formally entail an explicit contradiction.

3. CAN WE SHOW THAT THERE IS NO INCONSISTENCY HERE?

To summarize our conclusions so far: although many atheologians claim that the theist is involved in contradiction when he asserts the members of set A, this set, obviously, is neither *explicitly* nor *formally* contradictory; the claim, presumably, must be that it is *implicitly* contradictory. To make good this claim the atheologian must find some necessarily true proposition *p* (it could be a conjunction of several propositions) such that the addition of *p* to set A yields a set that is formally contradictory. No atheologian has produced even a plausible candidate for this role, and it certainly is not easy to see what such a proposition might be. Now we might think we should simply declare set A implicitly consistent on the principle that a proposition (or set) is to be presumed consistent or possible until proven otherwise. This course, however, leads to trouble. The same principle would impel us to declare the atheologian's claim—that set A is *in*consistent—possible or consistent. But the claim that a given set of propositions is implicitly contradictory is itself either necessarily true or necessarily false; so if such a claim is *possible*, it is not necessarily false and is, therefore, true (in fact, necessarily true). If we followed the suggested principle, therefore, we should be obliged to declare set A implicitly consistent (since it hasn't been shown to be otherwise), but we should have to say the same thing about the atheologian's claim, since we haven't shown *that* claim to be inconsistent or impossible. The atheologian's claim, furthermore, is necessarily true if it is possible. Accordingly, if we accept the above principle, we shall have to declare set A both implicitly consistent and implicitly inconsistent. So all we can say at this point is that set A has not been shown to be implicitly inconsistent.

Can we go any further? One way to go on would be to try to *show* that set A is implicitly consistent or possible in the broadly logical sense. But what is involved in showing such a thing? Although there are various ways to approach this matter, they all resemble one another in an important respect. They all amount to this: to show that a set S is consistent you think of a *possible state of affairs* (it needn't *actually obtain*) which is such that if it were actual, then all of the members of S would be true. This procedure is sometimes called *giving a model of S*. For example, you might construct an axiom set and then show that it is consistent by giving a model of it; this is how it was shown that the denial of Euclid's parallel postulate is formally consistent with the rest of his postulates.

There are various special cases of this procedure to fit special circumstances. Suppose, for example, you have a pair of propositions p and q and wish to show them consistent. And suppose we say that a proposition p_1 *entails* a proposition p_2 if it is impossible that p_1 be true and p_2 false—if the conjunctive proposition p_1 *and not* p_2 is necessarily false. Then one way to show that p is consistent with q is to find some proposition r whose conjunction with p is both possible, in the broadly logical sense, and entails q. A rude and unlettered behaviorist, for example, might hold that thinking is really nothing but movements of the larynx; he might go on to hold that

P Jones did not move his larynx after April 30

is inconsistent (in the broadly logical sense) with

Q Jones did some thinking during May.

By way of rebuttal, we might point out that P appears to be consistent with

R While convalescing from an April 30 laryngotomy, Jones whiled away the idle hours by writing (in May) a splendid paper on Kant's *Critique of Pure Reason.*

So the conjunction of P and R appears to be consistent; but obviously it also entails Q (you can't write even a passable paper on Kant's *Critique of Pure Reason* without doing some thinking); so P and Q are consistent.

We can see that this is a special case of the procedure I mentioned above as follows. This proposition R is consistent with P; so the proposition P *and R* is possible, describes a possible state of affairs. But P *and R* entails Q; hence if P *and R* were true, Q would also be true, and hence both P and Q would be true. So this is really a case of producing a possible state of affairs such that, if it were actual, all the members of the set in question (in this case the pair set of P and Q) would be true.

How does this apply to the case before us? As follows, let us conjoin propositions (1), (2), and (2′) and henceforth call the result (1):

(1) God is omniscient, omnipotent, and wholly good.

The problem, then, is to show that (1) and (3) (evil exists) are consistent. This could be done, as we've seen, by finding a proposition *r* that is consistent with (1) and such that (1) and *(r)* together entail (3). One proposition that might do the trick is

> (22) God creates a world containing evil and has a good reason for doing so.

If (22) is consistent with (1), then it follows that (1) and (3) (and hence set A) are consistent. Accordingly, one thing some theists have tried is to show that (22) and (1) are consistent.

One can attempt this in at least two ways. On the one hand, we could try to apply the same method again. Conceive of a possible state of affairs such that, if it obtained, an omnipotent, omniscient, and wholly good God would have a good reason for permitting evil. On the other, someone might try to specify *what God's reason is* for permitting evil and try to show, if it is not obvious, that it is a good reason. St. Augustine, for example, one of the greatest and most influential philosopher-theologians of the Christian Church, writes as follows:

> . . . some people see with perfect truth that a creature is better if, while possessing free will, it remains always fixed upon God and never sins; then, reflecting on men's sins, they are grieved, not because they continue to sin, but because they were created. They say: He should have made us such that we never willed to sin, but always to enjoy the unchangeable truth.
>
> They should not lament or be angry. God has not compelled men to sin just because He created them and gave them the power to choose between sinning and not sinning. There are angels who have never sinned and never will sin.
>
> Such is the generosity of God's goodness that He has not refrained from creating even that creature which He foreknew would not only sin, but remain in the will to sin. As a runaway horse is better than a stone which does not run away because it lacks self-movement and sense perception, so the creature is more excellent which sins by free will than that which does not sin only because it has no free will.[6]

In broadest terms Augustine claims that God could create a better, more perfect universe by permitting evil than He could by refusing to do so:

> Neither the sins nor the misery are necessary to the perfection of the universe, but souls as such are necessary, which have the power to sin if they so will, and become miserable if they sin. If misery persisted after their sins had been abolished, or if there were misery before there were sins, then it

might be right to say that the order and government of the universe were at fault. Again, if there were sins but no consequent misery, that order is equally dishonored by lack of equity.[7]

Augustine tries to tell us *what God's reason is* for permitting evil. At bottom, he says, it's that God can create a more perfect universe by permitting evil. A really top-notch universe requires the existence of free, rational, and moral agents; and some of the free creatures He created went wrong. But the universe with the free creatures it contains and the evil they commit is better than it would have been had it contained neither the free creatures nor this evil. Such an attempt to specify God's reason for permitting evil is what I earlier called a *theodicy;* in the words of John Milton it is an attempt to "justify the ways of God to man," to show that God is just in permitting evil. Augustine's kind of theodicy might be called a Free Will Theodicy, since the idea of rational creatures with free will plays such a prominent role in it.

A theodicist, then, attempts to tell us why God permits evil. Quite distinct from a Free Will Theodicy is what I shall call a Free Will Defense. Here the aim is not to say what God's reason *is*, but at most what God's reason *might possibly be*. We could put the difference like this. The Free Will Theodicist and Free Will Defender are both trying to show that (1) is consistent with (22), and of course if so, then set A is consistent. The Free Will Theodicist tries to do this by finding some proposition *r* which in conjunction with (1) entails (22); he claims, furthermore, that this proposition is *true*, not just consistent with (1). He tries to tell us what God's reason for permitting evil *really is*. The Free Will Defender, on the other hand, though he also tries to find a proposition *r* that is consistent with (1) and in conjunction with it entails (22), does *not* claim to know or even believe that *r* is true. And here, of course, he is perfectly within his rights. His aim is to show that (1) is consistent with (22); all he need do then is find an *r* that is consistent with (1) and such that (1) and *(r)* entail (22); whether *r* is *true* is quite beside the point.

So there is a significant difference between a Free Will Theodicy and A Free Will Defense. The latter is sufficient (if successful) to show that set A is consistent; in a way a Free Will Theodicy goes beyond what is required. On the other hand, a theodicy would be much more satisfying, if possible to achieve. No doubt the theist would rather know what God's reason *is* for permitting evil than simply that it's possible that He has a good one. But in the present context (that of investigating the consistency of set A), the latter is all that's needed. Neither a defense or a theodicy, of course, gives any hint to what God's reason for some *specific* evil—the death or suffering of someone close to you, for example—might be. And there is still another function—a sort of pastoral function[8]—in the neighborhood that neither serves. Confronted with evil in his own life or suddenly coming to realize more clearly than before the *extent* and *magnitude* of evil, a believer in God may undergo a crisis of faith. He may be tempted to follow the advice of Job's "friends"; he may be tempted to "curse God and die." Neither a Free Will Defense nor a Free Will Theodicy is designed to be of much help or comfort to one suffering from such a storm in the soul (although in a specific case, of course, one or the other could prove useful). Neither is to be thought of first of all as a means of pastoral counseling. Probably neither will enable someone to find peace with himself and with God in the face of the evil the world contains. But then, of course, neither is intended for that purpose.

4. THE FREE WILL DEFENSE

In what follows I shall focus attention upon the Free Will Defense. I shall examine it more closely, state it more exactly, and consider objections to it; and I shall argue that in the end it is successful. Earlier we saw that among good states of affairs there are some that not even God can bring about without bringing about evil: those goods, namely, that *entail* or *include* evil states of affairs. The Free Will Defense can be looked upon as an effort to show that there may be a very different kind of good that God can't bring about without permitting evil. These are good states of affairs that don't include evil; they do not entail the existence of any evil whatever; nonetheless God Himself can't bring them about without permitting evil.

So how does the Free Will Defense work? And what does the Free Will Defender mean when he says that people are or may be free? What is relevant to the Free Will Defense is the idea of *being free with respect to an action*. If a person is free with respect to a given action, then he is free to perform that action and free to refrain from performing it; no antecedent conditions and/or causal laws determine that he will perform the action, or that he won't. It is within his power, at the time in question, to take or perform the action and within his power to refrain from it. Freedom so conceived is not to be confused with unpredictability. You might be able to predict what you will do in a given situation even if you are free, in that situation, to do something else. If I know you well, I may be able to predict what action you will take in response to a certain set of conditions; it does not follow that you are not free with respect to that action. Secondly,

I shall say that an action is *morally significant,* for a given person, if it would be wrong for him to perform the action but right to refrain or *vice versa.* Keeping a promise, for example, would ordinarily be morally significant for a person, as would refusing induction into the army. On the other hand, having Cheerios for breakfast (instead of Wheaties) would not normally be morally significant. Further, suppose we say that a person is *significantly free,* on a given occasion, if he is then free with respect to a morally significant action. And finally we must distinguish between *moral evil* and *natural evil.* The former is evil that results from free human activity; natural evil is any other kind of evil.[9]

Given these definitions and distinctions, we can make a preliminary statement of the Free Will Defense as follows. A world containing creatures who are significantly free (and freely perform more good than evil actions) is more valuable, all else being equal, than a world containing no free creatures at all. Now God can create free creatures, but He can't *cause* or *determine* them to do only what is right. For if He does so, then they aren't significantly free after all; they do not do what is right *freely.* To create creatures capable of *moral good,* therefore, He must create creatures capable of moral evil; and He can't give these creatures the freedom to perform evil and at the same time prevent them from doing so. As it turned out, sadly enough, some of the free creatures God created went wrong in the exercise of their freedom; this is the source of moral evil. The fact that free creatures sometimes go wrong, however, counts neither against God's omnipotence nor against His goodness; for He could have forestalled the occurrence of moral evil only by removing the possibility of moral good.

I said earlier that the Free Will Defender tries to find a proposition that is consistent with

(1) God is omniscient, omnipotent, and wholly good

and together with (1) entails that there is evil. According to the Free Will Defense, we must find this proposition somewhere in the above story. The heart of the Free Will Defense is the claim that is *possible* that God could not have created a universe containing moral good (or as much moral good as this world contains) without creating one that also contained moral evil. And if so, then it is possible that God has a good reason for creating a world containing evil.

Now this defense has met with several kinds of objections. For example, some philosophers say that *causal determinism* and *freedom,* contrary to what we might have thought, are not really incompatible.[10] But if so, then God could have created free creatures who were free, and free to do what is wrong, but nevertheless were causally determined to do only what is right. Thus He could have created creatures who were free to do what was wrong, while nevertheless preventing them from ever performing any wrong actions—simply by seeing to it that they were causally determined to do only what is right. Of course this contradicts the Free Will Defense, according to which there is inconsistency in supposing that God determines free creatures to do only what is right. But is it really possible that all of a person's actions are causally determined while some of them are free? How could that be so? According to one version of the doctrine in question, to say that George acts freely on a given occasion is to say only this: *if George had chosen to do otherwise, he would have done otherwise.* Now George's action A is causally determined if some event E—some event beyond his control—has already occurred, where the state of affairs consisting in E's occurrence conjoined with George's *refraining* from performing A, is a causally impossible state of affairs. Then one can consistently hold both that all of a man's actions are causally determined and that some of them are free in the above sense. For suppose that all of a man's actions are causally determined and that he *couldn't,* on any occasion, have made any choice or performed any action different from the ones he did make and perform. It could still be true that if he *had* chosen to do otherwise, he would have done otherwise. Granted, he couldn't have chosen to do otherwise; but this is consistent with saying that *if* he had, things would have gone differently.

This objection to the Free Will Defense seems utterly implausible. One might as well claim that being in jail doesn't really limit one's freedom on the grounds that if one were *not* in jail, he'd be free to come and go as he pleased. So I shall say no more about this objection here. [11]

A second objection is more formidable. In essence it goes like this. Surely it is possible to do only what is right, even if one is free to do wrong. It is *possible,* in that broadly logical sense, that there would be a world containing free creatures who always do what is right. There is certainly no *contradiction* or *inconsistency* in this idea. But God is omnipotent; his power has no nonlogical limitations. So if it's possible that there be a world containing creatures who are free to do what is wrong but never in fact do so, then it follows that an omnipotent God could create such a world. If so, however, the Free Will Defense must be mistaken in its insistence upon the possibility that God is omnipotent but unable to create a world containing moral good without permitting moral evil. J. L. Mackie . . . states this objection:

If God has made men such that in their free choices they sometimes prefer what is good and sometimes what is evil, why could he not have made men such that they always freely choose the good? If there is no logical impossibility in a man's freely choosing the good on one, or on several occasions, there cannot be a logical impossibility in his freely choosing the good on every occasion. God was not, then, faced with a choice between making innocent automata and making beings who, in acting freely, would sometimes go wrong; there was open to him the obviously better possibility of making beings who would act freely but always go right. Clearly, his failure to avail himself of this possibility is inconsistent with his being both omnipotent and wholly good.[12]

Now what, exactly, is Mackie's point here? This. According to the Free Will Defense, it is possible both that God is omnipotent and that He was unable to create a world containing moral good without creating one containing moral evil. But, replies Mackie, this limitation on His power to create is inconsistent with God's omnipotence. For surely it's *possible* that there be a world containing perfectly virtuous persons—persons who are significantly free but always do what is right. Surely there are *possible worlds* that contain moral good but no moral evil. But God, if He is omnipotent, can create any possible world He chooses. So it is *not* possible, contrary to the Free Will Defense, both that God is omnipotent and that he could create a world containing moral good only by creating one containing moral evil. If He is omnipotent, the only limitations of His power are *logical* limitations; in which case there are no possible worlds He could not have created.

This is a subtle and important point. According to the great German philosopher G. W. Leibniz, *this* world, the actual world, must be the best of all possible worlds. His reasoning goes as follows. Before God created anything at all, He was confronted with an enormous range of choices; He could create or bring into actuality any of the myriads of different possible worlds. Being perfectly good, He must have chosen to create the best world He could; being omnipotent, He was able to create any possible world He pleased. He must, therefore, have chosen the best of all possible worlds; and hence *this* world, the one He did create, must be the best possible. Now Mackie, of course, agrees with Leibniz that God, if omnipotent, could have created any world He pleased and would have created the best world he could. But while Leibniz draws the conclusion that this world, despite appearances, must be the best possible, Mackie concludes instead that there is no omnipotent, wholly good God. For, he says, it is obvious enough that this present world is not the best of all possible worlds.

The Free Will Defender disagrees with both Leibniz and Mackie. In the first place, he might say, what is the reason for supposing that *there is* such a thing as the best of all possible worlds? No matter how marvelous a world is—containing no matter how many persons enjoying unalloyed bliss—isn't it possible that there be an even better world containing even more persons enjoying even more unalloyed bliss? But what is really characteristic and central to the Free Will Defense is the claim that God, though omnipotent, could not have actualized just any possible world He pleased.

5. WAS IT WITHIN GOD'S POWER TO CREATE ANY POSSIBLE WORLD HE PLEASED?

This is indeed the crucial question for the Free Will Defense. If we wish to discuss it with insight and authority, we shall have to look into the idea of *possible worlds*. And a sensible first question is this: what sort of thing is a possible world? The basic idea is that a possible world is a *way things could have been;* it is a *state of affairs* of some kind. Earlier we spoke of states of affairs, in particular of good and evil states of affairs. Suppose we look at this idea in more detail. What sort of thing is a state of affairs? The following would be examples:

Nixon's having won the 1972 election

7 + 5's being equal to 12

All men's being mortal

and

Gary, Indiana's, having a really nasty pollution problem.

These are *actual* states of affairs: states of affairs that do in fact *obtain*. And corresponding to each such actual state of affairs there is a true proposition—in the above cases, the corresponding propositions would be *Nixon won the 1972 presidential election, 7 + 5 is equal to 12, all men are mortal,* and *Gary, Indiana, has a really nasty pollution problem.* A proposition *p* corresponds to a state of affairs *s*, in this sense, if it is impossible that *p* be true and *s* fail to obtain and impossible that *s* obtain and *p* fail to be true.

But just as there are false propositions, so there are states of affairs that do *not* obtain or are *not* actual. *Kissinger's having swum the Atlantic* and *Hubert Horatio Humphrey's having run a mile in four minutes* would be examples. Some states of affairs that do not obtain are *impossible:* e.g., *Hubert's having drawn a square circle, 7 + 5's being equal to 75*, and *Agnew's having a brother who was an only child.* The propositions corresponding to these states of affairs, of course, are necessarily false. So there are states of affairs that *obtain* or *are actual* and also states of affairs that don't obtain.

Among the latter some are *impossible* and others are possible. And a possible world is a possible state of affairs. Of course not every possible state of affairs is a possible world; *Hubert's having run a mile in four minutes* is a possible state of affairs but not a possible world. No doubt it is an *element* of many possible worlds, but it isn't itself inclusive enough to be one. To be a possible world, a state of affairs must be very large—so large as to be *complete* or *maximal*.

To get at this idea of completeness we need a couple of definitions. As we have already seen a state of affairs A *includes* a state of affairs B if it is not possible that A obtain and B not obtain or if the conjunctive state of affairs A *but not* B—the state of affairs that obtains if and only if A obtains and B does not—is not possible. For example, *Jim Whittaker's being the first American to climb Mt. Everest* includes *Jim Whittaker's being an American*. It also includes *Mt. Everest's being climbed, something's being climbed, no American's having climbed Everest before Whittaker did*, and the like. *Inclusion* among states of affairs is like *entailment* among propositions; and where a state of affairs A includes a state of affairs B, the proposition corresponding to A entails the one corresponding to B. Accordingly, *Jim Whittaker is the first American to climb Everest* entails *Mt. Everest has been climbed, something has been climbed*, and *no American climbed Everest before Whittaker did*. Now suppose we say further that a state of affairs A *precludes* a state of affairs B if it is not possible that *both* obtain, or if the conjunctive state of affairs A *and* B is impossible. Thus *Whittaker's being the first American to climb Mt. Everest* precludes *Luther Jerstad's being the first American to climb Everest*, as well as *Whittaker's never having climbed any mountains*. If A precludes B, then A's corresponding proposition entails the denial of the one corresponding to B. Still further, let's say that the *complement* of a state of affairs is the state of affairs that obtains just in case A does not obtain. [Or we might say that the complement (call it $\bar{A}$) of A is the state of affairs corresponding to the *denial* or *negation* of the proposition corresponding to A.] Given these definitions, we can say what it is for a state of affairs to be *complete*: A is a complete state of affairs if and only if for every state of affairs B, either A *includes* B or A *precludes* B. (We could express the same thing by saying that if A is a complete state of affairs, then for every state of affairs B, either A includes B or A includes $\bar{B}$, the complement of B.) And now we are able to say what a possible world is: a possible world is any possible state of affairs that is complete. If A is a possible world, then it says something about everything; every state of affairs S is either included in or precluded by it.

Corresponding to each possible world W, furthermore, there is a set of propositions that I'll call *the book on* W. A proposition is in the book on W just in case the state of affairs to which it corresponds is included in W. Or we might express it like this. Suppose we say that a proposition P *is true in a world* W if and only if P *would have been true if* W *had been actual*—if and only if, that is, it is not possible that W be actual and P be false. Then the book on W is the set of propositions true in W. Like possible worlds, books are *complete;* if B is a book, then for any proposition P, either P or the denial of P will be a member of B. A book is a *maximal consistent set* of propositions; it is so large that the addition of another proposition to it always yields an explicitly inconsistent set.

Of course, for each possible world there is exactly one book corresponding to it (that is, for a given world W there is just one book B such that each member of B is true in W); and for each book there is just one world to which it corresponds. So every world has its book.

It should be obvious that exactly one possible world is actual. At *least* one must be, since the set of true propositions is a maximal consistent set and hence a book. But then it corresponds to a possible world, and the possible world corresponding to this set of propositions (since it's the set of *true* propositions) will be actual. On the other hand there is at *most* one actual world. For suppose there were two: W and W'. These worlds cannot include all the very same states of affairs; if they did, they would be the very same world. So there must be at least one state of affairs S such that W includes S and W' does not. But a possible world is maximal; W', therefore, includes the complement $\bar{S}$ of S. So if both W and W' were actual, as we have supposed, then both S and $\bar{S}$ would be actual—which is impossible. So there can't be more than one possible world that is actual.

Leibniz pointed out that a proposition p is necessary if it is true in every possible world. We may add that p is possible if it is true in one world and impossible if true in none. Furthermore, p *entails* q if there is no possible world in which p is true and q is false, and p *is consistent with* q if there is at least one world in which both p and q are true.

A further feature of possible worlds is that people (and other things) *exist* in them. Each of us exists in the actual world, obviously; but a person also exists in many worlds distinct from the actual world. It would be a mistake, of course, to think of all these worlds as somehow "going on" at the same time, with the same person reduplicated through these worlds and actually existing in a lot of different ways. This is not what is meant by saying that the same person exists in different possible worlds. What is meant, instead, is this: a person Paul exists in each of those possible worlds *W* which is such that, if *W had been actual*, Paul would have existed—actually existed. Suppose Paul had been an inch taller than he is, or a better tennis player. Then the world that does in fact obtain would not have been actual; some other world—*W'*, let's say—would have obtained instead. If *W'* had been actual, Paul would have existed; so Paul exists in *W'*. (Of course there are still other possible worlds in which Paul does not exist—worlds, for example, in which there are no people at all). Accordingly, when we say that Paul exists in a world *W*, what we mean is that Paul *would have* existed had *W* been actual. Or we could put it like this: Paul exists in each world W that includes the state of affairs consisting in Paul's existence. We can put this still more simply by saying that Paul exists in those worlds whose books contain the proposition *Paul exists*.

But isn't there a problem here? *Many* people are named "Paul": Paul the apostle, Paul J. Zwier, John Paul Jones, and many other famous Pauls. So who goes with "Paul exists"? Which Paul? The answer has to do with the fact that books contain *propositions*—not sentences. They contain the sort of thing sentences are used to express and assert. And the same sentence—"Aristotle is wise," for example—can be used to express many different propositions. When Plato used it, he asserted a proposition predicating wisdom of his famous pupil; when Jackie Onassis uses it, she asserts a proposition predicating wisdom of her wealthy husband. These are distinct propositions (we might even think they differ in truth value); but they are expressed by the same sentence. Normally (but not always) we don't have much trouble determining which of the several propositions expressed by a given sentence is relevant in the context at hand. So in this case a given person, Paul, exists in a world *W* if and only if *W's* book contains the proposition that says that *he*—that particular person—exists. The fact that the sentence we use to express this proposition can also be used to express *other* propositions is not relevant.

After this excursion into the nature of books and worlds we can return to our question. Could God have created just any world He chose? Before addressing the question, however, we must note that God does not, strictly speaking, *create* any possible worlds or states of affairs at all. What He creates are the heavens and the earth and all that they contain. But He has not created states of affairs. There are, for example, the state of affairs consisting in God's existence and the states of affairs consisting in His nonexistence. That is, there is such a thing as the state of affairs consisting in the existence of God, and there is also such a thing as the state of affairs consisting in the nonexistence of God, just as there are the two propositions *God exists* and *God does not exist*. The theist believes that the first state of affairs is actual and the first proposition true, the atheist believes that the second state of affairs is actual and the second proposition true. But, of course, both propositions *exist*, even though just one is true. Similarly, there are two states of affairs here, just one of which is actual. So both states of affairs *exist*, but only one *obtains*. And God has not created either one of them since there never was a time at which either did not exist. Nor has He created the state of affairs consisting in the earth's existence; there was a time when *the earth* did not exist, but none when the state of affairs consisting in the earth's existence didn't exist. Indeed, God did not bring into existence any states of affairs at all. What He did was to perform actions of a certain sort—creating the heavens and the earth, for example—which resulted in the *actuality* of certain states of affairs. God *actualizes* states of affairs. He actualizes the possible world that does in fact obtain; He does not create it. And while He has created Socrates, He did not create the state of affairs consisting in Socrates' existence.[13]

Bearing this in mind, let's finally return to our question. Is the atheologian right in holding that if God is omnipotent, then he could have actualized or created any possible world He pleased? Not obviously. First, we must ask ourselves whether God is a *necessary* or a *contingent* being. A *necessary* being is one that exists in every possible world—one that would have existed no matter which possible world had been actual; a contingent being exists only in some possible worlds. Now if God is not a necessary being (and many, perhaps most, theists think that He is not), then clearly enough there will be many possible worlds He could not have actualized—all those, for example, in which He does not exist. Clearly, God could not have created a world in which He doesn't even exist.

So, if God is a contingent being then there are many possible worlds beyond His power to create. But this is really irrelevant to our present concerns. For perhaps the atheologian can maintain his case if he revises his claim to avoid this difficulty; perhaps he will say something like this: if God is omnipotent, then He could have actualized any of those possible worlds *in which He exists*. So if He exists and is omnipotent, He could have actualized (contrary to the Free Will Defense) any of those possible worlds in which He exists and in which there exist free creatures who do no wrong. He could have actualized worlds containing moral good but no moral evil. Is this correct?

Let's begin with a trivial example. You and Paul have just returned from an Australian hunting expedition: your quarry was the elusive double-wattled cassowary. Paul captured an aardvark, mistaking it for a cassowary. The creature's disarming ways have won it a place in Paul's

heart; he is deeply attached to it. Upon your return to the States you offer
Paul $500 for his aardvark, only to be rudely turned down. Later you ask
yourself, "What would he have done if I'd offered him $700?" Now what
is it, exactly, that you are asking? What you're really asking in a way is
whether, under a *specific set of conditions,* Paul would have sold it. These
conditions include your having offered him $700 rather than $500 for the
aardvark, everything else being as much as possible like the conditions
that did in fact obtain. Let S' be this set of conditions or state of affairs.
S' includes the state of affairs consisting in your offering Paul $700 (in-
stead of the $500 you did offer him); of course it does not include his
accepting your offer, and it does not include his *rejecting* it; for the rest, the
conditions it includes are just like the ones that did obtain in the actual
world. So, for example, S' includes Paul's being free to accept the offer
and free to refrain; and if in fact the going rate for an aardvark was $650,
then S' includes the state of affairs consisting in the going rate's being
$650. So we might put your question by asking which of the following
conditionals is true:

> (23) If the state of affairs S' had obtained, Paul would have accepted
> the offer
> (24) If the state of affairs S' had obtained, Paul would not have ac-
> cepted the offer.

It seems clear that at least one of these conditionals is true, but naturally
they can't both be; so exactly one is.

Now since S' includes neither Paul's accepting the offer nor his rejecting it, the antecedent of (23) and (24) does not entail the consequent
of either. That is,

> (25) S' obtains

does not entail either

> (26) Paul accepts the offer

or

> (27) Paul does not accept the offer.

So there are possible worlds in which both (25) and (26) are true, and
other possible worlds in which both (25) and (27) are true.

We are now in a position to grasp an important fact. Either (23) or
(24) is in fact true; and either way there are possible worlds God could not
have actualized. Suppose, first of all, that (23) is true. Then it was beyond
the power of God to create a world in which (1) Paul is free to sell his
aardvark and free to refrain, and in which the other states of affairs in-

cluded in S' obtain, and (2) Paul does not sell. That is, it was beyond His power to create a world in which (25) and (27) are both true. There is at least one possible world like this, but God, despite His omnipotence, could not have brought about its actuality. For let W be such a world. To actualize W, God must bring it about that Paul is free with respect to this action, and that the other states of affairs included in S' obtain. But (23), as we are supposing, is true; so if God had actualized S' and left Paul *free* with respect to this action, he would have sold: in which case W would not have been actual. If, on the other hand, God had *brought it about* that Paul didn't sell or had *caused him* to refrain from selling, then Paul would not have been free with respect to this action; then S' would not have been actual (since S' includes Paul's being free with respect to it), and W would not have been actual since W includes S'.

Of course if it is (24) rather than (23) that is true, then another class of worlds was beyond God's power to actualize—those, namely, in which S' obtains and Paul *sells* his aardvark. These are the worlds in which both (25) and (26) are true. But either (23) or (24) is true. Therefore, there are possible worlds God could not have actualized. If we consider whether or not God could have created a world in which, let's say, both (25) and (26) are true, we see that the answer depends upon a peculiar kind of fact; it depends upon what Paul would have freely chosen to do in a certain situation. So there are any number of possible worlds such that it is partly up to Paul whether God can create them. [14]

That was a past tense example. Perhaps it would be useful to consider a future tense case, since this might seem to correspond more closely to God's situation in choosing a possible world to actualize. At some time t in the near future Maurice will be free with respect to some insignificant action—having freeze-dried oatmeal for breakfast, let's say. That is, at time t Maurice will be free to have oatmeal but also free to take something else—shredded wheat, perhaps. Next, suppose we consider S', a state of affairs that is included in the actual world and includes Maurice's being free with respect to taking oatmeal at time t. That is, S' includes Maurice's being free at time t to take oatmeal and free to reject it. S' does not include Maurice's taking oatmeal, however; nor does it include his rejecting it. For the rest S' is as much as possible like the actual world. In particular there are many conditions that do in fact hold at time t and are *relevant* to his choice—such conditions, for example, as the fact that he hasn't had oatmeal lately, that his wife will be annoyed if he rejects it, and the like; and S' includes each of these conditions. Now God no doubt knows what Maurice will do at time t, if S obtains; He knows which action

Maurice would freely perform if S were to be actual. That is, God knows that one of the following conditionals is true:

(28) If S' were to obtain, Maurice will freely take the oatmeal

or

(29) If S' were to obtain, Maurice will freely reject it.

We may not know which of these is true, and Maurice himself may not know; but presumably God does.

So either God knows that (28) is true, or else He knows that (29) is. Let's suppose it is (28). Then there is a possible world that God, though omnipotent, cannot create. For consider a possible world W' that shares S' with the actual world (which for ease of reference I'll name "Kronos") and in which Maurice does *not* take oatmeal. (We know there *is* such a world, since S' does not include Maurice's taking the oatmeal.) S' obtains in W' just as it does in Kronos. Indeed, everything in W' is just as it is in Kronos up to time t. But whereas in Kronos Maurice takes oatmeal at time t, in W' he does not. Now W' is a perfectly possible world; but it is not within God's power to create it or bring about its actuality. For to do so He must actualize S'. But (28) is in fact true. So if God actualizes S' (as He must to create W') and leaves Maurice free with respect to the action in question, then he will take the oatmeal; and then, of course, W' will not be actual. If, on the other hand, God causes Maurice to *refrain* from taking the oatmeal, then he is not *free* to take it. That means, once again, that W' is not actual; for in W' Maurice is free to take the oatmeal (even if he doesn't do so). So if (28) is true, then this world W' is one that God can't actualize, it is not within His power to actualize it even though He is omnipotent and it is a possible world.

Of course, if it is (29) that is true, we get a similar result; then too there are possible worlds that God can't actualize. These would be worlds which share S' with Kronos and in which Maurice *does* take oatmeal. But either (28) or (29) *is* true; so either way there is a possible world that God can't create. If we consider a world in which S' obtains and in which Maurice freely chooses oatmeal at time t, we see that whether or not it is within God's power to actualize it depends upon what Maurice would do if he were free in a certain situation. Accordingly, there are any number of possible worlds such that it is partly up to Maurice whether or not God can actualize them. It is, of course, up to God whether or not to create Maurice and also up to God whether or not to make him free with respect to the action of taking oatmeal at time t. (God could, if He chose, cause him to succumb to the dreaded *equine obsession*, a condition shared by some people and most horses, whose victims find it *psychologically impossible* to refuse oats or oat products.) But if He creates Maurice and creates him free with respect to this action, then whether or not he actually performs the action is up to Maurice—not God.[15]

Now we can return to the Free Will Defense and the problem of evil. The Free Will Defender, you recall, insists on the possibility that it is not within God's power to create a world containing moral good without creating one containing moral evil. His atheological opponent—Mackie, for example—agrees with Leibniz in insisting that *if* (as the theist holds) God is omnipotent, then it *follows* that He could have created any possible world He pleased. We now see that this contention—call it "Leibniz' Lapse"—is a mistake. The atheologian is right in holding that there are many possible worlds containing moral good but no moral evil; his mistake lies in endorsing Leibniz' Lapse. So one of his premises—that God, if omnipotent, could have actualized just any world He pleased—is false.

6. COULD GOD HAVE CREATED A WORLD CONTAINING MORAL GOOD BUT NO MORAL EVIL?

Now suppose we recapitulate the logic of the situation. The Free Will Defender claims that the following is possible:

> (30) God is omnipotent, and it was not within His power to create a world containing moral good but no moral evil.

By way of retort the atheologian insists that there are possible worlds containing moral good but no moral evil. He adds that an omnipotent being could have actualized any possible world he chose. So if God is omnipotent, it follows that He could have actualized a world containing moral good but no moral evil, hence (30), contrary to the Free Will Defender's claim, is not possible. What we have seen so far is that his second premise—Leibniz' Lapse—is false.

Of course, this does not settle the issue in the Free Will Defender's favor. Leibniz' Lapse (appropriately enough for a lapse) is false; but this doesn't show that (30) is possible. To show this latter we must demonstrate the possibility that among the worlds God could not have actualized are all the worlds containing moral good but no moral evil. How can we approach this question?

Instead of choosing oatmeal for breakfast or selling an aardvark, suppose we think about a morally significant action such as taking a bribe. Curley Smith, the mayor of Boston, is opposed to the proposed freeway route; it would require destruction of the Old North Church along with some other antiquated and structurally unsound buildings. L. B. Smedes, the director of highways, asks him whether he'd drop his opposition for $1 million. "Of course," he replies. "Would you do it for $2?" asks Smedes. "What do you take me for?" comes the indignant reply. "That's already established," smirks Smedes; "all that remains is to nail down your price." Smedes then offers him a bribe of $35,000; unwilling to break with the fine old traditions of Bay State politics, Curley accepts. Smedes then spends a sleepless night wondering whether he could have bought Curley for $20,000.

Now suppose we assume that Curley was free with respect to the action of taking the bribe—free to take it and free to refuse. And suppose, furthermore, that he would have taken it. That is, let us suppose that

(31) If Smedes had offered Curley a bribe of $20,000, he would have accepted it.

If (31) is true, then there is a state of affairs S' that (1) includes Curley's being offered a bribe of $20,000; (2) does not include either his accepting the bribe or his rejecting it; and (3) is otherwise as much as possible like the actual world. Just to make sure S' includes every relevant circumstance, let us suppose that it is a *maximal world segment*. That is, add to S' any state of affairs compatible with but not included in it, and the result will be an entire possible world. We could think of it roughly like this: S' is included in at least one world W in which Curley takes the bribe and in at least one world W' in which he rejects it. If S' is a maximal world segment, then S' is what remains of W when *Curley's taking the bribe* is deleted; it is also what remains of W' when *Curley's rejecting the bribe* is detected. More exactly, if S' is a maximal world segment, then every possible state of affairs that includes S', but isn't included by S', is a possible world. So if (31) is true, then there is a maximal world segment S' that (1) includes Curley's being offered a bribe of $20,000; (2) does not include either his accepting the bribe or his rejecting it; (3) is otherwise as much as possible like the actual world—in particular, it includes Curley's being free with respect to the bribe; and (4) is such that if it were actual then Curley would have taken the bribe. That is,

(32) if S' were actual, Curley would have accepted the bribe is true.

Now, of course, there is at least one possible world W' in which S' is actual and Curley does not take the bribe. But God could not have created W'; to do so, He would have been obliged to actualize S', leaving Curley free with respect to the action of taking the bribe. But under these conditions Curley, as (32) assures us, would have accepted the bribe, so that the world thus created would not have been S'.

Curley, as we see, is not above a bit of Watergating. But there may be worse to come. Of course, there are possible worlds in which he is significantly free (i.e., free with respect to a morally significant action) and never does what is wrong. But the sad truth about Curley may be this. Consider W', any of these worlds: in W' Curley is significantly free, so in W' there are some actions that are morally significant for him and with respect to which he is free. But at least one of these actions—call it A— has the following peculiar property. There is a maximal world segment S' that obtains in W' and is such that (1) S' includes Curley's being free *re* A but neither his performing A nor his refraining from A; (2) S' is otherwise as much as possible like W'; and (3) if S' had been actual, Curley would have gone wrong with respect to A.[16] (Notice that this third condition holds in fact, in the actual world; it does not hold in that world W'.)

This means, of course, that God could not have actualized W'. For to do so He'd have been obliged to bring it about that S' is actual; but then Curley would go wrong with respect to A. Since in W' he always does what is right, the world thus actualized would not be W'. On the other hand, if God *causes* Curley to go right with respect to A or *brings it about that* he does so, then Curley isn't free with respect to A; and so once more it isn't W' that is actual. Accordingly God cannot create W'. But W' was just any of the worlds in which Curley is significantly free but always does only what is right. It therefore follows that it was not within God's power to create a world in which Curley produces moral good but no moral evil. Every world God can actualize is such that if Curley is significantly free in it, he takes at least one wrong action.

Obviously Curley is in serious trouble. I shall call the malady from which he suffers *transworld depravity*. (I leave as homework the problem of comparing transworld depravity with what Calvinists call "total depravity.") By way of explicit definition:

> (33) A person P *suffers from transworld depravity* if and only if the following holds: for every world W such that P is significantly free in W and P does only what is right in W, there is an action A and a maximal world segment S' such that
>
> (1) S' includes A's being morally significant for P
> (2) S' includes P's being free with respect to A
> (3) S' is included in W and includes neither P's performing A nor P's refraining from performing A

and

(4) If S' were actual, P would go wrong with respect to A.

(In thinking about this definition, remember that (4) is to be true in fact, in the actual world—not in that world W.)

What is important about the idea of transworld depravity is that if a person suffers from it, then it wasn't within God's power to actualize any world in which that person is significantly free but does no wrong—that is, a world in which he produces moral good but no moral evil.

We have been here considering a crucial contention of the Free Will Defender: the contention, namely, that

(30) God is omnipotent, and it was not within His power to create a world containing moral good but no moral evil.

How is transworld depravity relevant to this? As follows. Obviously it is possible that there be persons who suffer from transworld depravity. More generally, it is possible that *everybody* suffers from it. And if this possibility were actual, then God, though omnipotent, could not have created any of the possible worlds containing just the persons who do in fact exist, and containing moral good but no moral evil. For to do so He'd have to create persons who were significantly free (otherwise there would be no moral good) but suffered from transworld depravity. Such persons go wrong with respect to at least one action in any world God could have actualized and in which they are free with respect to morally significant actions; so the price for creating a world in which they produce moral good is creating one in which they also produce moral evil.

NOTES

1. John Mackie, "Evil and Omnipotence," in *The Philosophy of Religion*, ed. Basil Mitchell (London: Oxford University Press, 1971), p. 92.

2. Ibid., pp. 92–93.

3. Ibid., p. 93.

4. More simply the question is really just whether any good state of affairs includes an evil; a little reflection reveals that no good state of affairs can include an evil that it does *not* outweigh.

5. In Plantinga, *God and Other Minds* (Ithaca, NY: Cornell University Press, 1967), chap. 5, I explore further the project of finding such propositions.

6. *The Problem of Free Choice*, Vol. 22 of *Ancient Christian Writers* (Westminster, MD: The Newman Press, 1955), bk. 2, pp. 14–15.

7. Ibid., bk. 3, p. 9.

8. I am indebted to Henry Schuurman (in conversation) for helpful discussion of the difference between this pastoral function and those served by a theodicy or a defense.

9. This distinction is not very precise (how, exactly, are we to construe "results from"?), but perhaps it will serve our present purposes.

10. See, for example, A. Flew, "Divine Omnipotence and Human Freedom," in *New Essays in Philosophical Theology,* eds. A. Flew and A. MacIntyre (London: SCM, 1955), pp. 150–153.

11. For further discussion of it see Plantinga, *God and Other Minds,* pp. 132–135.

12. Mackie, in *The Philosophy of Religion,* pp. 100–101.

13. Strict accuracy demands, therefore, that we speak of God as *actualizing* rather than creating possible worlds. I shall continue to use both locutions, thus sacrificing accuracy to familiarity. For more about possible worlds see my book *The Nature of Necessity* (Oxford: The Clarendon Press, 1974), chaps. 4–8.

14. For a fuller statement of this argument see Plantinga, *The Nature of Necessity,* chap. 9, secs. 4–6.

15. For a more complete and more exact statement of this argument see Plantinga, *The Nature of Necessity,* chap. 9, secs. 4–6.

16. A person goes wrong with respect to an action if he either wrongfully performs it or wrongfully fails to perform it.

Is Evil Evidence against the Existence of God?

MICHAEL MARTIN

In a recent article, Robert Pargetter[1] considers the existence of evil as the basis for a non-demonstrative argument for the non-existence of God. He maintains that the existence of evil has yet to be shown to be strong evidence for the non-existence of God. I believe that Pargetter has not given atheists their due; he has not presented the best nondemonstrative argument from evil to the non-existence of God that is available. In this paper I will outline a more adequate argument. First I will present the argument informally and then I will give a more formal presentation. Finally, I will answer some objections to the argument.

I

It is generally agreed that the following statements are logically compatible:

(1) God is all powerful.

(2) God is all good.

(3) Evil exists in great abundance.

This logical compatibility is suggested by the following considerations: (1) entails

    (1') God could prevent the great abundance of evil unless such evil were logically necessary.

and (2) entails

    (2') God would prevent the great abundance of evil unless God had a sufficient reason to allow the great abundance of evil.[2]

From *Mind* 87 (July 1978): 429–32. Used by permission of the editor.

(1′) and (2′) combined entail:

> (3′) Evil exists in great abundance only if either God had a sufficient
> reason to allow the abundance of evil or the great abundance of
> evil is logically necessary.

(3) *per se* does not conflict with (1) and (2). But unless certain assumptions are made, the existence of evil in great abundance does conflict
with the existence of God. One might speak of the existence of evil being
prima facie evidence against the existence of God.

For the purpose of this discussion *prima facie* evidence (where E is the
evidence, H is the hypothesis, A are the auxiliary assumptions) will be
defined as follows: E is *prima facie* evidence against H if E and H do not
entail a contradiction and E and A do not entail a contradiction and E and
H and A do entail a contradiction.

Now (1), (2), (3) together do not entail a contradiction, but (1), (2),
(3) together with

> (4) The existence of evil in great abundance is not logically necessary
> and there is no sufficient reason for God to allow evil in great
> abundance.

does entail

> (3′) Evil does not exist in great abundance

which conflicts with (3). Furthermore, (3) and (4) together do not entail
a contradiction. Consequently, the existence of evil in great abundance is
prima facie evidence against the existence of an all good, all powerful God.

However, this by itself does not give one any inductive reason to disbelieve in God unless one also has good reason to suppose that premise
(4) is true. There is no *a priori* way to demonstrate the truth of (4); however, all attempts to show that (4) is false have failed.[3] Apologists down
through the ages have failed to specify a sufficient reason for God allowing
evil; they have failed to show that this is the best of all logically possible
worlds. These failures should give us some confidence in (4). For if every
attempt to specify a needed explanation fails over a long period of time
this failure gives one good grounds to suppose that an explanation is
impossible.

Even if this failure did provide inductive support for (4) and consequently provide indirect evidence for the non-existence of God, this evidence would not necessarily outweigh evidence for the existence of God.
Given some positive evidence on balance disbelief in God would not be
rational. However, it is generally acknowledged even by many religious
persons that the traditional arguments for the existence of God are bank-

rupt. There is no positive evidence for belief in God that could outweigh the negative evidence. Consequently, the indirect negative evidence provided by the inductive support for (4) is crucial.

II

A more formal statement of the argument follows:

(1) If (a) there is no positive evidence that P, and
   (b) unless one assumes that R, evidence E would falsify that P, and
   (c) despite repeated attempts no good reason has been given for believing that R,
   then on rational grounds one should believe that P is false.

(2) There is no positive evidence that God exists.

(3) The existence of evil in great abundance would falsify the existence of God unless one assumes either that God has sufficient reason for allowing the existence of evil in great abundance or that evil in great abundance is logically necessary.

(4) Despite repeated attempts to do so, no one has provided a good reason to believe that God has sufficient reason to allow evil to exist in great abundance or that evil in great abundance is logically necessary.

(5) ∴ On rational grounds one should believe that God does not exist.

Although the above argument is formulated as a deductive argument, it is not a demonstrative argument that God does not exist; it only purports to show that on rational grounds one ought not believe that God exists. The argument can in fact be recast as a straightforward inductive argument rather than as a deductive argument with a conclusion about what one should believe. The general form of the argument would be:

(1) Evidence E falsifies H unless R.
(2) Repeated attempts to establish R have failed.
(3) There is no positive evidence that H.

(4) ~H.

H is not established by (1), (2), (3), but is made probable relative to (1), (2), (3). The atheistic argument from evil is achieved by substituting in the obvious variables.

No detailed defense of this inductive argument will be made here since the premises have been argued for by others[4] and the general form of the argument seems to be acceptable—indeed to be a type used in science and in rational discussion generally. The theist who would reject this means of argument better have excellent reasons, reasons that are not *ad hoc* and arbitrary. The present paper may be considered a challenge to the theist to come up with some non-arbitrary reasons for rejecting the argument.

III

Several objections might be made to the above argument.

(1) It might be argued that I have only specified two kinds of considerations that are relevant to saving the theist's position, viz (a) God has a sufficient reason for allowing evil, and (b) Evil is logically necessary. It may be argued that there could be other considerations. However, it is difficult to see what these other considerations could be since (a) and (b) seem to exhaust all possibilities. But no matter. If there are other considerations, these could be built into the structure of the argument quite easily. For example, in the formal statement of the argument in Part II one could add the disjunct

'or that there is another explanation for the existence of evil in great abundance compatible with theism'

to premises (3) and (4). The argument would proceed as before. Apologists have failed to specify what this other explanation might be. Consequently, one has good grounds for supposing that no other explanation compatible with theism exists.

(2) It may be argued that although God's existence may not be explained by the existence of evil, the non-existence of God does not explain anything, including evil.[5] However, if our argument is correct, it is not just that the existence of God does not explain evil but that the existence of evil provides inductive grounds for disbelief. Since there is no positive evidence for belief, evil is inconsistent with God's existence unless certain assumptions are made and there are inductive grounds to suppose these assumptions are wrong.

Of course, the non-existence of God does not explain evil. One might as well argue that the non-existence of spirits does not explain certain phenomena in a seance. But other non-spirit hypotheses are available, e.g. fraud, ESP. In the same way, there are a variety of non-theistic hypotheses to explain evil. Natural evil can be explained in terms of certain natural laws; for example, the birth of a defective baby by genetics. Moral evil can be explained in terms of certain psychological or sociological theories; for example the murder of an innocent bystander by the police in terms of motives and beliefs. There need be no general explanation for all evil.

There might be a problem with some particular naturalistic explanations. For example, some premises in some of the explanations could be false. There is *no* reason to suppose, however, that *all* such explanations would be false whereas we have seen that there is a general problem in the theistic account: we have grounds for supposing that evil and the existence of God are incompatible relative to certain inductively supported premises.

(3) It might be argued that to suppose that the existence of evil in great abundance is *prima facie* evidence against the existence of God relies upon some intuitively grasped relation between evil and the non-existence of God. However, such intuitions are unreliable and untrustworthy.[6]

But as I have shown above the *prima facie* conflict between the existence of God and the existence of evil can be defined and defended without appeal to intuition. The relation was defined in terms of entailment under certain conditions.

I believe that the above argument and refutation of objections to it meet Pargetter's challenge and show why the existence of evil is evidence against the existence of God in a way that is free of the problems he raised.

NOTES

1. Robert Pargetter, "Evil as Evidence against the Existence of God," *Mind*, 1976, pp. 242–245.

2. See for example N. Pike, "Hume on Evil," in *God and Evil*, ed. N. Pike (Englewood Cliffs, NJ: Prentice-Hall, 1964); A. Plantinga, *God and Other Minds* (Ithaca, NY: Cornell University Press, 1967).

3. Edward H. Madden and Peter H. Hare, *Evil and the Concept of God* (Springfield, IL: Charles C. Thomas, 1968).

4. Wallace I. Matson, *The Existence of God* (Ithaca, NY: Cornell University Press, 1967); Michael Scriven, *Primary Philosophy* (New York: McGraw-Hill, 1966); Madden and Hare, *op cit.*

5. Pargetter, p. 243.

6. Ibid., p. 243.

Evil as Evidence against God's Existence

DAVID BASINGER

Few atheologians still maintain that the existence of evil is logically incompatible with the existence of an omnipotent, omniscient, wholly good God. But many still wish to maintain not only that (a) the existence of evil in great abundance counts as evidence against the existence of an omnipotent, omniscient, wholly good God but also that the ability of the theist to respond to such evil is so limited that (b) on rational grounds one should believe that God does not exist. In a recent article, Michael Martin clearly sets forth what I consider to be the standard atheological argument for (a) and (b).[1] The purpose of this paper is not only to critique this argument but, in the process, to outline the set of tasks which I believe atheologians have yet to accomplish before it can be demonstrated that evil furnishes the basis for a good inductive argument against God's existence.

I.

Martin's version of the standard argument for (a) and (b) is the following:

(1) An omnipotent God could prevent the abundance of evil we experience unless such evil were logically necessary.

(2) A wholly good God would prevent the great abundance of evil unless he had a sufficient reason to allow it.

(3) Evil exists in great abundance only if either God has a sufficient reason to allow the abundance of evil or the great abundance of evil is logically necessary.

(4) If one has good reason to suppose that the existence of evil in great abundance is not logically necessary and that there is no

---

From *The Modern Schoolman* 58 (March 1981): 175–84. Used by permission of the author and editor.

sufficient reason for God to allow such evil, then the abundance of evil counts as strong evidence against the existence of God.

(5) One has good reason to believe that the existence of evil in great abundance is not logically necessary and that there is no sufficient reason for God to allow such evil if the theist fails over a long period of time to provide an acceptable explanation for the abundance of evil we experience.

(6) Despite repeated attempts, no one has provided a good reason to believe that God has a sufficient reason to allow evil to exist in great abundance or that such evil is logically necessary—that is, no one has been able to provide an acceptable explanation for the abundance of evil we experience.

(7) The abundance of evil we experience counts as strong evidence against God's existence.

(8) There is no (or little) positive evidence with respect to God's existence.

(9) If there exists strong evidence against God's existence and no (or even little) evidence that God exists, it is most reasonable to believe that God does not exist.

(10) It is most reasonable to believe that God does not exist.[2]

(1–4) seem acceptable, but (5) is in need of further discussion. Why exactly are we to believe that the failure of the theist to supply an acceptable explanation for the abundance of evil we experience constitutes a good reason to seriously question God's existence—that is, why are we to affirm (5)? Martin's answer is that "these failures should give us some confidence . . . (f) or if every attempt to specify a needed explanation fails over a long period of time this failure gives good grounds to suppose that an explanation is impossible."[3] But why exactly is such an explanation needed? Or, to phrase the question differently, even assuming that an explanation for the abundance of evil in the world will not be forthcoming, why exactly are we to consider this fact to be strong evidence for not believing in the existence of God?

The answer is that atheologians generally assume that

(11) An omnipotent, omniscient, wholly good God could create (could have created) possible worlds which contain less evil but no less good than does the actual world—that is, God could alleviate much of the evil we experience.

For unless the atheologian has good reason to believe that an omnipotent, omniscient, wholly good God could have done better, it can make little sense for him or her to declare that unexplained evil counts as strong evidence against God's existence. This fact seems to be at least implicitly acknowledged by many atheologians. Consider, for example, the following argument by Cornman and Lehrer:

> If you were all-good, all-knowing, and all-powerful, and you were going to create a universe in which there were sentient beings—beings that are happy and sad; enjoy pleasure, feel pain; express love, anger, pity, hatred—what kind of world would you create? Try to imagine what such a world would be like. Would it be like the one which actually does exist, this world we live in? Would you create a world such as this one if you had the power and know-how to create any logically possible world? If your answer is "no," as it seems that it must be, then you should begin to understand why the evil of suffering and pain in this world is such a problem for anyone who thinks God created this world.[4]

In short, it is not solely the fact that the theist can (supposedly) offer no explanation for the abundance of evil which troubles the atheologian. It is this fact, coupled with the belief that an omnipotent, omniscient, wholly good God could have done better, which leads the atheologian to claim that evil furnishes good inductive evidence against God's existence.

Now, of course, if it is assumed, as many persons do, that an omnipotent, omniscient, wholly good God can do anything he desires to do, (11) possesses *prima facie* plausibility. For it seems obvious that such a God would alleviate much of the evil we experience. But the interesting and relevant philosophical question is whether, given an objective analysis of an omnipotent, omniscient, wholly good God's actual creative options, (11) can in fact be affirmed. I shall argue that this is by no means a settled issue.

The root of the problem is that atheologians—for example, Cornman and Lehrer—normally assume without question that one or both of the following propositions are true:

(12) An omnipotent, omniscient, wholly good God can create any logically possible state of affairs—for example, he could have created a world in which moral agents would as a matter of fact always freely choose to do what is right;

(13) An omnipotent, omniscient, wholly good God, by benevolently intervening in the lives of individuals and/or in the natural environment could greatly reduce the amount of evil in our present world—for example, he could cure small children of cancer.

Now, of course, if either (12) or (13) is in fact true, then (11) is confirmed and the atheologian has a perfect right to demand a reason for the abundance of evil we experience. But (12) appears false and (13) is certainly debatable.

Let us consider (12) first. Most theists affirm an indeterministic sense of human freedom. That is, they maintain that

> (14) God cannot make a person (P) significantly free with respect to an action (A) and yet causally determine or bring it about that P go right with respect to A.

They also normally maintain that

> (15) An omniscient God knows with respect to any P exactly what P would do if he were made free with respect to any A.

But given (14) and (15), it can easily be shown that

> (16) It is not within the power of an omnipotent, omniscient God to create just any self-consistent (possible) state of affairs which is consistent with his goodness.

Consider, for example, two distinct, consistent possible worlds, W and W', which are identical in every way up to a time (t) when W a person (P) freely chooses to steal an apple while in W' P freely chooses not to steal the apple. And let us call this shared initial segment S. If P is in fact free with respect to an action (A) at time t, then while it is certainly the case that, given S, P might choose to do A or, given S, P might freely choose to do $\bar{A}$, it is not the case that, given S, P can perform both A and $\bar{A}$ at time t. That is, while it is the case that if S is in fact actualized, P will be free to do either A or $\bar{A}$, he can only make one decision. Now let us suppose that God, being omniscient, knows that, given S, P will freely choose to take the apple (perform A). Then God cannot actualize W', that possible world in which P freely chooses not to take the apple (chooses to perform $\bar{A}$). For to do so, he would obviously have to cause P to do what he would not have freely done, given S—that is, God would have to make it the case that P was not in fact free with respect to A in W'. On the other hand, let us suppose that God knows that, given S, P will freely perform $\bar{A}$. Then God obviously cannot actualize W, the world in which P freely chooses to do A.

In short, given that W and W' both contain S, God's creative options are limited by what he knows P will freely do. God might of course decide not to create W or W' or decide not to make P free with respect to A and simply cause P to do what he wants. But God cannot, as the pro-

ponent of (12) would have us believe, both make P free with respect to A
and yet remain free, himself, to create both W and W'.

Or to state this basic problem in more simplified terms, for P to be
free with respect to A means, by definition, that God cannot bring it
about that P do A (or Ā). But if God can in fact actualize any conceivable
world, then God can in fact bring it about that P do A (or Ā) and, accordingly, P cannot be considered free with respect to A. We must conclude, therefore, that if P is in fact free with respect to A, there exists at
least one conceivable state of affairs which God cannot actualize, that possible world in which P performs an action which he would not in fact
freely choose to perform if actualized and placed in the relevant context.[5]

Moreover, as Alvin Plantinga has clearly pointed out,

(17) It is possible that all creatures (creaturely essences) are such that
they would go wrong with respect to at least one action in any
world in which they were free with respect to morally significant actions.[6]

Accordingly, to be even more specific,

(18) It is possible that it was not within God's power to create a
world containing moral good but no moral evil.

(14–18), however, is not simply an argument against (12). It also
functions as a counter to (13) in relation to moral evil. For, given (14–18),
an omnipotent, omniscient, wholly good God cannot in fact control
(lessen) the amount of moral evil which will in fact eventuate in any given
possible world containing free moral agents—that is, the total responsibility for the amount of moral evil in any given world (including
the actual world) must be attributed to the relevant free moral agents
themselves.

The atheologian, of course, might wish to contend that, given the
abundance of moral evil in the actual world, it would have been better for
God not to have created any world or to have created a world containing
automata who always do what is right or at least to have created a world
in which humans possess less significant freedom (a lesser capacity to do
evil) and, accordingly, that an explanation for the abundance of evil we
experience in the actual world is still necessary. But that any of these creative options is better (more valuable) than a world in which humans possess the amount of significant freedom they do in the actual world, even
given the amount of moral evil therein generated, is not at all obvious. If
the atheologian wishes to base his or her affirmation of (11) upon this

claim, he or she needs a convincing argument to this end, an argument which to my knowledge has yet to be formulated.

Or the atheologian could challenge the reasonableness of (14), but there appears to be very little philosophical support for the contention that God could cause his created moral agents to freely do exactly what he desires that they do, even on the part of those who generally support a deterministic sense of human freedom in other contexts.[7]

In short, it seems to me that the theist need not at present grant the atheologian (12) or, in relation to moral evil, (13). This fact, however, must not be considered overly significant since many atheologians do not primarily base their acceptance of (11) or (12) or (13) as it relates to moral evil. Their affirmation of (11) is based rather on the belief that an omnipotent, omniscient, wholly good God could benevolently intervene in the natural environment in such a manner that the integrity of human freedom would be retained and the amount of good would not be lessened and yet there would be much less natural (physical) evil than there presently is—that is, it is based on the affirmation of (13) as this claim applies to natural evil. Consider, for example, a recent argument by William Rowe:

> It seems quite unlikely that all the instances of intense human and animal suffering occurring daily in our world lead to greater goods, and even more unlikely that if they all do, an omnipotent, omniscient being could not have achieved at least some of these goods without permitting the instances of suffering that lead to them. In the light of our experience and knowledge of the variety and scale of human and animal suffering in our world, the idea that none of these instances of suffering could have been prevented by an omnipotent being without the loss of a greater good seems an extraordinary, absurd idea, quite beyond our belief.[8]

This line of reasoning, admittedly, has a great deal of initial plausibility. For it does at first glance seem reasonable to contend that, for example, God could cure a small child or calm a severe storm without significantly affecting the integrity of human freedom or significantly lessening the amount of good which exists. But such *prima facie* plausibility may well be deceiving. Given the great number of diverse, widespread causal factors which continually generate natural evil in our world—for example, the harsh weather conditions, the incurable diseases, and so forth—it seems reasonable to maintain that

(19) God could not significantly lessen the amount of natural evil we experience unless he either directly intervened in our present

natural system in a continuous and widespread manner or modified our present natural system in some significant fashion.

But as many have pointed out, it seems extremely doubtful that God could continually circumvent or modify natural (including psychological) laws in a widespread manner without destroying our belief that anticipated consequences will normally follow given actions—that is, without destroying our belief in predictable regularities. But if we can no longer have the assurance that given consequences will normally follow given actions, we must seriously question whether we can retain a meaningful concept of "free choice." For example, what sense can it make to speak of a hot and thirsty individual meaningfully choosing to take a drink of water if he has no reasonable expectation that this action will have a thirst-quenching effect? Or, more significant, what sense can it make to speak of a terrorist meaningfully choosing to throw a bomb into a crowded room if we assume that such an individual has no reasonable expectation that significant destruction will follow? The answer, it seems to me, is that no sense can be made of the concept of "choice" under such conditions. The concept of "choosing to do X" is inextricably tied to the concept of "willing to bring about one state of affairs rather than another." Accordingly, if an individual has no reasonable expectation that one state of affairs rather than another will result if he performs A, it cannot be said that he has the capacity to exercise a meaningful sense of "choice" in relation to A. In short, it seems reasonable to maintain that

> (20) Continuous, widespread divine intervention into our present natural system would make meaningful human choice impossible (or at least greatly lessen its meaningfulness).[9]

Moreover, in order to demonstrate that some modification of our present natural system would greatly reduce the amount of physical evil we experience, the atheologian must do more than cite isolated contexts in which such modification would greatly help. He or she must demonstrate that, in the context of the entire world system of which it would be a part, such modification would actually result in a significant increase in the net amount of good in comparison to the actual world.

Now, it might be the case that the atheologian can, in fact, accomplish this task although there are, I shall argue later, some serious problems with "metaphysical" inductive arguments in general which will make any such attempt difficult. But the important point at present is that, at least in my estimation

(21) The atheologian has yet to demonstrate that God could create a
significantly modified natural system which, when considered
in terms of the entire world system of which it would be a part,
would produce significantly less natural evil and yet preserve
the integrity of human freedom and retain as much good as we
have in our present world.[10]

Accordingly, it seems to me that

(22) There is presently no good reason to believe that God could significantly lessen the amount of natural evil we experience—
that is, there is presently no good reason to affirm a "natural
evil" reading of (13).

But if this is so, there would seem to be no present necessity for the
theist to grant either (12) or (13) and consequently, no reason why the
theist need presently grant (11). But if (11) need not be granted, then (5)
need not be affirmed and the atheologian's attempt to demonstrate that
unexplained evil is strong evidence against God's existence fails.

But have I really demonstrated that (5) is questionable—that is,
that the atheologian may have no valid basis for claiming that unexplained
evil counts strongly against God's existence? Have I not actually argued
that the abundance of evil is logically necessary, given a proper understanding of God's creative options in relation to worlds containing sentient
creatures, that is, have I not actually attempted to set forth an acceptable
explanation for the abundance of evil we experience? And, accordingly,
have I not, by my use of (14–18) and (19–22) to counter (12) and (13),
actually affirmed implicitly that an explanation for evil is necessary—that
is, have I not implicitly affirmed (5)?

In one sense, this observation is correct. (14–18) and (19–22) certainly do stand as relevant "explanations" for the abundance of evil we
experience, and I certainly could have utilized them in this manner in the
context of (6). But these arguments need not be considered to be solely, or
even primarily, explanations for evil. They function equally well as criticisms of (11) and thus (5). Moreover, it seems to me more instructive in
the present context to utilize them as such. For to grant (5) and use (14–
18) and (19–22) solely in relation to (6) is to admit implicitly that there
is some self-evident, obvious sense in which the existence of evil in a world
created by an omnipotent, omniscient, wholly good God needs an explanation—that is, it is to admit implicitly that the onus is on the theist to
convince the atheologian that there exist good reasons to assume that evil
does not count strongly against God's existence. But to utilize these ar-

guments to challenge (11) in the context of (5) shifts the burden of proof. It places the onus on the nontheist to demonstrate why the theist ought to grant that there is some obvious, self-evident conflict between belief in God and the acknowledgment of evil in the world—that is, it places the onus on the atheologian to demonstrate that the abundance of evil we experience is in dire need of explanation by the theist.

However, whether (14–18) and (19–22) are in fact utilized in the context of (5) or (6)—function as "criticisms" or "explanations"—the end result is in one sense the same. To demonstrate successfully that evil counts strongly against God's existence, the atheologian must establish that there are in fact significantly better worlds which an omnipotent, omniscient, wholly good God could have created, that is, the atheologian must in either case offer convincing arguments for (11).

But let us assume for the sake of argument that both (5) and (6) are acceptable and move on to (7). In support of (7), Martin tells us only that "it is generally acknowledged even by many religious persons that the traditional arguments for the existence of God are bankrupt. There is no positive evidence for the belief in God that could outweigh the negative evidence."[11]

But this sort of argumentation will hardly do. First, it fails to distinguish explicitly between the "original" formulations of the traditional arguments for God's existence, which many do consider bankrupt, and contemporary reformulations of such arguments, which are still very much under serious discussion at this time.[12] Second, such argumentation at least implicitly perpetuates the widespread myth that, unless the theist can demonstrate the plausibility of one of the traditional arguments for God's existence, no positive evidence to this end exists. One need only briefly survey the literature to see that many sophisticated theists approach the question of God's existence from other evidential perspectives.[13] In short, the atheologian must give us more before (7) need be affirmed.

But there is a more basic, subtle problem with the general atheological argument in question which is not related specifically to a given premise. Martin and other atheologians who utilize such argumentation continually use such phrases as "positive evidence," "good reasons" and "rational grounds" throughout their discussions. But what exactly are these phrases to mean in the present context? What exactly, for example, must be true concerning a piece of data before it can be considered "positive evidence" for or against God's existence? And who is to make such a decision? The theist? The atheologian? Both? Or let us consider the concept of "rationality." Must the atheologian agree that the theist has

plausible responses to (supposed) difficulties such as evil before theistic belief can be considered rational? Or is theistic belief rational as long as it is
self-consistent and the atheologian has not conclusively demonstrated its
implausibility? Martin appears to adopt the former criterion, but why is
this superior to the latter? In short, a great deal of ambiguity surrounds
the key terms in the general atheological argument in question.

Such ambiguity would not, of course, be overly problematic if the
atheologian could establish that the theist and he both generally affirm
the same definitional criteria for the terms in question. But apart from the
fact that both the theist and atheologian do agree that the affirmation of
an inconsistent set of beliefs is irrational, there appear to be no definitional
givens in inter-world view discussions concerning the rationality of metaphysical beliefs. Nor do I see any satisfactory way to settle inductive,
inter-world view metaphysical disputes of this sort.

Take, for example, the question of whether the atheologian can conceive of an entire world system which an omnipotent, omniscient, wholly
good God could have created which is significantly better than our present
one—that is, can establish (13). The issue is not one of consistency; it is
one of comparative value. But how are we to proceed here? On what common ground are we to build? Both parties may well agree that in a comparison of two possible worlds the one containing the greatest net balance
of good over evil is superior. But how are we to assess the quantity of good
and evil in each? Let us suppose, for example, that in the mind of a given
atheologian the undeserved suffering of a single individual outweighs any
amount of good which might be generated in such a world, while in the
mind of a given theist the intrinsic value of "human freedom" outweighs
any amount of evil such freedom might entail. How would we determine
who is correct? I, for one, have no idea how an objective, nonquestion-
begging determination of this sort could be made.

In short, it seems to me that inductive inter-world view discussions
concerning metaphysical issues ultimately come down to a "difference of
opinion." Accordingly, I must agree with Alvin Plantinga, who has recently argued that, since the probability with respect to belief or disbelief
in God is relative to one's noetic structure, the whole program of an atheologian attempting to demonstrate that belief in God is irrational (or vice
versa) is totally misconceived.[14]

The atheologian may, of course, be able to respond adequately to
such a criticism. But the point is that such a response is necessary. The
unambiguous nature of the key concepts they frequently employ in this
context cannot simply be assumed.

II.

I have not been attempting to argue that there can be no convincing argument against the existence of God. I have attempted to argue, though, that before any atheologian can successfully demonstrate that the evil we experience furnishes the basis for a good inductive argument to this end, he or she must:

1. Set forth acceptable definitional criteria for "rationality," "evidence" and "good reasons" as these terms apply to inductive, inter-world view discussions concerning God's existence.

2. Demonstrate that the amount of evil we experience counts strongly against God's existence by demonstrating that an omnipotent, omniscient, wholly good God could, in fact, have created an entire world system containing not just significantly less evil but on the whole a much better balance of good over evil than that which exists in the actual world.

3. Demonstrate that no recent formulation of the traditional arguments and no other form of argumentation furnish positive evidence for God's existence or demonstrate that such evidence, if it exists, cannot outweigh the evidence against God's existence.

NOTES

1. Michael Martin, "Is Evil Evidence Against the Existence of God?" *Mind*, 1978, pp. 429–31.

2. Martin, pp. 429–31.

3. Martin, pp. 430.

4. J. Cornman and K. Lehrer, *Philosophical Problems and Arguments* (New York: Macmillan and Company, 1974), pp. 340–41.

5. See Alvin Plantinga, *The Nature of Necessity* (Oxford: Clarendon Press, 1974), pp. 169–84 for a fuller discussion of this point.

6. Plantinga, pp. 184–89.

7. See, for example, Antony Flew, "Divine Omnipotence and Human Freedom," in *New Essays in Philosophical Theology* (Macmillan, 1955), pp. 160–66.

8. William Rowe, *Philosophy of Religion* (Encino, CA: Dickerson, 1978), p. 89.

9. See David Basinger, "Human Freedom and Divine Providence: Some New Thoughts on an Old Problem," forthcoming in *Religious Studies*, for a fuller presentation of this argument.

10. See Bruce Reichenbach, "Natural Evils and Natural Laws: A Theodicy for Natural Evils," *International Philosophical Quarterly*, 1976, pp. 179–96.

11. Martin, p. 430.

12. See, for example, Plantinga, *The Nature of Necessity,* pp. 197–217.

13. See, for example, John Hick, *The Existence of God* (New York: Macmillan and Company, 1964), pp. 9–12.

14. Alvin Plantinga, "The Probabilistic Argument from Evil," *Philosophical Studies,* January, 1979.

On Regretting the Evils of This World

WILLIAM HASKER

The secret of happiness is to face the fact that the world is horrible.
—Bertrand Russell

Tell them I've had a wonderful life.
—Ludwig Wittgenstein

After everything was said about how unhappy her childhood had been—her father's casual death, her mother's craziness, her sullen older brother, the succession of boarding schools—there remained her sense that she would, now, be less of a person if it had happened any other way. She would be somebody else, somebody she had no desire to be.
—John Updike, *Marry Me*

I wish to address what is sometimes termed the "existential" form of the Problem of Evil—the form in which theism is questioned and/or rejected on the basis of moral protest, indignation, and outrage at the evils of this world. In the first section of the paper I shall ask the reader to participate in a meditative, highly personal sort of reflection, in the hope of eliciting therefrom a certain existential premise which is crucial to the argument. In the second section I present and discuss a thesis concerning personal identity, with the aim of establishing a connection between one's own existence and the world's past history. In the third section I introduce

From *Southern Journal of Philosophy* 19 (1981): 425–37. Used by permission of the author and editor.

certain principles of what might be termed the "logic of regret"—or, more generally, the logic of preference—and connect these with the results of the second section. The final section draws all of these threads together and shows their significance for the Problem of Evil.

I

The questions we shall be asking in this section are questions each person can only answer for himself. It is necessary, then, for you to meditate on your own life, and the meaning that is has for you; my own reflections will be set down here mainly as an aid to this. I ask myself, then, the following question: *Am I glad that I exist?* The question is not whether my life is all that it ought to be or all that it conceivably could be. It is not whether the pleasure-pain balance in my life to date has been, on the whole, favorable or unfavorable. It is not whether my life is, in general, a benefit to those who are affected by it. It is not even the question whether my life, all things considered, contains more good than evil. All of these questions are deeply interesting, and the answers to them, if known, might affect my answer to the question which I am asking. But the question is simply, am I glad that I am alive? Or is my existence, on the whole, something which I regret? Is my life something which I *affirm,* or do I wish, like Job, that I had never been? And what, I go on to ask, of my loved ones, of my wife and sons, and of others whom I know well enough that the question makes sense: Am I glad of their existence? If I could rewrite the script for the tale that we are living, would I leave their parts out?

It is my hope that as you reflect on these matters you will be able to say, as I must say, that I am glad for my existence. It is not that my life has been good without qualification and in every respect. It has had its share of pain—whether more or less than other lives, I cannot say. It has had times of deep anxiety, when the worth of living at all has come into question. Yet I can say, I must say, that it is good to live, that I am glad for my existence and would not wish to replace it with non-existence, either retrospectively or for the future. And when I think of certain "significant others," then I must emphatically say that I am glad that they exist, that I would not choose to rewrite the script without their parts, that their existence is something which I can and must affirm even as I affirm my own.

It is my hope that you are able to follow me in this, that you are able to be glad for your own existence, and the existence of those whom you love, even as I am glad for my existence and for the lives of those whom

I love. If this is so, then you have available to you a premise which you can use in the ensuing argument. For the argument to be developed is "person-relative," in the sense that each person who uses it to enlighten himself must make use of a different premise, one which applies only to himself and which can be affirmed only by himself. Assuming that you are able to affirm such a premise, let us see what can be derived from it.

II

In this section I shall suggest a partial answer to the question: What is necessary in order that you and I should exist as the individual human beings which we are? I shall not be concerned with those things, such as food, air, and water, which are necessary for the existence of any human being whatsoever, but only with what is necessary for one's *own* existence as distinct from the existence of some other person who might live in the same house, do the same job, and so on. In other words, I shall be proposing a thesis concerning personal identity. The thesis is not uncontroversial or universally acceptable, but I think its appeal is wide enough to make it worth pursuing. The thesis is that a human being is initially individuated by his body, so that, had that body not been conceived and born, that particular human being would never have existed. Or in other words:

(A) A necessary condition of my coming-into-existence is the coming-into-existence of my body.

This isn't acceptable to everyone, or course, but it is entailed by the most widely held views on the mind-body problem. It evidently must be accepted by materialists, identity theorists, etc., for whom the person *is* his body, as well as by epiphenomenalists and behaviorists for whom the mind results (in different ways, of course) from certain aspects of the functioning of the biological organism. More interestingly, however, the thesis must be accepted by some philosophers who hold more or less dualistic views. Thomists, for instance, hold that the soul, as a form, is individuated by the matter which it informs; the soul is created as the soul of *this particular body.* In order to dissent from the thesis, one must hold that the soul has an identity of its own which is at least logically prior, if not also temporally prior, to its embodiment.[1] To Cartesian dualists and others (if any) who hold such views, we now bid farewell, in order to explore the implications of the thesis we have proposed.

The chief advantage of this thesis is that it entitles us to include among the necessary conditions of *my* existence whatever is necessary for

my body's existence. But what *is* necessary for this? To begin with, it is
necessary that the individuals who are, in fact, my parents should have
had a child. Had my mother married someone else, none of their children
could have been *me*; none of their bodies could have been *this* body. But
clearly, not just any child of my parents would have been me. I believe it
would be widely accepted that personal identity requires an identical *genetic heritage*—that a child born to my parents at the same time that I was,
in fact, born but with a significantly different genetic endowment would
have been a different individual. But even genetic identity is not sufficient: identical twins are not identical *persons*, nor is either identical with
the individual who would have existed had twinning not occurred. Thinking along these lines, it seems clear that for my existence it is *at least* necessary that a particular pair of male and female reproductive cells should
have been joined to form a viable individual.[2]

It should already be clear that the coming into existence of any
particular human individual is, antecedently, an extremely improbably
event, one which is contingent upon a multitude of other highly improbable events.[3] Not to put too fine a point on it, let us consider some of
the contingencies involved, in some cases at least, in the fact that one's
parents happened to meet one another. My own father and mother came
from widely separated parts of the country and met as a result of a complex series of events, some of which affected many other individuals as
well. Not least among these was the First World War, which sent my father to France and brought my mother to Washington to work in the expanded Federal government, leading in each case to life-changing
experiences. Quite simply: had there been no war, I should not be here.
But this is not all, for behind my parents there stands the whole series of
their progenitors, persons whose own coming-into-being must have been
influenced in similar or even more striking ways by major and minor
events of their own times. The conclusion to which we are led, and which
is not at all too strong for the argument on which it rests, may be formulated thus:

> (B) Had major or significant events in the world's past history been
> different than they were, then in all probability neither I nor the
> persons whom I love would ever have existed.

III

By this time you may forsee the direction of my argument and the use that
I intend to make of the points established in the first two sections. But in

order to link those points together we need to establish some principles governing the logical relationships between certain attitudes—attitudes which are expressed by the phrases "being glad that . . . " and "being sorry that . . . " Attitudes such as these cannot be true or false, as beliefs are, yet it is my contention that they share with beliefs, moral judgments, and imperatives the property of being *rationally consistent or inconsistent*.[4] In order to see this, it is important to notice that "being glad that . . . " is not just a matter of having certain *feelings* of joy or gladness. Normally, indeed, being glad does involve feelings, but this is not true without exception. I am glad that the rate of unemployment declined by one tenth of a percent last month. But it would take a much bigger shift—or one sustained over several months' time—to trigger any noticeable *feeling* of gladness. What is the case, however, is that I *prefer* the rate's having declined to its having remained constant or climbed even higher. And this, I suggest, is true in general: my being glad that P entails my *preferring* that *P* be the case rather than not-*P*.[5] Conversely, I am *sorry*, or *regret* that P, this means that I *would prefer* that not-*P* be the case rather than *P*.[6] And it is in virtue of these preferences that the attitudes in question are, as I claimed above, rationally consistent or inconsistent.

But this is not sufficiently explicit. Suppose I am glad that Indiana won the NCAA basketball championship, defeating North Carolina in the final game. What is preferred to what? It is not that I would prefer Indiana's having won under all conceivable circumstances—for instance, if I had placed a large bet on North Carolina. What is the case is that I prefer the *actual situation*, in which Indiana won, to the state of affairs which *would have obtained* had Indiana failed to win[7]—presumably, a state of affairs in which Indiana is defeated by North Carolina in a final round. And on the other hand, my regretting Indiana's victory would entail my preferring that other state of affairs, in which North Carolina wins, to the one which actually obtains.

What logical principles apply to these attitudes? To begin with, we surely can say that:

(C) If I am glad that P, I rationally cannot be sorry that P.

One may, indeed, *feel* both gladness and sorrow about something; many events in life have such a "bitter-sweet" quality about them. But "being glad" in the sense which is of interest here involves preference, and clearly it cannot be true both that one *prefers* that P be the case and that one would prefer that it not be the case.

Another principle which may suggest itself is:

(D) If I am glad that P, and P entails Q, than I rationally must be glad that Q.

But there are objections to this. For one thing, I may be quite unaware that P entails Q, and if so I can hardly be expected to extend my gladness that P to include Q. This is easily remedied by adding to the antecedent of (D) a clause specifying that I am aware of the entailment. But even with this addition, (D) would still be false. The reason for this may be elicited by a further consideration of the basketball example. Clearly, Indiana's winning the NCAA basketball championship entails the existence of the National Collegiate Athletic Association and its national championship. But one might take the view that the NCAA's existence is on the whole a bad thing—that the very existence of such an organization with its national championships, television contracts, etc., inevitably fosters over-emphasis on athletics, commercialism, and the corruption of which we have recently been hearing so much. An Indiana fan who took this view might very well regret the NCAA's existence, even though Indiana's victory could not have occurred if there were no association. Yet it is still true that he is glad that Indiana won. For the alternative to Indiana's winning (the state of affairs which would have obtained had Indiana not won) would not include the (supposedly beneficent) disappearance of the NCAA; it would, no doubt, be simply a state of affairs in which Indiana was defeated in the final round of the tournament.

The fan we have just described is in no way irrational or inconsistent, and he does constitute a counter-example to (D). But his gladness about Indiana's victory is qualitatively different from that of typical fan who is less concerned about the undesirable aspects of national associations and their tournaments. The first fan is glad about Indiana's victory *under the circumstances*—circumstances which include the undesirable but inevitable fact that there *is* a tournament and it will be won by some other team if not by Indiana. We may also say, in the interests of brevity, that he is *circumstantially glad* that Indiana won, where

'A is circumstantially glad that P' = df 'A is glad that P, and there is some state-of-affairs Q such that A knows that if Q did not obtain neither would P, and A regrets that Q'.

The other fan, we may suppose, is *glad on the whole* that Indiana won. He may indeed, recognize that the national association and its championship tournament involve some undesirable consequences, but he definitely prefers Indiana's victory under these less-than-ideal circumstances to the alternative of no association, no tournament, and no championship for Indiana. More formally:

'A is glad on the whole that P' = df 'A is glad that P, and for any state-of-affairs Q such that A knows that if Q did not obtain neither would P, A is glad that Q'.

Being glad on the whole is a rather strong attitude of preference, but it is not an unfamiliar one: it is commonly expressed in the locution, "I wouldn't trade this for anything!" This may of course be said when it is not strictly true, but there is no reason to doubt that it is sometimes a true expression of one's attitude.[8]

Finally, we may say that a person *regrets on the whole* that P whenever he is clearly *not* glad on the whole that P—whenever, that is, he regrets that P or is only circumstantially glad that P.[9]

Given these definitions, we are able to proceed with some further principles. For instance, we can replace the objectionable (D) with:

(E) If I am glad on the whole that P, and I know that P entails Q, than I rationally must be glad on the whole that Q.

This is easily proved, given the definitions above. For suppose I am glad on the whole that P, but I am not glad on the whole that Q, where Q is a state of affairs which I know to be entailed by P. If I regret that Q, this is definitionally inconsistent with my being glad on the whole that P. (I may of course "regret" that Q, but this is consistent with my being glad on the whole that Q). Suppose, however, that I am circumstantially glad that Q. Then there is some state-of-affairs R such that I know that if R did not obtain neither would Q, and I regret that R. But since P entails Q, it follows that if R did not obtain neither would P. And this, once again, is inconsistent with the assumption that I am glad on the whole that P.

Clearly, our definitions entail not only (E) but also:

(F) If I am glad on the whole that P, and I know that if Q did not obtain neither would P, then I rationally must be glad that Q.[10]

These principles seem clearly correct. But when (F) is combined with the results from Section Two, a rather striking conclusion results. The reasoning is straightforward: My existence depends on the existence of my body, and that body would never have existed, had major events in the world's past history been different. Therefore.

(G) If I am glad on the whole about my own existence and that of those whom I love, then I must be glad that the history of the world, in its major aspects, has been as it has.

This conclusion, to be sure, does not follow deductively from (F) and (B) as they have been stated. For (F) speaks of my *knowing* that if Q did not obtain neither would P, whereas (B) says only that *in all probability* there is such a connection. What difference, if any, should this make in our attitude towards (G)? Very little, I believe. Note first of all that, given the truth of (A), it is *certain,* and not just probable, that subsequent to any major calamity, such as a war, many of the persons who come into existence are different individuals from those who would have existed had the calamity not occurred. Many persons who would otherwise have become parents die without having children. Those who would have been their mates have children with other partners, and so on. Within a few generations, it is likely that hardly anyone living in the affected area is identical with any individual who would have existed, had the calamity not occurred. What is more difficult is to show that this is true in the case of a given individual. But even in the individual case, the probabilities mount up very rapidly. Suppose, for example, that had the First World War not occurred there is one chance in ten that my parents would have met each other. (I am sure that this is too high. But at this point I can afford to be conservative.) Suppose, furthermore, that on just two previous occasions the meeting and mating of some of my earlier ancestors has been influenced in similar ways by calamitous events of their own times. Then neglecting all other factors (all of which, if considered, would further strengthen my argument), the likelihood of my existing, if just these three major calamities had not occurred, is no better than one in a thousand! The truth is, that I have no reason whatever to suppose that I would have existed, had the course of the world's history been substantially different. But what I have no reason to suppose true must for practical purposes be disregarded. So (G) must be accepted.

If the argument leading to (G) is as sound as it now seems to be, how are we to explain the fact that is has largely been ignored? Perhaps one reason is the non-obviousness of (A) and (B), for without these principles the connection between past historical events and my own existence would not obtain. [11] As a matter of fact the ideas expressed in (F) and (G) have received some attention, most frequently in connection with determinism. In a strict deterministic system, every event in a causal network is causally interlocked with every other event, so that one can't be glad or sorry on the whole about anything without being glad or sorry about everything. This is the source of the complaint urged by William James in "The Dilemma of Determinism"—that if determinism is true, one can't rationally regret any single event (a brutal murder, for instance) without implicating the entire universe in one's regret. Some determinists have seen this and have found it acceptable. Spinoza considers our ordinary judgments of good and bad to be irrational precisely because in making them we overlook the necessary connections between events; the only rational happiness is the joy with which we contemplate *deus sive natura* as one single, immutable fact. And Nietzsche, in "The Drunken Song" (*Zarathustra,* BK IV) enjoins us to love *all* of life and to will all of it back in "eternal return":

> All things are entangled, ensnared, enamored; if ever you wanted one thing twice, if ever you said, "You please me, happiness!" "Abide, moment!" then you wanted all back.

A final (to my mind wonderful) example, which is neither deterministic nor philosophical, comes from the Roman liturgy of the Easter vigil:

> O truly necessary sin of Adam, that is wiped out by death of Christ!
> O happy fault, that was worthy to have such and so great a redeemer. [12]

IV

Supposing the argument so far to be sound, and that the truth of (G) has been established, what follows for the Problem of Evil? Or better, who can be helped by our argument, and how can it help him? To begin with our argument can be of no help to the atheologian[13] who finds himself sincerely unable to affirm that he is glad for his own existence, and for the existence of persons whom he loves. If one on the whole regrets the sheer fact that he has lived at all—as opposed to regretting some, or many things that one has done, or that have happened to one—then his own life gives him no reason to be glad for the world's existence. If on the other hand you *are* glad on the whole that you exist then it follows (in the light of (G) above) that you must be glad also about the world's existence and about the general course its history has taken.

It may occur to you, however, that I am trying to extract too much from your admission that you are glad that you exist. Probably when you considered this question you weren't thinking at all about those tragic events which (as it turns out) are required for your existence. You were probably thinking just about your own life and its immediate surroundings, rather than about its connection with other lives and other events— and *this* is what you said you were glad about. If we agree to call this "gladness *simpliciter*" you may want to say that you are indeed glad *simpliciter* that you exist but that you are not necessarily glad on the whole that you exist.

Quite so. There is a difference between being glad *simpliciter* and being glad on the whole, and it's not at all impossible for a person to have one of these attitudes without having the other. But, now that we have clarified this distinction, I would like you to ask yourself, "Am I *on the whole* glad, or sorry, that I exist?" There are just three possible answers. If your answer, now that the issues have been clarified, is still "Yes," then the argument proceeds just as before. But perhaps you find that you can't easily give this answer, in the light of all those tragic events of the past. Perhaps, indeed, your reaction is one of bewilderment—you may feel, as a colleague suggested, that when you lump your life together with the whole past history of the world, you don't know *what* to say about it. Thus you may fail to have *any* "on the whole" attitude towards your own existence; you are neither glad on the whole nor sorry on the whole about it.

I can understand your feeling this way about the matter. The interesting point (which will emerge below) is that this failure to have an "on the whole" attitude towards your own existence leaves you just as unable to formulate a Problem of Evil as if you were definitely glad about it. In order to state a Problem of Evil (of the sort we are discussing) you must positively *regret* on the whole that you, your family, your friends, and all the rest of us, have lived. You must be able to say "Although my life has brought me some pleasures, I truly wish and would prefer that some other world, in which no one now living has a share, or perhaps no world at all, should exist in place of this present evil world of which I am (unhappily) a part." If this is your sincere attitude, then the argument I am presenting will necessarily fail to engage you. In this case the fact that I glad of my existence is of no help to you. But this point cuts both ways. If you are glad on the whole that you, and persons close to you, have lived, then it makes no difference that others might, or actually do, feel differently about *their* lives. In such matters as these, each of us is bound to the consequences of his own convictions and attitudes, regardless of whether they are shared by others or not.

It may be, however, that even an atheologian who is glad on the whole for his own existence will be unaffected by my argument. This will be the case, for instance, if he conceives and presents the Problem of Evil merely as an internal inconsistency in theistic belief. He may, for instance, allege that the famous triad "God is all-powerful, God is good, and the world contains evil" is either logically or probabilistically inconsistent, and that this shows the theist's position to be untenable. Such an atheologian does not need to commit himself to any substantive premises whatever; in particular, he need not commit himself to any moral principles, nor need he make any moral judgments of his own, or express any kind of dissatisfaction with the actual state of the world. His atheological argument does not depend in any way on his personal convictions, attitudes and commitments, so we can't expect the argument to be affected by our reminding him of these things.[14]

Typically, however, the Problem of Evil is not presented in this noncommittal kind of way. Not only is such a presentation generally lacking in the rhetorical force desired by atheologians, but it seems not to express the convictions which they wish to convey. Far more commonly, presentations of the Problem convey a strong sense that there is indeed something drastically wrong with the world from a moral point of view; that a supremely wise and powerful being such as God is alleged to be would, if he existed, *be morally at fault* for causing or permitting the world to be as it is; and sometimes that believers in God are not only logically obtuse but *morally insensitive*[15] for failing to recognize that the deplorable moral state of the world is a decisive objection to what they believe.

To this kind of presentation of the Problem of Evil, our present argument provides an effective answer. To see this, we have only to conjoin the "moral protest" involved in the presentation of the Problem with the results derived in the first three sentences of this paper. We then have, for instance, the following:

> (H) The world as we know it is morally so objectionable that a God who tolerated it could in no meaningful sense be called good— nevertheless, *I am glad for my own existence and therefore I am also glad that the world exists and that the main events and features of its history have been as they have.*

Or, in relation to the alleged moral insensitivity of theists, we have:

> (I) Those who would maintain that the world as we know it could be created and governed by a just and loving God "must have led sheltered lives and closed their heart to the voice of their brothers' blood," *nevertheless I am glad on the whole that I have been able to live in this world, and glad also that its history has been such as to give me that opportunity.*

Isn't it clear on the face of it that the admission in the latter parts of these two statements effectively *cancels out* the moral protest involved in the first part of each statement? That one simply *can't*, rationally and consistently, press home the complaint of the first part if one has the attitude expressed in the second part? The principle involved might be formulated something like this:

(J) I cannot reasonably *complain* to someone that P, or *blame* or *reproach* someone for its being the case that P, unless I myself sincerely *regret,* or *am sorry,* that P.[16]

This, I think, is intuitively evident, and applying it to the problem at hand, we have the following:

(K) If I am glad on the whole about my own existence, and that of persons close to me, then I cannot reproach God for the general character or the major events of the world's past history.

But this is just what the atheologian wants to do: it is just the "general character and major events," many of them tragic for the persons involved, which in his view render the world morally unsatisfactory and which, should God exist, would constitute a decisive objection against His goodness. Nor will it be feasible for the atheologian to develop a Problem of Evil based solely on events within his own lifetime, events therefore on which his own existence does not depend in the way in which it depends on those tragic events of the past. For the atrocities and tragedies of our lifetime are all of them the same *kinds* of events that have occurred countless times in the past; to protest loudly and indignantly against just these few calamities, while accepting with equanimity all the similar evils in the past which happen to have contributed to our own existence, is to adopt a moral stance which is too egocentric to deserve serious notice.

So much for the atheologian, at least for now. But what of the perplexed theist, who is troubled by the problem of reconciling the world's evil with the goodness of the God in whom he believes? Does our argument offer him any help?

To begin with, the argument cannot bear the weight of "positive theodicy"—that is, of the task of explaining *why* evil exists or why it is appropriate that God should allow it to exist. In order to do this along the lines of the present argument, we should have to assume that we, the persons actually existing, are uniquely valuable in comparison with any other persons whom God could have created—but I take it no one would want to assert this. These questions about the justification of evils must be answered, insofar as answers are possible at all, along other lines.

I think, however, that the argument is able to offer some help in another way—namely, by effecting a certain *change of perspective.* To be sure, the point of view presented here does not represent what philosophers would ordinarily be prone to describe as "viewing things in proper perspective." Ever since Plato, we have wanted to view such matters *sub specie aeternitatis,* taking our places as "spectators of all time and all existence." But are we really able to take this place? Can we actually *make* the innumerable judgments, both factual and evaluative, which are required if we are to sum things up from this point of view? Our argument suggests, on the contrary, that my judgments about the goodness or badness of existence as a whole are best made, not from the standpoint of "a cosmic ideal observer," but from *my own* standpoint as an individual existing human being—one who loves and struggles, who sorrows and rejoices, and who is glad for the opportunity to live out his life upon the earth. To sum it up in a word—the argument shows something about what it means to be a *creature.*[17]

NOTES

1. Presumably Alvin Plantinga has some view in mind, when he contemplates the question, whether or not it would have been possible for Socrates to be an alligator! See the *Nature of Necessity,* (Oxford: Oxford University Press, 1974), pp. 65–69. For the author's own preferred view of the mind-body problem, see "The Souls of Beasts and Men," in *Religious Studies,* Vol. 10 (1974) pp. 265–277.

2. See Saul Kripke, "Naming and Necessity," in Donald Davidson and Gilbert Harman, eds., *Semantics of Natural Language* (Dordrecht: Reidel, 1974), pp. 312–314. Even this may not be sufficient—for instance do the time and circumstances of my conception matter? If the same pair of cells had joined several days or weeks earlier would this make a difference to my identity? Or suppose my parents had had other children before me, and other circumstances of our life were different? On questions such as these, my own intuitions are far from clear— fortunately, for our present purpose there is no need to resolve them.

3. For instance: on any given occasion of conception, literally millions of viable sperm cells are available. It may well be that part of the historical attraction of doctrines of the pre-existence of the soul, (and of Cartesian dualism?) has been the desire to escape from this sense of the radical contingency, the fantastic improbability, of one's own existence. Whether this is something one ought to escape from, is another matter.

4. When I say that one "rationally must" (or "cannot") have a certain attitude, I mean that one must have it (or refrain from having it) on pain of inconsistency.

5. In order to avoid use-mention confusions I will use 'P' to stand for the sentence which expresses the proposition that P, and '*P*' as the name of the state of affairs such that P.

6. In certain contexts we may say that we "regret" that P when we do not, in fact, prefer that not-*P* be the case rather than *P.* This "polite" or "conventional" sense of "regret" entails nothing concerning one's actual preferences; thus it is too

weak to be of interest for the purposes of this essay. I shall refer to it only within
quotation marks, and then only when it seems advisable to distinguish it from
genuine regret.

7. This state of affairs may be identified, following the Lewis semantics for
counterfactuals, as that possible world most similar to the actual world in which
Indiana does not win.

8. Whether one is glad on the whole about something or only circumstantially glad about it depends in part on what, in a given context, are taken to be
reasonable topics for regret. In most everyday contexts, for example, the laws of
nature are seen simply as given facts that cannot reasonably be regretted. (When
I burn my finger it does not occur to me to regret that fire is hot.) And this is
probably true also of most events of the remote past. In the context of discussions
of the Problem of Evil, on the other hand, the scope of reasonable regret is often
held to be very wide indeed.

9. The various attitudes of preference then lend themselves to arrangement
in the following schema:

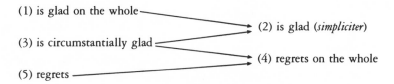

The ranking is of course from the greatest to the least degree of preference of the
state of affairs in question. The arrows represent entailment. (1) is incompatible
with (4), and so also with (3) and (5); (5) is incompatible with (2), and so also
with (1) and (3). There can be borderline or indeterminate cases between any of
the incompatible pairs. If we exclude these, and also the cases in which one has
no attitude of preference at all, we might say that (1) and (4) are *contradictory*
attitudes, as are (2) and (5); (1) and (3) are *contrary* attitudes, as are (1) and (5)
and (3) and (5); while (2) and (4) are *sub-contrary* attitudes.

10. Why not " . . . must be glad on the whole that Q"? The proof of this,
parallel to the proof given for (E), would require the inference-rule: From (if Q
did not obtain neither would P) and (if R did not obtain neither would Q), infer
(if R did not obtain neither would P). But this is not a valid rule of counter-
factual logic.

Some of the consequences of (E) and (F) may at first glance appear counter-
intuitive. If I am glad on the whole that Indiana won the championship, does it
follow that I am glad that: either Indiana won, or nuclear war is about to break
out in the Middle East? The answer is yes—and there is no problem here. Of
course (E) should not be understood to imply that I must actually consider the
entailed state of affairs, but only that if I were to consider it I must be glad about
it. And I *am* glad about this: I prefer the actual state of affairs, in which Indiana

won and war is (presumably) not imminent, to the state of affairs which would have obtained had Indiana not won. But it does *not* follow from this that *if Indiana had lost and nuclear war were imminent,* I would *then* be glad that: either Indiana won, or nuclear war is about to break out.

A similar treatment handles cases involving conjunction. If I am glad on the whole that P and Q, then I rationally must be glad on the whole that P, and also glad on the whole that Q. But it does not follow that *if it were true that P and false that Q,* I would *then* be glad that P.

11. But the argument does not lose *all* of its force even if (A) and (B) are denied. For those of us who are glad that we exist are in most cases glad not so much about the bare fact of having lived at all, as about specific things we have done, experiences we have had, persons we have known and loved. But a hypothetical life that "I" might have had, if my ego had been lodged in some other body, would in all likelihood be vastly different from my actual life in all of these respects. For many of us, preferring such a life to one's actual life might be nearly as difficult as preferring not to have lived at all. (I owe this point to Robert Rosenthal.)

12. I am indebted to Arthur Falk for these last two examples.

13. I use this word for convenience, while recognizing that one who propounds the Problem of Evil need not be attempting to demonstrate the non-existence of God. He may be a theist, or a concerned agnostic, whose own faith is troubled by the massiveness of the world's evil.

14. As Alvin Plantinga has shown (*God and Other Minds* (Ithaca: Cornell University Press, 1967)), it is extremely difficult to show that there is an inconsistency here. In order to do this, one would need to supply another proposition which is itself necessary, or at least obviously true, and which when conjoined with the "triad" yields a contradiction—but no such proposition is forthcoming. On the other hand, I am unconvinced by Plantinga's attempt to demonstrate positively that there is no inconsistency.

15. See Walter Kaufmann, *The Faith of a Heretic* (Garden City: Doubleday, 1963), p. 167: "Those who believe in God because their experience of life and the facts of nature prove his existence must have led sheltered lives and closed their hearts to the voice of their brothers' blood."

16. It is not enough that I "regret" that P! This principle shows that in order to formulate an existential Problem of Evil I must on the whole *positively regret* my own existence; the mere failure to be glad on the whole about it is insufficient.

17. I am indebted to Robert Merrihew Adams for the seed-thought of this essay; his own (rather different) development of the idea is given in "Existence, Self-Interest, and the Problem of Evil," published in *Nous* (1979). For comments on earlier drafts of this paper I wish to thank Arthur Falk, Henry Norton, Len Fleck, William Hawk, Michael Peterson, and Robert Rosenthal.

Redemptive Suffering: A Christian Solution to the Problem of Evil

Marilyn M. Adams

For the word of the cross is folly to those who are perishing, but to us who are being saved it is the power of God.

I Cor. 1:18

Christians believe that God is effectively dealing with the problem of evil through the cross—primarily the cross of Christ and secondarily their own. In the Gospel of Luke, Jesus follows the prediction of his own martyrdom (Luke 9:22) with a charge to his disciples: "If any man would come after me, let him deny himself and take up his cross daily and follow me. For whoever would save his life will lose it; and whoever loses his life for my sake, he will save it. For what does it profit a man if he gains the whole world and loses or forfeits himself?" (Luke 9:23–25). Yet these points are rarely mentioned in discussions of the problem of evil among analytic philosophers, no doubt because of their paradoxical nature, noted by St. Paul himself. How can the suffering of the innocent and loyal at the hands of the guilty and hard-hearted solve the problem of evil? Why is it not simply another witness against the goodness of God who commends it?

My purpose in this paper is to reintroduce reflection on the meaning of the cross into discussion (at least among Christian philosophers) of the problem of evil, in the hope that, as faith seeks understanding, our deepest contribution will become more articulate for us and less scandalous to others. My bold contention will be that the Christian approach to evil through redemptive suffering affords a distinctive solution to the problem of evil, for believers and unbelievers as well.

SOME METHODOLOGICAL REFLECTIONS

Discussions of the problem of evil among analytic philosophers of religion focused on *God's* responsibility for evils and have concentrated on the theoretical, or so-called logical, problem of evil. It is asked how the propositions

(T1) There is an omnipotent, omniscient, and perfectly good God

and

(T2) There is evil in the world

can be logically consistent in view of the assumption that

(T3) A perfectly good being would want to eliminate all of the evil that he could.

Proposed solutions involve arguing that even secular ethics admits exceptions to (T3), where the evils in question are prerequisite to or necessary consequences of greater goods. Nevertheless, it is conceded that

(T4) The fact that an evil was necessary for a greater good would provide an omniscient and omnipotent being with an excuse, only if the evil were a logically necessary prerequisite to or consequence of the good.

Defenses are then fleshed out by citing purported logically possible, morally legitimate excuses—either that the evils are logically necessary to the best of all possible worlds, or that each evil is logically connected with some great enough good, or that the risk of evil is logically implied by the good of free creatures. Philosophers usually dismiss the "factual" problem—that of whether (T1) and (T2) are both true—as philosophically intractable. After all, how could one establish that this *is* the best of all possible worlds or prove that each piece of evil was logically connected with some great enough good? Again, is it not overwhelmingly plausible—pace Plantinga[1]—that

(T5) God could do more than he does to prevent or eliminate evils,

even on the assumption that rational creatures have free will? When all is said and done, most Christians settle for "incomplete" as the most benign possible verdict on any attempted philosophical solution, and the rest is left to "pastoral care."[2]

I believe that Christianity does provide a distinctive resolution of the "logical" problem of evil and for believers an answer to the "factual" problem as well. To extract these results, however, it is necessary to approach the matter indirectly and to keep the following observations in mind.

First, it is necessary to remember that Christianity is primarily a religion, concerned to teach people how to live and serve God in the here and now. The problem of evil for Christians is posed by the question

(Q1) How can I trust (or continue to trust) God in a world like this (in distressing circumstances such as these)?

A Christian is committed to obey Christ in everything and to count on him to see to his good and preserve his life in any and every circumstance. Sometimes things happen in his life or in those of others close to him or in the world at large that radically shake his convictions. The Christian believer will not be reassured by the observation that it is *logically possible* for an omnipotent and omniscient being to prove trustworthy in and through these circumstances. For it is his *actual* commitments that are at issue; he needs to restore his confidence that God is *actually* trustworthy in the present situation. This problem is indeed a pastoral one, but it has a philosophical dimension in that it might be partially alleviated by some sort of explanations of how God is being good to created persons, even when he permits and/or causes evils such as these.

Second, evil is a problem for the Christian only insofar as it challenges his faith in God's goodness; yet, for the Christian, God's goodness remains at bottom a mystery. (*a*) For one thing, the typical Christian does not arrive at the conclusion that God is good by taking a Cliffordian survey of all the available data, tallying the evidence on both sides, and finding that the "scientific" case for God's goodness is stronger. Usually he is moved by personal and/or corporate experiences of deliverance from some concrete difficulty—"They cried to the Lord in their trouble; and He delivered them from their distress" (Ps. 107:6, 13, 19, 28)—or big or little theophanies in which the believer is permitted to "taste and see that the Lord is good" (Ps. 34:8). The Christian may come away deeply convinced of God's goodness and saving power without being able to articulate any clear recipe for predicting his behavior in future situations. (*b*) Further, it is fundamental to biblical religion that God's goodness cannot be comprehended by us in terms of a simple formula in this life. This is in part because the divine nature is eternally beyond the creature's conceptual grasp. But it is also part of God's deliberate design, since it is necessary to make possible the relationships He wants with us and for which we were created. For what God wants most from us is wholehearted trust and obedience. Yet it is conceptually impossible to trust someone if you know in advance every move that he will make. Again, even if such knowledge were possible, it would be a source of great temptation. For example, if God were known to have a fixed policy of rendering temporal goods for well-doing and temporal evils for wickedness, then the observant might even try to manipulate the equation to use God as a means to their ends.

These latter points are well illustrated by the story of Job, who apparently thought that divine goodness could be captured in the simple act-consequence principle. Job paid his social and religious dues, and God blessed him. When Satan was allowed to take away the temporal benefits and to afflict Job with a loss of material goods, family, health, and moral approval, however, Job was pressed to his limits and eventually demanded a hearing. Job had kept his side of the contract, but God was reneging on his; Job wanted a day in court. God answers Job with a theophany: Job is reprimanded for his insolence in presuming to grasp divine goodness in such a simplistic way; he is allowed to see and experience God's goodness but told he will have to trust God to save him in his own way, without advance billing of his plans. Job had loved God too much for his effects and benefits; now he has seen God and must love him for himself.

Third, while we cannot get a simple, clear analysis of divine goodness that will enable us to trace the hand of God in every situation the way the simple act-consequence principle promised to do, we can get a general idea of God's character, purposes, and policies from the collective experience of God's people over the centuries. The principal sourcebook for this general description is the Bible; a secondary source is the history of the Church. Nevertheless, the Christian story does not bridge the above-mentioned "incompleteness" gap by providing answers to such questions as

(Q2) Why does God not do more than he does to prevent or eliminate evils?

(Q3) Why did God make a world in which there are evils of the amounts and kinds found in this world, instead of one with fewer or less severe kinds?

(Q4) Why did God make a world such as this instead of one entirely free from evils?

To the extent that Christians do not know the answers to these questions, evil must remain a mystery from the Christian point of view. The Bible and church history do shed light on this question.

> (Q5) How does God fit evils, of the amounts and kinds we find in this world, into his redemptive purposes?

and thereby suggest an answer to

> (Q1) How can I trust (or continue to trust) God in a world like this (in distressing circumstances such as these)?

as well as a resolution of the philosopher's (logical and factual) problem of evil.

Finally, although the Christian religion does not hold that evil is an illusion or deny the grim fact that many have to struggle for survival and meaning in a world plagued by pain, disease, death, and wickedness, it teaches that the place to begin in grappling with the problem of evil is not the *evils without* but the *evils within,* not the evils that just happen or that are charged to others but one's own contributions to the problem. Christians believe that unless a person is willing to confront God's way of dealing with his own sin, he may not be able to appreciate God's approach to other evils or to discover the most fruitful way of living with them. To see how this works and how from this starting point it is possible to arrive at a Christian approach to the problem of evil through redemptive suffering, it is necessary to review briefly the doctrinal presuppositions of such a conclusion.

SIN AS THE PRIMARY EVIL FOR CHRISTIANS

Freedom and the actuality of sin. According to biblical religion,

> (T6) God's primary interest in creation is the rational creatures, particularly the human beings, whom he has made.

Further, as Psalm 8 eloquently reflects, God did not make us because human beings were just the touch he needed to make this the best of all possible worlds; rather

> (T7) God made human beings to enter into nonmanipulative relationships of self-surrendering love with himself and relationships of self-giving love with others.

So far from altering the characters to improve the plot, God is represented in the Old Testament as directing the course of history with the end of bringing his people into the relationship with himself that he desires. Nevertheless,

(T8) God cannot get the relationships he wants with human beings unless he makes them with incompatibilist free wills.

For if human beings are free in the compatibilist sense only, then their free and voluntary actions are the sorts of things that either have causes outside the agent himself or occur in part by chance. Surely, if God's primary purpose in creation is to enter into such loving relationships with human beings, he would not leave it simply to chance whether they cooperate with or reject him. On the other hand, if each free human choice or action is completely determined by a causal chain or chains whose first member is God, then God's relationships with human beings will be manipulative in the highest degree, like those of a computer expert with the robot he designs, builds, and completely programs. Again, how could God hold human beings accountable for their responses to his offers of friendship, if it were at his discretion whether they occurred by chance or were completely determined by him? Yet, these relationships are bought with a price, for

(T9) Not even an omnipotent God can introduce incompatibilist free creatures into the world without accepting the possibility, which he is powerless to exclude, that they will sin.

Although human beings are thus free to cooperate with God or not, it was his purpose in creation that we should, and

(T10) As creator, God has the right that we should submit to him in complete and voluntary obedience and offer ourselves in service to others.

We sin when we show contempt for God by willfully refusing to render what we owe. And as Christ taught in the Sermon on the Mount, sin is not only, or even primarily, a matter of misdeeds but of inner attitudes and emotions.

Second, God's response to the problem of human sin begins with divine judgment. Biblical religion conceives of divine goodness as righteous love. God's righteousness expresses itself in the desire for honest and open relationships with created persons, ones in which role expectations are clear and conflicts explicit and dealt with rather than glossed over or suppressed. Thus, God's judgment of sin is an expression of his righteousness, because

(T11) As righteous, God has a right to make us face the truth about who we are, who he is, who Christ is, and his rightful claims over us,

and

> (T12) God will not forgo this right of judgment.

He would not be wrong to judge us, even if no benefit accrued to us therefrom. Nevertheless, divine judgment is also an expression of his love, because

> (T13) God's interest in judgment is not condemnation and punishment but forgiveness and reconciliation.

As our creator, he knows that

> (T14) A human being's deepest longing is to be known and loved just as he is;

and he also realizes that

> (T15) Human beings, whether by nature or as a consequence of the fall, cannot really forget sin, whether their own or someone else's.

God therefore shows his love when in judgment he brings everything out on the table between him and the sinner, so that everyone knows that the love that follows is not based on false pretenses. We see this clearly in Jesus' encounter with the woman at the well: he tells her everything that she ever did, not to join the citizenry in condemning her scandal but to show that his offer to exchange drinks of water with her was made with full knowledge of what sort of sinner she was (John 4:7–30, 39–42).

The Christian's experience of divine judgment and the forgiveness of sins, his continued experience of the restored and ever-deepening relationship, convinces him of God's love at such a level that he is able to affirm in times of trial that

> (T16) God would not allow us to suffer evils that could not have, with our cooperation, a redemptive aspect,

and to keep trusting, his lack of answers for (Q2)–(Q4) notwithstanding.

GOD'S STRATEGY IN JUDGMENT

The direct approach. From a biblical point of view, God's right of judgment is in no way conditioned on any therapeutic effects it may have for us. And the book of Revelation implies that he has the means and will eventually force the unwilling to face the facts: "Behold, he is coming with the clouds, and every eye will see him, every one who pierced him; and all the tribes of the earth will wail on account of him" (Rev. 1:7). There is the

picture of Judgment Day on which all the secrets of our hearts will be
made known, not only to us but in front of everyone else.

Yet God knows that this sort of judgment would not usually be redemptive for fallen human beings. And the author of Revelation represents it as a method of last resort, to be used by God when time has run
out on his offer of salvation. When someone judges us, looking down
from a position of superior power or righteousness (the way the Pharisee
regarded the tax collector in the temple, Luke 18:11–12), our reaction is
apt to be hostile. We search wildly for countercharges and slander our
accuser; we blame someone else and/or rationalize our behavior as no worse
than others in our inferior position. No matter how much our judge insists
that he is telling us for our own good, we are apt to not to believe him but
to hate him for adding guilt and shame to the burden of our implicitly
recognized sin.

Indirect pedagogy. Since—by (T13)—God is interested in judgment as
an occasion for repentance and reconciliation, he confronts a pedagogical
problem; how to face us with our sin in such a way that we will accept the
verdict and repent. The best way is an indirect approach that does not ram
the truth down our throats but entices us to participate in arriving at the
verdict.

In the Old Testament, the prophets sometimes resort to stories or
speak in figures. Consider God's judgment of David for his affair with
Bathsheba and contrivance of Uriah's death. Nathan tells David the story
of a rich man who eats a poor man's pet lamb instead of taking an animal
from his own large flocks, and he elicits from David a verdict of guilty
and a sentence of death. Then Nathan proclaims, "You are the man," and
because David really loves God, he repents and God forgives him. The
first child dies, but another son, Solomon, becomes a great king and
builds the temple of the Lord (2 Sam. 11–12).

Jesus tells parables for a similar reason. For example, the Good Samaritan story is told to a self-righteous man who wants a definition of
'neighbor' so that he will not have to waste his efforts at being good on
people who do not fall into that category. Jesus does not use the confron-
tational approach: "You do not really love God or care about other people,
or else you would not be asking that question" or "You think you have
your 'religious act' together, but in God's eyes you are further from the
kingdom than the people you despise and exclude." Rather than provoke
hostility in his questioner, Jesus tells him a story about how to be neigh-
borly and commends the Good Samaritan's help of the needy man. The
young man can go away and ponder Jesus' answer and reflect on the dif-

ference between Jesus' starting point and his own. Dealt with in this gentler way, he may perhaps have a change of heart.

Sometimes such indirect approaches do not work, however. If the person is especially reluctant to see and if the sins in question are inner attitudes that are apparently easier to hide, he may successfully resist the conclusion that Jesus wants him to draw. The Pharisees and Sadducees were like this. Their outward acts were correct and legal, so that it was easy for them to defend themselves and to argue that they were better than most people. They repeatedly refused the insight that they were self-righteous and contemptuous of others and that they had lost faith in the redemptive power of God. In cases of this sort, God is left with a more expensive, noncoercive strategy: redemptive suffering as epitomized in martyrdom and the cross.

GOD'S COSTLY APPROACH TO THE PROBLEM OF EVIL: MARTYRDOM AND THE CROSS

What is a martyr? A martyr is simply a witness, in the sense relevant here, someone who gives testimony about a person, some events, or an ideal and who is made to pay a price for doing it. Usually the cost involves the loss of some temporal goods, for example, the experience of social disapproval or exclusion, the deprivation of educational and professional opportunities, economic losses, moral disapproval, imprisonment, exile, and death. The price a martyr is willing to pay is a measure of his love for and loyalty to what he believes to be the truth and/or that to which he bears witness. Martyrdom in the good sense is not a subtle manipulative maneuver to get one's way in the long run by making people feel guilty about one's short-term sufferings. On the contrary, the martyr usually does not actively seek martyrdom, both because he is diffident about his being able to pay the price and because he does not wish to provoke others to evil. Given this characterization, I want to suggest that martyrdom is an expression of God's righteous love toward the onlooker, the persecutor, and even the martyr himself.

Martyrdom as a vehicle of God's goodness to the onlooker. For onlookers, the event of martyrdom may function as a prophetic story, the more powerful for being brought to life. The martyr who perseveres to the end presents an inspiring example. Onlookers are invited to see in the martyr the person they ought to be and to be brought to a deeper level of commitment. Alternatively, onlookers may see themselves in the persecutor and be moved to repentance. If the onlooker has ears to hear the martyr's testimony, he may receive God's redemption through it.

Martyrdom as potentially redemptive for the persecutor. In martyrdom, God shows his goodness—both his righteous judgment and his redemptive mercy—not only in relation to the onlooker but also in relation to the persecutors. First of all, the martyr's sacrifice can be used as an instrument of divine judgment, because it draws the persecutor an external picture of what he is really like—the more innocent the victim, the clearer the focus. Consider the case of a businessman who commutes to New York City from the suburbs everyday; he loves his family and works hard to provide them with a nice home, his children with an Ivy League education, his wife with an attractive social circle, and so on. As the pressures of his business increase, he falls increasingly silent and follows his 8:30 P.M. dinner with more and more drinks. His patient and loving wife tries to get him to talk, but he insists that nothing is wrong. One night after he has drunk even more than usual, his wife says quietly but firmly, "I think you've had enough." He protests that everything is fine, but she repeats, "I think you've had enough," whereupon he hits her and knocks her out. At first he thinks he has killed her, but she recovers and no charges are pressed. In this incident, the man's anger and hostility, which he had been so carefully hiding (more from himself than from everyone else) by drowning in drink, is externalized on a comparatively innocent victim. He cannot rationalize away his behavior in terms of any commensurate attack from her. It is an occasion of judgment, in which the man is brought face to face with who he really is and with the choice of seeking help or pursuing ruin.[3]

In attempting to bring reconciliation out of judgment (T13), God may find no more promising vehicle than martyrdom for dealing with the hard-hearted. What Pharisee would give the "holier than thou" posture a hearing? When indirect approaches fail, Jesus repeatedly confronts the Pharisees in the Gospels, but they will not listen. Finally, he bears the cost of divine judgment upon them by accepting martyrdom at their hands. In allowing himself to be crucified, he permits their sinful attitudes to be carried into action and externalized in his own flesh. Because he is a truly innocent victim, his body is the canvas on which the portrait of their sins can be most clearly drawn. In their great jealousy and mistrustfulness toward God, they had subjected his Messiah to a ritually accursed death. Unable to hear divine judgment through other media, there was at least a chance that they would be moved by the love of such a martyr and accept the painful revelation.

Nevertheless, the strategy is noncoercive, as it must be to accord with divine purposes (T7 and T8), and it does not always work. Our commuter chose to admit his need, seek help, and change his life-style; by contrast, the Pharisees and Sadducees who handed Jesus over to be crucified used their superior knowledge of the law and the prophets to assure themselves against the ambiguous evidence that Jesus could not be the Messiah: he was born at the wrong address and was following the wrong script, associating himself too closely with God on the one hand and with sinners on the other. They rationalized their action—"it was expedient that one man should die for the people" (John 18:14)—and then took his death by crucifixion as clinching evidence that Jesus was not the one. Surely it would be some kind of pragmatic contradiction for God's Messiah to be ritually unclean and hence unfit to enter God's presence!

The cross of Christ is the primary expression of God's goodness in a fallen world. First, it is the principal means of divine judgment, because Christ is the only truly innocent victim, the clearest picture of who his persecutors are. The Christian disciple is called to share his Master's redemptive work by taking up his cross daily (Luke 9:23–25). But the disciple's sins give his persecutors many handles for explaining away their behavior. Christians can be martyrs and fill up the sufferings of Christ (Col. 1:24) only to the extent that he cleanses them first. That is why continual repentance is not only necessary for the Christian's own reconciliation with Christ but also the best contribution he can make toward solving the problem of evil.

Second, the cross of Christ is the chief expression of God's love for the persecutor. If the persecutor is moved to repentance by the love of the martyr, it is the martyr whom he will thank and love. According to Christian belief, God was so eager to win our love that he became incarnate and volunteered for martyrdom himself (John 3:16–18).

Martyrdom as a vehicle of God's goodness to the martyr. For the potential religious martyr, the threat of martyrdom is a time of testing and judgment. It makes urgent the previously abstract dilemma of whether he loves God more than the temporal goods that are being extracted as a price. Especially if the price is high (but surprisingly even when the price is low), he will have to struggle with his own divided loyalties. Whatever the outcome, the martyr will have had to face a deeper truth about himself and his relations to God and temporal goods than ever he could in fair weather.

Nevertheless, the time of trial is also an opportunity for building a relationship of trust between the martyr and that to which he testifies.

Whether because we are fallen or by the nature of the case, trusting relationships have to be built up by a history of interactions. If the martyr's loyalty to God is tested, but after a struggle he holds onto his allegiance to God and God delivers him (in his own time and way), the relationship is strengthened and deepened. The Bible is full of such stories. God calls Abraham and makes him a promise to multiply his descendants. But accepting the promise involves trials: "Do you trust me enough to leave your homeland?" (Gen. 12). Abraham grows old: "Do you trust me enough to do this in your old age?" (Gen. 15, 18). When God provides Isaac, Abraham feels called by God to sacrifice him: "Do you trust me to keep my promise to you even though I am asking you to do something that would seem to make that impossible?" (Gen. 22). Abraham trusted God, and their relationship is celebrated as a hallmark by Jews and Christians to this day. Again, with the children of Israel God repeatedly asks: "Do you trust me enough to get you out of Egypt? . . . to give you food and water in the desert? . . . to bring you victorious into the land I have promised you?" The story records the tests they failed (see Ps. 106). Nevertheless, they looked back on the exodus experience as central to building their relationship with God. Despite their disobedience and his punishment of them, they were his and he was theirs in a way that would have been impossible had they stayed in Egypt with its fleshpots, leeks, and cucumbers.

Further, through his pioneering redemptive act (Heb. 2:10), God in Christ turns martyrdom into an opportunity for intimacy and identification with him. If one person loves another, he not only wants to know what it is like *for* that person, he wants to know what it is like to *be* that person. If the cross of Christ does not unveil the mystery of why God permits so much suffering in the first place (that is, the mystery of why [T5] is true), it does reveal his love in becoming incarnate to suffer with us. He is not content to be immutable and impassible, to watch his writhing creation with the eye of cool reason. He unites himself to a human consciousness and takes the suffering to himself. Thus, he knows from experience what it is like for pain to drive everything else from a finite consciousness and to press it to the limits of its endurance. When the martyr regains his wits enough to notice, he can recognize Christ crucified as providing the company that misery loves. Beyond that, the more the believer loves his Lord, the more he wants to know what it was like for him, what it is like to be him. The cross of Christ permits the martyr to find in his deepest agonies and future death a sure access to Christ's experience. No doubt it was this perspective that made the early church rejoice in being counted worthy to suffer for the Name (Acts 5:41). Moreover, as the believer enters into the love of Christ and shares his love for the world, he will also be able to appreciate his own suffering as a welcome key into the lives of others.

Thus God uses the harassments of his people by sinners both as instruments of divine judgment and as opportunities for relationship building, intimacy, and identification. The religious martyr who perseveres at the cost of his life wins his highest good. For in loving God more than any temporal good and trusting God to see to his good in the face of death, he is rightly related to God. He is also freed from the power of evil, because evil controls us only by bribing us with temporal goods we want more than we want to obey God. There is no remaining capital with which to "buy off" the martyr who is willing to pay the highest price for his loyalty. Finally, such a martyr has become heir to Christ's promise that "the pure in heart . . . shall see God" (Matt. 5:8).

THE MARTYRDOM MODEL AND ITS LIMITATIONS

I have proposed martyrdom as a paradigm of redemptive suffering. And the redemptive potential of many other cases that, strictly speaking, are not martyrdoms can be seen by extrapolation from the considerations of the preceding section. (*a*) For instance, there is suffering in which the victim not only will not but cannot obtain the benefits of relationship development. Some are too witless to have relationships that can profit and mature through such tests of loyalty. Some people are killed or severely harmed too quickly for such moral struggles to take place. At other times the victim is an unbeliever who has no explicit relationship with God to wrestle with. Even so, this type of suffering may provide the persecutor and onlooker with opportunities for reconciliation. (*b*) Alternatively, much suffering comes through natural causes—disease, natural disaster, or death—and so apparently involves no personal persecutor (other than God) who can be moved to repentance by the victim's plight. Here, nevertheless, the victim's faith in God may be tried and emerge stronger.

When all is said and done, however, not all suffering can be seen to have a redemptive value via this model. For example, what about cases at the intersection of types (*a*) and (*b*), where no one observes suffering naturally inflicted on the young or mentally deficient?

Further, some would argue that the cost/benefit ratio for such a "redemptive" strategy renders it morally unconscionable: the price for the victim is too high and the success rate is too low, both in relation to God's goals with the persecutor and in relation to his purposes with the martyr. Martyrdom often deepens the cruelty of the tormentor and tempts the victim beyond what he can bear (for example, in modern brainwashing). The possible conversion of the persecutor and onlooker and the possible enriching of the victim's faith are not, it is claimed, goods great enough or (often) probable enough to justify such losses on the victim's side. In short, it seems there would have to be more in it for those who suffer in order for such divine license to sinners and noninterference with nature to be morally justifiable. Yet, what further goods could there be?

THE VISION OF GOD AND THE PROBLEM OF EVIL

In my opinion, suffering cannot seem a wise, justifiable, or loving redemptive strategy except when embedded in the larger context of a Christian world view.

> *Intimacy with God as the incommensurate good.* Christians believe that
>
> (T17) The best good is intimacy with God and the worst evil is his absence.

Human beings were made to be happy enjoying a "face-to-face" intimacy with God. Genesis implies that Adam and Eve experienced it in the garden (Gen. 2–3) and it is that to which the saints look forward in heaven. By contrast, hell will be some sort of existence entirely bereft of God's presence. Unbelievers may find this latter point difficult to credit, since they deny the existence of God and yet find in the world as it is many goods to be enjoyed and satisfactions to be taken. A Christian will not be surprised at human pleasure in things here below, because he insists that the whole earth is full of the glory of God. When we appreciate a beautiful mountain scene or immerse ourselves in Mozart or are lost in a Cezanne painting, we are experiencing God shining through the mask of his creatures. When humans share deep, satisfying intimacy, part of the joy they taste is God in the middle of it. And this is so whether or not he is recognized there. Since ordinary human experience is thus "God-infested", we are in no position to imagine the horror of a creation in which he was entirely hidden from view. St. Paul speaks for Christians when he acknowledges that "now we see in a mirror dimly, but then face to face. Now I know in part; then I shall understand fully, even as I have been understood" (I Cor. 13:12). Nevertheless, for a few saints and perhaps on rare moments in the lives of most Christians, it seems as if God drops his mask to give the believer a more direct if still unclear view. Maybe it was out of such rapturous experience that St. Paul wrote with confidence that "the sufferings of this present time are not worth comparing with the glory that is to be revealed to us" (Rom. 8:18) and counted "everything as loss because of the surpassing worth of knowing Christ Jesus as my Lord" (Phil. 3:8). In other words,

> (T18) The good of "face-to-face" intimacy with God (the evil of his total absence) is simply incommensurate with any merely temporal evils (goods).

St. Stephen cannot help forgiving his murderers when he sees Jesus (Acts 7:56–8:1); the martyrs "have forgot their bitter story in the light of Jesus' glory."

Morally sufficient reasons and the incommensurate good. If a face-to-face vision of God is an incommensurate good for human beings, that will surely guarantee, for any cooperative person who has it, that the balance of goods over evils will be overwhelmingly favorable. Indeed, strictly speaking, there will be no *balance* to be struck. And no one who received such benefits would have any claim against God's justice or complaint against his love. God will have bestowed on those who see him "up close" as great a good as such a finite container can take. If so, it seems that God's justice and love toward creatures can be vindicated apart from any logically necessary connection between the evils suffered here below and some great enough good. In short, where 'excuse' is taken to mean 'morally sufficient reason',

> (T4) The fact that an evil was necessary for a greater good would provide an omniscient and omnipotent being with an excuse, only if the evil were a logically necessary prerequisite to or consequence of the good,

is false. This is not to say that, subjectively speaking, a person in the middle of terrible suffering might not complain, doubt, or rail against God. Nevertheless, retrospectively, from the viewpoint of the beatific vision, no one would be disposed to blame God for not eliminating or preventing various evils or to regard God's love as limited or insufficient. And St. Paul is able to adopt this position even in prospect (Rom. 8:18).

Divine wisdom, temporal evils, and the meaning of life. What about the interpretation of (T4) on which 'excuse' means 'prudential justification'? After all, if God wants the saints to enjoy the beatific vision (which ex hypothesi has no logically necessary connection with temporal evils), is not their sojourn through this vale of tears a waste (foolish management) for him as well as "a pain" for them? Could God really be serious about this life if his principal response to its ills were simply to obliterate it in a final cloud of glory? Would not such a scenario rob our earthly suffering of any meaning? Once again, does not the conjunction of (T4) and (T5) combine to show that God is foolish?

This objection assumes that the only way that an omnipotent, omniscient God's permission of evils could be rationalized is by a logically necessary connection between the actual evils and great enough goods. Traditionally, Christians have disagreed. After all, the rationality of a person's behavior is in part a function of his purposes and his consistency and efficiency in pursuing them. No doubt God could have "brought many sons to glory" (Heb. 2:10) without a detour through the temporal world. His not doing so is explained by his wider and over-arching purpose in creation, which is to raise the finite and temporal above itself into relationship with the infinite and eternal. His persistent commitment to relationships with created persons (T6 and T7) reaches a radical focus in the Incarnation. The evils of sin, sickness, and death were not part of God's original intentions but a by-product of his creation of free persons and/or a plurality of mutually interfering natures (for example, humans, birds, and mosquitoes), and the Christian does not know (T5) why he permits so many of them. (For Christians, the answers to Q2–Q4 remain a mystery.) Nevertheless, the Christian revelation does say that God incarnate faces evils in deadly earnest, ultimately on the cross. It would not be consistent for the God who is so committed to the temporal order as to enter it and suffer in it himself to snatch his people out of it in some gnostic ascent. Thus enduring temporal suffering, God's people share in the divine commitment to the temporal order.

Suffering as a vision of the inner life of God. For all that, I believe Christian mysticism would not hesitate to admit a logically necessary connection between temporal suffering and a very great good, on the ground that temporal suffering itself is a vision into the inner life of God. The relation is thus not one of logically necessary means or consequence but rather that of identity. Perhaps—pace impassibility theorists—the inner life of God itself includes deep agony as well as ecstatic joy. Alternatively, the divine consciousness may be something beyond both joy and sorrow. Just as for Otto human beings can only experience the divine presence now as *tremendum* (a deep dread and anxiety), now as *mysterium* (an attraction beyond words), so perhaps our experiences of deepest pain as much as those of boundless joy are themselves direct (if still imperfect) views into the inner life of God. Further, just as lesser joys and pleasures (for example, the beauty of nature, music, or painting) may be more obscure visions of the glory of God, so also lesser degrees of suffering.

Instructed by Christian mysticism, I suggest that a Christian might endorse not only

(T18) The good of face-to-face intimacy with God (the evil of his total absence) is simply incommensurate with any merely temporal evils (goods)

but also

(T19) Any vision into the inner life of God has a good aspect, this goodness at least partly a function of the clarity of the vision.

He need not go so far as to maintain that *any* vision of God, however obscure or painful, has an *incommensurately* good aspect. Nor need he deny that

(T20) Experiences of suffering have an evil aspect proportionate to the degree of suffering involved.

Nevertheless, he might be led to reason that the good aspect of an experience of deep suffering is great enough that, from the standpoint of the beatific vision, the victim would not wish the experience away from his life history, but would, on the contrary, count it as an extremely valuable part of his life.

Note that, unless the Christian maintains that any experience of suffering whatever has an incommensurately good aspect, he will not claim to rest his whole defense on this putative logically necessary connection of identity alone. Rather, his vindication of divine goodness might still rely heavily on the incommensurate goodness of the beatific vision itself. Nevertheless, Christians believe that God intends to be *good* to his people in calling them to share his dogged pursuit of relationships within the temporal order. The fact of (T19) might be seen to lend credibility to the wisdom in this divine purpose, by giving a depth of meaning to their temporal suffering independently of its *external* relations to *other* logically independent goods, whether eternal or temporal.

Objections. The danger in this Christian-mystical suggestion (as Ivan Karamazoff and J. S. Mill contended about other attempts to draw a logically necessary connection between temporal evils and great enough goods) is that it runs the risk of making suffering seem too good. To begin with, someone might object that if suffering were a vision of the inner life of God, there would be nothing wrong with our hurting people, and especially with our causing them great suffering. For such experiences are alleged in (T19) to have a good aspect in some direct proportion to their intensity. A Christian could reply, "Non sequitur." God is the one who is responsible for ensuring that each person's life is, with that person's cooperation, a great good to him on the whole. Christians believe that God calls his people to share in his work. But God is the one who defines the finite person's responsibility for another's good. Christians could agree with secular moralists that sometimes one person has an obligation or at least a right to cause another person to suffer for his own good—for example, by spanking the two-year old that runs into the street or by speaking a painful word of correction. But Christian mysticism would neither compel nor countenance this suggestion that any created person has a vocation to sadism (or to masochism, either).

Again, someone might charge, on this view it would be fully compatible with divine goodness if human beings suffered eternally in hell forever. Indeed, insofar as suffering lasted forever, it would constitute for the damned soul an infinite good.

A twofold reply is possible: First of all, given (T11) and (T12), Christians do not believe that God would be wrong to consign sinners to eternal punishment. Second, it is arguable whether, given (T18), it is accurate to conceive of hell as the continuance of temporal evils, however sinister, rather than as the absence of God. As noted above, I doubt that we have any notion of how devastating that would be, although we might speculate with C. S. Lewis that the absence of God would bring a total disintegration of created personality.[4] In any event, hell considered as everlasting temporal punishment is not the "good" Christians believe God to have in mind for his people. For one thing, not every good is fitting for every sort of creature. As Aristotle observed in rejecting Platonic forms long ago, the putative metaphysical good of immutability is logically (metaphysically) ruinous to plant and animal natures. Similary, some adult freedoms and pleasures are harmful for children. Perhaps omnipotence would be inappropriate for created persons of limited wisdom and good will. And even if the everlasting temporal suffering of a created person would have a good aspect, and indeed accumulate toward an infinite sum, it is a good that would break down and destroy the creature (in something of the way the tortures of brainwashing do). A loving God would not, any more than a loving parent, want to give his children goods that would naturally tend to destroy them.

A more profound answer to this second objection reverts to (T7) and the nature of the relationships for which God created us, namely, relationships of intimate sharing and loving self-giving. He wants us to share not merely his agony (or the aspect we experience in this life as agony) but also his joy. He wants us to enjoy our relationship with him and wants to make us happy in it. Needless to say, the experience of everlasting temporal torment does not "fill the bill"; for that we need a more balanced view of God.

CONCLUSION

Christians will not want to depreciate the awfulness (awefulness) of suffering in this life, by the innocent and the guilty, by the intelligent and the witless alike. They will not appear beside racks of torture to proclaim that it does not really matter or to exhort the victim to gratitude. Nevertheless, they see in the cross of Christ a revelation of God's righteous love and a paradigm of his redemptive use of suffering. Christian mysticism invites the believer to hold that a perfectly good God further sanctifies our moments of deepest distress so that retrospectively, from the vantage point of the beatific vision, the one who suffered will not wish them away from his life history—and this, not because he sees them as the source of some other resultant good, but inasmuch as he will recognize them as times of sure identification with and vision into the inner life of his creator.

For Christians as for others in this life, the fact of evil is a mystery. The answer is a more wonderful mystery—God himself.

NOTES

I owe whatever is right in this paper to those who, at various times in my life, have tried to teach me how to follow Christ—most recently, A. Orley Swartzentruber, rector of All Saints' Episcopal Church, Princeton, New Jersey; Allan Wolter, OFM, of Catholic University of America; James Loder of Princeton Theological Seminary; Jon Olson of Bloy House and Christ Church, Ontario, California; and many friends at the Community of Jesus in Orleans, Massachusetts. The sharp objections and subtle reflections of my colleague Roger Albritton and of my critics, especially David A. Conway of the University of Missouri, St. Louis, have—at least at times—restrained me from claiming too much. Finally, I am indebted to my husband, Robert Adams, who, by living with me, practices what I preach! The errors are due to my own sinful confusion.

1. Alvin Plantinga. *God, Freedom and Evil* (New York: Harper and Row, 1974), pp. 49–64.

2. Ibid., p. 64.

3. I owe this example to James Loder's lectures.

4. C. S. Lewis, *The Problem of Pain* (New York: Macmillan, 1962), pp. 125–26.

PART THREE

Traditions in Theodicy

Augustinian Theodicy
Irenaean Theodicy
Process Theodicy

A Good Creation's Capacity for Evil

ST. AUGUSTINE

BK XI, CHAP. 17. *That the flaw of wickedness is not nature, but contrary to nature, and has its origin, not in the Creator, but in the will*

It is with reference to the nature, then, and not to the wickedness of the devil, that we are to understand these words, "This is the beginning of God's handiwork";[1] for, without doubt, wickedness can be a flaw or vice only where the nature previously was not vitiated. Vice, too, is so contrary to nature, that it cannot but damage it. And therefore departure from God would be no vice, unless in a nature whose property it was to abide with God. So that even the wicked will is a strong proof of the goodness of the nature. But God, as He is the supremely good Creator of good natures, so is He of evil wills the most just Ruler; so that, while they make an ill use of good natures, He makes a good use even of evil wills. Accordingly, He caused the devil (good by God's creation, wicked by his own will) to be cast down from his high position and to become the mockery of His angels—that is, He caused his temptations to benefit those whom he wishes to injure by them. And because God, when He created him, was certainly not ignorant of his future malignity, and foresaw the good which He Himself would bring out of his evil, therefore says the psalm, "This leviathan whom Thou has made to be a sport therein,"[2] that we may see that, even while God in His goodness created him good, He yet had already foreseen and arranged how He would make use of him when he became wicked.

From *City of God*, Book XI, chaps. 17, 18, 21, 22 and Book XII, chap. 3. Translated by Marcus Dods.

BK XI, CHAP. 18. *Of the beauty of the universe, which becomes, by God's ordinance, more brilliant by the opposition of contraries*

For God would never have created any, I do not say angel, but even man, whose future wickedness He foreknew, unless He had equally known to what uses in behalf of the good He could turn him, thus embellishing the course of the ages, as it were an exquisite poem set off with antitheses. For what are called antitheses are among the most elegant of the ornaments of speech. They might be called in Latin "oppositions," or, to speak more accurately, "contra-positions"; but this word is not in common use among us, though the Latin, and indeed the languages of all nations, avail themselves of the same ornaments of style. In the Second Epistle to the Corinthians the Apostle Paul also makes a graceful use of antithesis, in that place where he says, "By the armour of righteousness on the right hand and on the left, by honour and dishonour, by evil report and good report: as deceivers, and yet true; as unknown, and yet well known; as dying, and, behold, we live; as chastened, and not killed; as sorrowful, yet always rejoicing; as poor, yet making many rich; as having nothing, and yet possessing all things."[3] As, then, these oppositions of contraries lend beauty to the language, so the beauty of the course of this world is achieved by the opposition of contraries, arranged, as it were, by an eloquence not of words, but of things. This is quite plainly stated in the Book of Ecclesiasticus, in this way: "Good is set against evil, and life against death: so is the sinner against the godly. So look upon all the works of the Most High, and these are two and two, one against another."[4]

BK XI, CHAP. 21. *Of God's eternal and unchangeable knowledge and will, whereby all he has made pleased him in the eternal design as well as in the actual results*

For what else is to be understood by that invariable refrain, "And God saw that it was good," than the approval of the work in its design, which is the wisdom of God? For certainly God did not in the actual achievement of the work first learn that it was good, but, on the contrary, nothing would have been made had it not been first known by Him. While, therefore, He sees that that is good which, had He not seen it before it was made, would never have been made, it is plain that He is not discovering, but teaching that it is good. Plato, indeed, was bold enough to say that, when the universe was completed, God was, as it were, elated with joy.[5] And Plato was not so foolish as to mean by this that God was rendered more blessed by the novelty of His creation; but he wished thus to indicate that the work now completed met with its Maker's approval, as it had while yet in design. It is not as if the knowledge of God were of various kinds, knowing in different ways things which as yet are not, things which are, and things which have been. For not in our fashion does He look forward to what is future, nor at what is present, nor back upon what is past; but in a manner quite different and far and profoundly remote from our way of thinking. For He does not pass from this to that by transition of thought, but beholds all things with absolute unchangeableness; so that of those things which emerge in time, the future, indeed, are not yet, and the present are now, and the past no longer are; but all of these are by Him comprehended in His stable and eternal presence. Neither does He see in one fashion by the eye, in another by the mind, for He is not composed of mind and body; nor does His present knowledge differ from that which it ever was or shall be, for those variations of time, past, present, and future, though they alter our knowledge, do not affect His, "with whom there is no variableness, neither shadow of turning."[6] Neither is there any growth from thought to thought in the conceptions of Him in Whose spiritual vision all things which He knows are at once embraced. For as without any movement that time can measure, He Himself moves all temporal things, so He knows all times with a knowledge that time cannot measure. And therefore He saw that what He had made was good, when He saw that it was good to make it. And when He saw it made, He had not on that account a twofold nor any way increased knowledge of it; as if He had less knowledge before He made what He saw. For certainly He would not be the perfect worker He is, unless His knowledge were so perfect as to receive no addition from His finished works. Wherefore, if the only object had been to inform us who made the light, it had been enough to say, "God made the light"; and if further information regarding the means by which it was made had been intended, it would have sufficed to say, "And God said, Let there be light, and there was light," that we might know not only that God had made the world, but also that He had made it by the word. But because it was right that three leading truths regarding the creature be intimated to us, viz., who made it, by what means, and why, it is written, "God said, Let there be light, and there was light. And God saw the light that it was good." If, then, we ask who made it, it was "God." If, by what means, He said, "Let it be," and it was. If we ask, why He made it, "it was good." Neither is there any author more excellent than God, nor any skill more efficacious than the word of God, nor any cause better than that good might be created by the good God. This also Plato has assigned as the most sufficient reason for the creation of the world, that good works might be made by a good God;[7]

whether he read this passage, or, perhaps, was informed of these things by those who had read them, or, by his quick-sighted genius, penetrated to things spiritual and invisible through the things that are created, or was instructed regarding them by those who had discerned them.

BK XI, CHAP. 22. *Of those who do not approve of certain things which are a part of this good creation of a good Creator, and who think that there is some natural evil*

This cause, however, of a good creation, namely, the goodness of God—this cause, I say, so just and fit, which, when piously and carefully weighed, terminates all the controversies of those who inquire into the origin of the world, has not been recognized by some heretics,[8] because there are, forsooth, many things, such as fire, frost, wild beasts, and so forth, which do not suit but injure this thin-blooded and frail mortality of our flesh, which is at present under just punishment. They do not consider how admirable these things are in their own places, how excellent in their own natures, how beautifully adjusted to the rest of creation, and how much grace they contribute to the universe by their own contributions as to a commonwealth; and how serviceable they are even to ourselves, if we use them with a knowledge of their fit adaptations—so that even poisons, which are destructive when used injudiciously, become wholesome and medicinal when used in conformity with their qualities and design; just as, on the other hand, those things which give us pleasure, such as food, drink, and the light of the sun, are found to be hurtful when immoderately or unseasonably used. And thus divine providence admonishes us not foolishly to vituperate things, but to investigate their utility with care; and, where our mental capacity or infirmity is at fault, to believe that there is a utility, though hidden, as we have experienced that there were other things which we all but failed to discover. For this concealment of the use of things is itself either an exercise of our humility or a leveling of our pride; for no nature at all is evil, and this is a name for nothing but the want of good. But from things earthly to things heavenly, from the visible to the invisible, there are some things better than others; and for this purpose are they unequal, in order that they might all exist. Now God is in such sort a great worker in great things, that He is not less in little things—for these little things are to be measured not by their own greatness (which does not exist), but by the wisdom of their Designer; as, in the visible appearance of a man, if one eyebrow be shaved off, how nearly nothing is taken from the body, but how much from the beauty!—

for that is not constituted by bulk, but by the proportion and arrangement of the members. But we do not greatly wonder that persons, who
suppose that some evil nature has been generated and propagated by a
kind of opposing principle proper to it, refuse to admit that the cause of
the creation was this, that the good God produced a good creation. For
they believe that He was driven to this enterprise of creation by the urgent
necessity of repulsing the evil that warred against Him, and that He
mixed His good nature with the evil for the sake of restraining and con-
quering it; and that this nature of His, being thus shamefully polluted
and most cruelly oppressed and held captive, He labours to cleanse and
deliver it, and with all His pains does not wholly succeed; but such part
of it as could not be cleansed from that defilement is to serve as a prison
and chain of the conquered and incarcerated enemy. The Manichaeans
would not drivel, or rather, rave in such a style as this, if they believed the
nature of God to be, as it is, unchangeable and absolutely incorruptible,
and subject to no injury; and if, moreover, they held in Christian sobriety
that the soul which has shown itself capable of being altered for the worse
by its own will, and of being corrupted by sin, and so, of being deprived
of the light of eternal truth—that this soul, I say, is not a part of God, nor
of the same nature as God, but is created by Him, and is far different from
its Creator.

BK XII, CHAP. 3. *That the enemies of God are so, not by nature, but by will,
which, as it injures them, injures a good nature; for if vice does not injure, it is
not vice*

In Scripture they are called God's enemies who oppose His rule, not
by nature, but by vice; having no power to hurt Him, but only themselves. For they are His enemies, not through their power to hurt, but by
their will to oppose Him. For God is unchangeable, and wholly proof
against injury. Therefore the vice which makes those who are called His
enemies resist Him, is an evil not to God, but to themselves. And to them
it is an evil, solely because it corrupts the good of their nature. It is not
nature, therefore, but vice, which is contrary to God. For that which is
evil is contrary to the good. And who will deny that God is the supreme
good? Vice, therefore, is contrary to God, as evil to good. Further, the
nature it vitiates is a good, and therefore to this good also it is contrary.
But while it is contrary to God only as evil to good, it is contrary to
the nature it vitiates, both as evil and as hurtful. For to God no evils are
hurtful; but only to natures mutable and corruptible, though, by the

testimony of the vices themselves, originally good. For were they not good, vices could not hurt them. For how do they hurt them but by depriving them of integrity, beauty, welfare, virtue, and, in short, whatever natural good vice is wont to diminish or destroy? But if there be no good to take away, then no injury can be done, and consequently there can be no vice. For it is impossible that there should be a harmless vice. Whence we gather, that though vice cannot injure the unchangeable good, it can injure nothing but good; because it does not exist where it does not injure. This, then, may be thus formulated: Vice cannot be in the highest good, and cannot be but in some good. Things solely good, therefore, can in some circumstances exist; things solely evil, never; for even those natures which are vitiated by an evil will, so far indeed as they are vitiated, are evil, but in so far as they are natures they are good. And when a vitiated nature is punished, besides the good it has in being a nature, it has this also, that it is not unpunished.[9] For this is just, and certainly everything just is a good. For no one is punished for natural, but for voluntary vices. For even the vice which by the force of habit and long continuance has become a second nature, had its origin in the will. For at present we are speaking of the vices of nature, which has a mental capacity for that enlightenment which discriminates between what is just and what is unjust.

NOTES

1. Job 40:14
2. Psalms 104:26
3. II Corinthians 6:7–10
4. Ecclesiastes 33:15
5. *Timaeus* 37
6. James 1:17
7. *Timaeus* 29
8. The Manichaeans
9. Compare Plato, *Gorgias*

Augustine and the Denial of Genuine Evil

DAVID RAY GRIFFIN

Augustine repeatedly affirmed God's omnipotence and goodness. And he was acutely aware of the problem of evil that is occasioned by this combination of divine attributes and the apparent existence of evil. In his early Christian writings against the Manichaeans, he stressed that God created all natures, and that all natures are *good,* insofar as they are—i.e., whatever is, is good (e.g., C VII. 18).[1] There is no nature that is evil, even the devil's. Evil is due to will, not to nature (*CG* XII. 3). All evil can be accounted for in terms of the misuse of free will (*FW* III. 17, 48). Hence, although God is the creator of all natures, God is absolved from the responsibility for evil.

In his later writings Augustine retracted some of his statements about free will that were used by the Pelagians. And he emphasized predestination much more, insisting that predestination is not based upon God's prevision of faith and good works, but that faith and good works are the result of grace which follows from eternal predestination to salvation. But he never explicitly gave up the free-will defense of God's goodness. He continued to maintain that evil ultimately comes from the free choice of creatures, so that God is not responsible for sin and hence is justified in inflicting evil as a punishment for sin. In this chapter, I will examine whether the tracing of evil to creaturely free will is compatible with Augustine's doctrine of God's power, and hence whether his defense of God's goodness is tenable.

From *God, Power, and Evil: A Process Theodicy* (Philadelphia: Westminster, 1976), 55–71. Rpt. University Press of America, forthcoming. Used by permission of author and publisher.

197

THE SUPERNATURALISTIC FRAMEWORK
OF AUGUSTINE'S THEODICY

In regard to the question as to why good people suffer and seem to get the same rewards and punishments in this life as sinful people, Augustine states flatly that good and evil persons are treated the same way by God in regard to material goods. There are several reasons for this evenhandedness. It will encourage us not to covet material goods and not to cultivate religion for rewards in this life. (*CG* I. 8; XXII. 22). It will help us realize that there are future rewards and penalties as well as present ones (*CG* I. 8). Whereas suffering is punishment for bad persons, it helps good ones prove their perfections or correct their imperfections (*CG* I. 29). For example, when virgins are raped this helps destroy their pride, actual or potential (*CG* I. 28). Furthermore, the good people in a community, as well as the bad, love this present life, and thus deserve punishment (*CG* I. 9). And in losing temporal goods, the good really lose nothing important, for they do not thereby lose their faith and their godliness (*CG* I. 10 and 28). God even permits baptized infants, who are unsurpassed in innocence, to be tormented, in order to teach us to bewail the calamities of this life and desire the life to come (*CG* XXII. 22). However, God does sometimes interfere, delivering present rewards and punishments, so that we will believe in his providence (*CG* I. 8).

From these statements one can see that Augustine's view of the meaning and end of life is almost totally supernatural, so that the question of the balance of goods and evils that we experience in this life is not really very important. They can all be justified in terms of their relation to the supernatural end of life. However, although he offers many possible justifications for the way things happen, he admits that God's judgments are finally unsearchable. But, he says, speaking of the day of judgment,

> we shall then recognize the justice of all God's judgments . . . and . . . we shall also recognize with what justice so many, or almost all, the just judgments of God in the present life defy the scrutiny of human sense or insight, though in this matter it is not concealed from pious minds that what is concealed is just. (*CG* XX. 2)

Faced with this answer to the question as to why evil has been caused or allowed by an omnipotent God, many people would want to stand with Ivan in the chapter entitled "Rebellion" in Dostoevsky's *The Brothers Karamazov*. Ivan admits that at the end of the world a "higher harmony" may be realized, and that if he is there, he may then cry aloud with the rest, "Thou art just, O Lord, for Thy ways are revealed." But, both in spite of this possibility and because of it, he wants to get his protest on the record in advance. He announces that he hopes he will not join that chorus, for he cannot accept the idea that any "higher harmony" could justify the evils that were allegedly necessary for this harmony, such as the suffering of innocent children.

However, whether or not we can share Augustine's faith that it will be revealed to us some day that the distribution of good and evil in this life reflects wholly just judgments on God's part, this does provide a possible answer to the problem of evil. That is, although one might not believe it, or might rebel against it, there is nothing necessarily self-contradictory in the answer. In a context where belief in an omnipotent God and a future life is already accepted on other grounds, it is possible consistently to maintain that all presently unanswerable questions as to why God caused or at least permitted certain things will be answered in and by this future life. Later I will argue that today one cannot simply assume the existence of an omnipotent God and a future life when dealing with the problem of evil. But it would be anachronistic to criticize Augustine on these grounds.

Accordingly, this examination of Augustine's theodicy must be primarily concerned with the problem of evil as it emerged in terms of his own central ideas. This means dealing with his attempt or reconcile the doctrine of supernatural rewards and punishments for this life with the assertion of God's absolute goodness. Whereas this discussion will not directly be of much interest to those who do not believe in a future life (especially one understood in terms of rewards and punishments), or to those who at least do not believe that a future state should be the primary focus of the religious life, this examination of Augustine's position will be indirectly relevant to the possibility of "justifying God's ways to humanity" simply in terms of the good and evil in our present existence. For, this discussion will be relevant to the possibility of reconciling the belief in a good and omnipotent God with the reality of any type of genuine evil whatsoever.

THE FREE-WILL DEFENSE

One absolutely clear teaching of Augustine regarding the future life is that it will not be a pleasant experience for all persons. In fact, a majority will be condemned to eternal punishment (CG XXI. 12; E XXIV. 97). And equally clear, at least in his later writings, is the teaching that the question as to who will be saved is settled entirely by God (GFW XLV; PS XI,

XIX, XXXIV). In regard to how it can be just of God unilaterally to elect some for salvation and to condemn the rest to punishment apart from any question of merit, Augustine has a two-part response: On the one hand, in reference to the question as to why God chooses the particular persons chosen for salvation, Augustine refers to Paul's statement in Rom. 9:20 about the potter and the clay, saying that this statement reminds us to consider the limits of our capacities (*E* XXV. 99; *PS* XVI). The other half of Augustine's answer deals with the more general question of the justice of saving some and not the rest. The answer to this is that all people have freely sinned, and therefore all people deserve punishment (*CG* XII. 8). God would be perfectly just if all of them were condemned to eternal punishment. The fact that God graciously chooses to save some simply shows that God is merciful as well as just (*E* XXV. 99; *PS* XVI).

Augustine's entire theodicy hinges on this argument. If he cannot consistently claim that all people (except the God-man, of course) deserve eternal punishment, his theodicy fails.

The context for this argument is his doctrine of original sin and its effects. The first people had the possibility of not sinning (*posse non peccare*) and yet sinned. As they were our parents, we all sinned "in" them. Because of this, we do not have the possibility of not sinning (*non posse non peccare*). We can do no good unless we are freed from our bondage to sin by God's grace, which returns us to Adam's state of having the ability not to sin. (The third possible state, that of not having the ability to sin [*non posse peccare*], will characterize those who attain eternal life.)

There are three crucial aspects of Augustine's argument that all people deserve eternal punishment. First, he must argue that the punishment is just in the sense of being proportional to the crime. And this he does, arguing that Adam's sin was very heinous, partly because it was such an easy sin to avoid (*CG* XIV. 12). Second, he must argue for the intelligibility of the idea that the rest of humanity sinned "in" Adam, and hence is responsible for this first sin. Both of these arguments have seemed weak to many. But the debate about these issues does not have relevance to the more general problem of reconciling omnipotent goodness and genuine evil. Hence I will not rehearse this debate, but will move to the third crucial step in the argument, the idea that we could be said to have sinned freely. In order to broaden the issue, so that the rather archaic and questionable idea of humanity's sinning in Adam can be ignored, I will examine the question as to whether anyone could sin freely in the Augustinian universe, be they angels, humans before the fall, humans after the fall but before receiving grace, or humans after grace.

Augustine certainly means to affirm the reality of free choice. He sees that the whole idea of precepts would be nonsensical unless we had freedom to choose to obey them (*GFW* II, IV), and that unless sin is voluntary, it would not be sin (*TR* XIV. 27). Furthermore, he sees that unless there is volition that does not come from God, God would be the author of sin (*SL* LIV). For Augustine, the evil will is the one thing in the universe that God did not create (*CG* V. 8, 10). The devil's wicked will came from the devil himself, not from God (*NOG* 32). And the original sin of humanity resulted from human free will (*NAG* III).

It cannot be overstressed how central to Augustine's thought is this affirmation of free will. In his early writings he was especially concerned with Manichaeanism, and stressed that all beings are created by a good God and are therefore good. Evil is not to be explained on the basis of any being whose nature is bad, whether this being be created or uncreated. In order to account for evil, then, Augustine distinguished between the created "nature," which all beings have, and the "will," which free beings have. The will as such is also created. But God does not create its evil volitions; in fact, these evil volitions have no efficient cause at all, but only a "deficient" cause (*CG* XII. 6, 7).

Only upon this basis could Augustine simultaneously reject Manichaean dualism and yet avoid suggesting that his own monotheistic God was responsible for the world's evil. He saw evil willing as the source of all evil; he said that there is no evil other than sin and its punishment (*TR* XII. 23).

But is this affirmation of free choice on the part of some of God's creatures compatible with Augustine's doctrine of God? *Prima facie* it seems incompatible with his doctrine that God is both immutable and omniscient. And it seems incompatible with his doctrine of God's omnipotence. I will first examine the compatibility of creaturely free will with an immutably omniscient God and then turn to the problem raised by Augustine's doctrine of omnipotence.

FREE WILL AND DIVINE OMNISCIENCE

By itself the doctrine of an immutable being would not be prejudicial to the freedom of worldly beings, if this immutable being did not know the world, as was the case with Aristotle's God. And by itself, the doctrine of an omniscient being would not be prejudicial to worldly free choice, since this doctrine could simply mean that this being knows all things that are knowable, and one could maintain that a free choice is not knowable until after it is made. In other words, the omniscient being would not know the future (except insofar as some more or less abstract characteristics of the future are already settled in the present). But Augustine holds that God is both omniscient and immutable; and he explicitly points out that this entails that God is not affected by anything, so that there can be no increase in the content of the divine knowledge (*CG* XII. 17; XI. 21). Accordingly, omniscience includes prescience. In fact, Augustine takes this characteristic to belong to the defining essence of deity, saying that "one who is not prescient of all future things is not God" (*CG* V. 9). This makes the reality of free choice on the part of the creatures quite dubious.

Augustine argues that God's prescience of all things does not mean that our wills are not genuine causes, since God, in foreknowing all things, foreknows the causes of all things. Human wills, which are genuine causes of human actions, are included in that order of causes which God foreknows (*CG* V. 9). And in foreknowing what will be in the power of our wills, God does not foreknow simply nothing (*CG* V. 10).

This reconciliation seems purely verbal. The meaning of the "freedom" that is thereby allowed to us is not such as to make us responsible in the sense that Augustine's theodicy requires. The word "freedom" can be defined in many ways, of course, and different meanings can be relevant in different contexts. But when one is asking whether an action is "free" in a context in which the issue is whether the agent could justifiably be held responsible in the sense of being liable to incur blame, one must be asking whether the agent *could have done otherwise*. Or, since some people (such as Augustine) distinguish between willing and doing, one could be asking whether a person's *willing* is blameworthy. One would then have to be asking whether the individual could have willed something different from what he in fact did will.

Free choice in this sense is not compatible with an omniscient being who knows the details of what is still the future for us. If this being knows infallibly that next year I will do A, instead of B or C, then it is necessary that I will do A. It may seem to me then as if I make a real choice among genuine alternatives, but this will be illusory. I really could not do otherwise. If I were to do otherwise, God's immutable, infallible knowledge would be in error, and this is impossible. So in what meaningful sense will I be responsible for that choice? The response often made here is that, although I will not have been able to choose B or C, I will choose A because I *want* to choose A. And if A is a wicked deed, then I am blameworthy for wanting to do something wicked. But here we only need to focus on willing or wanting instead of doing, or to see willing as a type of doing. In any case, we can ask whether I shall be able at that future moment to *will* to do either B or C (even though I shall actually have to *do* A). Here the answer must be: If God knows that I shall will to do A, then I shall necessarily will to do A. And how can I be blameworthy for willing something when there was absolutely no possibility that I could have willed otherwise? If at this point the response is made that I shall necessarily will A at that future moment because of my character, and that I am in part responsible for forming my own character, the same objection must be stated. That is, to the extent that we form our own characters we do this by the choices we make, especially those kinds which we reinforce by frequent repetition. But if there is a being who eternally knows all things, then every single "choice" in my life prior to wicked deed A and the desire to do it is as devoid of real alternatives as the wicked deed A itself. Hence I am not responsible for my character any more than I will be for that particular decision.

If this analysis is correct, then an immutably omniscient God (who would certainly know that it is correct) would be unjustified in condemning anyone to punishment for sinning. For, from the moment of conception, a person's life could not have been one iota different from its actual course. So the person exercises no freedom in any sense that would justify blame. This conclusion follows merely from the definition of God as an omniscient being who is also immutable in all respects.

FREE WILL AND DIVINE OMNIPOTENCE

When Augustine's notion of omnipotence is brought into focus, the self-contradictory character of his reconciliation of God's goodness with worldly evil becomes even more apparent. The previous discussion about omniscience was based upon allowing tentative validity to Augustine's claim that God could foreknow some things, i.e., evil wills, without causing them (*PS* XIX). But now it will become apparent that this claim cannot be maintained.

For Augustine, omnipotence belongs to the defining essence of deity as fully as does immutable omniscience. He stresses that the first sentence of the creed is a confession of faith in God the Father Almighty. Then he adds: "For he is called Almighty for no other reason than that he can do whatsoever he willeth and because the efficacy of his omnipotent will is not impeded by the will of any creature." To deny this, he says, would be to undermine our confession of faith (*E* XIV. 96). Elsewhere he says that "he who denies that all things, which either angels or men can give us, are in the hand of the one Almighty, is a madman" (*CG* X. 14).

However, one meaning of "omnipotence" that might be suggested by these statements (that all things are in God's hands and that nothing can impede the divine will) is not the full Augustinian meaning. That is, these statements could be compatible with the following sketch of the world, which Augustine sometimes suggests: God created the world, willing that everything be good. God included beings with free will in this good creation. Some of these beings (some of the angels, and all of the humans, except the God-man) use their free will to sin, which means willing in a way that is contrary to God's will (*E* XXVI. 100). Of course, God foresees this sin, and builds appropriate responses to it into the divine eternal plan. On the one hand, God includes a plan of mercy:

> But since he did foreknow that man would make bad use of his free will—that is, that he would sin—God prearranged his own purpose so that he could do good to man, even in man's doing evil, and so that the good will of the Omnipotent should be nullified by the bad will of men, but should nonetheless be fulfilled. (*E* XXVIII. 104)

On the other hand, God includes punishments for the sin:

> Unbelievers indeed do contrary to the will of God when they do not believe His gospel; nevertheless they do not therefore overcome His will. . . . God's will is forever invincible; but it would be vanquished, unless it devised what to do with such as despised it, or if these despisers could in any way escape from the retribution which He has appointed for such as they. (*SL* LVIII)

These passages suggest that God's ideal plan, in which there would be no evil, is upset by the free will of creatures who go contrary to the divine will, and that God, foreseeing this misuse of free will, forms the plan so as to bring good out of evil. On the one hand, to some of the sinful creatures God returns good for evil, thereby manifesting the divine mercy, which is a good thing to do. On the other hand, God plans a punishment for the rest of the sinful creatures, thereby manifesting the divine justice, which is also a good thing to do.

Essential to this account is the idea that creatures can really will and act contrary to the divine will. That idea is suggested in each of the preceding quotations as well as in the following one: "But, however strong the wills either of angels or of men, whether good or evil, whether they will what God willeth or will something else, the will of the Omnipotent is always undefeated" (*E* XXVI. 102). And Augustine defines humanity's sin as doing what it willed, not what God had willed (*E* XXVI. 100). God's will is always undefeated because deity can arrange things in such a way that its will concerning the creatures will be done whether the creatures act according to it or contrary to it (*E* XXVI 100; XXVII. 107).

However, although this is the sense that Augustine often gives to the notion that creatures cannot impede the divine will, and although this is the sense which he must suggest if his statement that creatures are justifiably punished for their actions is to have some plausibility, this is not the stronger sense which he gives to the notion elsewhere, and which his doctrine of God requires. According to this stronger sense, *nothing* happens other than what God wills to happen. For example, Augustine stresses "how certain, immutable, and effectual is the will of God," and that God "willeth nothing he cannot do." In regard to the Psalm which states that God has done all things that he would (composed inexactly from Ps. 115:3 and 135:6), Augustine says:

> This obviously is not true, if there is anything that he willed to do and did not do, or, what were worse, if he did not do something because man's will prevented him, the Omnipotent, from doing what he willed. Nothing, therefore, happens unless the Omnipotent wills it to happen. He either allows it to happen or he actually causes it to happen. (*E* XXIV. 95)

And, whether God is said to "cause" something or merely to "allow" it, if it happens this is because God wills it: "For it would not be done without his allowing it—and surely his permission is not unwilling but willing" (*E* XXVI. 100).

Not leaving any ambiguity, Augustine insists that we are not on any account "to underrate the fully omnipotent will of God." For, "if he willeth, then what he willeth must necessarily be." And, after offering his interpretation of a Scriptural passage that seems to cast doubt on this view, Augustine says: "We could interpret it in any other fashion, as long as we are not compelled to believe that the Omnipotent hath willed anything to be done which was not done." He then adds: "There must be no equivocation on this point" (*E* XXVII. 103). (The Scriptural passage in question is I Tim. 2:4, which states that God "desires all men to be saved." Augustine's interpretation of this is that it does not really mean "all men" but "all kinds of men," i.e., some from every class of human beings, e.g., rich and poor, rulers and subjects, etc.)

This would seem to imply that even sinful choices are willed by God. And Augustine does not flinch from making this application. Whereas he had insisted that God does not *create* evil wills, he does say that God *rules* them (*CG* XI. 17). He states that those wills "which follow the world are so entirely at the disposal of God, that He turns them whithersoever He wills, and whensoever He wills" (*GFW* XLI). God "does in the hearts of even wicked men whatsoever He wills" (*GFW* XLII).

Some passages suggest that the wicked willing is done independently by the creatures, and that God only then uses this self-determined wicked will. For example, Augustine says:

> It is not unjust that the wicked should receive power to harm so that the patience of the good should be proved and the iniquity of the bad should be punished. By the power given to the devil Job was proved that his justice might be made apparent; Peter was tempted so that he might not think too highly of himself. . . . God himself . . . did all things justly by the power he gave to the devil. Not for performing these just actions, but for the wicked will to do hurt, which came from the devil himself, will he in the end be awarded punishment. (*NOG* 32)

However, this element of autonomy cannot be granted. The previous statements about omnipotence do not allow it. Also Augustine elsewhere says explicitly that even the willing is done by God: "The Almighty sets in motion even in the innermost hearts of men the movement of their will, so that He does through their agency whatsoever He wishes to perform through them" (*GFW* XLII). And further: "God works in the hearts of men to incline their wills whithersoever He wills, whether to good deeds according to His mercy, or to evil after their own deserts" (*GFW* XLIII).

Augustine recognizes, of course, that this idea that sinning is willed by God and thereby necessitated seems to negate the creatures' freedom and responsibility, and hence to throw God's justice for punishing them into question. Accordingly, he makes a distinction between two kinds of sin. Some sins are penalties for previous sin. God causes these "by a counsel most secret to Himself, indeed, but beyond all doubt most righteous" (*GFW* XLI). It is righteous because these sins that are caused by God are brought about in us because of previous sin on our part:

> [God's judgment is] sometimes manifest, sometimes secret, but always righteous. This ought to be the fixed and immovable conviction of your heart, that there is no unrighteousness with God. Therefore, whenever you read in the Scriptures of Truth, that men are led aside, or that their hearts are blunted and hardened by God, never doubt that some ill deserts of their own have first occurred, so that they justly suffer these things. (*GFW* XLIII)

This first wickedness on their part "was not made by Him, but was either derived originally from Adam, or increased by their own will" (*ibid.*).

But can this be? Can there have been an original sin, by the wicked angels, the first humans, and/or by each human being, i.e., some act or even desire that was contrary to the will of God? Not in light of what has already been reviewed about the divine omnipotence. Nothing happens but what God wills to happen; and what God wills necessarily happens. So there is no way to distinguish between those sins which Augustine admits that God causes and those which he sometimes implies that God does not cause.

Augustine's way of overcoming the apparent contradiction—that we are responsible for evil willing and acting even though God causes them—is simply to *assert* that God's causation does not take away our free agency. For example, he says that faith and works are commanded and also shown to be God's gifts to us so that "we may understand both that we do them, and that God makes us to do them" (*PS* XXII). And in regard to the Biblical statement that God "hardened" Pharaoh's heart and then punished him, Augustine says: "Thus it was that both God hardened him by His just judgment, and Pharaoh by his own free will" (*GFW* XLV). But is this both-and position tenable? If God "makes" us do something, then do "we" do it at all? In a statement quoted previously, Augustine said that God sets in motion even the movement of people's wills, "so that He does through their agency whatsoever He wishes to perform through them" (*GFW* XLII). But if God "does" the act, do the people really have any "agency" at all? Is it not self-contradictory and therefore simply nonsense to say that an act is B's act, if the act was totally determined by A? Most theists have held that God cannot do the self-contradictory, e.g., make a round square. Is it not saying that the self-contradictory is done when it is said that *God* performs certain acts without causing these acts not to be *our* acts?

The argument against this doctrine of double causation, which was suggested by Augustine and later developed as the doctrine of "primary and secondary causation," will be continued later, especially in the chapter on the theodicy of James Ross. For the present I will simply state somewhat dogmatically that the doctrine is not intelligible, and hence does not help absolve God from the charge of injustice, if people are punished for sins which God causes "them" to commit.

SIN AND THE DIVINE WILL(S)

Furthermore, how can there even be any sin in the Augustinian universe? Augustine's definition of sin includes the idea of going contrary to the will

of God. And yet Augustine has so defined God's omnipotence that nothing can happen which God does not will. He tries to overcome this contradiction by making a distinction between two "wills" in God. Whereas
we go against God's will in one sense when we sin, Augustine says, we
nevertheless fulfill God's *eternal* will. This distinction is suggested in a
passage in which Augustine says that the fall of the wicked angels was
ordained although not approved by God (*CG* XI. 19–20). Elsewhere he
states that God inspires people to pray for things which God then does not
grant. Regarding this, Augustine states that we can say:

> God wills and does not perform—meaning that He Who causes them to
> will these things Himself wills them. But if we speak of that will of His
> which is eternal as His foreknowledge, certainly He has already done all
> things in heaven and on earth that He has willed. (*CG* XXII. 2)

This same distinction is seen in the following passage, in which Augustine
is speaking about those angelic and human creatures who have sinned:

> For, as far as they were concerned, they did what God did not will that they
> do, but as far as God's omnipotence is concerned, they were quite unable
> to achieve their purpose. In their very act of going against his will, his will
> was thereby accomplished. . . . In a strange and ineffable fashion even that
> which is done against his will is not done without his will. (*E* XXVI. 100)

It is in terms of this distinction between two meanings of "God's
will' that all those passages in Augustine must be interpreted which seem
to say that the creatures have some freedom vis-à-vis God by which they
can go contrary to the divine will, and hence be genuinely responsible.
With this distinction made explicit, it becomes clear that nothing happens
that is not willed and thereby necessitated by God's eternal will. Accordingly, there is no original sinful free choice on the part of the creatures by
which they can then be justly caused to commit further sins, and then
justly punished for both types of sin.

ANALYSIS OF AUGUSTINE'S POSITION[2]

What, then, is Augustine's position on the problem of evil? He clearly
would not reject either premise 1 or premise 2 (i.e., that God is perfect,
and that this perfection includes omnipotence). Could Augustine reject
premise 3, which says that God could have created a world without evil in
it? There is, indeed, one passage in which Augustine seems to foreshadow
those who will suggest that evil, or at least the possibility of evil, is metaphysically necessary, since the world is made out of nothing, and the
"nothingness" in it has some power to resist God's power:

> Now, nature could not have been depraved by vice had it not been made out of nothing. Consequently, that it is a nature, this is because it is made by God; but that it falls away from Him, this is because it is made out of nothing. (*CG* XIV. 13)

However, Augustine's numerous statements on God's omnipotence show that this condition of being made out of nothing is not a sufficient (or even a necessary) condition for the occurrence of evil. And he explicitly says elsewhere that "it is undoubtedly as easy not to allow to exist what he does not will, as it is for him to do what he does will" (*E* XXIV. 96). And he asks rhetorically: "For who will dare to believe or say that it was not in God's power to prevent both angels and men from sinning" (*CG* IV. 27)? Furthermore, the fact that the "nothing" out of which God created the world is "absolute nothingness" (*ouk ōn*), rather than "relatively nothing" (*mē ōn*) with some kind of autonomy, is indicated by Augustine's rejection of the idea that evil is necessitated by the fact that God created the world out of some pre-existent stuff (*C* VII. 5).

What about premise 4, which asserts that perfection includes moral perfection? There is indeed a strain in Augustine's position which could be taken as a denial that God is moral in any sense that corresponds with our ideas of morality. Augustine refers approvingly to Paul's statement that the clay cannot criticize the potter. One could take this to mean "might makes right." And in one passage Augustine even says that "there is a very great difference between what it is fitting for man to will and what is fitting for God" (*E* XXVI. 101). However, the passages quoted four paragraphs above, plus numerous similar passages (e.g., *PS* XVI), including the passage quoted in the fourth paragraph of this chapter, clearly show that Augustine would not consider rejecting the idea that perfection includes moral goodness and that this is a moral goodness that we will be able to recognize as good when we can see things from a larger perspective. And, of course, the defense of God's moral goodness is the main point at issue in theodicy.

To reject statement number 6 would mean to reject the validity of logic when thinking about God and the world. Some of Augustine's statements might be so interpreted, as he often appeals to the mystery of God's ways, and the inability of the human mind to fathom God's "unsearchable" judgments (*PS* XVI). However, I do not believe Augustine means to be making the formal point that logic has to be suspended in these matters. Rather, his intention is that now we often cannot understand how the content of God's judgments is compatible with God's righteousness. He has no doubt that at the day of judgment we will understand the compatibility of omnipotent goodness and worldly evil. And just as there is no suggestion that this will involve seeing that God is "beyond good and evil," there is no suggestion that this will involve transcending the formal laws of thought.

This leaves premises 5 and 7 to be considered. In the "simple statement" of the problem of evil (given in the Introduction), the equivalent of premise 5 is stated as follows: "If God is perfectly good, he would want to prevent all evil." In concluding this discussion of Augustine, I will argue that, although he would reject this premise, the insertion of the qualifier "genuine" before "evil" in the expanded statement of the problem requires that we see the rejection of premise 7 ("There is genuine evil in the world") as the Augustinian solution.

THE DENIAL OF GENUINE EVIL

What kind of evil does Augustine think there is in the universe? He specifically says that there is no "natural evil" (*CG* XI. 22). According to his use of this term, this means in the first place that there is nothing whose "nature" is evil, nothing that is "naturally" bad. Whatever is, is good. For all natures are created by God, and were created good (*NOG* 1). And there is no uncreated being, as the Manichaeans supposed, whose nature is evil. The devil is a creature; and even the devil's nature is good. Accordingly, nothing is by nature intrinsically evil.

In denying all "natural evil," Augustine also means that there is no genuine evil in the universe below the level of creatures with freedom. As was stated in the previous paragraph, there is no intrinsic evil in this realm. Things such as fire, frost, and wild beasts are excellent in their own natures (*CG* XI. 22). All things are good, even though we may not like all things (*C* VII. 22). Augustine also believes there is no genuine instrumental evil arising from this realm. Some sufferings caused in us by this realm, which are *prima facie* evil, are in reality punishments from God, and as such are just (*ibid.*). And the things that cause these sufferings are actually useful to us, and hence are instrumentally good; we should believe this even when we do not yet see their utility (*CG* XI. 22). Furthermore, the irrational beings that sometimes cause suffering in us contribute grace and beauty to the universe as a whole; although we cannot see this from our limited perspectives, we should believe it (*CG* XI. 22; XII. 4). In short, in the realm of subhuman nature everything is intrinsically good; everything has positive instrumental value for us; and everything contributes to the good of the whole, so that there is no genuine evil in this realm.

good; everything has positive instrumental value for us; and everything contributes to the good of the whole, so that there is no genuine evil in this realm.

What about the suffering that is caused in us by the sin of other people? It is not genuinely evil, for the suffering inflicted is just:

> Nor can any other nature which is less than divine be hurt unjustly. No doubt some people by sinning do harm unjustly. Their will to harm is counted against them, but the power by which they are permitted to do the harm comes only from God, who knows, though they do not, what those ought to suffer whom he permits them to harm. (*NOG* II)

Augustine explains more fully: "It is not unjust that the wicked should receive power to harm so that the patience of the good should be proved and the iniquity of the bad should be punished" (*NOG* 32). Accordingly, suffering due to the sin of other people is not genuine evil, for it does not make the universe a worse place than it would otherwise be. To put it otherwise, sin, considered in regard to its instrumental effects on other beings, is not genuinely evil.

The only possible candidates for genuine evil, then, are moral evil, or sin, and its penalty. The penalty is caused by God, and hence, by definition (since there is no unrighteousness in God), cannot be genuinely evil. That is, once sin has occurred, it is better that it be punished than that it go unpunished. Accordingly, it is only sin itself that might be genuinely evil. And when Augustine speaks of evil, it is almost exclusively sin that he has in mind. He considers it intrinsically evil. But the question is whether this judgment of evil is a *prima facie* judgment only, or whether he thinks that sin is genuinely evil, so that the universe would have been a better place without it.

The answer to this must be that he sees it as only apparently evil. He constantly repeats the theme that God, who could have prevented all evil, allowed it only because he could bring good out of it. Assuming that the good that God brings out of the evil were perfectly balanced by the resulting good, then the *prima facie* evil would be neither good nor bad, all things considered, but simply neutral. But if the resulting good more than compensates for the *prima facie* evil which was a necessary condition for the resulting good, then the *prima facie* evil is not simply neutral, but is instrumentally good. And this is what Augustine holds. He says that the beauty of the world is achieved by the opposition of contraries. God is thereby able to use the wickedness of humans and angels for good, "thus embellishing the course of the ages, as it were an exquisite poem set off with antitheses" (*CG* XI. 18). "To the eye that has skill to discern it, the universe is beautified even by sinners, though, considered by themselves, their deformity is a sad blemish" (*CG* XI. 23).

Several other passages indicate that God not only compensates for *prima facie* evil, but more than compensates for it, so that it is really good that the *prima facie* evil occurred. Augustine says that God allowed man to be tempted by the devil "because He foresaw that by the man's seed, aided by divine grace, this same devil himself should be conquered, to the greater glory of the saints" (*CG* XIV. 27). "In this universe, even what is called evil, when it is rightly ordered and kept in its place, commends the good more eminently, since good things yield greater pleasure and praise when compared to the bad things" (*E* III. 11). "God judged it better to bring good out of evil than not to permit any evil to exist" (*E* VIII. 27). "If it were not good that evil things exist, they would certainly not be allowed to exist by the Omnipotent Good" (*E* XXIV. 96).

In summary, Augustine's position is that there is only one thing that is clearly evil intrinsically, and this is sin, or evil willing. But this *prima facie* evil is only apparently evil, for the universe is a better place with sin than it would have been without it. The one other thing that might be considered intrinsically evil, i.e., suffering, is never genuinely evil, for it is always a just punishment for sin and/or an aid toward achieving eternal life, which is such a great good that it more than compensates for any suffering. And those things which seem instrumentally evil within a limited context or from a partial perspective are not evil within the context of the universe as a whole. Accordingly there is no genuine evil in reality.

This is a possible position to hold in the sense that it is not necessarily inconsistent (even though each person holding such a position may have inconsistencies in his thought). But two questions can be asked: First, is this position adequate to our experience? Or do we have intuitions abut the reality of genuine evil which should be given higher credibility than at least one of the traditional Christian premises about the nature of a "perfect reality"? Second, is this conclusion that there is no genuine evil in the world adequate to Christian faith itself?

I believe we must answer these questions differently from the way Augustine did. His position, that there is no genuine evil, was necessitated by the particular way in which he tried to combine Greek and Hebrew ideas of deity. The idea of divine power that resulted from affirming God's knowledge of and influence upon the world, on the one hand, and divine immutability and impassibility, on the other, implied that God caused all things. This belief, added to the idea that God is morally perfect, implied that there is no imperfection in the universe. Only a thoroughgoing revision of the idea of God can allow one consistently to affirm the virtually universal intuition that not everything is as good as it could have been.

NOTES

1. Below are given the works to which the symbols refer, along with the translations from which quotations are made:

C   *The Confessions*. Tr. by Edward Bouverie Pusey.

CG   *The City of God*. Tr. by Marcus Dods.

E   *Enchiridion*. Tr. by J. F. Shaw.

FW   *On Free Will*. Tr. by John H. S. Burleigh.

GFW   *Grace and Free Will*. Tr. by P. Holmes.

NAG   *Nature and Grace*. Tr. by John H. S. Burleigh

NOG   *The Nature of the Good*. Tr. by John H. S. Burleigh.

PS   *On the Predistination of the Saints*. Tr. by P. Holmes.

SL   *On the Spirit and the Letter*. Tr. by P. Holmes.

TR   *Of True Religion*. Tr. by John H. S. Burleigh.

The Confessions can be found in Robert M. Hutchins (ed.), *Great Books of the Western World* (Encyclopedia Britannica, Inc., 1952), Vol. 18.

The City of God, Enchiridion, Grace and Free Will, Nature and Grace, On the Predestination of the Saints, and *On the Spirit and the Letter* are found in *Basic Writings of St. Augustine* (2 vols.), edited and with an introduction and notes by Whitney J. Oates (Random House, 1948).

On Free Will, The Nature of the Good, and *Of True Religion* are found in *Augustine: Earlier Writings*, Vol. VI of the Library of Christian Classics (The Westminster Press, 1953).

2. Augustine's position on the problem of evil, as well as the positions of other thinkers, can be analyzed by reference to a formal statement of the problem of evil. Throughout my analysis I will refer to the following eight-step version of the theoretical problem of evil:

1. God is perfect reality. (Definition)
2. A perfect reality is an omnipotent being. (By definition)
3. An omnipotent being could unilaterally bring about an actual world without any genuine evil. (By definition)
4. A perfect reality is a morally perfect being. (By definition)
5. A morally perfect being would want to bring about an actual world without any genuine evil. (By definition)
6. If there is genuine evil in the world, then there is no God. (Logical conclusion from 1 through 5)
7. There is genuine evil in the world. (Factual statement)
8. Therefore, there is no God. (Logical conclusion from 6 and 7)

I believe this argument is valid, which means that the final conclusion follows from the premises. That is, 6 follows from 1 through 5, while 8 follows from 6 and 7. The question then is whether the argument is *sound,* which requires that, besides being valid, all its premises must be acceptable. [As presented earlier in Griffin's *God, Power and Evil.*]

The World as a Vale of Soul-Making

JOHN HICK

I. THE NEGATIVE TASK OF THEODICY

At the outset of an attempt to present a Christian theodicy—a defence of
the goodness of God in face of the evil in His world—we should recognize
that, whether or not we can succeed in formulating its basis, an implicit
theodicy is at work in the Bible, at least in the sense of an effective reconciliation of profound faith in God with a deep involvement in the realities of sin and suffering. The Scriptures reflect the characteristic mixture
of good and evil in human experience. They record every kind of sorrow
and suffering from the terrors of childhood to the "stony griefs of age":
cruelty, torture, violence, and agony; poverty, hunger, calamitous accident; disease, insanity, folly; every mode of man's inhumanity to man and
of his painfully insecure existence in the world. In these writings there is
no attempt to evade the clear verdict of human experience that evil is
dark, menacingly ugly, heart-rending, crushing. And the climax of this
biblical history of evil was the execution of Jesus of Nazareth. Here were
pain and violent destruction, gross injustice, the apparent defeat of the
righteous, and the premature death of a still-young man. But further, for
Christian faith, this death was the slaying of God's Messiah, the one in
whom mankind was to see the mind and heart of God made flesh. Here,
then, the problem of evil rises to its ultimate maximum; for in its quality
this was an evil than which no greater can be conceived. And yet throughout the biblical history of evil, including even this darkest point, God's
purpose of good was moving visibly or invisibly towards its far-distant
fulfilment. In this faith the prophets saw both personal and national tragedy as God's austere but gracious disciplining of His people. And even the

greatest evil of all, the murder of the son of God, has been found by subsequent Christian faith to be also, in an astounding paradox, the greatest
good of all, so that through the centuries the Church could dare to sing on
the eve of its triumphant Easter celebrations, "O felix culpa, quae talem
ac tantum meruit habere redemptorem."[1] For this reason there is no room
within the Christian thought-world for the idea of tragedy in any sense
that includes the idea of finally *wasted* suffering and goodness.[2]

In all this a Christian theodicy is latent; and our aim must be to try
to draw it out explicitly. The task, like that of theology in general, is one
of "faith seeking understanding," seeking in this case an understanding of
the grounds of its own practical victory in the face of the harsh facts of
evil. Accordingly, from the point of view of apologetics, theodicy has a
negative rather than a positive function. It cannot profess to create faith,
but only to preserve an already existing faith from being overcome by this
dark mystery. For we cannot share the hope of the older schools of natural
theology of inferring the existence of God from the evidences of nature;
and one main reason for this, as David Hume made clear in his *Dialogues,*
is precisely the fact of evil in its many forms. For us today the live question
is whether this renders impossible a rational belief in God: meaning by
this, not a belief in God that has been arrived at by rational argument (for
it is doubtful whether a religious faith is ever attained in this way), but
one that has arisen in a rational individual in response to some compelling
element in his experience, and decisively illuminates and is illuminated by
his experience as a whole. The aim of a Christian theodicy must thus be
the relatively modest and defensive one of showing that the mystery of
evil, largely incomprehensible though it remains, does not render irrational a faith that has arisen, not from the inferences of natural theology, but
from participation in a stream of religious experience which is continuous
with that recorded in the Bible.

2. THE TRADITIONAL THEODICY BASED
UPON CHRISTIAN MYTH

We can distinguish, though we cannot always separate, three relevant fac-
ets of the Christian religion: Christian experience, Christian mythology,
and Christian theology.

Religious experience is "the whole experience of religious persons,"[3]
constituting an awareness of God acting towards them in and through the
events of their lives and of world history, the interpretative element within
which awareness is the cognitive aspect of faith. And distinctively *Chris-*

tian experience, as a form of this, is the Christian's seeing of Christ as his "Lord and Saviour," together with the pervasive recreative effects of this throughout his life, transforming the quality of his experience and determining his responses to other people. Christian faith is thus a distinctive consciousness of the world and of one's existence within it, radiating from and illuminated by a consciousness of God in Christ. It is because there are often a successful facing and overcoming of the challenge of evil at this level that there can, in principle at least, be an honest and serious—even though tentative and incomplete—Christian theodicy.

By *Christian mythology* I mean the great persisting imaginative pictures by means of which the corporate mind of the Church has expressed to itself the significance of the historical events upon which its faith is based, above all the life, death, and resurrection of Jesus who was the Christ. The function of these myths is to convey in universally understandable ways the special importance and meaning of certain items of mundane experience.

By *Christian theology* I mean the attempts by Christian thinkers to speak systematically about God on the basis of the data provided by Christian experience. Thus it is a fact of the Christian faith-experience that "God was in Christ";[4] and the various Christological theories are attempts to understand this by seeing it in the context of other facts both of faith and of nature. Again, it is another facet of this basic fact of faith that in Christ God was "reconciling the world unto Himself";[5] and the various atonement theories are accordingly attempts to understand this further aspect of the experience. The other departments of Christian doctrine stand in a similar relationship to the primary data of Christian experience.

In the past, theology and myth have been closely twined together. For the less men knew about the character of the physical universe the harder it was for them to identify myth as myth, as distinct from history or science. This fact has profoundly affected the developments of the dominant tradition of Christian theodicy. Until comparatively recent times the ancient myth of the origin of evil in the fall of man was quite reasonably assumed to be history. The theologian accordingly accepted it as providing "hard" data, and proceeded to build his theodicy upon it. This mythological theodicy was first comprehensively developed by Augustine, and has continued substantially unchanged within the Roman Catholic Church to the present day. It was likewise adopted by the Reformers of the sixteenth century and has been virtually unquestioned as Protestant doctrine until within approximately the last hundred years. Only during this latest period has it been possible to identify as such its mythological basis, to apply a theological criticism to it, and then to go back to the data of Christian experience and build afresh, seeking a theodicy that can hope to make sense to Christians in our own and succeeding centuries.

But first, in order to see how the hitherto dominant theodicy has arisen, and why it is now utterly unacceptable, we must trace the outline of the mythology that underlies it. The story of the fall of man is part of a more comprehensive cosmic story. In this great amalgam of Jewish and Christian themes, God created spiritual beings, the angels and arch-angels, to be His subjects and to love and serve Him in the heavenly spheres. But a minority of them revolted against God in envy of His su-premacy, and were defeated and cast into an abode suited to their now irreconcilably evil natures. Either to replenish the citizenry of heaven thus depleted by the expulsion of Satan and his followers, or as an independent venture of creation, God made our world, and mankind within it consist-ing initially of a single human pair. This first man and woman, living in the direct knowledge of God, were good, happy, and immortal, and would in due course have populated the earth with descendants like them-selves. But Satan, in wicked spite, successfully tempted them to disobey their Creator, who then expelled them from this paradisal existence into a new situation of hardship, danger, disease, and inevitable death. This was the fall of man, and as a result of it the succeeding members of the human race have been born as fallen creatures in a fallen world, participating in the effects of their first parents' rebellion against their Maker. But God in Christ has made the atonement for man's sin that His own eternal justice required and has offered free forgiveness to as many as will commit them-selves to Christ as their Saviour. At the last judgement, when faith and life alike will be tested, many will enter into eternal life whilst others, preferring their own darkness to God's light, will linger in a perpetual living death.

This great cosmic drama is the official Christian myth. With only minor variations it has constituted the accepted framework of thought of the great majority of Christians in the past, and still fulfils this role for the great majority today. By means of it Christian faith, which began as a crucial response of trust towards one in whom the disciples had experi-enced God directly at work on earth, broadened out into a comprehensive vision of the universe. The great creation-fall-redemption myth has thus brought within the scope of the simplest human soul a pictorial grasp of the universal significance of the life and death of Jesus. Jesus himself was not a mythological figure; he lived in Palestine and his life and death and resurrection made their impact upon living people, and through them

upon others in a long succession of faith down to ourselves today. But the
cosmic picture, sketched by St. Paul and completed by St. Augustine, of
the beginning of our present human situation in the fall of humanity from
a condition of paradisal perfection into one of sin and pain and death, and
of its end in the separation of mankind into those destined for the eternal
bliss or torment of heaven or hell, is a product of the religious imagination. It expresses the significance of the present reality of sin and
sorrow by seeing them as flowing from a first dramatic act of rebellion;
and the significance of the experience of reconciliation with God by
means of the picture of a juridical arrangement taking place within the
councils of the Trinity and being transacted in time on the cross of Christ;
and the significance of man's inalienable personal responsibility by the
picture of a divine administration directing souls to their appropriate final
destinations.

This great cosmic drama in three acts has constituted a valid myth
in the sense that it has successfully fulfilled the conserving and communicating function of a myth in the minds of countless people. By means of
natural images it has vividly brought home to the simplest understandings the claim that Christ stands at the centre of the universe and is
of crucial importance for all men. And when religious myths thus work
effectively it is as absurd to criticize them for being myths rather than
science or history as it would be for us today to insist that they *are* science
or history and to proceed to draw scientific or historical conclusions
from them.

Because we can no longer share the assumption, upon which traditional Christian theodicy has been built, that the creation-fall myth is
basically authentic history,[6] we inevitably look at that theodicy critically
and see in it inadequacies to which in the past piety has tended to blind
the eyes of faith.

For, in general, religious myths are not adapted to the solving of
problems. Their function is to illumine by means of unforgettable imagery the religious significance of some present or remembered fact of experience. But the experience which myth thus emphasizes and illumines is
itself the locus of mystery. Hence it is not surprising that Christian mythology mirrors Christian experience in presenting but not resolving the
profound mystery of evil. Nor is it surprising that when this pictorial presentation of the problem has mistakenly been treated as a solution to it,
the 'solution' has suffered from profound incoherences and contradictions.

This traditional solution (representing the theological, in distinction from the philosophical, side of Augustine's thought on the theodicy

problem) finds the origin of evil, as we have seen, in the fall, which was the beginning both of sin and, as its punishment, of man's sorrows and sufferings.[7] But this theory, so simple and mythologically satisfying, is open to insuperable scientific, moral, and logical objections. To begin with less fundamental aspects of the traditional solution, we know today that the conditions that were to cause human disease and mortality and the necessity for man to undertake the perils of hunting and the labours of agriculture and building, were already part of the natural order prior to the emergence of man and prior therefore to any first human sin, as were also the conditions causing such further 'evils' as earthquake, storm, flood, drought, and pest. And, second, the policy of punishing the whole succeeding human race for the sin of the first pair is, by the best human moral standards, unjust and does not provide anything that can be recognized by these standards as a theodicy. Third, there is a basic and fatal incoherence at the heart of the mythically based "solution." The Creator is preserved from any responsibility for the existence of evil by the claim that He made men (or angels) as free and finitely perfect creatures, happy in the knowledge of Himself, and subject to no strains or temptations, but that they themselves inexplicably and inexcusably rebelled against Him. But this suggestion amounts to a sheer self-contradiction. It is impossible to conceive of wholly good beings in a wholly good world becoming sinful. To say that they do is to postulate the self-creation of evil *ex nihilo!* There must have been some moral flaw in the creature or in his situation to set up the tension of temptation; for creaturely freedom in itself and in the absence of any temptation cannot lead to sin. Thus the very fact that the creature sins refutes the suggestion that until that moment he was a finitely perfect being living in an ideal creaturely relationship to God. And indeed (as we have already seen) the two greatest upholders of this solution implicitly admit the contradiction. Augustine, who treats of evil at its first occurrence in the fall of Satan and his followers, has to explain the eruption of sin in supposedly perfect angels by holding that God had in effect predestined their revolt by withholding from them the assurance of eternal bliss with which, in contrast, He had furnished the angels who remained steadfast.[8] And Calvin, who treats the subject primarily at the point of the fall of man, holds that "all are not created in equal condition; rather, eternal life is foreordained for some, eternal damnation for others."[9] Thus the myth, when mistakenly pressed to serve as a theodicy, can be saved only by adding to it the new and questionable doctrine of an absolute divine predestination. And this in turn only leads the theodicy to contradict itself. For its original intention was to blame evil upon the misuse of creaturely free will. But now this misuse is itself said to fall under the divine predestinating decrees. Thus the theodicy collapses into radical incoherence, and its more persistent defenders have become involved in ever more desperate and implausible epicycles of theory to save it. For example, to salvage the view of the fall of man as a temporal event that took place on this earth some definite (if unknown) number of years ago, it has been suggested that after emerging from his subhuman precursors man lived in the paradisal state for only a very brief period, lasting perhaps no more than a matter of hours. Again, attempts have been made to protect the fall doctrine from the encroachments of scientific research by locating the primal calamity in a pre-mundane sphere. In the third century Origen had taught that some of the spirits whom God created rebelled against the divine majesty and were cast down into the material world to constitute our human race;[10] and in the nineteenth century the German Protestant theologian Julius Müller, impressed by the overwhelming difficulties of affirming an historical fall, in effect revived Origen's theory as an explanation of the apparently universal evil propensities of man. All men are sinful, he suggested, because in another existence prior to the present life they have individually turned away from God.[11]

The difficulties and disadvantages of such a view are, I think, not far to seek. The theory is without grounds in Scripture or in science, and it would have claim to consideration only if it could provide a solution, even if a speculative one, to the question of the origin of moral evil. But in fact it is not able to do this. It merely pushes back into an unknown and unknowable realm the wanton paradox of finitely perfect creatures, dwelling happily and untempted in the presence of God, turning to sin. Whether on earth or in heaven, this still amounts to the impossible self-creation of evil *ex nihilo*. If evil could thus create itself out of nothing in the midst of a wholly good universe, it could do so in a mundane Garden of Eden as easily as, or perhaps more easily than, in the highest heaven. Nothing, then, is gained for theodicy by postulating a pre-mundane fall of human souls.

As a variation which he regarded as superior to the notion of a pre-mundane fall of individuals, N. P. Williams proposed the idea of "a collective fall of the race-soul of humanity at an indefinitely remote past."[12] This collective fall occurred, according to Williams, during the long period between the first emergence of man as a biological species and his subsequent development to the point at which there were primitive societies, and therefore moral laws which could be transgressed. "We must," he says, "postulate some unknown factor or agency which interfered to arrest the development of corporate feeling, just when man was becoming man, some mysterious and maleficent influence which cut into the stream of the genetic evolution of our race at some point during the twilit age which separates pre-human from human history."[13] This evil influence which attacked and corrupted mankind is also "the mysterious power which vitiates the whole of sub-human life with cruelty and selfishness,"[14] and thus accounts not only for moral evil but also for the disorder, waste, and pain in nature. Accordingly the original calamity was not merely a fall of man but of the Life-Force itself, which we must conceive "as having been at the beginning, when it first sprang forth from the creative fecundity of the Divine Being, free, personal, and self-conscious."[15] This World-Soul was created good, but "at the beginning of Time, and in some transcendental and incomprehensible manner, it turned away from God and in the direction of Self, thus shattering its own interior being, which depended upon God for its stability and coherence, and thereby forfeiting its unitary self-consciousness, which it has only regained, after aeons of myopic striving, in sporadic fragments which are the separate minds of men and perhaps of superhuman spirits."[16]

Williams is, I think, justified in claiming that such a speculation cannot be excluded *ab initio* as impermissible to a responsible Christian theologian. As he points out,

> Such a substitution of the idea of a corruption of the whole cosmic energy at some enormously remote date for the idea of a voluntary moral suicide of Man in comparatively recent times would be no greater a revolution than that which was effected by St. Anselm, when he substituted a satisfactional theory of the Atonement for the view which regarded the death of Christ as a ransom paid to the Devil—a view which had behind it the venerable authority of a thousand years of Christian history.[17]

Williams' suggestion preserves the central thought of the Augustinian fall doctrine that the ultimate source of evil lies in an original conscious turning away from God on the part of created personal life. But precisely because of its faithfulness to that tradition his theory fails to throw any new light upon the problem of evil. Whether the self-creation of evil *ex nihilo* be located in an historical Adam and Eve, or in a multitude of souls in a pre-mundane realm, or in a single world-soul at the beginning of time, it is equally valueless from the point of view of theodicy. In order for a soul or souls to fall there must be, either in them or in their environment, some flaw which produces temptation and leads to sin; and this flaw in the creation cannot be traced back to any other ultimate source than the Creator of all that is. Thus Williams' theory is open to the same objection as Müller's: namely, that it is a speculation whose only point would be to solve or lighten the problem of evil, but that it fails to do this.[18]

3. THE "VALE OF SOUL-MAKING" THEODICY

Fortunately there is another and better way. As well as the "majority report" of the Augustinian tradition, which has dominated Western Christendom, both Catholic and Protestant, since the time of Augustine himself, there is the "minority report" of the Irenaean tradition. This latter is both older and newer than the other, for it goes back to St. Irenaeus and others of the early Hellenistic Fathers of the Church in the two centuries prior to St. Augustine, and it has flourished again in more developed forms during the last hundred years.

Instead of regarding man as having been created by God in a finished state, as a finitely perfect being fulfilling the divine intention for our human level of existence, and then falling disastrously away from this, the minority report sees man as still in process of creation. Irenaeus himself expressed the point in terms of the (exegetically dubious) distinction between the "image" and the "likeness" of God referred to in Genesis 1. 26: "Then God said, Let us make man in our image, after our likeness."[19] His view was that man as a personal and moral being already exists in the image, but has not yet been formed into the finite likeness of God. By this "likeness" Irenaeus means something more than personal existence as such; he means a certain valuable quality of personal life which reflects finitely the divine life. This represents the perfecting of man, the fulfilment of God's purpose for humanity, the "bringing of many sons to glory,"[20] the creating of "children of God" who are "fellow heirs with Christ" of his glory.[21]

And so man, created as a personal being in the image of God, is only the raw material for a further and more difficult stage of God's creative work. This is the leading of men as relatively free and autonomous persons, through their own dealings with life in the world in which He has placed them, towards that quality of personal existence that is the finite likeness of God. The features of this likeness are revealed in the person of Christ, and the process of man's creation into it is the work of the Holy Spirit. In St. Paul's words, "And we all, with unveiled faces, beholding the glory of the Lord, are being changed into his likeness ($\varepsilon i \varkappa \acute{\omega} \nu$) from one degree of glory to another; for this comes from the Lord who is the Spirit";[22] or again, "For God knew his own before ever they were, and also

ordained that they should be shaped to the likeness (εἰχών) of his Son."[23]
In Johannine terms, the movement from the image to the likeness is a
transition from one level of existence, that of animal life (*Bios*), to another
and higher level, that of eternal life (*Zoe*), which includes but transcends
the first. And the fall of man was seen by Irenaeus as a failure within the
second phase of this creative process, a failure that has multiplied the perils and complicated the route of the journey in which God is seeking to
lead mankind.

In the light of modern anthropological knowledge some form of
two-stage conception of the creation of man has become an almost unavoidable Christian tenet. At the very least we must acknowledge as two
distinguishable stages the fashioning of *homo sapiens* as a product of the
long evolutionary process, and his sudden or gradual spiritualization as a
child of God. But we may well extend the first stage to include the development of man as a rational and responsible person capable of personal
relationship with the personal Infinite who has created him. This first
stage of the creative process was, to our anthropomorphic imaginations,
easy for divine omnipotence. By an exercise of creative power God caused
the physical universe to exist, and in the course of countless ages to bring
forth within it organic life, and finally to produce out of organic life personal life; and when man had thus emerged out of the evolution of the
forms of organic life, a creature had been made who has the possibility of
existing in conscious fellowship with God. But the second stage of the
creative process is of a different kind altogether. It cannot be performed by
omnipotent power as such. For personal life is essentially free and self-
directing. It cannot be perfected by divine fiat, but only through the un-
compelled responses and willing co-operation of human individuals in
their actions and reactions in the world in which God has placed them.
Men may eventually become the perfected persons whom the New Testament calls "children of God," but they cannot be created ready-made
as this.

The value-judgement that is implicitly being invoked here is that
one who has attained to goodness by meeting and eventually mastering
temptations, and thus by rightly making responsible choices in concrete
situations, is good in a richer and more valuable sense than would be one
created *ab initio* in a state either of innocence or of virtue. In the former
case, which is that of the actual moral achievements of mankind, the individual's goodness has within it the strength of temptations overcome, a
stability based upon an accumulation of right choices, and a positive and
responsible character that comes from the investment of costly personal

So we are involved in our own creation

effort. I suggest, then, that it is an ethically reasonable judgement, even though in the nature of the case not one that is capable of demonstrative proof, that human goodness slowly built up through personal histories of moral effort has a value in the eyes of the Creator which justifies even the long travail of the soul-making process.

The picture with which we are working is thus developmental and teleological. Man is in process of becoming the perfected being whom God is seeking to create. However, this is not taking place—it is important to add—by a natural and inevitable evolution, but through a hazardous adventure in individual freedom. Because this is a pilgrimage within the life of each individual, rather than a racial evolution, the progressive fulfilment of God's purpose does not entail any corresponding progressive improvement in the moral state of the world. There is no doubt a development in man's ethical situation from generation to generation through the building of individual choices into public institutions, but this involves an accumulation of evil as well as of good.[24] It is thus probable that human life was lived on much the same moral plane two thousand years ago or four thousand years ago as it is today. But nevertheless during this period uncounted millions of souls have been through the experience of earthly life, and God's purpose has gradually moved towards its fulfilment within each one of them, rather than within a human aggregate composed of different units in different generations.

If, then, God's aim in making the world is "the bringing of many sons to glory,"[25] that aim will naturally determine the kind of world that He has created. Antitheistic writers almost invariably assume a conception of the divine purpose which is contrary to the Christian conception. They assume that the purpose of a loving God must be to create a hedonistic paradise; and therefore to the extent that the world is other than this, it proves to them that God is either not loving enough or not powerful enough to create such a world. They think of God's relation to the earth on the model of a human being building a cage for a pet animal to dwell in. If he is humane he will naturally make his pet's quarters as pleasant and healthful as he can. Any respect in which the cage falls short of the veterinarian's ideal, and contains possibilities of accident or disease, is evidence of either limited benevolence or limited means, or both. Those who use the problem of evil as an argument against belief in God almost invariably think of the world in this kind of way. David Hume, for example, speaks of an architect who is trying to plan a house that is to be as comfortable and convenient as possible. If we find that "the windows, doors, fires, passages, stairs, and the whole economy of the building were the

teleo from telos = the end (or purpose)

NT

pleasure as supreme

again: is God not all good or all powerful?

source of noise, confusion, fatigue, darkness, and the extremes of heat and cold" we should have no hesitation in blaming the architect. It would be in vain for him to prove that if this or that defect were corrected greater ills would result: "still you would assert in general, that, if the architect had had skill and good intentions, he might have formed such a plan of the whole, and might have adjusted the parts in such a manner, as would have remedied all or most of these inconveniences."[26]

But if we are right in supporting that God's purpose for man is to lead him from human *Bios,* or the biological life of man, to that quality of *Zoe,* or the personal life of eternal worth, which we see in Christ, then the question that we have to ask is not, Is this the kind of world that an all-powerful and infinitely loving being would create as an environment for his human pets? (or,) Is the architecture of the world the most pleasant and convenient possible? The question that we have to ask is rather, Is this the kind of world that God might make as an environment in which moral beings may be fashioned, through their own free insights and responses, into "children of God"?

Such critics as Hume are confusing what heaven ought to be, as an environment for perfected finite beings, with what this world ought to be, as an environment for beings who are in process of becoming perfected. For if our general conception of God's purpose is correct the world is not intended to be a paradise, but rather the scene of a history in which human personality may be formed towards the pattern of Christ. Men are not to be thought of on the analogy of animal pets, whose life is to be made as agreeable as possible, but rather on the analogy of human children, who are to grow to adulthood in an environment whose primary and overriding purpose is not immediate pleasure but the realizing of the most valuable potentialities of human personality.

Needless to say, this characterization of God as the heavenly Father is not a merely random illustration but an analogy that lies at the heart of the Christian faith. Jesus treated the likeness between the attitude of God to man, and the attitude of human parents at their best towards their children, as providing the most adequate way for us to think about God. And so it is altogether relevant to a Christian understanding of this world to ask, How does the best parental love express itself in its influence upon the environment in which children are to grow up? I think it is clear that a parent who loves his children, and wants them to become the best human beings that they are capable of becoming, does not treat pleasure as the sole and supreme value. Certainly we seek pleasure for our children, and take great delight in obtaining it for them; but we do not desire for

suffering 227 *coeur*

them unalloyed pleasure at the expense of their growth in such even greater values as moral integrity, unselfishness, compassion, courage, humour, reverence for the truth, and perhaps above all the capacity for love. We do not act on the premise that pleasure is the supreme end of life; and if the development of these other values sometimes clashes with the provision of pleasure, then we are willing to have our children miss a certain amount of this, rather than fail to come to possess and to be possessed by the finer and more precious qualities that are possible to the human personality. A child brought up on the principle that the only or the supreme value is pleasure would not be likely to become an ethically mature adult or an attractive or happy personality. And to most parents it seems more important to try to foster quality and strength of character in their children than to fill their lives at all times with the utmost possible degree of pleasure. If, then, there is any true analogy between God's purpose for his human creatures, and the purpose of loving and wise parents for their children, we have to recognize that the presence of pleasure and the absence of pain cannot be the supreme and overriding end for which the world exists. Rather, this world must be a place of soul-making. And its value is to be judged, not primarily by the quantity of pleasure and pain occurring in it at any particular moment, but by its fitness for its primary purpose, the purpose of soul-making.[27]

In all this we have been speaking about the nature of the world considered simply as the God-given environment of man's life. For it is mainly in this connection that the world has been regarded in Irenaean and in Protestant thought.[28] But such a way of thinking involves a danger of anthropocentrism from which the Augustinian and Catholic tradition has generally been protected by its sense of the relative insignificance of man within the totality of the created universe. Man was dwarfed within the medieval world-view by the innumerable hosts of angels and archangels above him—unfallen rational natures which rejoice in the immediate presence of God, reflecting His glory in the untarnished mirror of their worship. However, this higher creation has in our modern world lost its hold upon the imagination. Its place has been taken, as the minimizer of men, by the immensities of outer space and by the material universe's unlimited complexity transcending our present knowledge. As the spiritual environment envisaged by Western man has shrunk, his physical horizons have correspondingly expanded. Where the human creature was formerly seen as an insignificant appendage to the angelic world, he is now seen as an equally insignificant organic excrescence, enjoying a fleeting moment of consciousness on the surface of one of the planets of a minor star. Thus the truth that was symbolized for former ages by the existence of the angelic hosts is today impressed upon us by the vastness of the physical universe, countering the egoism of our species by making us feel that this immense prodigality of existence can hardly all exist for the sake of man—though, on the other hand, the very realization that it is not all for the sake of man may itself be salutary and beneficial to man!

However, instead of opposing man and nature as rival objects of God's interest, we should perhaps rather stress man's solidarity as an embodied being with the whole natural order in which he is embedded. For man is organic to the world; all his acts and thoughts and imaginations are conditioned by space and time; and in abstraction from nature he would cease to be human. We may, then, say that the beauties and sublimities and powers, the microscopic intricacies and macroscopic vastnesses, the wonders and the terrors of the natural world and of the life that pulses through it, are willed and valued by their Maker in a creative act that embraces man together with nature. By means of matter and living flesh God both builds a path and weaves a veil between Himself and the creature made in His image. Nature thus has permanent significance; for God has set man in a creaturely environment, and the final fulfilment of our nature in relation to God will accordingly take the form of an embodied life within "a new heaven and a new earth."[29] And as in the present age man moves slowly towards that fulfilment through the pilgrimage of his earthly life, so also "the whole creation" is "groaning in travail," waiting for the time when it will be "set free from its bondage to decay."[30]

And yet however fully we thus acknowledge the permanent significance and value of the natural order, we must still insist upon man's special character as a personal creature made in the image of God; and our theodicy must still centre upon the soul-making process that we believe to be taking place within human life.

This, then, is the starting-point from which we propose to try to relate the realities of sin and suffering to the perfect love of an omnipotent Creator. And as will become increasingly apparent, a theodicy that starts in this way must be eschatological in its ultimate bearings. That is to say, instead of looking to the past for its clue to the mystery of evil, it looks to the future, and indeed to that ultimate future to which only faith can look. Given the conception of a divine intention working in and through human time towards a fulfilment that lies in its completeness beyond human time, our theodicy must find the meaning of evil in the part that it is made to play in the eventual outworking of that purpose; and must find the justification of the whole process in the magnitude of the good to which it leads. The good that outshines all ill is not a paradise long since lost but a kingdom which is yet to come in its full glory and permanence.

From this point of view we must speak about moral evil; about pain, including that of the lower animals; about the higher and more distinctively human forms of suffering; and about the relation between all this and the will of God as it has been revealed in Jesus Christ.

NOTES

1. *"O certe necessarium Adae peccatum, quod Christi morte deletum est! O felix culpa, quae talem ac tantum meruit habere redemptorem!"* (O truly necessary sin of Adam, which is cancelled by Christ's death! O fortunate crime [*or*, O happy fault], which merited [to have] such and so great a redeemer!) These famous phrases occur in the Roman Missal in the *Exsultet* for the evening before Easter Day. The date and authorship of this *Exsultet* are uncertain. It has been attributed, but without adequate evidence, to St. Augustine, to St. Ambrose, and to Gregory the Great. As part of the Easter liturgy it goes back at least to the seventh century and possibly to the beginnings of the fifth century. On its history see Arthur O. Lovejoy, *Essays in the History of Ideas*, 1948 (New York: Capricorn Books, 1960), pp. 286.

2. Cf. D. D. Raphael, *The Paradox of Tragedy* (London: George Allen and Unwin, Ltd., 1960), pp. 43 f.

3. William Temple, *Nature, Man and God* (London: Macmillan & Co. Ltd, 1934), p. 334.

4. 2 Corinthians 5:19.

5. Ibid.

6. One of the most eloquent recent presentations of the traditional conception of the temporal fall of man is that of C. S. Lewis in *The Problem of Pain* (London: The Centenary Press, 1940), pp. 65f.

7. See Chapter 3 [in Hick's *Evil and the God of Love*].

8. *City of God*, bk. xi, chaps. 11 and 13; bk. xii, chap. 9 [in *City of God*, trans. Marcus Dods, George Wilson, and J. J. Smith (New York: Random House, 1950)].

9. *Institutes*, bk. 3, chap. 21, para. 5 [in *Calvin: Institutes of the Christian Religion*, ed. John T. McNeil, trans. Ford Lewis Battles (London and Philadelphia: S.C.M. Press and Westminster Press, 2 vol., 1961)].

10. *De Principiis*. bk. II, chap. i, para. 1. Cf. ibid., chap. ix, para. 6.

11. *The Christian Doctrine of Sin* [5th ed., trans. W. Urick (Edinburgh: T. & T. Clark, 1868)], bk. IV, chap. 4. Cf. bk. III, pt. i, chap. 3, sect. 1, and chap. 4, sect. 3.

12. N. P. Williams, *The Ideas of the Fall and of Original Sin* (London: Longmans, Green, 1927), p. 513.

13. Ibid., pp. 518–19.

14. Ibid., p. 520.

15. The application of the notion of a pre-mundane fall to evil in nature [is discussed in Chapter 15 of Hick's *Evil and the God of Love*].

16. Williams, *Ideas of the Fall*, p. 526.

17. Ibid., p. 524.

18. A pre-mundane fall has been propounded by Canon Peter Green in *The Problem of Evil* (London: Longmans, Green, 1920), chap. 7, and in *The Pre-Mundane Fall* (London: A. R. Mowbray & Co., 1944); and by C. W. Formby in *The Unveiling of the Fall* (London: Williams & Norgate, 1923).

19. *Against Heresies*, v.vi.1 Translation in the Ante-Nicene Library.

20. Hebrews 2:10.

21. Romans 8:17.

22. 2 Corinthians 3:18.

23. Romans 8:29. Other New Testament passages expressing a view of man as undergoing a process of spiritual growth within God's purpose, are: Ephesians 2:21; 3:16; Colossians 2:19; John 3:2; 2 Corinthians 4:16.

24. This fact is symbolized in early Christian literature both by the figure of the antichrist, who continually opposes God's purposes in history, and by the expectation of cataclysmic calamity and strife in the last days before the end of the present world order.

25. Hebrews 2:10.

26. *Dialogues Concerning Natural Religion*, pt. xi. Kemp-Smith's ed. (Oxford: Clarendon Press, 1935), p. 251.

27. The phrase "the vale of Soul-making" was coined by the poet John Keats in a letter written to his brother and sister in April 1819. He says, "The common cognomen of this world among the misguided and superstitious is a 'vale of tears' from which we are to be redeemed by a certain arbitrary interposition of God and taken to Heaven—What a little circumscribed straightened notion! Call the world if you Please 'The vale of Soul-making'." In this letter he sketches a teleological theodicy. "Do you not see," he asks, "how necessary a World of Pains and troubles is to school an Intelligence and make it a Soul?" (*The Letters of John Keats*, ed. by M. B. Forman. London: Oxford University Press, 4th ed., 1952, pp. 334–5.)

28. Thus Irenaeus said that "the creation is suited to [the wants of] man; for man was not made for its sake, but creation for the sake of man" (*A. H.* v. xxix.1), and Calvin said that "because we know that the universe was established especially for the sake of mankind, we ought to look for this purpose in his governance also" (*Inst.* I.xvi.6.).

29. Revelation 21:1.

30. Romans 8:21–22. .

The Loving God: Some Observations on Hick's Theodicy

ROLAND PUCCETTI

Philosophers of religion divide neatly into two camps on the problem of evil: those who think it fatal to the concept of a loving God and those who do not. The latter have established a wide array of defensive positions down through the centuries, but none that has proved impregnable to sceptical attack. In his new book Mr Hick[1] wisely abandons these older fortifications and falls back on highly mobile reserves. Not for him the "Fall of Man" thesis, with its unexplained choice to give up finite perfection; nor the Plotinian principle of plenitude, evil being an inevitable petering out of God's goodness; nor the "aesthetic" gambit where the horrors of life constitute mere "shadows" designed to highlight the beauty of creation; nor the "cosmic Toryism," as someone called it, of Leibniz's "best of all possible worlds;" nor even, one might say gratefully, the gaseous obscurantism of Karl Barth's "das Nichtige." All of these defences, and others besides, Mr Hick lumps together under what he calls "the majority report" in Christian theodicy: the Augustinian tradition or type. In place of these venerable ramparts Hick elects the more fluid defence afforded, he thinks, by Irenaeus, Eastern Christianity and, in modern times, by Schleiermacher and a few contemporary thinkers.

I shall not attempt to review all of Hick's manoeuvres here: his book is but the occasion of my renewed assault.[2] Indeed I shall have very little to say about one side of the problem of evil, the issue of moral evil. It seems to me that on this front Hick's Irenaean type of defence holds up rather well, and in any case I am sure my fellow sceptics—Anthony Flew, J. L. Mackie, and H. J. McCloskey—will soon open fire there. Instead

From *Religious Studies* 2 (1967): 255–68. © Cambridge University Press, 1967. Reprinted with permission of Cambridge University Press.

and in the meantime I want to attack on the other flank, concentrating my resources on the problem of physical evil. It is here, I think, that we shall find Hick's reserves unguarded and really unprepared. But more important, I hope by this flanking movement not only to carry the battle but also the campaign. I hope to show not merely that Hick's "theodicy for today" fails, but that theodicy in general is a subject without a proper object.

I. FOUR CRUCIAL CASES

What we need to begin with are some instances of innocent suffering or pain that are completely noncontroversial. By this I mean cases where any sane theist would agree (*a*) that the subject really did undergo torment, and (*b*) that this is clearly unrelated to his moral character or past conduct. For we are obviously disinclined to recognise a problem of evil in, for example, the profligate's being stricken by syphilis, or Adolf Hitler's coming to a violent end. Still it should not prove difficult to find cases of the kind we want: there is so much to choose from.

Case I: The Trapped Rabbit. This animal lives by foraging for food in the fields. One day he is caught by a farmer's cat, who carries him back to the farmhouse relatively unharmed. Then the cat bites his hindquarters, partially hamstringing the rabbit. He lets the rabbit hop a few steps, then pounces on him again, tearing at his flesh. This is repeated several times. When the cat tires of this he settles down and begins to gnaw at the back of the rabbit's head. The rabbit lies there, bleating, its eyes still open, until death comes.

Case II: The Infant Toddler. A woman takes her eighteen-months old daughter to the club every afternoon, where she lets the child play while chatting with friends. Often enough the little girl wanders towards the swimming-pool, which leads to her mother or some other person dashing to the rescue. But one afternoon it happens no one is looking as the child toddles to the edge of the pool, falls in, and goes straight under. No one is in the pool either; by the time anyone realises what has happened she is dead.

Case III: The Cancer Patient. We have an aged woman down with advanced carcinoma of the stomach and bowels. Exploratory surgery reveals that it is widespread, malignant, inoperable. The doctors put her on morphine sedation but her agony increases without lethal collapse. Everyone hopes she will die quickly, for her sake. But she lingers on during still another week of suffering. Seven days. One hundred and sixty-eight hours. Ten thousand and eighty minutes. Six hundred and four thousand eight hundred seconds.

Case IV: The Brilliant Pianist. Here we have a man thirty-five years old with a fine musical career behind him and an even more brilliant future predicted by all who know him. One day while practising at the keyboard he notices a trembling of his fingers. This gets worse in succeeding weeks. In time tiny involuntary muscle spasms occur. In a few months he cannot play any more. During the same period he becomes irritable, slovenly, aggressive. Finally his family and friends insist upon medical attention. The diagnosis is Huntington's Chorea. He is told he has at the most fifteen years left to live: fifteen years during which he will progressively deteriorate psychically as well as physically. His end will come in a mental institution, a crippled shell of a man, unable to care for himself. And if he had children, half of them may expect exactly the same end.

II. PARING AWAY TANGENTIAL MATTERS

In order to preserve the purity of these examples as instances of physical evil, let us look briefly at the peripheral issues sometimes introduced in discussions of this kind.

In the first case one might say the rabbit was a pest we are well rid of. Certainly the farmer is not sorry his cat caught the rabbit, and I suppose most of us would understand that attitude. But the rabbit could have been shot, or even killed quickly by the cat. Taking him out of the ecological and agricultural picture does not require this kind of death. Further, there is no genuine moral element in the story. The rabbit has no moral character. Nor did he do anything to deserve this. He is just a rabbit, and rabbits eat what they can find in fields. In fact the cat did not kill him for eating the farmer's crops, but just because he is a rabbit. It would be a mistake also to interpret the incident as an example of feline cruelty. There is no evidence that cats enjoy the suffering of their victims. This is how they train themselves to catch prey. What is at issue here is merely the painful death of the rabbit.

The case of the Infant Toddler is different in that our victim does have a (developing) moral character. But no one is going to say that is an established bad character: not at eighteen months. Nor will it make sense to say she was a bad little girl that morning and deserved to drown. Still, one might introduce compensatory features. One might suppose that as a result of this death her mother became a better person: more serious, responsible, perhaps more dedicated to others. All such considerations are beside the point. Quite apart from the fact that, as in most cases of this kind, the overall effect on others is unrelieved tragedy, nothing compensatory to the infant victim is suggested. Her life and potentialities have come to an end.

The Cancer Patient Case presents us with a fully developed moral character, and a long series of morally responsible acts in the past. Here it is always possible to suppose the victim deserved her fate, because of a particularly evil character or secret life of vice. But this qualifying move will succeed only if we can plausibly maintain that suffering in this life really is justly proportionate to one's moral record. Was every cancer victim unusually evil, and everyone who died peacefully in his sleep morally upright? That seems inherently unlikely to anyone with a measure of experience in human affairs.

The last case, the Case of the Brilliant Pianist, differs in some respects from all these. For while the Cancer Patient was at the end of her normal life anyway, he is still young. And while she had only a few weeks of agony before her, he faces fifteen years of gradual but irreversible deterioration, during which his mind, his body, his whole personality structure will be destroyed. And in this there cannot be even a hypothetical question of retribution. He inherited the disease by genetic transmission the moment he was conceived, long before he developed a moral character or became morally responsible for his acts. It makes absolutely no difference to the onset of the disease whether his early life was saintly or the opposite.

III. THE THEOLOGICAL PROBLEM

The difficulty for anyone who believes in a loving God is to reconcile that concept with such states of affairs. It is to Hick's credit that he faces this problem uncompromisingly. Not only does he reject, as I said, the major theological and metaphysical escape-mechanisms of the Augustinian tradition; he joins Augustine (and others) in rejecting any dualistic "solution" which seeks a transcendental source of evil other than God. For that can be purchased only at the cost of limiting God's power. The absolute monotheism of the Judeo-Christian faith is, he says, just "not negotiable" (p. 35).

> We are undoubtedly here at one of the major watersheds of theodicy. On the
> one hand, we must treat sin as *wrong* and evil as *bad*. We want to see them,
> as they are seen in the New Testament, as manifestations of a principle that
> is irreconcilably at enmity with both God and man. But, on the other

hand, we must not so magnify this contrary power as to create a final dualism. Ultimately God alone is sovereign, and evil can exist only by his permission. This means that God has willed to create a universe in which it is better for Him to permit sin and evil than not to permit them. And this brings us back, however reluctantly, to some kind of instrumental view of evil. (p. 239)

But how could a loving God find it better to permit sin and evil than not? How can a being" . . . than which nothing more perfect can be conceived," in Hick's (p. 35) as well as Anselm's phrase, choose to use evil as an *instrument?* Could not any good God wanted to secure be obtained directly, without tolerating evil means to that end? These questions lead directly into Hick's "theodicy for today."

IV. THE "VALE OF SOUL-MAKING"

Hick's particular instrumentalist approach to the problem of evil is reflected in the phrase (taken from a Keats letter) that our world is not a "vale of tears" so much as a "vale of soul-making." God did not will, of course, that men should sin and suffer in this or that particular instance: but he did will to create a world where sin and suffering take place. He did so because there is no other way for men to win for themselves a place beside him as his 'children'. Following Irenaeus, Hick affirms that man is born in God's 'image' but not his 'likeness'. To achieve a likeness to God men must perfect themselves, or at least begin to perfect themselves, in this life. If they were created perfect by God there would be no further development, no struggle to forge a soul. It is quite true, Hick concedes, that God could create men such that they would always freely choose to do the right. But our notions of love, worship, and faith are such that it would be contradictory to speak of God 'fixing' these in his creatures in advance. To be genuine they must come from a free commitment or response to God which rules out any such scheme. Thus our world is really better than alternative utopian conceptions. It has a higher moral value in God's eyes precisely because its imperfections and challenges provide the conditions under which men may become 'God-like' by their own efforts.

Something very like this account constiutes the essence of Hick's theodicy. As I said at the beginning of this paper, I intend to leave his treatment of moral evil to others and concentrate on physical evil. Our question now will be how well Hick's instrumentalist view explains the latter, and here we have to enter into more detail than heretofore.

V. THE STERN HEADMASTER

According to Hick, the great mistake of antitheistic writers is to assume a loving God would ineluctably create a hedonistic paradise.

> They think of God's relation to the earth on the model of a human being building a cage for a pet animal to dwell in. If he is humane he will naturally make his pet's quarters as pleasant and healthful as he can. Any respect in which the cage falls short of the veterinarian's ideal, and contains possibilities of accident or disease, is evidence of either limited benevolence or limited means, or both. . . . Men are not to be thought of on the analogy of animal pets, whose life is to be made as agreeable as possible, but rather on the analogy of human children, who are to grow to adulthood in an environment whose primary and overriding purpose is not immediate pleasure but the realising of the most valuable potentialities of human personality. . . . I think it is clear that a parent who loves his children, and wants them to become the best human beings they are capable of becoming, does not treat pleasure as the sole and supreme value . . . we do not desire for them unalloyed pleasure at the expense of their growth in such even greater values as moral integrity, unselfishness, compassion, courage, humour, reverence for the truth, and perhaps above all the capacity for love. (pp. 293-4)

There is something suspect in the way Hick presents this contrast. I cannot speak for other antitheists, but I at least never regarded it the duty of a loving God to provide his creatures with a hedonistic paradise. The Humane Veterinarian need not give his pets LSD or heroin, but he should at least shorten their suffering. The model of the Loving Parent is similarly misleading. True, we often sacrifice our children's pleasure for their moral gain: but we also try to spare them pain when it is not necessary for that purpose, and it is just this which Hick's postulated "Father of us all" does not seem concerned to do.

Perhaps a more appropriate analogy for Hick's theodicy would be that of the Stern Headmaster, who prizes moral character highly but is indifferent to hardships. For this reason he designs a school, let us say, where the buildings are unsafe, the food often contaminated, the playing-fields dangerous, and the surrounding grounds unhealthy. In this way his charges are frequently ill or injured, which gives them ample opportunity to develop certain desirable values. So far so good. But suppose there are some accidents which are permanently disabling or even fatal, some diseases which become epidemic? And suppose further that in each case the Stern Headmaster knew what was going to happen and could have pre-

vented it, but decided not to? Can one also say he is infinitely loving?
That is the problem Hick confronts.

omnipotence

VII. THE ALL-OR-NOTHING GAMBIT

At several points in the last part of his book Hick formulates the issue in
this same misleading way.

For example, he attacks Hume's suggestion that our world could be
improved if men and animals were motivated to satisfy their natural needs
by diminution of pleasure rather than the incidence of pain. Hick counters
this by saying pleasure is a relative and variable thing; once we cut painful
experiences off entirely the hedonic scale shifts so that formerly less pleasant experiences become painful. So we cannot escape pain entirely.

Again, he ridicules the utopian notion of a world where pain-
producing situations would be systematically thwarted by special adjust-
ments to the course of nature, so that sentient organisms would never have
their pain mechanisms activated. This, he says, would be " . . . as though
each living creature were individually watched over by a miracle-working
guardian angel charged with protecting it from pain" (p. 341). Life
would have no stable environment of natural law as in such a world. Evolution could not have taken place. Or, if we imagine these pain-avoiding
suspensions to come into effect after human evolution, then men could not
have developed the physical sciences and technology. There would be no
need for exertion, no challenge, no demand for human skill or inventive-
ness; no occasion for co-operation, the development of culture, or the creation of human civilisation. The race would consist of " . . . feckless
Adams and Eves, harmless and innocent, but devoid of positive character and without the dignity of real responsibilities, tasks, and achievements" (p. 343).

It is comforting to find a Christian philosopher so devoted to evolution and the emergence of the physical sciences, and so unattracted by
the picture of a primordial state of bliss. But of course there is no need to
choose between a completely painless world and the actual world. Just as
there could be a far more painful scheme of things without changing the
stable environment of natural laws, so could there be a far less painful one.
It is not at all clear, for example, that God would be obliged to create the
organic world as we now know it through evolution. I see no contradiction
in an Omnipotent Being starting the world off exactly as it was six thousand or so years ago without any past history whatsoever. Nor do I see a
contradiction in his creating it so that all sentient beings live off plants:

after all, some of the most intelligent and adaptable higher mammals, such as the great apes, are herbivorous. It would still be our world, except that nature would not be "red in tooth and claw." And surely in these respects, at least, it would be less painful while yet a "vale of soul-making."

VIII. A BACKWARD GLANCE

Hick's remarks about a painless utopia lead back to the crucial cases of physical evil I instanced earlier. He has said it would be ridiculous to imagine a world where each living creature is individually watched over by a miracle-working guardian angel charged with protecting it from pain. But once we decline the All-or-Nothing Gambit it becomes not at all absurd to ask why a loving God could not intervene to curtail suffering, and so arrange things as to prevent certain types of suffering from occurring at all.

Take our Trapped Rabbit. Hick has quite a few assuaging things to say on animal pain. The lower species are probably not even conscious; higher vertabrates other than men are mostly doomed to die violently, as parts of a self-sustaining organic system; animals have a "happy blindness" to the inevitability of death, which is therefore not a "problem" to them; animals live "from instant to instant" merely, and cannot carry their past experience with them in conscious memory; and in any case the problem of animal pain is subordinate to human sin and suffering, since animal life merely provides "the natural origin and setting" of human life (pp. 345–53). Be that as it may, our furry friend does suffer, and pretty much the way a man does when being devoured by a lion. Why does not God put him out of his misery? That is what the Humane Veterinarian does with an animal facing painful death. Surely the answer cannot be that this animal's torment is necessary to the "vale of soul-making" in any direct way: for according to Hick's theology neither the rabbit nor the cat has a soul anyway.

Or look at the case of the Infant Toddler. If it became subsequently known that a *man* witnessed the child's falling into the pool and could have saved her, yet did nothing at all about it, we should certainly not consider him benevolent. Yet we are expected to believe, or at least not hold it an irrational belief, that God did just that. But for what conceivable reason? The child has not gained any higher moral values from drowning: she is dead. And even if it is true that without real dangers in life—which can and therefore sometimes must lead to disaster—our world would have to be completely, perhaps unpalatably, restructured:

still one is not asking for a complete restructuring. One is asking no more
of God than one expects from a loving parent, to use Hick's own preferred
analogy: that he intervene to prevent such a completely senseless loss.

The Cancer Patient case sharpens these difficulties. For the victim's
"soul" was fully formed—at least as far as this world is concerned—in a
normal course of life. She is dying "in her time," and nothing further is
to be gained for her character or conduct from an agonising end. Let us say
that in the final week of her life she was in conscious torment just half that
time. This still makes three hundred and two thousand four hundred separate seconds of agony completely unnecessary to her death. The humane
doctor, and indeed probably her relatives and fellow-patients as well, regard each of these seconds as sheer loss. They would in most cases actually
prefer that someone give her an overdose of morphine, or inject a few c.c.
of air into her bloodstream. Yet we are supposed to believe that an all-
knowing and all-powerful being who is also infinitely loving could not,
because of a higher imperative, remove her from this "vale of soul-
making." Not even the last day? The last hour? The last minute? The last
second?

Finally, consider again the case of the Brilliant Pianist. As we saw,
the disease is strictly hereditary. Therefore nothing he did in the "vale of
soul-making" before its onset will affect its actually occuring to him.
More disheartening still, nothing he did in his earlier life will in any way
mitigate the course of the disease. Within five to fifteen years he will be
in exactly the same deteriorated state, psychically and physically, as the
village wastrel or drunk would be given the same dominant gene. Indeed
there is a kind of reverse moral process here: the more one achieves in one's
early life the more one loses when the disease sets in. The "vale of soul-
making" theodicy is particularly strained in this example: one cannot resist asking why a loving God finds it desirable to perpetuate diseases like
Huntington's Chorea.

IX. THE DIVINE PROVIDENT FUND

Hick is not, as we shall see in a later section of this paper, entirely unaware
of the formidable difficulties facing his "vale of soul-making" theodicy.
But before we reach what I take to be his final desperate stand, let us look
at the reserves he is able to bring up in this critical juncture.

For Hick the "vale of soul-making" is not complete with the end of
life in this world. Rather our experience in this life is but one stage in the
perfecting process Christianity envisages. Beyond death lies a further

stage in which one may hope for the resurrection or recreation or recon-
stitution of the human personality.

> The Christian claim is that the ultimate life of man—after what further
> scenes of soul-making we do not know—lies in that Kingdom of God
> which is depicted in the teachings of Jesus as a state of exultant and blissful
> happiness, symbolised as a joyous banquet in which all and sundry, having
> accepted God's gracious invitation, rejoice together. And Christian theod-
> icy must point forward to that final blessedness, and claim that this infinite
> future good will render worthwhile all the pain and travail and wickedness
> that has occurred on the way to it. . . . We must thus affirm in faith that
> there will in the final accounting be no personal life that is unperfected and
> no suffering that has not eventually become a phase in the fulfillment of
> God's good purpose. Only so, I suggest, is it possible to believe both in the
> perfect goodness of God and in His unlimited capacity to perform His will.
> For if there are finally wasted lives and finally unredeemed sufferings, ei-
> ther God is not perfect in love or He is not sovereign in rule over His cre-
> ation. (p. 376)

When one reads these sentences there leaps to the mind an idea that
God will redeem innocent suffering by proportionate rewards in the next
life. In that case our Cancer Patient and Brilliant Pianist, at any rate,
would get unusually large "settlements" compared to the ordinary run of
mortals. But of course this does not make sense when one considers that
their suffering was innocent and could have been prevented by God in the
first place. It would be like a human parent letting his children get sick
or injured unnecessarily, then giving them Christmas presents each year in
accordance with how much each suffered. A parent could do that, of
course, but he would not be called "loving"at the same time. Fortunately,
Hick rejects the Insurance Scheme concept of divine providence, correctly
noting that it implies no one will enjoy endless or infinite bliss, since no
one suffers an unending or unlimited injury.

In place of this "book-keeping view," as he calls it, Hick offers another scheme which I shall designate the Divine Provident Fund idea.
Here disproportionate individual suffering leads ultimately to everyone
sharing in an infinite pool of heavenly rewards. As Hick puts it,

> . . . these sufferings—which for some people are immense and for others
> relatively slight—will in the end lead to the enjoyment of a common good
> which will be unending and therefore unlimited, and which will be seen by
> its participants as justifying all that has been endured on the way to it. The
> 'good eschaton' will not be a reward or a compensation proportioned to

each individual's trials, but an infinite good that would render worth while any finite suffering endured in the course of attaining it. (p. 377)

At first sight this seems entirely satisfactory. One thinks though in some ways inappropriately, of several people winning the Sweepstakes together: who will quibble about one winner having been poor all his life and another well off so long as each is getting an enormous sum? But then we return to our crucial cases and measure the idea against them. Our Trapped Rabbit, poor beast, does not even have a claim-slip under this scheme. The Infant Toddler gets no more than other souls whose mortal lives were fully and perhaps not unenjoyably lived out. The Cancer Patient gets nothing additional for that last week's torment, nor the Brilliant Pianist for his wasted later life.

It is no good saying, either, that this reasoning is wrong because one cannot get more than infinite good. For if these are the same persons, their total lives include a finite period of disproportionate good or evil plus an infinite period of perfect good. Thus in the total reckoning they have been differently treated by God and no talk of an ultimate infinite reward can gloss that over. To go back to the picture I suggested before, our human parent not only lets his children get sick or injured unnecessarily but after a time rewards all them equally no matter how differently they fared. If anything, this is less just than the Insurance Scheme Hick wisely repudiates.

X. THE "INTERMEDIATE STATE"

But I have not been entirely fair to Hick in the above criticism. For he also allows room in his eschatological plan for an Intermediate State between the end of this life and the "joyous banquet" of eternal salvation in which we are all to share one day. This is in fact referred to in the long passage I quoted, where Hick inserts the qualifier "after what further scenes of soul-making we do not know"; and goes on to say that in the final accounting no personal life will go 'unperfected'. Indeed it is for this reason that he denies any kind of "bad eschaton," including the belief in eternal, irredeemable suffering in Hell." . . . God will eventually succeed in His purpose of winning all men to Himself in faith and love" (p. 378). It is on this ground that, one might say, Hick chooses to make a final and rather desperate stand.

For Hick the primary purpose of this Intermediate State is what he calls, following some Protestant theologians, "progressive sanctification after death." This ties in with the notion of "soul-making" quite directly, as the continuation of a sanctifying process begun on earth and carried through to completion before one is invited to share in the "joyous banquet" referred to above. How long this postgraduate course in purification will last depends, according to Hick, on the " . . . degree of *un*sanctification remaining to be overcome at the time of death" (p. 383). One should imagine that in some cases it would take an unconscionably long time, and one hope others will not be kept waiting for them. But since these issues touch more intimately on the problem of moral evil I shall leave them and pass on to the relevance this notion of an Intermediate State has, if any, to innocent pain and suffering.

It seems fairly clear to me that it can have no relevance except in one totally unacceptable way. For whatever one postulates beyond this life, each person's total history, at least, begins here. If we divide that total history into two, three, or even a much larger number of "states" the first one is completed in this life. Thus as I said in the previous section of this paper, not even infinite rewards in the last state can really atone for inequities in the first. There is one way, however, that the concept of an Intermediate State could do that. We could suppose God metes out pain and suffering to everyone who enters the Intermediate State in such compensating proportions that they all face the final state on a strictly equal footing. Unfortunately for this ingenious alternative, it implies that God not only permits innocent suffering in the first state for some, but imposes it on previously more fortunate souls in the second. Which carries us even farther from the notion of a loving God.

XI. SHOWING THE WHITE FLAG

It is not surprising, then, that Hick ends up by taking refuge in obscurity on the problem of physical evil. I shall cite just two passages to support this charge, but each will be unmistakably germane to the critical issues I have been raising.

In the first, symptomatically subsumed under the topic "Soul-making and Mystery," he says this:

> Our 'solution', then, to this baffling problem of excessive and undeserved suffering is a frank appeal to the positive value of mystery. Such suffering remains unjust and inexplicable, haphazard and cruelly excessive. The mystery of dysteleological suffering is a real mystery, impenetrable to the rationalizing human mind. (p. 371)

In the second, where Hick is considering whether endless heavenly joy could heal the scars of human suffering, he answers as follows:

... we do not know what is possible, let alone what is probable, in realms of being so far beyond our present experience. We can think only in terms of what Plato called 'likely tales'. It may be that personal scars and memories of evil remain forever, but are transfigured in the light of the universal mutual forgiveness and reconciliation on which the life of heaven is based. Or it may be that the journey to the heavenly Kingdom is so long, and traverses such varied spheres of existence, involving so many new and transforming experiences, that in the end the memory of our earthly life is dimmed to the point of extinction. (pp. 386–7)

Does one not detect a small white flag waving in the smoke there? For if, on the one hand, innocent suffering presents a mystery the rational mind cannot penetrate; or on the other, its compensation in a future life requires conjectures beyond all present experience, then surely the "problem of evil" remains unsolved? Now it is true that in the first pages of his book Hick more or less disclaims any intention of solving it. He even says—a doubleedged remark indeed—that "It may be that what the theodicist is searching for does not exist" (p. 8). All Hick claims to be doing is exploring a more adequate approach to a solution than various others. Yet if the problem really has no solution, as Hick's final appeal to mystery seems to concede, then it is no longer a problem. It is no longer a problem, not merely because all genuine problems have solutions, but also and more importantly because this particular problem, if insoluble, would no longer have a subject. But more on that in a moment. We have first to consider the final defensive manoeuvre open to theodicists when the whole front threatens to collapse.

XII. THE PERMANENT ESCAPE-CLAUSE

Surprisingly, Hick does not make use of this manoeuvre, though he knows it is available (cf. footnote 1, p. 345). But since as I said in the beginning I aim to carry the campaign as well as the battle, I shall examine it anyway.

The move I have in mind has probably never received such a precise and shrewd formulation as in the hands of Nelson Pike.[3] Pike asks us to consider these three propositions:

(1) The world contains instances of suffering.
(2) God exists—and is omnipotent, omniscient, and perfectly good.
(3) An omnipotent and omniscient being would have no morally sufficient reason for allowing instances of suffering.

I think we have to insert the word "innocent" before "suffering" in (1) and (3) above to be faithful to the terms of our problem, but apart from that these propositions will do.

Now according to Pike, it is impossible that all three of these propositions should be true. If (1) and (3) are true, then (2) is false. That is, of course, what the sceptic claims. On the other hand, if (2) and (3) are true, then (1) must be false. But no theist concerned with this problem would say that: precisely because if (1) is false there is no problem of [physical] evil. Still there is a third possibility. That is that (1) and (2) are true but (3) is false. Thus in order to claim God does not exist or, what amounts to the same, that the so-called problem of evil is radically insoluble, a sceptic must show (3) to be true.

But the only way to do that, again according to Pike, is to affirm (3) as a *necessary truth*. This one cannot do. One can only take all the suggested explanations for God allowing innocent suffering offered by the theodicist one by one, as I have been doing, and show them lacking. When the theodicist has exhausted these he can still retreat to "unexamined reasons" no matter how complete the list of examined reasons (pp. 89–90). It is always open to the theist, having abandoned all his attempts at positive theodicy, to say God *could* have a morally sufficient reason for allowing innocent pain and suffering, even if we do not and perhaps never will understand what that is.

But will such a defence really work? That depends, of course, upon what you mean by "work." Consider the following blasphemous-sounding but pertinent analogy. Suppose someone who knew Adolf Eichmann well and wants to defend him says this: "I agree that Eichmann did all the things you cite and I know of no reason which could justify his doing them. Perhaps no reason will ever be discovered. But because I believe him to have been a fundamentally good person I am confident he has—indeed he must have had—a morally sufficient reason for acting the way he did. Now to exclude this possibility entirely you have to show his not having such a reason to be a necessary truth. But it cannot be a necessary truth, since it will never be self-contradictory to maintain that he had one."

This defence "works" in the sense that one cannot make necessary truths out of negative statements about someone's motives. But it patently fails to work in the sense that, having had that pointed out to us, we must agree to suspend all further judgement on Eichmann's character and guilt. For one thing, if we did this in the present case we would have to do it, if we wanted to be consistent, in every case. Which means no one would be guilty or bad, so far as we can know; and that in turn would

If no one is bad can no one be good??

mean no one is innocent or good; not even God. For another, the logic of decision in such matters is not, to use John Wisdom's contrasting terms, "vertical" but "horizontal." That is to say it is not part of our decision-making process in such cases to ask if it is *logically* possible someone had a morally sufficient reason for what he did, or failed to do. We ask only if it is *practically* possible, that is, whether any reason has been put forward plausible enough to warrant an acquittal or suspension of judgement. When that is not forthcoming we regard the matter as closed.

But does the believer? Often and obviously he does not. This leads into my final remarks.

XIII. THE PROBLEM OF BELIEF

Theists sometimes talk of the "problem of unbelief" in our time, but to the unbeliever there is a parallel problem of belief. Why does the theodicist, when his proffered reasons for the existence of evil in a God-oriented world have been examined and shown lacking, retreat to "unexamined reasons"? Why does he not simply lay down his arms and go home to better things? For unlike the example used above, there would then be nothing left to defend. God is truly unique in the sense that if he is "guilty"—even of indifference only—then he disappears. He is a loving God, after all.

Perhaps the solution to this problem of belief can be found along lines suggested by Pike. At the end of his essay he concludes that when the existence of God is accepted, as it is by most theologians, 'prior to any rational consideration of the status of evil in the world', then the traditional problem of evil " . . . reduces to a noncrucial perplexity of minor importance" (p. 102). That may be a philosophical overstatement, as Hick insists (*ibid.*). But it may yet be psychologically valid, for there is no doubt most theists remain singularly untouched in their faith by self-confessed failures to understand God's tolerance of innocent suffering.

One gets the image, indeed, of two classes of people interested in the philosophy of religion. On the one hand there are sceptics, like myself, who move from the world to a God-hypothesis which they feel compelled by reason to dismiss. On the other hand there are believers who move from a God-postulate to the world, prepared to endlessly explain away, or even leave admittedly unexplained, whatever the world contains that cannot be logically entailed in that postulate. Thus it is that in the final analysis theodicists retreat either, as in the case of Hick, to "divine mystery," or, in the case of others, to "unexamined reasons" for God's indifference.

But it is important to note that at just these points theists cease to be theodicists at all. They are no longer "explaining" evil in the world: they are either "explaining it away" or saying it cannot be explained. And in both cases they are in effect admitting they have no rational defence to offer. Which means that despite appearances they really are abandoning the battlefield.

It is, finally, just because I think that despite their credentials philosophical theists are only derivatively interested in the problem of evil that I really despair of any decisive outcome on this issue. Perhaps in the end the sceptical philosopher of religion must affirm: unbelief cannot argue with belief: it can only preach to it.

NOTES

1. John Hick, *Evil and the God of Love* (Macmillan, 1966).

2. Cf. Roland Puccetti, "The Concept of God," *The Philosophical Quarterly,* vol. 14, no. 56 (July 1964).

3. *Hume on Evil,* reprinted in *God and Evil,* ed. Nelson Pike (Prentice-Hall, 1964), pp. 85–102.

Divine Persuasion and the Triumph of Good

LEWIS FORD

In Archibald MacLeish's *J. B.*, Nickles hums a little tune for Mr. Zuss:

> I heard upon his dry dung heap
> That man cry out who cannot sleep:
> "If God is God He is not good,
> If God is good He is not God;
> Take the even, take the odd,
> I would not sleep here if I could . . . "

These words epitomize the unyielding difficulty confronting classical theism, for it cannot seem to reconcile God's goodness with his power in the face of the stubborn reality of unexplained evil. The process theism of Alfred North Whitehead and Charles Hartshorne was clearly designed to circumvent these persistent difficulties. The time has now come, perhaps, to probe the adequacy of this solution. While it may handle the problem of evil, does not process theism's critique of classical omnipotence open up a Pandora's box of its own? If God lacks the power to actualize his own ends in the world, how can we be certain that the good will ultimately be achieved? In a recent article, Edward H. Madden and Peter H. Hare contend that process theism lies shipwrecked in the very same shoals it sought to avoid.[1] If God's power is curtailed in order to absolve him of responsibility for evil, they suggest, then the guarantee for the ultimate triumph of good has been undermined. The process theist may say that

> natural events do not thwart (God) but are the occasions for his exercise of creative power, but he still must admit that on his view of the matter God is still limited in the sense that he neither creates nor wholly controls actual

From *The Christian Scholar* 50 (Fall 1967): 235–50. Used by permission of the author and the editor of *Soundings* which was the successor of *The Christian Scholar*.

occasions. Moreover, if God does not wholly control actual occasions, it is difficult to see how there is any real assurance of the ultimate triumph of good. The two elements of traditional theism reinforce each other. The unlimited power of God insures the triumph of good, and the latter requires the notion of God's unlimited power. The mutual reinforcement, however, is wholly lacking in Whitehead's system. The absence points up a fundamental difficulty with his quasi-theism.[2]

Madden and Hare implicitly construe divine power to be coercive, limited by the exercise of other coercive powers in the world. We contend that divine power is neither coercive nor limited, though we agree that God does not wholly control finite actualities. This means we must recognize their contention that process theism does preclude any *necessary* guarantee that good will triumph on the stage of worldly endeavour. Yet should there be such a guarantee? Far from being required by theism, we shall argue that such a philosophical guarantee would undermine genuine religious commitment, and that the ultimate redemption from evil moves on a very different plane. With respect to any such guarantee we find, as Kant did on another occasion, that it becomes "necessary to deny knowledge, in order to make room for faith."[3]

I

Now clearly, if power is exerted only to the extent that control is maintained, then Whitehead's God is limited. But power may be defined more broadly as the capacity to influence the outcome of any process of actualization, thereby permitting both persuasive and coercive power. Coercive power directly influences the outcome, since the process must conform to its control. Persuasive power operates more indirectly, for it is effective in determining the outcome only to the extent that the process appropriates and reaffirms for itself the aims envisioned in the persuasion. Thus the measure of control introduced differs; coercive power and control are commensurate, while persuasive power introduces the additional variable of acceptance by the process in actualization. That God's control is in fact limited by the existence of evil would signify a limited coercive power, but it is compatible with unlimited persuasive power.

Whitehead's thesis is that God possesses no coercive power at all. Whether limited or unlimited, such power is incompatible with divine perfection. In the official formulation of Christian doctrine, Whitehead complains, "the deeper idolatry, of the fashioning of God in the image of the Egyptian, Persian, and Roman imperial rulers, was retained. The

Church gave unto God the attributes which belonged exclusively to Caesar" (*PR* 520). The concept of divine coercive power, both in its pure and modified forms, has led to grave difficulties.

Consider the extreme instance in which God is conceived as exerting unlimited coercive power, thereby controlling and determining all things. God is the master potter, moulding the clay of the world by the force of his creative activity, except that God has no need of any clay with which to work; he makes his own. On this exception the analogy breaks down, for the potter's vase asserts it own reality apart from the human potter precisely because it had already existed separately as clay. Could a world moulded completely by God's coercive power assert any independent existence of its own? To do so the world must possess some power. Pure coercive power transforms *creatio ex nihilo* into *creatio ex deo*, with the world possessing no more independent actuality than an idea in the divine mind would have. Even if it were to exist apart from the divine mind, it could not enrich God's experience, for he fully experiences in imagination any world he could completely determine.

Most views of divine power are less extreme, but they all share the same basic defects insofar as they ascribe coercive power to God. To the extent that God exercises such power, creaturely freedom is restricted, the reality of the world is diminished, and the divine experience is impoverished. Creaturely freedom is all important, for without it God is deprived of the one thing the world can provide which God alone cannot have: a genuine social existence. Abandoning the angelic marionettes who merely echo his thought as further extensions of his own being, God has elected to enter into dialogue with sinful, yet free, men.

Divine persuasive power maximizes creaturely freedom, respecting the integrity of each creature in the very act of guiding that creature's development toward greater freedom. The image of God as the craftsman, the cosmic watchmaker, must be abandoned. God is the husbandman in the vineyard of the world, fostering and nurturing its continuous evolutionary growth throughout all ages; he is the companion and friend who inspiries us to achieve the very best that is within us. God creates by persuading the world to create itself. Nor is this persuasion limited by any defect, for as Plato pointed out long ago, the real good is genuinely persuasive, in contrast to the counterfeit of the apparent good we confront on all sides.

This vision appears to many as too bold, for its seems to ascribe mind and consciousness to all beings. In ordinary discourse only those who are consciously sensitive to the directives and promptings of others can be persuaded, although we are beginning to recognize the subliminal influence of the "hidden persuaders." Whitehead is urging us to broaden our understanding of persuasion, for otherwise we lack the means for penetrating the nature of creation. Without the alternative of divine persuasion, we confront two unwelcome extremes: divine determinism or pure chance. In neither instance can God create. If determined by God, the world lacks all ontological independence. It makes no difference even if God only acts through the secondary causes of the natural order. To exist apart from God, either the world as a whole or its individual parts must possess a self-activity of its own. This self-activity is denied to the world as a whole if God is its primary (coercive) cause, and it is denied to the individual parts if they are determined by the secondary causes of the natural order acting in God's stead. Chance, on the other hand, ignores God's role in the evolutionary advance entirely and renders this advance itself unintelligible. We need not anthropocentrically imagine the evolutionary process to culminate in man, for it is quite conceivable that in time it might bypass man and the entire class of mammals to favor some very different species capable of a greater complexity than man can achieve; if not here on earth, then in some other planetary system. Nevertheless it seems impossible to deny that there has been an evolutionary advance in the sense of increasing complexity of order over the past several billion years. This increasing complexity cannot be satisfactorily accounted for simply in terms of the chance juxtaposition of component elements, and calls for a transcendent directing power constantly introducing richer possibilities of order for the world to actualize. God proposes, and the world disposes. This response is the necessary self-activity of the creature by which it maintains its own existence. The creature may or may not embody the divine urge toward greater complexity, but insofar as that ideal is actualized, an evolutionary advance has been achieved. Any divine power which so influences the world without violating its integrity is properly called persuasive, while the necessary self-activity of the creature insures the spontaneity of response. This spontaneity may be minimal for protons and electrons, but in the course of the evolutionary advance, sustained until now, it has manifested itself in ever richer forms as the vitality of living cells, the conscious activity of the higher animals, and the self-conscious freedom of man. Spontaneity has matured as freedom. On this level it becomes possible for the increasing complexity of order to be directed toward the achievement of civilization, and the means of divine persuasion to become ethical aspiration (see *RM* 119). The devout will affirm that in the ideals we envision we are being persuaded by God, but this self-conscious awareness is not necessary for its effectiveness. Not only we ourselves, but the entire created order, whether consciously or unconsciously, is open to this divine persuasion, each in its own way.

II

The model of divine coercive power persisted so long primarily because God's activity is usually conceived in terms of efficient causality. The effect must conform to its cause; this is the basis for all causal law. Yet Aristotle's insight that God influences the world by final causation is more insightful, though it must be reformulated so that God can *act* to provide each actuality with its own final cause, and not just inspire the world as a whole through the perfection of his *being*. Whitehead suggests that God experiences the past actual world confronting each individual occasion in process of actualization, and selects for it that ideal possibility which would achieve the maximum good compatible with its situation. The occasion's past actual world consists in the totality of efficient causal influences impinging upon it which it must take into account and integrate into its final actualization. The efficient causal influences provide the means whereby actualization occurs, but the way in which they may be integrated can vary, depending upon the complexity of the situation. God's directive provides an initial aim for this process of integration, but unlike the efficient causal influences, that aim can be so drastically modified that its original purpose could be completely excluded from physical realization in the final outcome.[4] Insofar as the occasion actualizes its initial aim, the divine persuasion has been effective. God furnishes the initial direction, but the occasion is responsible for its actualization, whether for good or for evil.

In presenting this theory of divine activity, Whitehead unfortunately concentrated his attention upon the primordial nature of God as the locus of possible values to be presented to individual occasions, at the expense of the consequent nature's role in determining which possibility would be most appropriate for the particular contingent situation. As John B. Cobb, Jr. has convincingly demonstrated,[5] Whitehead's "principle of concretion" only gradually takes on flesh and blood as he subjects his conception of God to the categoreal obligations of his own metaphysical vision during the years 1924–1929. Any statements taken from *Science and the Modern World* or *Religion in the Making* about the nature of God are systematically worthless unless proleptically interpreted in terms of Whitehead's mature position. Taken in isolation they only serve to muddy the waters.[6] Even in *Process and Reality* the transformation of God into an actual entity is not wholly complete, and to that extent there is some truth in the assertion that "what little influence Whitehead's God has on the actual world . . . he has as a principle, not as a being or person, and insofar as God is a personal being, he is without any effect on the actual world."[7] On the other hand, it is possible to modify Whitehead's presentation in the direction of greater consistency with his own categoreal scheme, indicating the very active role the consequent nature plays in providing the initial aim. William A. Christian recognizes the interweaving of the primordial and consequent natures when he writes:

> As prehended by a certain actual occasion, God is *that* unity of feelings which result from the integration of his primordial nature with his prehensions of the past actual world of *that* actual occasion.[8]

Cobb also develops this point:

> Whitehead speaks of God as having, like all actual entities, an aim at intensity of feeling. . . . This aim is primordial and unchanging, and it determines the primordial ordering of eternal objects. But if this eternal ordering is to have specified efficacy for each new occasion, then the general aim by which it is determined must be specified for each occasion. That is, God must entertain for each new occasion the aim for its ideal satisfaction.[9]

Cobb recognizes that his account goes "a little beyond the confines of description of Whitehead's account in *Process and Reality* in the direction of systematization,"[10] but he is prepared to defend his interpretation in detail.[11] What is important for our purposes is the fact that the involvement of God's consequent nature in divine persuasion renders that activity intensely personal. For God thus serves as a dynamic source of value, personally responding anew to the concrete situation confronting each creature in turn, and providing it individually with its own particular initial aim. Through this ever ongoing activity God becomes the ultimate source for all value, though not one which is static and impersonal like Plato's Form of the Good.

III

If there is no fixed, final end towards which God and the world are moving, what governs God in his choice of the good? Socrates once asked Euthyphro (10 A), "whether the pious or holy is beloved by the gods because it is holy, or holy because it is beloved of the gods?" In response to the corresponding ethical question, Duns Scotus declared that what God wills is good because God wills it, rather than that he wills it because it is good. If in affirming God as the dynamic source of value we agree with Scotus, what prevents our God from being utterly capricious in what he chooses to be good?

In order to grapple with this question we must first appreciate Whitehead's analysis of the good. Because he subordinates goodness to beauty, he runs a serious risk of being misunderstood. He has been accused of a general aestheticism which fails to take seriously the tragic conflict between good and evil, though his own motives are quite different. He does not seek to trivialize the good, but to enhance it by placing it in relation to an all-embracing value which would not be restricted to the limited context of human conduct. Beauty, the name of this all-embracing value, cannot be interpreted simply in terms of aesthetic categories. It is evoked by natural occurrences and by works of art, to be sure, but also by conduct, action, virtue, ideas, and even by truth (AI 342f.).

Goodness is essentially subordinate to beauty for two reasons. As Whitehead uses these terms, goodness is primarily instrumental while beauty is intrinsically valuable, actualized in experience for its own sake. It is a quality of experience itself, while that which occasions our experience of beauty (such as the good) is more properly called "beautiful" (AI 328). Moreover, goodness is rooted in Reality, the totality of particular finite actualizations achieved in the world, while beauty pertains also to Appearance, our interpretative experience of Reality:

> For Goodness is a qualification belonging to the constitution of reality, which in any of its individual actualizations is better or worse. Good and evil lie in depths and distances below and beyond appearance. They solely concern interrelations within the real world. The real world is good when it is beautiful (AI 345).

We are apt to dismiss appearance as unimportant in contrast to reality, regarding it as largely illusory. Appearance need be neither unimportant nor illusory. It is presupposed by truth, which as "the conformation of Appearance to Reality" (AI 309) could not exist without it. It is the basis for the intelligibility of our experience, and as we shall see in the final section, appearance plays a crucial role in the establishment of the kingdom of heaven. In any event, whether appearance is significant or trivial, that value which includes it along with reality is clearly the more inclusive.

The good, therefore, is to be understood in terms of its contribution to beauty. Beauty, in turn, is described as "the internal conformation of the various items of experience with each other, for the production of maximum effectiveness" (*AI* 341). This effectiveness is achieved by the conjoint operation of harmony and intensity. Harmony is the mutual adaptation of several items for joint inclusion within experience, while intensity refers to the wealth and variety of factors jointly experienced, particularly in terms of the degree of contrast manifest. In effect, then, actuality is good insofar as it occasions an intrinsic experience of harmonious intensity.

By the same token, evil is the experience of discord, attesting to the presence of destruction. "The experience of destruction is in itself evil" and in fact constitutes its meaning (*AI* 333). This definition is fully serviceable, once we realize that what is destroyed is not what is but what might have been. We tend to think of existence only in terms of continued persistence of being, but whatever has once achieved actual existence remains indestructible as determinate fact, regardless of the precariousness of its future continuation. In like manner, we ordinarily restrict destruction to the loss of anticipated continuing existence. Such continuing existence, however, if destroyed, never was but only might have been. As such it is merely a special case of what might have been, along with lost opportunities, thwarted experiences, disappointed anticipations. Whenever what is is less than what might have been there is destruction, no matter how slight.

Whitehead is emphatic in insisting upon the finitude of actuality, which in its exclusiveness affords the opportunity for evil.

> There is no totality which is the harmony of all perfections. Whatever is realized in any one occasion of experience necessarily excludes the unbounded welter of contrary possibilities. There are always 'others', which might have been and are not. This finiteness is not the result of evil, or of imperfection. It results from the fact that there are possibilities of harmony which either produce evil in joint realization, or are incapable of such conjunction. . . . History can only be understood by seeing it as the theatre of diverse groups of idealists respectively urging ideals incompatible for conjoint realization. You cannot form any historical judgment of right or wrong by considering each group separately. The evil lies in the attempted conjunction (*AL* 356f.; see *AI* 375, *MT* 75).

This conflict of values in attempted actualization is experienced as discord, and engenders destruction. "There is evil when things are at cross purposes" (*RM* 97). "The nature of evil is that the characters of things are mutually obstuctive" (*PR* 517).

While evil is the disruption of harmony, it need not detract from intensity. In fact, the intensity of evil may be preferred to the triviality of some dead-level achievement of harmony, for the intense clash may be capable of resolution at a much higher level of complexity. The unrelieved "good life" may be rather dull, yielding no more zest of value than the perfectly harmonious repetition of dominant fifth chords in C major. "Evil is the half-way house between perfection and triviality. It is the violence of strength against strength" (*AI* 355).

In his consequent nature God experiences both the good and the evil actualized in the world. His own aim, like that of the creature, is at beauty. "God's purpose in the creative advance is the evocation of intensities" (*PR* 161), but these intensities must be balanced to overcome the mutual obstructiveness of things. God therefore seeks in his experience of the world the maximum attainment of intensity compatible with harmony that is possible under the circumstances of the actual situation. In order to insure this richness of experience for his consequent nature, God therefore provides to each occasion that initial aim which, if actualized, would contribute maximally to this harmonious intensity. This is the aim God wills as good for that creature in his role as the dynamic source of value. It is not capricious for it seeks the well-being both of the creature and of God. Were God to select any other aim for that occasion he would be frustrating his own aim at beauty.

Because of the intrinsic unity of the divine experience, all the finite actualities of the world must be felt together in their measure of harmony and discord. Insofar as they are individually intense and vivid, these occasions contribute to the maximum intensity of experience for God. Insofar as the several occasions are mutually supportive of one another, they also contribute, but should they clash, or be individually trivial, they detract from this final unity of all actuality within God. Divine love and justice may serve as primary symbols for God's aim at the harmonious intensity of beauty. Love expresses God's concern and appreciation for the particular intensity achieved by each individual, who finds ultimate significance in this divine feeling of appreciation for its particular contribution. Justice, on the other hand, expresses God's concern for the social situation of the togetherness of all occasions, since his experience of the world necessarily includes all the harmonies and clashes between individual achievements. Human justice tends to be cold and impartial, because our own partiality is so imperfect and limited to permit fair adjudication.

Our sympathy and participation in the needs and claims of one party usually precludes any adequate participation in the rival needs and claims of others, particularly if the rival claimant is "society as a whole." Divine justice, on the other hand, is not abstract, following inexorably from the character of the primordial nature, but is concrete, the natural and spontaneous activity of the consequent nature integrating God's individual appreciations of the several occasions. Far from being impartial, God is completely partial, fully participating in the needs and claims of every creature. But because he is partial to all at once, he can judge the claims of each with respect to all others, valuing each to the extent to which this is consonant with all rival claims. Justice is ultimately the divine appreciation for the world, that is, the divine love simply seen in its social dimension.

This analysis of divine activity as the source of human value enables us to make sense out of the competing claims of rival ethical theories by assigning each a subordinate role within a wider explanation. Hedonistic and emotivistic theories emphasize the necessity to locate intrinsic value solely in subjective experience, though they tend to ignore the divine experience in this connection. Utilitarian theories stress the need for individual achievements of value to support and enhance one another. Their rule of "the greatest happiness for the greatest number" is strictly applicable, but it is spontaneously and non-calculatively calibrated to balance the claims to individual experience both qualitatively and quantitatively in the divine experience. Theories of duty, including Plato's vision of the Forms, see both the ideal character of the initial aim for each individual as well as the transcendent character of its source.

Religion seeks to enhance the role of ethical aspiration embodied in initial aims by concentrating upon their source in God. God is supremely worthy of worship because he is the ultimate source of value, as well as being that actuality in which all other actualities achieve their ultimate significance. The metaphysical description of God serves to purify the religious tradition of accidental accretions, while the religious experience of God gives concrete embodiment to these philosophical abstractions.

IV

Is there then any ultimate triumph of good? The Christian and the Jew alike wait with confident expectation for that day when the wolf shall lie down with the lamb. Classical theism, construing omnipotence in terms of coercive power, provides a philosophical guarantee that that day will in fact come to pass, or argues that it is already taking place (Leibniz' best of all possible worlds). This guarantee, however, transforms a confident expectation into a determinate fact, whether that fact be regarded as present or future. From the standpoint of faith, this appears to be nothing more than an emphatic underscoring of an intense trust in God. From the standpoint of logic, however, the fact of the triumph of good vitiates all need to strive for it. As in the case of the Marxist vision of a classless society, if its coming is inevitable, why must we work for it?

In process theism the future is an open risk. God is continuously directing the creation toward the good, but his persuasive power is effective only insofar as the creatures themselves affirm that good. Creaturely evil is an ever-present contingency, unless Origen is correct that we cannot resist the grace of God forever. On the other hand, the absence of any final guarantee now makes it genuinely possible for the expectation of the good to become a matter of faith. By faith I do not mean its rationalistic counterfeit: a belief based upon insufficient evidence. Rather I mean what Kierkegaard meant by truth for the existing individual: "an objective uncertainty held fast in an appropriation-process of the most passionate inwardness."[12] Faith is belief in spite of doubt, sustained by trust, loyalty, and devotion. The future is now doubtful, risky, uncertain. Yet the theist is sustained by his confident expectation that if we as creatures all have faith in God, that is, if all rely upon his guidance (given in the initial aim of each occasion), trusting him sufficiently to actualize the good which he proposes as novel possibility, then the good *will* triumph. The continued persistence of evil, both in man and in the natural order, testifies to the very fragmentary realization of creaturely faith in God. Nonetheless we may hope that the grace of God may be received and permeate all beings, and in that hope do our part in the great task. Such hope prohibits other worldly withdrawal, but calls upon us to redouble our efforts to achieve the good in this world with all its ambiguities for good and evil.

Faith in this sense is reciprocal. Just as the world must trust God to provide the aim for its efforts, so God must trust the world for the achievement of that aim. As Madden and Hare point out, "he is apparently so weak that he cannot guarantee his own welfare."[13] This is true to the Biblical image of God's vulnerability toward man's waywardness. We read that "God repented that he had made man, and it grieved him to his heart."[14] Israel remembers God's suffering and anguish over his chosen people,[15] a suffering most poignantly revealed to the Church in the crucifixion of Jesus of Nazareth. The world is a risky affair for God as well as for us. God has taken that risk upon himself in creating us with freedom through persuasion. He has faith in us, and it is up to us to respond in faith to him.

V

Thus far we have spoken concerning the actualization of the good in the world. Here the good will not triumph unless we achieve that victory. Nevertheless there is an ultimate consummation, not in the world but in the divine experience, that accomplishes our redemption from evil.

Whitehead provides an extremely detailed analysis of experience as a process of integration whereby an initial multiplicity of direct feelings of other actualities fuse together with the help of supplemental feelings to achieve a unified outcome. This distinction between initial, physical, conformal feelings and supplemental, conceptual feelings can by significantly applied to the divine experience. In this initial phase God experiences each actuality just as it is for itself, with all its joy and/or suffering. As Christian documents so well, God's initial conformal feelings are perfect, reenacting the same feeling with all of the intimacy and poignancy that the creature felt, without any loss or distortion. [16] Here God is completely vulnerable, completely open to all the evil and the tragedy that the world has seen. "God is the great companion—the fellow-sufferer who understands" (PR 532). Moreover, the early phases in his integration of these several conformal feelings introduce dimensions of suffering the world has not known. God experiences fully the discord between incompatible achievements of value, since he honors and appreciates the value of each wholeheartedly, refusing to moderate the cause of any party in the interests of easy compromise. He also faces the disappointment of the disparity between the initial ideal he proposed for any occasion and its subsequent faulty actualization. God is a most sensitive individual, with the highest ideals, constantly thwarted at every turn, yet who resolutely refuses to give up his grip on either ideality or actuality. At the same time, however, he is also a most imaginative being, whose unlimited conceptual resources enable him to transmute this suffering into joy and peace.

In his analysis of beauty and evil, Whitehead discusses four ways of dealing with the suffering of disharmony (AI 334f.). The first three are inhibitory, directly or indirectly, excluding and rejecting some elements for the sake of the final harmony. Since God is hospitable to all, refusing none, none of these approaches is finally satisfactory. Yet there is hope in the final approach.

This fourth way is by spontaneity of the occasion so directing its mental functionings as to introduce a third system of prehensions, relevant to both the inharmonious systems. This novel system is such as radically to alter the distribution of intensities throughout the two given systems, and to change the importance of both in the final intensive experience of the occasion. This way is in fact the introduction of Appearance, and its use to preserve the massive qualitative variety of Reality from simplification by negative prehensions (i.e., by inhibitory exclusions) (*AI* 335).

Here we can best understand Whitehead's point by analogy with works of the imagination, since this fourth way calls upon the resources of conceptual possibility to heal the wounds inflicted by actuality. Art and poetry transform the dull, ugly, irritating commonplaces of life into vibrant, meaningful realities by inserting them within fresh and unexpected contexts. Dramatic insight at the hands of Sophocles can suffuse the tragic deeds and suffering of Oedipus the King with dignity and honor by skillfully weaving these actions into an artful whole. Imaginative reason in the form of a speculative philosophy such as Whitehead's can surmount the interminable conflicts between man and nature, mind and body, freedom and determinism, religion and science, by assigning each its rightful place within a larger systematic framework. The larger pattern, introduced conceptually, can bring harmony to discord by interrelating potentially disruptive elements in constructive ways. Since God's conceptual feelings as derived from his primordial nature are inexhaustible, he has all the necessary resources to supplement his initial conformal feelings perfectly, thereby achieving a maximum harmonious intensity from any situation.

As the last sentence of our quotation indicates, the shift from initial conformal feelings to supplemental conceptual feelings marks a shift from reality to appearance. The objective content of conformal feelings constitutes reality as experienced, for it embodies our direct confrontation with other actualities (*AL* 269). The difference between this objective content and the content arising out of the integration of conformal feeling with supplemental conceptual feelings (the "mental pole") is felt as "appearance."

In other words, "appearance" is the effect of the activity of the mental pole, whereby the qualities and coordinations of the given physical world undergo transformation. It results from the fusion of the ideal with the actual—The light that never was, on sea or land (*AI* 270).

Appearance plays little or no role in simpler actualities, for they tend simply to conform to the realities of the immediate situation. Appearance

becomes of the utmost importance with the emergence of sensory
perception, for his complex mental functioning provides the means
whereby the bewildering bombardment of causal influences can be reduced to a vivid awareness for perceptive discernment. We tend to despise
appearance for its occasional lapses from reality, but this is short-sighted
thinking. Appearance, Whitehead argues, is the locus for perception,
novelty, intelligibility, and even consciousness. We constantly strive to
encounter reality directly, but such an effort simply takes us back to a
preconscious physical interaction with our surroundings. What is needed
is not reality but truthful appearance, that is, conscious perceptive
experience which is directly derived from and rooted in reality. Appearance becomes illusory only to the extent that the final integration
achieves completion by the inhibitory exclusion of some elements of
reality.

Clearly, divinely experienced Appearance is thoroughly truthful, in-
corporating all Reality within its comprehension, yet infusing it with an
intensity and harmony that Reality failed to achieve for itself. Goodness,
as pertaining solely to the achievement of Reality, is left behind in this
final experience of Beauty, though its contribution forms its necessary basis. In this way Truth, as the conformation of Appearance to the Reality
in which it is rooted, enhances Beauty (see *AI* 342f.). In Beauty the goodness of the world is saved and preserved whole, while its evil is redeemed
and purged of all its wickedness.

Hopefully this technical analysis will illuminate Whitehead's lyrical
words towards the end of *Process and Reality:*

> The wisdom of the divine subjective aim prehends every actuality for
> what it can be in such a perfected system—its sufferings, its sorrows, its
> failures, its triumphs, its immediacies of joy—woven by rightness of feel-
> ing into the harmony of the universal feeling. . . . The revolts of destruc-
> tive evil, purely self-regarding, are dismissed into their triviality of merely
> individual facts; and yet the good they did achieve in individual joy, in in-
> dividual sorrow, in the introduction of needed contrast, is yet saved by its
> relation to the completed whole. The image—and it is but an image—the
> image under which this operative growth of God's nature is best conceived,
> is that of a tender care that nothing be lost.
>
> The consequent nature of God is his judgment on the world. He
> saves the world as it passes into the immediacy of his own life. It is the
> judgment of a tenderness which loses nothing that can be saved. It is also
> the judgment of a wisdom which uses what in the temporal world is mere
> wreckage (*PR* 525).

(The last two sentences recall to mind the ancient vision of a law-giver, the leader of a second exodus, who humbly fulfills the task of the suffering servant:

> A bruised reed he will not break,
> and a dimly burning wick he will not quench;
> he will faithfully bring forth justice.)[17]

George F. Thomas, while most sensitive to the metaphorical power of these words of Whitehead, offers a searching critique which must be answered:

> The nature of the process by which God "saves" the world is not entirely clear. "He saves the world," says Whitehead, "as it passes into the immediacy of his own life." This means that in some way the values realized by actual entities are saved by being included in the experience of God as a "completed whole." But does it mean that the world is transformed and the evil in it overcome, or only that it is included in the harmony of God's experience? The method by which it is "saved" is said to be rationality rather than force. . . . But the "over-powering rationality of his conceptual harmonization" (PR 526) seems to be effective not in transforming the *world* and overcoming its evil but in harmonizing its discords in the experience of *God*.[18]

Yet is it God's task to transform the world? Clearly the ancient Hebrew looked to Yahweh to bring about the prosperity of his nation. Thomas reaffirms that hope, but is it a realistic and justifiable expectation?

Samuel H. Beer argues that this expectation was transformed by the proclamation of Jesus:

> The gospel of the kingdom is that there is another order beyond our earthy existence. Things of the world as we find it are moral and so without consequence and meaning, except as they may be preserved in that saving order. Here the covenant with man is not that he and his children shall thrive and prosper in history. It is rather that they shall sooner or later die in history but that they shall yet live in an order which transcends history. The meek, the merciful, the pure in heart, shall inherit it, not on earth, but in heaven.[19]

We are to seek "a kingdom not of this world" (PR 520), a kingdom which both Beer and Whitehead find exemplified in the consequent nature of God (PR 531).

Were God to transform the world, he would usurp our creaturely function in the moral economy. Yet suppose he were to usher in a perfected world tomorrow, the fulfillment of all our wishful dreaming. That would certainly redeem the world from all the evil which it would otherwise fall heir to tomorrow, but would it purge the world of today's evil? Remembering Ivan Karamazov's words, would such a perfect world even compensate for the innocent suffering of one baby in today's world? For what has already happened is past and cannot be altered; no future transformation can affect it. Nevertheless it can be transformed in the divine experience of the world, and this is where its redemption is to be sought. Finite actualization is necessarily transient. Far from saving and perfecting the past, the present blocks out the immediacy of the past by its own presence. If "the nature of evil is that the character of things are mutually obstructive" (PR 517), then the constant displacement and loss of the past through the activity of the present is most evil, however unavoidable, and no present or future achievement of the world can remedy that situation. "The ultimate evil in the temporal world . . . lies in the fact that the past fades, that time is a 'perpetual perishing' " (PR 517). This perishing can only be overcome within a divine experience which savors every occasion, no matter how distantly past with respect to ourselves, as happening now in an everlasting immediacy which never fades.

> Each actuality in the temporal world has its reception into God's nature. The corresponding element in God's nature is not temporal actuality, but is the transmutation of that temporal actuality into a living, ever-present fact (PR 531).[20]

Finally, however, it may be objected that this ultimate consummation of all things is fine for God, but has no value for us. Thomas argues that Whitehead's God is not "the *Redeemer* of the world who transforms His creatures by the power of His grace and brings new life to them."[21] In response Whitehead speaks of "four creative phases in which the universe accomplishes its actuality" (PR 532),[22] which culminates in the impact of God's consequent experience upon the world.

> For the perfected actuality passes back into the temporal world, and qualifies this world so that each temporal actuality includes it as an immediate fact of relevant experience. For the kingdom of heaven is with us today (PR 532).

This follows from his general 'principle of relativity,' whereby any actuality whatever causally influences all subsequent actualities, however negligibly (PR 33). As it stands, this brief description of our intuition of the kingdom of God in the last two paragraphs of *Process and Reality* is exceedingly cryptic, and must be explicated by means of the final chapter of *Adventures of Ideas* on "Peace." In this chapter, however, there is a tentativeness, a suggestive inarticulateness struggling with a far wider vision than we can possibly do justice to. Whitehead tells us he chose "the term 'Peace' for that Harmony of Harmonies which calms destructive turbulence and completes civilization" (*AI* 367). "The experience of Peace is largely beyond the control of purpose. It comes as a gift" (*AI* 368). I take it to be the way in which we participate in the divine life through an intuitive foretaste of God's experience. "It is primarily a trust in the efficacy of Beauty" (*AI* 367), presumably that Beauty realized in God's perfected experience of all actuality. It is here that the good finally triumphs in all her glory—or, more precisely, as engulfed by all the divine glory as well.

NOTES

1. E. H. Madden and P. H. Hare, "Evil and Unlimited Power," *The Review of Metaphysics*, 20, 2 (December 1966), pp. 278–89. This article has been revised and reprinted in Hare and Madden, *Evil and the Concept of God* (Springfield, IL: Charles C. Thomas, 1968). Throughout the revision the original phrase "triumph of good" has been softened to "growth of value." In the present essay we shall quote from the original article, adding in parentheses a reference to the corresponding passage from the book.

2. Ibid., 281f. (117).

3. Immanuel Kant, *Critique of Pure Reason*, B 30. Norman Kemp Smith, trans. (London: Macmillan, 1929), p. 29.

4. The subjective aim cannot be rejected in the sense that the aim could be excluded (i.e., negatively prehended) in its entirety at some phase in concrescence, thereby leaving the occasion bereft of any direction whatsoever. There must be continuity of aim throughout concrescence, for the process of unification is powerless to proceed in the absence of some direction. Nonetheless it is possible for the subjective aim to be so continuously modified in concrescence that the final outcome could express the contrary of the initial aim. Though genetically related to the initial aim, such a final outcome has excluded that initial purpose from realization.

5. John B. Cobb, Jr., *A Christian Natural Theology* (Philadelphia: Westminster, 1965), pp. 135–85.

6. *Contra* Madden and Hare, p. 282f. (118).

7. Ibid., 285f. (121).

8. William A. Christian, *An Interpretation of Whitehead's Metaphysics* (New Haven: Yale University Press, 1959), p. 396; italics his. See also pp. 286, 275.

9. Cobb, p. 156. He continues: "Such an aim is the feeling of a proposition of which the novel occasion is the logical subject and the appropriate eternal object is the predicate. The subject form of the propositional feeling is appetition,

that is, the desire for its realization." We agree, except for the identification of the logical subject, which we take to be the multiplicity of actual occasions constituting the past actual world of the novel occasion, as reduced to the status of bare logical subjects for God's propositional feeling.

10. Ibid., p. 157.

11. Ibid., pp. 157–68, 176–85.

12. Søren Kierkegaard, *Concluding Unscientific Postscript*, David F. Swenson, trans. (Princeton: Princeton University Press, 1944), p. 182.

13. Madden and Hare, *op. cit.*, p. 288 (125). In *Evil and the Concept of God*, p. 121f., Madden and Hare insert three paragraphs summarizing and criticizing the argument thus far of this paper (except for the discussion of evil in section II). Their summary is succinct and accurate, and they introduce the interesting analogy that Whitehead's God is like "an especially effective leader of an organization . . . who is powerful enough to guarantee the success of the organization *if* most of the members pitch in and help." They propose two objections to the existence of such a conditional guarantee of the triumph of good. "First, if cases can be found in which there has been widespread human cooperation and yet there has been no success, these cases would count as evidence against the existence of such a conditional guarantee. Such cases seem easy to find." Yet none are mentioned. I suspect all such instances would turn out to be problematic, for the theist and the naturalist would evaluate "widespread human cooperation" and "success" rather differently. Only widespread human cooperation *with God* can count as the proper fulfillment of the condition attached to the guarantee. Here the Christian might point to the rise of the early church, and the Muslim to the initial spread of Islam, both of which were eminently successful. Ancient Israel always understood her success in terms of her obedience to God, and her failures in terms of a widespread lack of cooperation with him. Secondly, they argue that the amount of evil in the world suggests that God is not a very persuasive leader. "It is a little too convenient simply to attribute all the growth to God's persuasive power and all the evil to the worlds' refusal to be persuaded." Now convenience, by itself, is not objectionable; in this instance, it may indicate that we have hit upon a proper solution. The measure of persuasion, moreover, is not how many are actually persuaded at any given time, but the intrinsic value of the goal envisaged. The only really satisfactory motive for action must be the achievement of the good, which alone is purely persuasive. All other "persuasion" is mixed with apparent, counterfeit goods and with indirect coercion. Divine persuasion may be a "still, small voice" amid the deafening shouts and clamourings of the world, but it is most effective in the long run—it brought this mighty universe into being out of practically nothing.

14. Genesis 6:6.

15. Hosea 11:8, Jeremiah 31:20, Isaiah 63:15. See also Kazoh Kitamori, *Theology of the Pain of God* (Richmond: John Knox Press, 1965), and Abraham J. Heschel, *The Prophets* (New York: Harper and Row, 1962), chaps. 12–15.

16. Christian, pp. 351–53.

17. Isaiah 42:3.

18. George F. Thomas, *Religious Philosophies of the West* (New York: Charles Scribner's Sons, 1965), p. 368.

19. Samuel H. Beer, *The City of Reason* (Cambridge: Harvard University Press, 1949), p. 131. Beer is Professor of Government at Harvard and very distinguished in that field, yet quite versatile. In this remarkable book he sought "to state a philosophy of liberalism based on A. N. Whitehead's metaphysics of creative advance" (p. vii). See particularly chap. 12, "A Saving Order," which considers most of the themes of this final section.

20. For a detailed development of this point, see my article, "Boethius and Whitehead on Time and Eternity," *International Philosophical Quarterly,* vol. 8, 1 (March 1968), pp. 38–67.

21. George F. Thomas, p. 389.

22. The first three phases are (a) God's originating activity in providing initial aims, (b) finite actualizations in the world, and (c) God's complete experience of the world in his consequent nature.

Evil and Persuasive Power

PETER HARE AND EDWARD MADDEN

Although they have exercised much influence on Protestant theology, process theists have had disappointingly little influence on philosophical discussions of the problem of evil. Despite the fact that leading process theists have devoted a substantial part of their writings to the discussion of evil, we find publication after publication by philosophers on the problem of evil with hardly a mention of process theism. Nelson Pike's widely used anthology, *God and Evil,*[1] contains no discussion of process theism and John Hick's *Evil and the God of Love,*[2] generally considered the most comprehensive treatment of the problem of evil to date, virtually ignores process theism. Although we might have hoped for a change of attitude, M. B. Ahern, the author of the latest philosophical book devoted to the problem of evil, persists in ignoring process theism.[3] In our book, *Evil and the Concept of God,*[4] we seem to have been the exception in taking nontraditional as well as traditional forms of theism seriously.

In this paper we shall not attempt a full-scale reply to critics of our discussion of nontraditional theism. Instead we hope to make a further contribution to the philosophical discussion of nontraditional theism by examining in more detail than we did in our book one strand of thought that plays a crucial, and philosophically fascinating, role in process theism's treatment of the problem of evil. Basic to this strand is the view that God's power is persuasive, not coercive.

Our argument will proceed as follows: (1) we accept many of the metaphysical and moral reasons given for supposing that God's power is in some degree, and in some respects, persuasive rather than coercive, but we do not find that any good reason has been given why God's power must and should be exclusively persuasive; (2) even in those contexts where per-

From *Process Studies* 2 (1972): 44–48. Reprinted by permission of the authors and the editor.

suasive and not coercive power is appropriate we find that process theists have made no attempt to provide a theodicy that explains how the high proportion remaining unpersuaded is compatible with the exercise of great persuasive power; (3) if it is replied that a persuasive God can be expected to maximize only creativity and freedom, and not good acts and experiences, we point out that process theists have no more produced a theodicy that shows that the limitations of creativity and freedom in this world are compatible with the exercise of great persuasive power than they have produced a theodicy showing that the extent and distribution of evil acts and experiences are compatible with great persuasive power; (4) if no theodicy is produced to explain these purported compatibilities, then we may as reasonably believe that great *evil* persuasive power is being exercised as that great persuasive power for the good is being exercised; and (5) if the process theist wishes to circumvent this need for a theodicy by claiming that process theism, like any metaphysics, can never be disproved by experiential findings but only by a demonstration of its conceptual incoherence, then we insist that the notion of persuasive power as used by process theists must be shown to be, contrary to appearances, a coherent concept. If, as we believe, such a *conceptual* theodicy can only succeed by modifying the concept of persuasive power in such a way than an *experiential* theodicy is again needed, then there is no way of circumventing the need for an experiential theodicy, a theodicy that, as we have already indicated, no process theist has produced.

(1) The arguments, both metaphysical and moral, given for supposing that God's power is persuasive rather than coercive are too well known to readers of process philosophy to need repeating in detail here. Let us begin by granting that the idea of God's power as totally coercive is morally repugnant as well as conceptually incoherent. Process theists make a useful point when they insist that such coercive power is incompatible with divine goodness. They are also right in claiming that it is "double talk" to say that "God decides my decisions . . . yet they are truly mine."[5] However, process theists fail to notice that while *totally* coercive power may be objectionable, solely *persuasive* power may also be objectionable. Why must we suppose that God's power is solely coercive or solely persuasive? Why must we consider coerciveness and persuasiveness to be mutually exclusive?

Process theists excuse God of evil by saying that he quite properly respects the freedom of his creatures and only tries to persuade them to do good. Although we agree that it would be morally repugnant for God to take all freedom from his creatures, we fail to see why there are not many situations in which a certain amount of coercive power is morally required. We cannot agree with John Cobb when he says that "[t]he only power capable of any worthwhile result is the power of persuasion."[5] Consider an analogy. It would not do to excuse a mother for the grossly evil habits of her child by appealing to her use of persuasion only, when sometimes there have been situations in which some coercion was morally required. To be sure, a mother who uses coercion frequently destroys the child's individuality and, in so doing, destroys, in a sense, her power over him. However, no reasonable person is asking for the frequent use of coercion. Rather the reasonable person asks for whatever mixture of coercion and persuasion is appropriate to a particular situation. The reasonable person asks of God also the same appropriate mixture of coercion and persuasion. Consequently, it is not enough to show that this or that evil in the world is compatible with divine persuasive power for the good; it must also be shown that this or that situation is one in which the exercise of *only* persuasive power is morally appropriate. If it is not a situation in which only persuasive power is appropriate, then it must be asked why God did not use a degree of coercion. Once one recognizes that is not a question of whether God's power is to be conceived of as either totally coercive or totally persuasive, one must ask the crucial question whether the extent and distribution of evil in the world are compatible with the existence of a God who always exercises the mixture of coercion and persuasion that is morally required.

We recognize that in a metaphysics of social process "coercive power" is considered a self-contradictory term and existence of any kind, sentient or non-sentient, entails freedom. However, choice of terminology is unimportant. Surely in any plausible metaphysics it is possible to distinguish *degrees* of creativity, freedom, etc. Hartshorne admits as much when he says that "all creatures have *some* [our emphasis] freedom."[7] When such distinctions are made, something equivalent to degrees of coercion are recognized and one can meaningfully ask whether the morally appropriate degree of coercive power is being exercised in a particular situation.

(2) Persuasive power alone is appropriate, however, in at least some contexts. But even in those situations process theists have left important questions unanswered. Is the extent and distribution of evil in those contexts compatible with the exercise of great persuasive power for the good? We cannot be satisfied with Lewis Ford's assertion that any evil is "compatible with unlimited persuasive power."[8] In ordinary contexts we quite reasonably cease to believe that great persuasive power is being exercised if we find that a high proportion of those who should be persuaded remain

unpersuaded. We all recognize that a high enough proportion remaining unpersuaded makes unlikely the exercise of great persuasive power and no reason is given why this isn't also the case with God. It is hardly adequate to answer, as Ford does, that the "measure of persuasion . . . is not how many people are actually persuaded at any given time, but the intrinsic value of the goal proposed."[9] We agree that the intrinsic merit of unself-ishness, for example, is very great and we applaud a mother who tries strenuously to convince her child to be unselfish, but if she generally fails, then we think that she does not have much persuasive power in spite of the excellence of her goals.

Our point is simply that process theists have not taken the problem of the large number that remain unpersuaded seriously. Any process theodicy that pretends to be adequate must provide an answer to this ques-tion and not content itself with saying that the exercise of persuasive power entails the existence of at least *some* who are unpersuaded. Clearly we agree to that. John Hick in his theodicy has attempted to explain in detail in terms of soul-making how the existence of *traditional* theistic power is compatible, not just with *any* evil, but with the extent and distribution of actual evil in the world, but process theists have made no parallel attempt to explain how the very high proportion remaining unpersuaded is com-patible with the exercise of great persuasive power by God, though they have shown with little difficulty how the existence of some who are un-persuaded is compatible with great persuasive power.

(3) Process theists are sometimes inclined to minimize the problem of explaining the large number that remain unpersuaded by emphasizing the intrinsic value of the creativity and freedom that God promotes, albeit entailing risk of evil. Let us grant that God may have set up the laws of nature for the development of the intrinsic values of creativity and free-dom, and that he may do many other things to promote these values. However, if this is the case, an adequate theodicy must show that creativ-ity and freedom are being maximized in this world by a great persuasive power. It is not sufficient to point to the fact that all process involves emergent novelty in some degree and infer from such emergent novelty a God exercising great persuasive power to foster creativity and freedom. Nor is it sufficient to pronounce creativity the ultimate metaphysical prin-ciple and say: "*To be is to create.*" In ordinary contexts we would find un-acceptable an analysis of a society which pointed to the fact that even men in solitary confinement exercise some freedom of choice and inferred from that freedom that this is a society in which creativity and freedom are be-ing fostered by a great persuasive power. An adequate analysis of a society

must take seriously the question of whether *more* creativity and freedom are feasible. While it is clear that there is genuine creativity and freedom everywhere in this world, it would seem to us that there are many situations in which we would like to see a great deal more creativity and freedom, and an adequate theodicy must show that this additional creativity and freedom cannot be achieved by even unlimited persuasive power. If the process theist is right in supposing that God's power is the power to inspire freedom in others, then he must answer the question of whether more freedom could be inspired—or whether the maximum amount has been achieved.

(4) One cannot avoid answering the above questions with impunity. If such questions are not answered, then we do not know that there is not a great persuasive power for *evil!* How do we know that the good acts in the world are not acts of resistance to an evil persuasive power? If we do not take the trouble to estimate on the basis of good and evil in the world the degree and kind of persuasive power being exercised, we may as reasonably believe that unlimited and evil persuasive power is being exercised as that great persuasive power for good is being exercised.

(5) Some process theists appear to be inclined to circumvent all these questions by insisting that process theism, like any metaphysics, cannot be disproven by the experiential facts of evil or by any other experiential findings. A metaphysics, Hartshorne argues, is to be judged on the basis of its conceptual coherence. The metaphysics of traditional theism he criticizes not on the grounds that empirical facts are incompatible with it but instead on the grounds that, e.g., the concept of omnipotence in traditional theism is incoherent:

> Who could want anyone, even God, to make all his decisions for him? And if this occurred, how could the decisions be "his" at all? The difficulty here is logical, does not depend on the facts. . . . My conclusion is: the idea of omnipotence, as it figures in the classical problem of evil, is a pseudo-idea; it would not make sense no matter what the empirical world happened to be like.[11]

Let us suppose that we accept this account of how a metaphysics is to be judged. The important question is then whether such concepts as persuasive power in theism are coherent. It is by no means clear to us that the concept of persuasive power as used by Hartshorne is coherent. Does it make conceptual sense to speak of a sort of power whose nature and extent is in principle impossible to estimate experientially? In ordinary contexts power is always something that can be, at least indirectly and roughly, measured experientially. To speak of completely unmeasurable power appears to be as much a "pseudo-idea" as to speak of weight that can never require force to lift.

If the concept of persuasive power in process theism is incoherent, then the metaphysics of process theism fails to pass the very test that Hartshorne proposes. If, on the other hand, persuasive power is made coherent by making such power experientially measurable, then the process theist is obliged to produce a theodicy in which it is shown that the proportion of goods to evils in the world is compatible with the exercise of great persuasive power for the good, and, as we have seen, no such theodicy has been produced.

NOTES

1. Nelson Pike (ed.), *God and Evil* (Englewood Cliffs, NJ: Prentice-Hall, 1964).

2. John Hick, *Evil and the God of Love* (New York: Harper & Row, 1966).

3. M. B. Ahern, *The Problem of Evil* (London: Routledge & Kegan Paul, 1971).

4. Edward H. Madden and Peter H. Hare, *Evil and the Concept of God* (Springfield, IL: Charles C. Thomas, 1968), pp. 104–36.

5. Charles Hartshorne, "A New Look at the Problem of Evil," in F. C. Dommeyer (ed.), *Current Philosophical Issues: Essays in Honor of Curt John Ducasse* (Springfield, IL: Charles C. Thomas, 1966), p. 203.

6. John B. Cobb, Jr. *God and the World* (Philadelphia: Westminster Press, 1969), p. 90.

7. Hartshorne, "A New Look . . . ," p. 205.

8. Lewis S. Ford, "Divine Persuasion and the Triumph of Good" in Delwin Brown, Ralph E. James, Jr., and Gene Reeves (eds.). *Process Philosophy and Christian Thought* (Indianapolis: Bobbs-Merrill, 1971), p. 289.

9. Ford in Brown *et al.*, p. 298n13.

10. Hartshorne, *Creative Synthesis and Philosophic Method* (LaSalle, IL: Open Court, 1970), p. 1.

11. Hartshorne, "A New Look . . . ," p. 202f.

PART FOUR

Issues in the Problem of Evil

God and the Best Possible World
Natural Evils and Natural Laws
Defense and Theodicy
Theoretical and Practical Theodicy

Must God Create the Best?

ROBERT M. ADAMS

I

Many philosophers and theologians have accepted the following proposition:

> (P) If a perfectly good moral agent created any world at all, it would have to be the very best world that he could create.

The best world that an omnipotent God could create is the best of all logically possible worlds. Accordingly, it has been supposed that if the actual world was created by an omnipotent, perfectly good God, it must be the best of all logically possible worlds.

In this paper I shall argue that ethical views typical of the Judeo-Christian religious tradition do not require the Judeo-Christian theist to accept (P). He must hold that the actual world is a good world. But he need not maintain that it is the best of all possible worlds, or the best world that God could have made.[1]

The position which I am claiming that he can consistently hold is that *even if* there is a best among possible worlds, God could create another instead of it, and still be perfectly good. I do not in fact see any good reason to believe that there is a best among possible worlds. Why can't it be that for every possible world there is another that is better? And if there is no maximum degree of perfection among possible worlds, it would be unreasonable to blame God, or think less highly of His goodness, because He created a world less excellent than He could have created.[2] But I do not claim to be able to prove that there is no best among possible worlds, and in this essay I shall assume for the sake of argument that there is one.

Reprinted from *The Philosophical Review* 99 (1990): 131–155 by permission of the publisher and author.

Whether we accept proposition (P) will depend on what we believe are the requirements for perfect goodness. If we apply an act-utilitarian standard of moral goodness, we will have to accept (P). For by act-utilitarian standards it is a moral obligation to bring about the best state of affairs that one can. It is interesting to note that the ethics of Leibniz, the best-known advocate of (P), is basically utilitarian.[3] In his *Theodicy* (Part I, Section 25) he maintains, in effect, that men, because of their ignorance of many of the consequences of their actions, ought to follow a rule-utilitarian code, but that God, being omniscient, must be a perfect act utilitarian in order to be perfectly good.

I believe that utilitarian views are not typical of the Judeo-Christian ethical tradition, although Leibniz is by no means the only Christian utilitarian. In this essay I shall assume that we are working with standards of moral goodness which are not utilitarian. But I shall not try either to show that utilitarianism is wrong or to justify the standards that I take to be more typical of Judeo-Christian religious ethics. To attempt either of these tasks would unmanageably enlarge the scope of the paper. What I can hope to establish here is therefore limited to the claim that the rejection of (P) is consistent with Judeo-Christian religious ethics.

Assuming that we are not using utilitarian standards of moral goodness, I see only two types of reason that could be given for (P). (1) It might be claimed that a creator would necessarily wrong someone (violate someone's rights), or be less kind to someone than a perfectly good moral agent must be, if he knowingly created a less excellent world instead of the best that he could. Or (2) it might be claimed that even if no one would be wronged or treated unkindly by the creation of an inferior world, the creator's choice of an inferior world must manifest a defect of character. I will argue against the first of these claims in Section II. Then I will suggest, in Section III, that God's choice of a less excellent world could be accounted for in terms of His grace, which is considered a virtue rather than a defect of character in Judeo-Christian ethics. A counterexample, which is the basis for the most persuasive objections to my position that I have encountered, will be considered in Sections IV and V.

II

Is there someone *to* whom a creator would have an obligation to create the best world he could? Is there someone whose rights would be violated, or who would be treated unkindly, if the creator created a less excellent world? Let us suppose that our creator is God, and that there does not exist any being, other than Himself, which He has not created. It follows that if God has wronged anyone, or been unkind to anyone, in creating whatever world He has created, this must be one of His own creatures. To which of His creatures, then, might God have an obligation to create the best of all possible worlds? (For that is the best world He could create.)

Might He have an obligation to the creatures in the best possible world, to create them? Have they been wronged, or even treated unkindly, if God has created a less excellent world, in which they do not exist, instead of creating them? I think not. The difference between actual beings and merely possible beings is of fundamental moral importance here. The moral community consists of actual beings. It is they who have actual rights, and it is to them that there are actual obligations. A merely possible being cannot be (actually) wronged or treated unkindly. A being who never exists is not wronged by not being created, and there is no obligation to any possible being to bring it into existence.

Perhaps it will be objected that we believe we have obligations to future generations, who are not yet actual and may never be actual. We do say such things, but I think what we mean is something like the following. There is not merely a logical possibility, but a probability greater than zero, that future generations will really exist; and *if* they will in fact exist, we will have wronged them if we act or fail to act in certain ways. On this analysis we cannot have an obligation to future generations to bring them into existence.

I argue, then, that God does not have an obligation to the creatures in the best of all possible worlds to create them. If God has chosen to create a world less excellent than the best possible, He has not thereby wronged any creatures whom He has chosen not to create. He has not even been unkind to them. If any creatures are wronged, or treated unkindly, by such a choice of the creator, they can only be creatures that exist in the world He has created.

I think it is fairly plausible to suppose that God could create a world which would have the following characteristics:

(1) None of the individual creatures in it would exist in the best of all possible worlds.

(2) None of the creatures in it has a life which is so miserable on the whole that it would be better for that creature if it had never existed.

(3) Every individual creature in the world is at least as happy on the whole as it would have been in any other possible world in which it could have existed.

It seems obvious that if God creates such a world He does not thereby wrong any of the creatures in it, and does not thereby treat any of them with less than perfect kindness. For none of them would have been benefited by His creating any other world instead.[4]

If there are doubts about the possibility of God's creating such a world, they will probably have to do with the third characteristic. It may be worth while to consider two questions, on the supposition (which I am not endorsing) that no possible world less excellent than the best would have characteristic (3), and that God has created a world which has characteristics (1) and (2) but not (3). In such a case must God have wronged one of His creatures? Must He have been less than perfectly kind to one of His creatures?

I do not think it can reasonably be argued that in such a case God must have wronged one of His creatures. Suppose a creature in such a case were to complain that God had violated its rights by creating it in a world in which it was less happy on the whole than it would have been in some other world in which God could have created it. The complaint might express a claim to special treatment: "God ought to have created *me* in more favorable circumstances (even though that would involve His creating some *other* creature in less favorable circumstances than He could have created it in)." Such a complaint would not be reasonable, and would not establish that there had been any violation of the complaining creature's rights.

Alternatively, the creature might make the more principled complaint, "God has wronged me by not following the principle of refraining from creating any world in which there is a creature that would have been happier in another world He could have made." This also is an unreasonable complaint. For if God followed the stated principle, He would not create any world that lacked characteristic (3). And we are assuming that no world less excellent than the best possible would have characteristic (3). It follows that if God acted on the stated principle He would not create any world less excellent than the best possible. But the complaining creature would not exist in the best of all possible worlds; for we are assuming that this creature exists in a world which has characteristic (1). The complaining creature, therefore, would never have existed if God had followed the principle that is urged in the complaint. There could not possibly be any advantage to this creature from God's having followed that principle; and the creature has not been wronged by God's not following the principle. (It would not be better for the creature if it had never existed; for we are assuming that the world God created has characteristic [2].)

The question of whether in the assumed case God must have been unkind to one of His creatures is more complicated than the question of whether He must have wronged one of them. In fact it is too complicated to be discussed adequately here. I will just make three observations about it. The first is that it is no clearer that the best of all possible worlds would possess characteristic (3) than that some less excellent world would possess it. In fact it has often been supposed that the best possible world might not possess it. The problem we are now discussing can therefore arise also for those who believe that God had created the best of all possible worlds.

My second observation is that if kindness to a person is the same as a tendency to promote his happiness, God has been less than perfectly (completely, unqualifiedly) kind to any creature whom He could have made somewhat happier than He has made it. (I shall not discuss here whether kindness to a person is indeed the same as a tendency to promote his happiness; they are at least closely related.)

But in the third place I would observe that such qualified kindness (if that is what it is) toward some creatures is consistent with God's being perfectly good, and with His being very kind to all His creatures. It is consistent with His being very kind to all His creatures because He may have prepared for all of them a very satisfying existence even though some of them might have been slightly happier in some other possible world. It is consistent with His being perfectly good because even a perfectly good moral agent may be led, by other considerations of sufficient weight, to qualify his kindness or beneficence toward some person. It has sometimes been held that a perfectly good God might cause or permit a person to have less happiness than he might otherwise have had, in order to punish him, or to avoid interfering with the freedom of another person, or in order to create the best of all possible worlds. I would suggest that the desire to create and love all of a certain group of possible creatures (assuming that all of them would have satisfying lives on the whole) might be an adequate ground for a perfectly good God to create them, even if His creating *all* of them must have the result that some of them are less happy than they might otherwise have been. And they need not be the best of all possible creatures, or included in the best of all possible worlds, in order for this qualification of His kindness to be consistent with His perfect goodness. The desire to create *those* creatures is as legitimate a ground for Him to qualify His kindness toward some, as the desire to create the best of all possible worlds. This suggestion seems to me to be in keeping with the aspect of the Judeo-Christian moral ideal which will be discussed in Section III.

These matters would doubtless have to be discussed more fully if we were considering whether the *actual* world can have been created by a perfectly good God. For our present purposes, however, enough may have been said—especially since, as I have noted, it seems a plausible assumption that God could make a world having characteristics (1), (2), and (3). In that case He could certainly make a less excellent world than the best of all possible worlds without wronging any of His creatures or failing in kindness to any of them. (I have, of course, *not* been arguing that there is *no* way in which God could wrong anyone or be less kind to anyone than a perfectly good moral agent must be.)

III

Plato is one of those who held that a perfectly good creator would make the very best world he could. He thought that if the creator chose to make a world less good than he could have made, that could be understood only in terms of some defect in the creator's character. Envy is the defect that Plato suggests.[5] It may be thought that the creation of a world inferior to the best that he could make would manifest a defect in the creator's character even if no one were thereby wronged or treated unkindly. For the perfectly good moral agent must not only be kind and refrain from violating the rights of others, but must also have other virtues. For instance, he must be noble, generous, high-minded, and free from envy. He must satisfy the moral ideal.

There are differences of opinion, however, about what is to be included in the moral ideal. One important element in the Judeo-Christian moral ideal is *grace*. For present purposes, grace may be defined as a disposition to love which is not dependent on the merit of the person loved. The gracious person loves without worrying about whether the person he loves is worthy of his love. Or perhaps it would be better to say that the gracious person sees what is valuable in the person he loves, and does not worry about whether it is more or less valuable than what could be found in someone else he might have loved. In the Judeo-Christian tradition it is typically believed that grace is a virtue which God does have and men ought to have.

A God who is gracious with respect to creating might well choose to create and love less excellent creatures than He could have chosen. This is not to suggest that grace in creation consists in a preference for imperfection as such. God could have chosen to create the best of all possible creatures, and still have been gracious in choosing them. God's graciousness in creation does not imply that the creatures He has chosen to create must be less excellent than the best possible. It implies, rather, that even if they are the best possible creatures, that is not the ground for His choosing them. And it implies that there is nothing in God's nature or character which would require Him to act on the principle of choosing the best possible creatures to be the object of His creative powers.

Grace, as I have described it, is not part of everyone's moral ideal. For instance, it was not part of Plato's moral ideal. The thought that it may be the expression of a virtue, rather than a defect of character, in a creator, *not* to act on the principle of creating the best creatures he possibly could, is quite foreign to Plato's ethical viewpoint. But I believe that thought is not at all foreign to a Judeo-Christian ethical viewpoint.

This interpretation of the Judeo-Christian tradition is confirmed by the religious and devotional attitudes toward God's creation which prevail in the tradition. The man who worships God does not normally praise Him for His moral rectitude and good judgment in creating *us*. He thanks God for his existence as for an undeserved personal favor. Religious writings frequently deprecate the intrinsic worth of human beings, considered apart from God's love for them, and express surprise that God should concern Himself with them at all.

> When I look at thy heavens, the work of thy fingers, the
>   moon and the stars which thou hast established;
> What is man that thou art mindful of him, and the son of
>   man that thou dost care for him?
> Yet thou hast made him little less than God, and dost crown
>   him with glory and honor.
> Thou hast given him dominion over the works of thy hands;
>   thou hast put all things under his feet [Psalm 8: 3–6].

Such utterances seem quite incongruous with the idea that God created us because if He had not He would have failed to bring about the best possible state of affairs. They suggest that God has created human beings and made them dominant on this planet although He could have created intrinsically better states of affairs instead.

I believe that in the Judeo-Christian tradition the typical religious attitude (or at any rate the attitude typically encouraged) toward the fact of our existence is something like the following. "I am glad that I exist, and I thank God for the life He has given me. I am also glad that other people exist, and I thank God for them. Doubtless there could be more excellent creatures than we. But I believe that God, in His grace, created us and loves us; and I accept that gladly and gratefully." (Such an attitude need not be complacent; for the task of struggling against certain evils may be seen as precisely a part of the life that the religious person is to accept and be glad in.) When people who have or endorse such an attitude say that God is perfectly good, we will not take them as committing themselves to the view that God is the kind of being who would not create any other world than the best possible. For they regard grace as an important part of perfect goodness.

IV

On more than one occasion when I have argued for the positions I have taken in Sections II and III above, a counterexample of the following sort has been proposed. It is the case of a person who, knowing that he intends to conceive a child and that a certain drug invariably causes severe mental retardation in children conceived by those who have taken it, takes the drug and conceives a severely retarded child. We all, I imagine, have a strong inclination to say that such a person has done something wrong. It is objected to me that our moral intuitions in this case (presumably including the moral intuitions of religious Jews and Christians) are inconsistent with the views I have advanced above. It is claimed that consistency requires me to abandon those views unless I am prepared to make moral judgments that none of us are in fact willing to make.

I will try to meet these objections. I will begin by stating the case in some detail, in the most relevant form I can think of. Then I will discuss objections based on it. In this section I will discuss an objection against what I have said in Section II, and a more general objection against the rejection of proposition (P) will be discussed in Section V.

Let us call this Case (A). A certain couple become so interested in retarded children that they develop a strong desire to have a retarded child of their own—to love it, to help it realize its potentialities (such as they are) to the full, to see that it is as happy as it can be. (For some reason it is impossible for them to *adopt* such a child.) They act on their desire. They take a drug which is known to cause damaged genes and abnormal chromosome structure in reproductive cells, resulting in severe mental retardation of children conceived by those who have taken it. A severely retarded child is conceived and born. They lavish affection on the child. They have ample means, so that they are able to provide for special needs, and to insure that others will never be called on to pay for the child's support. They give themselves unstintedly, and do develop the child's capacities as much as possible. The child is, on the whole, happy, though incapable of many of the higher intellectual, aesthetic, and social joys. It suffers some pains and frustrations, of course, but does not feel miserable on the whole.

The first objection founded on this case is based, not just on the claim that the parents have done something wrong (which I certainly grant), but on the more specific claim that they have *wronged the child*. I maintained, in effect, in Section II that a creature has not been wronged by its creator's creating it if both of the following conditions are satisfied.[6] (4) The creature is not, on the whole, so miserable that it would be better for him if he had never existed. (5) No being who came into existence in better or happier circumstances would have been the same individual as the creature in question. If we apply an analogous principle to the parent-child relationship in Case (A), it would seem to follow that the retarded child has not been wronged by its parents. Condition (4) is satisfied: the child is happy rather than miserable on the whole. And condition (5) also seems to be satisfied. For the retardation in Case (A), as described, is not due to prenatal injury but to the genetic constitution of the child. Any normal child the parents might have conceived (indeed any normal child at all) would have had a different genetic constitution, and would therefore have been a different person, from the retarded child they actually did conceive. But—it is objected to me—we do regard the parents in Case (A) as having wronged the child, and therefore we cannot consistently accept the principle that I maintained in Section II.

My reply is that if conditions (4) and (5) are really satisfied the child cannot have been wronged by its parents' taking the drug and conceiving it. If we think otherwise we are being led, perhaps by our emotions, into a confusion. If the child is not worse off than if it had never existed, and if *its* never existing would have been a sure consequence of its not having been brought into existence as retarded, I do not see how *its* interests can have been injured, or *its* rights violated, by the parents' bringing it into existence as retarded.

It is easy to understand how the parents might come to feel that they had wronged the child. They might come to feel guilty (and rightly so), and the child would provide a focus for the guilt. Moreover, it would be easy, psychologically, to assimilate Case (A) to cases of culpability for

prenatal injury, in which it is more reasonable to think of the child as having been wronged.[7] And we often think very carelessly about counterfac-
tual personal identity, asking ourselves questions of doubtful
intelligibility, such as, "What if I had been born in the Middle Ages?" It
is very easy to fail to consider the objection, "But that would not have
been the same person."

It is also possible that an inclination to say that the child has been
wronged may be based, at least in part, on a doubt that conditions (4) and
(5) are really satisfied in Case (A). Perhaps one is not convinced that in real
life the parents could ever have a reasonable confidence that the child
would be happy rather than miserable. Maybe it will be doubted that a
few changes in chromosome structure, and the difference between damaged and undamaged genes, are enough to establish that the retarded
child is a different person from any normal child that the couple could
have had. Of course, if conditions (4) and (5) are not satisfied, the case
does not constitute a counterexample to my claims in Section II. But I
would not rest any of the weight of my argument on doubts about the
satisfaction of the conditions in Case (A), because I think it is plausible
to suppose that they would be satisfied in Case (A) or in some very similar case.

V

Even if the parents in Case (A) have not wronged the child, I assume that
they have done something wrong. It may be asked *what* they have done
wrong, or *why* their action is regarded as wrong. And these questions may
give rise to an objection, not specifically to what I said in Section II, but
more generally to my rejection of proposition (P). For it may be suggested
that what is wrong about the action of the parents in Case (A) is that they
have violated the following principle:

> (Q) It is wrong to bring into existence, knowingly, a being less ex-
> cellent than one could have brought into existence.[8]

If we accept this principle we must surely agree that it would be wrong for
a creator to make a world that was less excellent than the best he could
make, and therefore that a perfectly good creator would not do such a
thing. In other words, (Q) implies (P).

I do not think (Q) is a very plausible principle. It is not difficult to
think of counterexamples to it.

Case (B): A man breeds goldfish, thereby bringing about their existence. We do not normally think it is wrong, or even prima facie wrong,

for a man to do this, even though he could equally well have brought about the existence of more excellent beings, more intelligent and capable of higher satisfactions. (He could have bred dogs or pigs, for example.) The deliberate breeding of human beings of subnormal intelligence is morally offensive; the deliberate breeding of species far less intelligent than retarded human children is not morally offensive.

Case (C): Suppose it has been discovered that if intending parents take a certain drug before conceiving a child, they will have a child whose abnormal genetic constitution will give it vastly superhuman intelligence and superior prospects of happiness. Other things being equal, would it be wrong for intending parents to have normal children instead of taking the drug? There may be considerable disagreement of moral judgment about this. I do not think that parents who chose to have normal children rather than take the drug would be doing anything wrong, nor that they would necessarily be manifesting any weakness or defect of moral character. Parents' choosing to have a normal rather than a superhuman child would not, at any rate, elicit the strong and universal or almost universal disapproval that would be elicited by the action of the parents in Case (A). Even with respect to the offspring of human beings, the principle we all confidently endorse is not that it is wrong to bring about, knowingly and voluntarily, the procreation of offspring less excellent than could have been procreated, but that it is wrong to bring about, knowingly and voluntarily, the procreation of a human offspring which is deficient by comparison with normal human beings.

Such counterexamples as these suggest that our disapproval of the action of the parents in Case (A) is not based on principle (Q), but on a less general and more plausible principle such as the following:

(R) It is wrong for human beings to cause, knowingly and voluntarily, the procreation of an offspring of human parents which is notably deficient, by comparison with normal human beings, in mental or physical capacity.

One who rejects (Q) while maintaining (R) might be held to face a problem of explanation. It may seem arbitrary to maintain such a specific moral principle as (R), unless one can explain it as based on a more general principle, such as (Q). I believe, however, that principle (R) might well be explained in something like the following way in a theological ethics in the Judeo-Christian tradition, consistently with the rejection of (Q) and (P).[9]

God, in His grace, has chosen to have human beings among His creatures. In creating us He has certain intentions about the qualities and goals of human life. He has these intentions for us, not just as individuals, but as members of a community which in principle includes the whole human race. And His intentions for human beings as such extend to the offspring (if any) of human beings. Some of these intentions are to be realized by human voluntary action, and it is our duty to act in accordance with them.

It seems increasingly possible for human voluntary action to influence the genetic constitution of human offspring. The religious believer in the Judeo-Christian tradition will want to be extremely cautious about this. For he is to be thankful that we exist as the beings we are, and will be concerned lest he bring about the procreation of human offspring who would be deficient in their capacity to enter fully into the purposes that God has for human beings as such. We are not God. We are His creatures, and we belong to Him. Any offspring we have will belong to Him in a much more fundamental way than they can belong to their human parents. We have not the right to try to have as our offspring just any kind of being whose existence might on the whole be pleasant and of some value (for instance, a being of very low intelligence but highly specialized for the enjoyment of aesthetic pleasures of smell and taste). If we do intervene to affect the genetic constitution of human offspring, it must be in ways which seem likely to make them *more* able to enter fully into what we believe to be the purposes of God for human beings as such. The deliberate procreation of children deficient in mental or physical capacity would be an intervention which could hardly be expected to result in offspring more able to enter fully into God's purposes for human life. It would therefore be sinful, and inconsistent with a proper respect for the human life which God has given us.

On this view of the matter, our obligation to refrain from bringing about the procreation of deficient human offspring is rooted in our obligation to God, as His creatures, to respect His purposes for human life. In adopting this theological rationale for the acceptance of principle (R), one in no way commits oneself to proposition (P). For one does not base (R) on any principle to the effect that one must always try to bring into existence the most excellent things that one can. And the claim that, because of His intentions for human life, we have an obligation to God not to try to have as our offspring beings of certain sorts does not imply that it would be wrong for God to create such beings in other ways. Much less does it imply that it would be wrong for God to create a world less excellent than the best possible.

In this essay I have argued that a creator would not necessarily wrong anyone, or be less kind to anyone than a perfectly good moral agent must be, if he created a world of creatures who would not exist in the best world he could make. I have also argued that from the standpoint of Judeo-Christian religious ethics, a creator's choice of a less excellent world need not be regarded as manifesting a defect of character. It could be understood in terms of his *grace*, which (in that ethics) is considered an important part of perfect goodness. In this way I think the rejection of proposition (*P*) can be seen to be congruous with the attitude of gratitude and respect for human life as God's gracious gift which is encouraged in the Judeo-Christian religious tradition. And that attitude (rather than any belief that one ought to bring into existence only the best beings one can) can be seen as a basis for the dispproval of the deliberate procreation of deficient human offspring. [10]

NOTES

1. What I am saying in this paper is obviously relevant to the problem of evil. But I make no claim to be offering a complete theodicy here.

2. Leibniz held (in his *Theodicy,* pt. I, sec. 8) that if there were no best among possible worlds, a perfectly good God would have created nothing at all. But Leibniz is mistaken if he supposes that in this way God could avoid choosing an alternative less excellent than others He could have chosen. For the existence of no created world at all would surely be a less excellent state of affairs than the existence of some of the worlds that God could have created.

3. See Gaston Brua, *Jurisprudence universelle et théodicée selon Leibniz* (Paris, 1953), pp. 210–218.

4. Perhaps I can have a right to something which would not benefit me (e.g., if it has been promised to me). But if there are such non-beneficial rights, I do not see any plausible reasons for supposing that a right not to be created could be among them.

5. *Timaeus,* 29E–30A.

6. I am not holding that these are necessary conditions, but only that they are jointly sufficient conditions, for a creature's not being wronged by its creator's creating it. I have numbered these conditions in such a way as to avoid confusion with the numbered characteristics of worlds in sec. II.

7. It may be questioned whether even the prenatally injured child is the same person as any unimpaired child that might have been born. I am inclined to think it is the same person. At any rate there is *more* basis for regarding it as the same person as a possible normal child than there is for so regarding a child with abnormal genetic constitution.

8. Anyone who was applying this principle to human actions would doubtless insert an "other things being equal" clause. But let us ignore that, since such a clause would presumably provide no excuse for an agent who was deciding an issue so important as what world to create.

9. I am able to give here, of course, only a very incomplete sketch of a theological position on the issue of "biological engineering."

10. Among the many to whom I am indebted for help in working out the thoughts contained in this paper, and for criticisms of earlier drafts of it, I must mention Marilyn McCord Adams, Richard Brandt, Eric Lerner, the members of my graduate class on theism and ethics in the fall term of 1970 at the University of Michigan, and the editors of the *Philosophical Review*.

God, Moral Perfection, and Possible Worlds

PHILIP L. QUINN

According to the theistic religions, human persons are called upon to worship God. Theists typically hold that reverence and adoration are the appropriate human responses to him. This view presupposes that God deserves or merits worship. If a being were not worthy of worship, then surely worship directed toward that being would be wildly inappropriate. But what features must a being have to be a fitting and proper object of worship? It seems clear that only a morally perfect being could be worthy of the unqualified devotion typical of theistic worship. Moral goodness falling short of perfection might earn a being admiration but never adoration. This is why it is essential to theistic orthodoxy that God be thought of as perfectly good.

Theists also hold that God created the heavens and the earth. God is, therefore, responsible for at least some of the good and evil in the cosmos of contingent things. Theists cannot avoid grappling with the problem of evil. How could a perfectly good being create a cosmos containing as much evil as we find in the world? Possible answers to this question, ranging from a free-will defense to a soul-making theodicy, are common currency among philosophers and theologians. But it is less widely recognized that theists must also confront a problem of good. Evil apart, the created cosmos seems to contain less good than it might have contained. How could a perfectly good being create a cosmos containing less good than the very best he could have created? And if a being worthy of worship would create the best cosmos he could, is a theist

From *God: The Contemporary Discussion*, ed. Frederick Sontag and M. Darrol Bryant (New York: 1982), 199–215, by permission of Rose of Sharon Press.

committed to holding that this is the best of all possible worlds? We all know that Voltaire ridiculed the Leibnizian doctrine that this is indeed the best of all possible worlds. But is the doctrine really ridiculous, fit only for satire? And, ridiculous or not, is it a doctrine orthodox theists are stuck with, like it or not, in virtue of holding that the creator deserves their worship? In this paper, I propose to discuss these and related questions.

In an ingenious paper called "Must God Create the Best?" Robert M. Adams tries to refute the doctrine according to which God, if he creates at all, must create the best of all logically possible worlds.[1] Adams supposes that those who would defend such a view would do so because they accept something like the following principle:

(1) If a perfectly good moral agent created any world at all, it would have to be the very best world that he could create.[2]

Adams claims that a theist, or at least a typical Judeo-Christian theist, need not accept this principle. He holds that it is plausible to suppose that God could create a world such that (i) none of the individual creatures in it would exist in the best of all possible worlds; (ii) none of the creatures in it has a life which is so miserable on the whole that it would be better for that creature if it had never existed; and (iii) every individual creature in it is at least as happy on the whole as it would have been in any other possible world in which it exists.[3] If God were to create such a world, Adams says, he would not thereby wrong any of the creatures in it, nor would he thereby treat any of them with less than perfect kindness, nor would he thereby exhibit any flaw or defect of moral character. Hence, according to Adams, God's creating such a world would not preclude his being a perfectly good moral agent. But because such a world could not be the best of all possible worlds, or even one of the best if there are several tied for first place, Adams concludes that there simply is no requirement, logical or moral, that God create the best of all possible worlds.

It seems to me clear enough that a being who created a cosmos satisfying the three conditions Adams states would be a good moral agent. What needs further exploration, I think, is the question of whether such a being would be morally perfect in the sense necessary for being worthy of worship. But before beginning such an exploration, I need to give some attention to a fundamental conceptual issue.

According to Alvin Plantinga, a possible world is a state of affairs of a certain sort, and states of affairs are not the kinds of things that can be either created or destroyed.[4] On this view, even God could not, literally speaking, create a possible world. What he can do is bring it about that certain states of affairs obtain or are actual, and so we ought to speak of God actualizing rather than creating a possible world. Of course, we may suppose that God can create ordinary contingent individuals such as tables and chairs or even extraordinary individuals such as angels and demons. But such creatures are not a possible world; they are its inhabitants or denizens. In actualizing a possible world, God, we may suppose, creates its contingent denizens. Some possible worlds, however, have only necessary beings such as numbers and properties as their denizens, and if God were to actualize such a world, he would refrain from creating any contingent individual. Thus strict accuracy forbids us to speak of God creating possible worlds, because this way of talking suggests a power to alter modal status which most theists do not attribute even to God.

Is it plausible to suppose that God could actualize a possible world satisfying conditions (i)–(iii)? It certainly appears to be. Because each of those conditions implicitly involves universal quantification over creatures, a world without creatures would vacuously satisfy them. Surely Judeo-Christian theists would not deny that God could have chosen to actualize a possible world without creatures, for to do so would be to imply that God as a matter of logical necessity had to create something or other. Moreover, if each creature is a denizen of only one possible world, as modern counterpart theorists believe and as Leibniz seems to have held, then any possible world that is less than maximally good in which no creature has a life so miserable that it would have been better for it if it had never existed will satisfy these conditions. A problem arises, however, if we do not accept counterpart theory and consider possible worlds containing creatures. For all I know, every possible world which contains creatures at all contains at least one which could be happier than it is in that world. Or perhaps there is no possible world in which any creature is as happy as it could be; maybe for every possible world w and each creature capable of being happy that exists in w, there is some possible world w' such that w' is diverse from w and that creature also exists in w' and is happier in w' than it is in w. This is not to suggest that any creature could be unboundedly happy, so to speak; it could happen if creatures approached, asymptotically as it were, without ever reaching their upper limits of happiness as possible worlds varied. So it might be, for all I know, that condition (iii) cannot be satisfied except vacuously; but, then again, perhaps condition (iii) can be nonvacuously satisfied. The trouble is that I do not know enough about possible worlds and their creaturely denizens to be able to tell for sure whether what Adams assumes is really plausible. In this situation, the reasonable thing to do seems to be to allow, for the sake of argument, that there are possible worlds with creatures that satisfy (i)–(iii) but to reserve judgment on just how plausible this assumption really is.

But even if this concession is made, some problems remain. A possible world with creatures that satisfies conditions (i)–(iii) is such that every creature in it is as happy as that creature could be, but perhaps another possible world containing the very same creatures is morally better though less replete with felicity. Why should we rule out of court the possibility that a possible world which fails to satisfy condition (iii) but includes compensating exercises of moral virtue in the face of adversity on the part of some of its creatures is a morally better world than another which contains the very same creatures and satisfies condition (iii) but lacks such exercises of virtue? If this is possible, should we not admit that a perfectly good moral agent would prefer a possible world with more moral goodness and less happiness to a possible world with more happiness and less moral goodness? Adams makes use of intuitive notions of the goodness of possible worlds and of the moral goodness of agents without exploring in much detail the philosophical questions such notions give rise to. What are we to understand by the relational predicate '———— is a better world than . . . ' applied to pairs of possible worlds? How are we to interpret the expression '———— is a better moral agent than . . . ' applied to pairs of persons or personlike entities? And what connections are there between the moral goodness of a creator and the goodness of the individuals he creates? Does morality ask for no more from a perfectly good creator than that he wrong none of his creatures, treat none of them with less than perfect kindness and manifest no defect of moral character? I next turn to an exploration of some of these issues.

II

When we assume that possible worlds can be compared with respect to their goodness, we suppose that there are features of possible worlds on which such comparisons are based. But which features are these? Should we say that the goodness of a possible world is a monotonically increasing function of the total amount of moral goodness contained in it? On this view, one possible world would be better than another just in case the first contained more moral goodness than the second. Or should we claim that the goodness of a possible world is a function of some of its apparently nonmoral features? For example, one possible world might be judged better than another just in case the first ranked higher on a scale combining considerations of simplicity and variety, appropriately weighted, than did the second.[5] Of course, it is by no means evident that possible worlds which are very simple and chock full of variety are also particularly morally edifying. Perhaps simplicity and variety constitute an appropriate basis for comparative judgments of aesthetic goodness and yet are utterly irrelevant to moral goodness.

So we need to make some assumptions about which varieties of goodness a morally perfect creator would be concerned about in comparing possible worlds with an eye to actualizing one. I shall assume that the sort of goodness which would be important from the point of view of a perfectly good moral agent envisaging actualizing a possible world is moral goodness, and so I shall suppose that there is a relation expressed by the phrase '————— is a morally better world than . . . ' which does relate pairs of possible worlds. But I shall not give an account of what moral goodness is. In particular, I shall not assume that a possible world in which every creature is as happy as it could be but no pity for suffering is ever felt is morally better than one in which some suffering evokes pity but some creature could be happier than it is. Nor shall I assume that a possible world of the second kind is morally better than one of the first kind. Similarly, I shall remain neutral about whether justice contributes more, or less, than creaturely happiness to the moral goodness of a possible world. All I shall suppose is that, however the moral goodness of possible worlds is determined, some are morally better than others.

What format properties should we attribute to the relation expressed by the phrase '————— is a morally better world than . . . '? Doubtless there would be widespread agreement that such a relation must be asymmetric and transitive. From this it follows that it must also be irreflexive and, hence, that it induces a strict partial ordering on the set of all possible worlds.[6] This much seems obvious, but beyond this point things quickly become murky. Is it the case that for any possible worlds w and w', if w is distinct from w', then either w is a morally better world than w' or w' is a morally better world than w? Not obviously so, for perhaps there are two distinct possible worlds exactly equal in moral goodness. Is it even the case that every pair of possible worlds is commensurable with respect to moral goodness? Again the answer is not obvious; maybe there are distinct possible worlds w and w' such that w is not a morally better world than w', w' is not a morally better world than w, and yet neither are w and w' equal in moral goodness. And even if any two possible worlds are morally commensurable, must we suppose that one possible world is the best of all? Once more it is not clear what the answer is. Perhaps for each possible world there is another which is morally better, or, if there is a possible world than which no other is morally better, maybe there are many such possible worlds of maximal moral goodness. Since I can see no way to provide uncontroversial answers to questions such as these, I propose to leave them open in this discussion. Thus I intend to see how far I can get in exploring the topic of this paper with nothing stronger than the assumption that the set of possible worlds is strictly partially ordered.

A simple observation will serve to motivate a definition linking possible worlds with the power needed to actualize them. It may, for all I know, be the case that even an omnipotent being is not able to actualize just any world which is logically possible.[7] Suppose, for instance, there were an inhabitant of some but not all possible worlds such that in every possible world where it exists it is uncreated. Such a thing would be contingent but essentially uncreated. Let us also assume that actualizing a possible world involves at least creating all its denizens which do not exist necessarily. Any possible world which has among its inhabitants a contingent but essentially uncreated being would then be unactualizable. But maybe the best of all possible worlds, if there is a unique one, is for this reason, or for some other, unactualizable. Or perhaps every possible world better than some particular world is unactualizable. In order not to beg any questions about such matters, I suggest that the notion of an actualizable world be defined as follows:

> (2) w is an actualizable world = df w is such that it is possible that there is an x such that x is omnipotent and x actualizes it.

Less formally, an actualizable world is one which an omnipotent being could actualize. It may or may not be the case that every logically possible world is also actualizable. I take no stand on this issue.

I shall not assume that there is a best actualizable world or that, if there is one, it is unique. But even without such strong assumptions several definitions of kinds of moral goodness that pertain to actualizable worlds can be formulated. First, there is a notion analogous to the idea of being a best possible world; it is the concept of an actualizable world whose moral goodness cannot be surpassed. This notion is defined as follows:

> (3) w is an actualizable world of unsurpassable moral goodness = df w is an actualizable world, and, for all w', if w' is an actualizable world, then w' is not a morally better world than w.

An actualizable world of unsurpassable moral goodness is an actualizable world such that no actualizable world is morally better than it is. Obviously this definition does not entail that there are any such worlds, and it is consistent with there being several if there are any. For all that I have said, two actualizable worlds of unsurpassable moral goodness might either be equally morally good or be incommensurable with respect to moral goodness. A Leibnizian of the strict persuasion would, I suppose, be as unhappy with the suggestion that there are many actualizable worlds of unsurpassable moral goodness as with the suggestion that there are none. In either case it would seem that God could have no Sufficient Reason for actualizing exactly one possible world, and this, after all, is the most he can do. However, if there are several such worlds, God can at least appeal to the principle of Insufficient Reason and decide which among them to actualize by some divine analogue of the process of rolling fair dice. Or nonmoral considerations might serve in such a case to break ties for first place.

Next we need to frame some definitions having to do with possible worlds of the sort Adams holds God could actualize without moral fault. I begin by defining those possible worlds, if any, whose denizens are happy in the appropriate ways. They are to be thought of as possible worlds whose creaturely inhabitants enjoy a felicity as complete as is possible for them. The definition of such completely felicitous actualizable worlds goes as follows:

(4) w is a completely felicitous actualizable world $=$ df w is an actualizable world, and w is such that (i) none of the creatures in w has a life in w so miserable on the whole that it would be better for that creature if it did not exist in w, and (ii) every creature in w is at least as happy on the whole in w as it is in any w' distinct from w in which it exists.

As I mentioned above, for all I know, there are no completely felicitous actualizable worlds other than those vacuously so in virtue of containing no creatures. Moreover, if there are some, some or all of them may, as far as I can tell, also be actualizable worlds of unsurpassable moral goodness. The definitions do not preclude this. Whether or not one thinks this is the case will depend at least in part, I imagine, on one's views of the relations of felicity and moral goodness, and so I would expect opinions on this matter to differ as moral theories vary. Thus, in order to follow Adams in focusing attention on possible worlds less good than the best actualizable, we need to define the notion of a morally surpassable but completely felicitous actualizable world. This concept is defined as follows:

> (5) w is a morally surpassable completely felicitous actualizable world = df w is a completely felicitous actualizable world, and there is a w' such that w' is an actualizable world and w' is a morally better world than w.

For all I have said so far, it may be that no actualizable world is morally better than any completely felicitous actualizable world. So perhaps no possible worlds satisfy this definition. But maybe some actualizable worlds which are not completely felicitous are morally better than some which are. After all, there may be features other than felicity which contribute to the moral goodness of possible worlds, and some such features may be weightier than felicity by itself.

A final idea that I will have occasion to use in subsequent arguments is the notion of a possible world which is, among completely felicitous actualizable worlds, morally unsurpassable. It is defined as follows:

> (6) w is a morally unsurpassable completely felicitous actualizable world = df w is a completely felicitous actualizable world, and, for all w', if w' is a completely felicitous actualizable world, then w' is not a morally better world than w.

It is evident that this definition does not entail that there are any morally unsurpassable completely felicitous actualizable worlds, and it does not preclude there being several if there are any. Moreover, our definitions entail nothing about whether some morally unsurpassable completely felicitous actualizable worlds, if there are any, are also actualizable worlds of unsurpassable moral goodness.

The point of this somewhat cumbersome battery of definitions is to allow us to pose some rather precise questions about what a perfectly good and omnipotent moral agent would do if he were to actualize a possible world. Would such a being actualize a world of unsurpassable moral goodness even if no such world were completely felicitous? Might such a being actualize a morally surpassable yet completely felicitous world? Must such a being at least actualize a morally unsurpassable completely felicitous world?

Adams seems to hold, in effect, that such a being might actualize a completely felicitous world that is morally surpassable. Is this correct? Before we can return any confident answer to this question, we must reflect a bit on what is involved in being a perfectly good moral agent.

III

Our discussion of the perfections of moral agents may begin with an observation about English grammar. There are many English expressions whose general form is 'a perfectly A N,' where substituends for 'A' are adjectival phrases which admit of the comparative and substituends for 'N' are noun phrases which function as count nouns. Examples are such things as 'a perfectly flat surface,' 'a perfectly splendid dinner,' 'a perfectly frictionless plane' and 'a perfectly respectable place to live.' Among expressions of this sort, there is one difference of logical functioning that has some importance in the present context. In some cases at least, a perfectly A N would be such that it is not possible that there be an N more A than it is. For example, a perfectly flat surface would be such that it is not possible that there be a surface flatter than it is. It is clear that this is one of the features of perfectly flat surfaces, perfectly frictionless planes and perfectly rigid rods which makes them such useful idealizations in physics. In other cases, however, a perfectly A N would be such that it is possible that there be an N more A than it is. Thus, a perfectly respectable place to live may nonetheless be such that it is possible that there be a place to live more respectable than it is. For example, though Rye is a perfectly respectable place to live, Scarsdale is a more respectable place to live than Rye is.

When theists apply the phrase 'a perfectly good moral agent' to God, it may not be obvious whether they intend their usage to be assimilated to cases of the first sort or to cases of the second sort. In order to circumvent any ambiguities, I shall define different locations to express two interpretations which might be placed on that phrase. The weaker locution is defined as follows:

> (7) x is a thoroughly good moral agent = df x is a moral agent, x performs some actions, x does nothing morally wrong, and x exhibits no defects of moral character.

A thoroughly good moral agent is, so to speak, morally good through and through. However, a thoroughly good moral agent may be such that it is possible that there be a moral agent better than he is, for of two moral agents both of whom exhibit sterling characters and neither of whom does anything wrong, one may effectuate more widespread beneficence, perhaps of a supererogatory kind, than another. I believe my definition of a thoroughly good moral agent reflects all those features of moral agents to which Adams makes explicit reference in his statement of what God might properly do in creating, since I take kindness to be a moral character trait. There is, however, another degree of moral excellence. The stronger locution which expresses it may be defined as follows:

> (8) x is a superlatively good moral agent = df x is a thoroughly good moral agent, and x is such that there is no possible world in which there is some y such that y is a better moral agent in that world than he is in the actual world.

There could be no moral agent better than a superlatively good moral agent actually is. Of course, comparing the goodness of moral agents is probably no easier than comparing the goodness of possible worlds. Many questions arise. What features of moral agents are to be considered in making such comparisons? What sort of ordering does this relation induce on sets of moral agents? Moral theories can be expected to disagree about the answers to such questions. However, it does seem clear enough that many theists are committed to holding that God is a superlatively good moral agent and, indeed, the only superlatively good moral agent. Such theists would not, I think, be satisfied to maintain that God is merely a thoroughly good moral agent, though he is at least that, or even essentially a thoroughly good moral agent; they would insist that God has to be a superlatively good moral agent, and perhaps essentially so, if he is to be worthy of the kind of worship they believe they owe him. The question such people need to ponder seems to me to be this: What sort of possible world would an omnipotent and superlatively good moral agent actualize if he actualized any world at all? Or, at any rate, since this is a question I find puzzling, I shall next consider some answers to it.

IV

As a preliminary to our discussion of superlatively good moral agents, let us consider briefly what a thoroughly good moral agent would do in creating. A principle with some plausibility is the following:

> (9) If an omnipotent and thoroughly good moral agent were to actualize a possible world, he would actualize some completely felicitous actualizable world.

This principle strikes me as acceptable provided we assume, at least for the sake of argument, that the value properly most cherished by such an agent is the happiness of his creatures. An argument in support of the acceptability of this principle goes as follows. Suppose an omnipotent and thoroughly good moral agent actualizes a world. Since he is omnipotent,

it can be any actualizable world. Because he is thoroughly good, he will
do no wrong and exhibit no flaw of character in actualizing a world. Assuming that depriving a creature of happiness it might have enjoyed is the
only way a creator might wrong that creature or exhibit a moral flaw in
creating it, a thoroughly good moral agent might actualize any completely
felicitous actualizable world. So if there are some such worlds with creatures in them, he will actualize one of them. I think this is the important
positive insight Adams has got hold of, even though I remain somewhat
skeptical about the exclusive emphasis on happiness in his treatment.
However, it should be noted that it is consistent with (9) that the world
actualized by an omnipotent and thoroughly good moral agent be neither
a morally unsurpassable completely felicitous actualizable world nor an actualizable world of unsurpassable moral goodness. This is interesting but
perhaps not very surprising. After all, it would seem that a thoroughly
good moral agent could omit certain moral perfections from his creation
without diminishing the happiness of any of its creatures. The difficulty is
that (9), though it is at least arguably correct, is not really an answer to
the question posed by a theist who wishes to know what sort of world
a superlatively good moral agent would actualize if he actualized any
world at all. So we should next consider some principles that do address
that question.

The first such principle may be stated in the following way:

(10) If an omnipotent and superlatively good moral agent were to
actualize a possible world, he would actualize some completely
felicitous actualizable world.

It seems to me that this principle is at best misleading. There are some
relations among possible worlds which may hold, consistent with everything I have assumed so far, such that if they did hold there would be
certain completely felicitous actualizable worlds that an omnipotent and
superlatively good moral agent would not actualize. Let me explain why.
Suppose an omnipotent and superlatively good moral agent actualizes a
world, and assume the world he actualizes is a completely felicitous actualizable world but is also a morally surpassable completely felicitous actualizable world. On these assumptions, it is possible that something
actualizes a morally better world than the one which, by hypothesis, he
actualizes, since it is morally surpassable. But then it surely seems possible that there is a better moral agent than he actually is, namely, one
who actualizes a morally better world than he, by hypothesis, has actualized. This, however, contradicts the assumption that he is a superlatively

good moral agent. Hence, if there are completely felicitous actualizable worlds that are also morally surpassable, and a world without creatures would indicate that there are, then an omnipotent and superlatively good moral agent would actualize none of them. He would actualize instead some morally better world.

This line of reasoning suggests that we examine next a somewhat stronger principle. It may be formulated as follows:

> (11) If an omnipotent and superlatively good moral agent were to actualize a possible world, he would actualize some morally unsurpassable completely felicitous actualizable world.

But even this principle seems not to capture the doctrine we are searching for. It is consistent with everything I have assumed so far to suppose that there are actualizable worlds morally better than any morally unsurpassable completely felicitous actualizable world. This would be the case, for example, if there is some actualizable world in which happiness is proportioned to virtue and some suffer on account of their sins which is morally better than any completely felicitous actualizable world. But perhaps there are some such worlds; certainly many theists have thought there are. If there are, and if an omnipotent being were nevertheless to actualize a morally unsurpassable completely felicitous actualizable world, then there would be actualizable worlds morally better than the one that he, by hypothesis, had actualized. But then it surely seems to be possible that there is a better moral agent than he, by hypothesis, actually is. Thus he would not be a superlatively good moral agent. So if there are actualizable worlds morally better than any morally unsurpassable completely felicitous actualizable world, as there may well be, then an omnipotent and superlatively good moral agent would actualize one of them and not some morally unsurpassable completely felicitous actualizable world.

These considerations suggest that the correct principle about actualization by a superlatively good moral agent is the following:

> (12) If an omnipotent and superlatively good moral agent were to actualize a possible world, he would actualize some actualizable world of unsurpassable moral goodness.

The reasons that support this principle are easy to state. Suppose an omnipotent and superlatively good moral agent actualizes a world. Assume for the sake of argument that the one he actualizes is not an actualizable world of unsurpassable moral goodness. Then either it is not an actualizable world at all, which contradicts the supposition that an omnipotent being actualizes it, or there is another possible world which is both actualizable and morally better than it is. But, in this case, it surely seems to be possible that there is a better moral agent than he who, by hypothesis, actualized a world of surpassable moral goodness, namely, one who actualizes a morally better actualizable world. And this contradicts the supposition that our creator is a superlatively good moral agent. So an omnipotent and superlatively good moral agent would actualize an actualizable world of unsurpassable moral goodness. As was noted above, it is consistent with our definitions that such a world also be a morally unsurpassable completely felicitous actualizable world. What these arguments show, therefore, is only that, if an omnipotent and superlatively good moral agent had to choose between less than complete felicity and surpassable moral goodness when actualizing a possible world, he would choose less than complete felicity.

It is obvious that (12) is a good deal like (1). Since (1) expresses a view Adams rejects, an argument in favor of (12) can reasonably be interpreted as an argument against a position of the general sort Adams defends. I intend the arguments I have given to be successful arguments of this kind. But are my arguments sound? An attentive reader will have observed that in several of them I infer from the premise that there are morally better actualizable worlds than the one which, by hypothesis, has been actualized the conclusion that it is at least possible that there is a better moral agent than its hypothetical actualizer is. Are such inferences in any way dubious? Their validity, it would appear, can be guaranteed by assuming as an additional premise the following principle:

(13) Necessarily, for all w, w' and x, if w is an actualizable world and w' is an actualizable world and w is a morally better world than w', then if x is an omnipotent moral agent and x actualizes w', then x is such that there is some possible world in which there is a y such that y is a better moral agent in that world than he is in w'.

As far as I can tell, (13) expresses a fairly obvious truth. An omnipotent moral agent can actualize any actualizable world. If he actualizes one than which there is a morally better, he does not do the best he can, morally speaking, and so it is possible that there is an agent morally better than he is, namely, an omnipotent moral agent who actualizes one of those morally better worlds.

Another nice feature (13) has is that it does not fall prey to certain counter-examples Adams cites in order to refute a principle he suggests as something which implies (1). The principle in question goes as follows:

(14) It is wrong to bring into existence, knowingly, a being less excellent than one could have brought into existence.[8]

Examples involving animal breeding, e.g., breeding goldfish rather than golden retrievers, and human procreation, e.g., having normal children instead of chemically altered supergeniuses, seem to refute (14), if we allow that what people do in such cases is genuinely to bring something into existence. But clearly such examples do not serve also to refute (13). For one thing, since its scope is restricted to the actualization of possible worlds, no example which concerns bringing something into existence could be so much as relevant to refuting it. For another, (13) does not assert that it would be wrong to actualize a world than which there is a morally better one could actualize; instead it asserts that a being who acted in this way would not do the best that could be done, which in turn implies that such a being would not be a superlatively good moral agent.

From all of this, I conclude that I have gone a long way towards meeting the challenge to the Leibnizian philosophical tradition raised by Adams. For I have formulated a principle, namely (12), which is akin to his principle (1), and I have argued in support of it from a premise, namely (13), which is not refuted by his counter-examples to (14) or by any other examples known to me. In addition, I have tried to indicate why theists are indeed committed to defending some position of this general sort in virtue of their view that God deserves or merits worship of the extreme kinds they typically believe it appropriate to direct toward him.[9]

NOTES

1. Robert M. Adams, "Must God Create the Best?", *The Philosophical Review* 81 (1972), pp. 317–32.

2. *Ibid.*, p. 317.

3. *Ibid.*, p. 320.

4. Alvin Plantinga, *The Nature of Necessity* (Oxford: Clarendon, 1974), pp. 44–45.

5. Leibniz seems to have held a view of this sort. See Section V of *Discourse on Metaphysics* and Paragraph 58 of *Monadology*.

6. The technical terms from the theory of relations are defined in many set theory texts. See, for instance, Patrick Suppes, *Axiomatic Set Theory* (New York: Van Nostrand, 1960), pp. 68–72.

7. The supposition that an omnipotent being could actualize any logically possible world has been baptized "Leibniz' Lapse" by Alvin Plantinga. See Plantinga, *op. cit.*, pp. 180–84. His examples involve the complexities of free actions.

8. Adams, *op. cit.*, p. 329.

9. I read earlier versions of this material at the University of Illinois at Chicago Circle and at the University of Rhode Island. I thank my audiences on those occasions for helpful discussion.

Natural Evil

RICHARD SWINBURNE

I

The problem of evil is the difficulty raised for theism, the belief that there is a God, by the existence of evil. God is, by definition, omnipotent, omniscient and perfectly good. He is omnipotent in the sense, roughly, that he can do whatever it is logically possible to do. He is omniscient in the sense that he knows all true propositions (or perhaps, we should say, all true propositions which it is logically possible to know). He is morally good in the sense that he does no morally bad action. Now, the atheist argues, an omniscient God would know when evil would occur, if he did not act to prevent it. Being omnipotent, he would be able to prevent the occurrence of evil, and, being perfectly good, would choose to do so. But in fact there is evil in the world. Hence there is no God.

Down the centuries theists have displayed various defences against the atheist's argument. The defense which has appealed most to modern man has been the free-will defense. This claims that a good God might well permit men to have free will despite the danger that they will bring about evil rather than good, because of the goodness of their having freedom. The trouble with this defense is that although it may explain why a good God might permit evil, it only explains why he might permit evil of a certain kind—moral evil. I understand by moral evil that evil brought about intentionally by human agents, to be contrasted with natural evil which is that evil not brought about intentionally by human agents—primarily evil such as famine, disease, and earthquake, which are brought about by natural processes. Hence, because of the way the free-will defense works, it immediately allows the construction of a slightly different

From *American Philosophical Quarterly* 15 (Oct. 1978): 295–301. Reprinted by permission of the editor.

argument against the existence of God—an argument not from evil as such but from the occurrence of natural evil, an argument which appears much more difficult to refute. The purpose of this paper is to argue that if the free-will defense works in explaining why God might permit the existence of moral evil, then it also provides an explanation of why God might bring about the existence of much natural evil. Contrary to what might appear at first sight, if the free-will defense works with respect to moral evil, it also has the force to defeat an argument from natural evil.

II

I begin by developing the free-will defense in the way necessary if it is to give an explanation of why God permits the existence not merely of moral evil as such, but of moral evil of the kind and quantity which we do in fact find in the world. The free-will defense claims that God might well give to men a kind of free will in which how an agent acts is not fully determined by preceding causes but depends, at least in part, on the agent's uncaused choice at the instant of action. It has been argued convincingly[1] that it is not logically possible that God should have given men free will of this kind and at the same time have predetermined what they would do. Rather, if men had free will of this kind, what they did must be truly up to them. God could of course have given men such free-will without allowing them to make any significant difference to the world by their exercise of it. However it is plausible to suppose that a good God might well give to free agents the power through their free choices to make a significant difference to the world and to each other, including the power to influence the course of history for quite a considerable time ahead. In giving men such free-will God would be giving men a share in his own creative work.

Now God could have given men only the power to benefit their fellows or to withhold benefit from them, but not the power to inflict harm on each other or on themselves. He could have created a world in which men could give to their fellows chocolate, or help them to build a TV set, without creating a world in which men could risk their own lives, inflict pain on their fellows or deprive them of anything which they really valued. However it is plausible to suppose that a good God might well wish to give to men a real share in his work of planning the development of the world and mankind. To allow men a real choice in this respect, he must give them the choice of doing what is objectively harmful. Having himself the powers to benefit and harm, he would give men a substantial share in his creative work, by giving to them both powers (although perhaps to a lesser degree). Thereby he would show real trust in men and they would have substantial responsibility for themselves and their fellows. If my responsibility to you is limited to whether or not I give you chocolate or a TV set, I hardly have much responsibility for you.

Clearly too the greater the share in his creative work which a God chooses to give to men, the greater the powers to benefit and to harm each other he must give to them. He must for example not merely give men the power to bruise each other, but also give men the power to become heroin addicts, to persuade other men to become heroin addicts, and to drop atom bombs. A God who greatly limits the harm which men can do to each other greatly limits the control over their destiny which he gives to men—just as an over-protective parent who preserves his child from almost every possible physical or moral danger does not allow him to run his own life, and in his turn to make through his own choice a difference to the lives of others.

The free-will defense must be developed in the above way if it is to explain why God allows the existence of moral evil of the kind and quantity which we find in the world. It is, I have briefly suggested, a plausible defense—although I am not concerned to argue that. The claim is that God allowed man to cause evil because only by so doing would he give to man a significant choice of destiny and share in his own creative work. God does not make men abuse the powers which he gives them, nor wish man to abuse them. But their having these powers allows them to bring about significant evil, and God cannot stop them doing so without depriving them of their powers.

The free-will defense does not claim that God has to create a world in which men may bring about evil, only that it would not be wrong for him to do so. The free-will defense does not deny that there must be a limit to the amount of harm which a good God would allow man to do to others deliberately or through negligence. Clearly in our world there is such a limit because there is a limit to the amount of harm which men can suffer. Men only live for so long, and if you inflict too much pain on them during their life they become unconscious. It is in no way obvious that the limit to human suffering inflicted by other men is drawn in the wrong place—that if there is a God he has given to men too great a control of their own destiny.

Now suppose that the free-will defense does work in providing an explanation of why God permits the existence of the moral evil which we find in the world. My concern is to show that in that case there is also an explanation of why God brings about much natural evil. Superficially, the free-will defense does not have much to do with natural evil, for by definition natural evil is evil not brought about through man's choice. Many theists have of course claimed that natural evils are really brought about by free agents other than men, viz. fallen angels, and hence that a defense similar to the free-will defense can be used to give the same kind of account of them as of moral evils. But this looks very much like an ad hoc hypothesis added to theism to save it from falsification by evidence which would otherwise falsify it. Although this hypothesis may save theism from formal falsification, it would seem that natural evil still greatly disconfirms theism, if the only way to save theism from falsification is by adding to it an ad hoc hypothesis. If the fallen-angel defense is to be taken more seriously, we need evidence of the existence of fallen angels, other than that provided by the existence of natural evil. My argument is a different one—that the free-will defense already outlined could only work in providing an explanation of why God allows moral evil, if in fact there is also natural evil. This is because there must be natural evils if men are to have the *knowledge* which they need to have in order to bring about moral evils.

III

To see this, let us ask how men acquire knowledge, in particular knowledge of what will follow in the future from a present state. There are two routes to such knowledge. The normal route is by induction from what is known to have happened in the past. The simplest such case is where I infer that a present state of affairs C will be followed by a future state E from the fact that in the past states of affairs like C on all occasions of which I have knowledge have been followed by states like E. Because on the many occasions of which I have knowledge, a piece of chalk being liberated from the hand has fallen to the floor, I can infer that the next time chalk is liberated it will fall. However induction may take a more complicated form. From a vast collection of data about the positions of planets a scientist may infer a consequence of a different kind, e.g. that there will be a very high tide on Earth when the planets are in such and such positions. Here the data provide evidence for a complicated scientific theory of which the prediction about the high tide is a somewhat remote consequence.

Whether the inference is simple or complicated, certain obvious points can be made about the claim to knowledge of the future which results from it. The first is that the more past data there are, the better established is a claim to such knowledge. This is because the data support a claim about the future by supporting a theory or a simple universal (or statistical) generalization (e.g. "states like C are always followed by states like F") which in turn licenses the claim about the future. The more data there are, the more they show that the theory or generalization holds in many different circumstances and so is more likely to hold in the future instance in question. (However similar the circumstances under which the past data are observed are in many respects, they are almost bound to differ from each other in some observable or unobservable respects; if the generalization holds despite many differences, that gives it greater reliability.)

Secondly, the surer my knowledge that the past data occurred as stated, the better grounded is my claim to knowledge of the future. If the data are mental experiences of mine or events which I myself have seen, or events which many independent observers have reported to me, then my knowledge of their occurrence is sure. If they are experiences of others or events about which only one or two observers have told me, then I have some doubt whether they occurred. I have more doubt still if I need to make a complicated inference from other data to prove their occurrence. Clearly in so far as an inference is licenced by certain data, then to the extent to which it is doubtful whether the data are correct, it is doubtful whether the inference is justifiable.

Thirdly, in so far as the data are qualitatively very dissimilar from what is predicted, and a complicated scientific theory is needed to generate the prediction, the claim to knowledge will be less surely based. Thus suppose that by a process of complex extrapolation from a number n of astronomical data I reach a very complex theory of mechanics, from which I conclude that in a very unusual set of circumstances (when the planets are in just such and such configurations relative to an observer) if I let go a bit of chalk it will rise into the air. And suppose that these circumstances are manifested on Earth uniquely in my study during this hour. Do I *know* that when shortly I let go of the chalk it will rise? Doubtfully so. Clearly I do know it and know it a lot better if I have already actually let go of the chalk in my study n times during the hour, and it has risen.

Fourthly, if a complex inference is needed in order to reach a prediction, then in so far as the inference is of a kind which has proved successful before, or is made by persons with known predictive success from this kind of work in the past, that is grounds for believing the prediction. These four points about the strength of knowledge obtained by induction may be summarized by saying that our claims to knowledge are better justified, the closer they are to our experience.

Now if men are knowingly to bring about states of affairs, or to allow states of affairs to come about through neglecting to prevent them, they must know what consequences will follow from their actions. Inductive knowledge of consequences, it follows from what has just been said, is to be obtained as follows. Consider an action A which I am contemplating doing in circumstances X. Suppose that A consists in bringing about a state of affairs C. This we will call the result of A. (A result of an action is to be distinguished from a consequence or effect of the action. The consequence is an effect distinct from the action, caused by it. Thus the result of the action of pulling a trigger is that a trigger is pulled. The consequence may be that a bullet is fired, or a man killed.)[2] How am I to know what its effects will be, what will follow from it? Most certainly, by having done such an action myself many times before in similar circumstances, and having observed the effects of its result. I come to know most surely what will result from pulling the trigger of a certain loaded gun when it is pointing at a man's head by having done such an action often before. I know the effect less surely by having seen the effects of others doing the action, or by having seen the effects of the result of the action when this was brought about unintentionally, all in similar circumstances to those in which I am considering doing the action; or by others telling me what happened on different occasions when they pulled triggers of loaded guns. I know that pulling the trigger will kill the man less surely, because I suspect that maybe it does not work with me, or that others have a special way of pulling the trigger which I do not know, and so on. Less sure knowledge still is obtained by observing the result occur in somewhat different circumstances (e.g., when the gun was pointing at a man's stomach instead of at his head). Still less sure knowledge is obtained by having observed goings-on only somewhat similar, and having to make allowance for the difference—e.g., I may only have seen guns fired at cardboard targets, or arrows fired at men. Or my knowledge may depend on reports given by a few others who depended in turn on other witnesses for their information; then it will be still less certain.

The least certain knowledge of all is that which is reached by a process of more complicated inference from goings-on remotely similar to A. However it is difficult to see how a theory which predicted the occurrence of such evils as pain or death could have any justification unless the data on which the theory was built were cases of pain and death. If you had no knowledge of anything causing pain, how could other kinds of data substantiate predictions about pain? For pain is so different from other kinds of goings-on and has no natural connection with particular brain or nerve conditions rather than with others. (There is no reason for supposing that stimulation of this nerve will cause pain and of that one will cause pleasure, other than that provided by knowledge that that is what has happened in the past.)

So proximity to experience gives more certain knowledge. It is notorious that people are much more inclined to take precautions against disaster if they have suffered before themselves or if a similar disaster has happened to those close to them than if they are warned of the need for precaution by some impersonal distant authority. A man is far more inclined to take precautions against fire or burglary if he or his neighbors have suffered than if the police warn him that these things have happened in the next village. My point is that this is not just irrational perversity. It is the height of rationality to be influenced more by what is known better. People know better that it can happen to them if they know that it has happened to them or to others like them. With a mere police warning, they always have some reason for suspecting that police exaggerate or that things are different in the next village. What is irrational is not being influenced at all by the police warning; what is not irrational is being influenced more by goings-on closer to hand of which we have more intimate experience.

IV

One thing that follows from all this, is that if we are to know the effects of our actions, things must behave in regular ways. Only if my action is going to have an effect similar to that of similar actions done by others on other occasions, can I know what effect that action is going to have. Only if I know what effects my actions will have can I set about making a difference to things. It follows that if agents are to mould the world and themselves, the world has to be on the whole a pretty deterministic sort of place; deterministic laws of nature have to operate fairly universally. There would not need to be complete determinism—agents themselves could be exempt from the full rigours of determinism, and there might be violation of natural laws from time to time. But basically the world has to be governed by laws of nature if agents are to be able to control it.

The main things however for our purposes which follows from what has been said so far is that we can only come to know that certain of our actions will have harmful consequences through prior experience (in some degree) of such harmful consequences. I come to know that drinking alcohol will give me a hangover most surely by having had it happen to me before, less surely by my having seen it happen to others before, less surely by others telling me that it has happened to them before and least surely still by its being a remote prediction of some complex scientific theory.

With the case of the worst evils it is not possible that my knowledge should be based on experience of what has happened to *me* before. I cannot know by experience that taking more and more heroin over a long period will cause death by having had it happen to me before. In such cases the most sure knowledge will be given by seeing it happen to many friends; less sure knowledge by seeing it happen on television (as in the British TV documentary "Gale is Dead"); still less sure knowledge by reading in a book that this happened before. Loss of limbs too is a consequence about which I can learn only by seeing or hearing of the experiences of others. But here too actually seeing a friend have to have his arm amputated as a result of walking too close to the edge of a cliff and falling over it, is rightly going to deter me from walking close to the edge of the cliff much better than is a notice which says "Dangerous" (for the former gives me surer knowledge of a possible consequence of my action). It follows generally that my actions or negligence can only to my knowledge have really bad consequences if others have suffered such really bad consequences before. Among such really bad consequences are prolonged incurable suffering or death. These can only be among the evils which I can knowingly inflict on others, or through my negligence allow others to suffer, if others have suffered before.

Further, for any evil which men knowingly inflict on each other, there must have been a first time in human history at which this was done. There must have been a first murder, a first murder by cyanide poisoning, a first deliberate humiliation, and so on. The malevolent agent in each case knows the consequences of the result of his action (e.g., that imbibing cyanide will lead to death). *Ex hypothesi,* he cannot know this through having seen an agent give another cyanide for this purpose. His knowledge that cyanide poisoning causes death must come from his having seen or others having told him that on other occasions taking cyanide accidentally led to death. (If in my example, you think that knowledge of the effects of imbibing cyanide might be gained by seeing the effects of taking similar chemicals, the argument can be put more generally. Some man must have taken previously a similar poison by accident.) What applies to the malevolent agent also applies to the man who knowingly refrains from inflicting evil on another or stops evil occurring to another. There must be natural evils (whether caused by natural processes or brought about accidentally by men) if men are to know how to cause evils themselves or are to prevent evil occurring.

And there have to be *many* such evils, if men are to have sure knowledge, for as we saw, sure knowledge of what will happen in future comes only by induction from many past instances. A solitary instance of a man dying after taking cyanide will not give to others very sure knowledge that in general cyanide causes death—maybe the death on the occasion studied had a different cause, and the cyanide had nothing to do with it. And unless men have been bringing about evils of a certain kind deliberately recently, there have to be many recent naturally occurring evils if men are currently to have sure knowledge of how to bring about or prevent such evils.

Thus we know that rabies causes a terrible death. With this knowledge we have the possibility of preventing such death (e.g. by controlling the entry of pet animals into Britain), or of negligently allowing it to occur or even of deliberately causing it. Only with the knowledge of the effects of rabies are such possibilities ours. But for us to gain knowledge of the effect of rabies it is necessary that others die of rabies (when the rabies was not preventable by man), and be seen to have done so. Generally, we can only have the opportunity to prevent disease affecting ourselves or others or to neglect to do so, or the opportunity to spread disease deliberately (e.g., by indulging in biological warfare), if there are naturally occurring diseases. And men can only have the opportunity to prevent incurable diseases or to allow them to occur, if there are naturally occurring incurable diseases.

V

What applies to individuals in the short term, applies also in the longer term and to races. If men are to have the opportunity by their actions or negligence to bring about evil consequences in the distant future, or to avoid doing so, they must know the long-term consequences of their actions, and the most sure inductive knowledge of those consequences can only come from past human history. How are men to have the opportunity to stop future generations catching asbestosis, except through knowledge of what causes asbestosis and how is that to be obtained except through records which show that persons in contact with blue asbestos many years ago have died from asbestosis thirty years later? Or suppose that men are to have the choice of building cities along earthquake belts, and so risking destruction of whole cities and their populations hundreds of years later, or of avoiding doing so. How can such a choice be available to them unless they know where earthquakes are likely to occur and what their probable consequences are? And how are they to come to know this unless earthquakes have happened due to natural and unpredicted causes, like the Lisbon earthquake of 1755.

The scope for long-term choice available to future generations must not be underestimated. They may have the choice not merely of whether to build cities so as to avoid earthquakes, but of whether to drive the earth nearer to the sun or further from it, to take air and water to Mars and live there instead, to extend the life span, to produce new man-like organisms in laboratories, and so on. But rational choices on these matters can only be made in the light of knowledge of the consequences of alternative actions. The *most* sure knowledge can come only from the records of the effects on men of natural disasters, and of naturally caused changes of environment and constitution. If men are knowingly to determine the fate of future generations through making such choices they can do so most surely by having knowledge of the disasters which have befallen past generations.

I argued that what has happened to men very different from ourselves gives less sure knowledge than what has happened to ourselves. It does nevertheless give knowledge. And what has happened to sentient creatures other than men also gives knowledge, though very much less sure knowledge. Indeed a great deal of our knowledge of the disasters for man which would follow some action come from study of the actual disasters which have befallen animals. For millenia it has been normal to discover the effects of drugs or surgery or unusual circumstances on man, by deliberately subjecting animals to those drugs or surgery or circumstances. Before putting men into space, men put animals into space and saw what happened to them. Such experiments do not give very sure knowledge of what would happen to men—because from the nature of the case, there are very considerable differences between animals and men—but they do give considerable knowledge. The evils which have naturally befallen animals provide a huge reservoir of information for men to acquire knowledge of the choices open to them, a reservoir which men have often tapped—seeing the fate of sheep, men have learnt of the presence of dangerous tigers; seeing the cows sink into a bog, they have learnt not to cross that bog, and so on.

As regards *very* long-term consequences of changes of circumstances, environment or climate, the story of animal evolution provides our main information. Human history so far is too short to provide knowledge of the very long-term consequences of our actions (including the knowledge needed to make some of the choices to which I referred two paragraphs back). To take another example—future biologists will have the power to produce much good or ill by inducing various genetic mutations. Human history does not provide the data which will give them any knowledge of the consequences of their actions. Their surest knowledge of those consequences will come from a study of the evolutionary history of the consequences in animals of various naturally occurring mutations.

Apart from such detailed results the story of pre-human nature "red in tooth and claw" provides some very general information crucially relevant to our possible choices. For suppose that animals had come into existence at the same time as man (e.g., B.C. 4004) always in situations where men could save them from any suffering. Naturally it would then seem a well-confirmed theory that (either through act of God or nature) suffering never happens to animals except such as men can prevent. So men would seem not to have the opportunity to do actions which would cause suffering to later generations of animals of a subsequently unpreventable kind, or the opportunity to prevent such suffering. The story of evolution tells us that that is not so—the causation or prevention of long-term suffering is indeed within our power; such suffering can happen because it has happened. The story of pre-human evolution reveals to man just how much the subsequent fate of animals is in his hands—for it will depend on the environment which he causes for them and their genes which he may cause to mutate.

In any case it is not only men who learn from animal suffering. Animals learn themselves. They do of course avoid many situations and do many actions instinctively; but in those cases they cannot be said to be doing the action or avoiding the situation through knowledge of its consequences. If it is good (as it might well appear) that they too should save their lives and those of their offspring through knowledge of consequences, this is only to be had by experience thereof. Other animals must suffer if some animals are to learn to avoid suffering for themselves and their offspring.

In connection with animal suffering, it is appropriate to make the obvious point that presumably this is far less intense than human suffering. For if man suffers and inanimate matter and plants do not, then suffering presumably increases with mental and nervous complexity. Animals in general are far less intelligent and have a far less developed nervous organization than men; one would expect their suffering to be

correspondingly much less. This is presumably why men do not interfere
very much to stop animals hurting and killing each other.

VI

My main argument so far has been that *if* men are to have the opportunity
to bring about serious evils for themselves or others by actions or negligence, or to prevent their occurrence, and *if* all knowledge of the future
is obtained by induction, then there must be serious natural evils occurring to man or animals. We saw earlier that a developed free-will defense
must claim that a good God might give to men the opportunity to do to
each other serious harm for the sake of the freedom and responsibility
which he would thereby be giving them and which they cannot otherwise
have. It follows that if they are to have this opportunity, there must be
serious naturally occurring evils too—unless God were to give to men
non-inductive knowledge of the consequences of their actions.

I turn briefly to consider this latter alternative. Inductive inference
from the past is not our only route to knowledge of the future. In so far
as what will happen lies within the power of an agent, we can learn what
will happen, not merely by studying the agent's past behavior and so inferring by induction how he will behave in future, but by his telling us
what he intends to do. I can learn that you will be in London tomorrow
by your telling me so. I can learn that if I omit to pay your bills, you will
prosecute me, by your telling me so. Such knowledge of the future I will
call verbal knowledge. If there is a God, ought he not to convey to men
knowledge of the consequences of their actions verbally, in order to avoid
having to bring about natural evils? His giving us verbal knowledge of the
consequences of our actions would involve his saying out loud such things
as "if you walk near the cliff, you will fall over," or "if you want to kill
your neighbor, cyanide is very effective."

Such a procedure would make men know for certain that there was
a God, with all that that involves.[3] Then not merely would many men
reasonably believe that there was a God; all men without exception would
know for certain that all that happened (except for human actions) was due
to the immediate action of God. Whether morally good or bad, whether
they would otherwise concern themselves with matters religious or not; the
existence of God would be for them an item of evident common knowledge. Knowing that there was a God, men would know that their most
secret thoughts and actions were known to God; and knowing that he was

just, they would expect for their bad actions and thoughts whatever punishment was just. Even if a good God would not punish bad men further, still they would have the punishment of knowing that their bad actions were known to God. They could no longer pose as respectable citizens; God would be too evident a member of the community.

Further, in seeing God, as it were, face to face, men would see him to be good and worshipful, and hence would have every reason for conforming to his will. In such a world men would have little temptation to do wrong—it would be the mark of both prudence and reason to do what was virtuous. Yet a man only has a genuine choice of destiny if he has reasons for pursuing alternative courses of action, for a man can only perform an action which he has some reason to do. Further too, in such a world, men could not choose whether to acquire knowledge or what kinds of knowledge to seek, but knowledge would surround them. In this way too men would have no choice of destiny.

I conclude that a world in which God gave to men verbal knowledge of the consequences of their actions would not be a world in which men had a significant choice of destiny, of what to make of themselves and of the world. God would be too close for them to be able to work things out for themselves. But the whole point of the free-will defense is that a good God might give to man a choice of destiny; if he gave to men verbal knowledge of the consequences of their actions, he would not be able to give that choice. Proximity to God is no doubt a good thing; but a God has reason to ensure that we only get to that state as a result of our own choice (e.g., in another world as a result of our conduct in this one).

But if you do not have verbal knowledge of the consequences of your actions, your knowledge must be obtained by inference from what has happened in the past, and the only justified inference from what has happened in the past is that things will continue to behave as they have behaved, and the supposition that this is so is what characterizes inductive inference. It follows that only by giving to men inductive knowledge of the bad consequences of some of their possible actions can a God give to men substantial responsibility for their destiny and that of their fellows. But the giving of such knowledge involves a God in producing natural evils. There must be natural evils if men are to have a significant choice of destiny; which is why a good God might well bring them about. Contrary to what might at first sight appear, if the Free Will Defense can cope with evils produced by man, it can cope with natural evils as well.

NOTES

1. See, for example, Alvin Plantinga, *God and Other Minds* (London and Ithaca, 1967), chaps. 5 and 6.

2. For this distinction see G. H. Von Wright, *Norm and Action* (London, 1963), pp. 39ff.

3. I assume that in discovering that there was an omnipotent omniscient and perfectly free creator (which is what God's successful predictions would suggest) men would have discovered the existence of a being of a kind such that he is also necessarily perfectly good. See R. G. Swinburne, "Duty and the Will of God," *Canadian Journal of Philosophy* (1974), vol. 4, pp. 213–227, especially pp. 219–222.

Knowledge, Freedom, and the Problem of Evil

ELEONORE STUMP

INTRODUCTION

In his recent book *The Existence of God*,[1] Richard Swinburne offers a so-phisticated, promising solution to the problem of evil. Why is there evil in the world if there is an omniscient, omnipotent, perfectly good God? If God is perfectly good, he wants to prevent all the evil he knows about and is able to prevent; if he is omnipotent, he is able to prevent any evil he knows about; and if he is omniscient, he knows about all instances of evil. So if God exists, he will know about all evil, be able to prevent it, and want to do so; hence there will be no evil in the world. Philosophers have sometimes thought this argument implied that the existence of evil is log-ically incompatible with the existence of God;[2] and since there is unde-niably evil in the world, such philosophers have taken the existence of evil to be conclusive proof that God does not exist. This argument has been countered by what has come to be called the free-will defense. Argued re-cently by Alvin Plantinga[3] among others, it maintains that a perfectly good, omniscient, omnipotent God will not necessarily prevent all evil. God might give some of his creatures free will, and allowing free will is not compatible with preventing all evil if that free will is exercised for evil. The free-will defense successfully rebuts the claim that the presence of evil in the world is logically incompatible with God's existence. But many people, theists as well as atheists, feel that the free-will defense leaves some of the most important questions about evil unanswered. If there is a

From *International Journal for Philosophy of Religion* 14 (1983): 49–58. © 1983, Klu-wer Academic Publishers. Reprinted by permission of Kluwer Academic Publishers.

God, the *nature* and *quantity* of evil in the world still remain a puzzle; and even if they do not support a conclusive argument, they still seem to provide strong evidence against the probability of God's existence. In particular, natural evils such as diseases, congenital defects, earthquakes, and droughts, need to be given some plausible explanation which shows their existence to be compatible with God's goodness. It is the problem of evil in this sense which Swinburne addresses in Chapter 11 of *The Existence of God*. In what follows, I will describe Swinburne's solution and give reasons for thinking it unacceptable.

SWINBURNE'S SOLUTION

Swinburne begins his solution[4] to the problem of evil with two assumptions (which he gives some arguments for earlier in the book), namely, that men have free will, and that free will is very valuable. His thesis is this:

> the existence of many natural evils . . . is logically necessary for the existence of a world of the type which I have already described. For they are necessary if agents are to have the *knowledge* of how to bring about evil or prevent its occurrence, knowledge which they must have if they are to have a genuine choice between bringing about evil and bringing about good. (pp. 202–203)

It is clear that knowledge is necessary for significant choices between good and evil, but why should Swinburne think natural evil is necessary for such knowledge? His reasons for thinking so have to do with his views of the acquisition of the knowledge in question.

> Now if agents are knowingly to bring about states of affairs, or to allow states of affairs to come about through neglecting to prevent them, they must know what consequences will follow from their actions. Normal inductive knowledge of consequences . . . is to be obtained as follows. Consider an action A which I am contemplating doing in circumstances X. . . . How am I to know what its effects will be, what will follow from it? Most certainly, by having done such an action myself many times before in similar circumstances, and having observed the effects of its results. . . . I know the effect less surely by having seen the effects of others doing the action. . . . Less sure knowledge still is obtained by observing the result occur in somewhat different circumstances. . . . Still less sure knowledge is obtained by having observed goings-on only somewhat similar, and having to make allowance for the difference. . . . Or my knowledge may depend on reports given by others; then it will be still less certain. . . . The

least certain knowledge of all is that which is reached by a process of more complicated inference from goings-on only remotely similar. . . .

So proximity to experience gives more certain knowledge. It is notorious that people are much more inclined to take precautions against disaster if they have suffered before themselves or if a similar disaster has happened to those close to them. . . . It follows from all this that we can only come to know that certain of our actions will have harmful consequences through prior experience (in some degree) of such harmful consequences. . . . It follows generally that my actions or negligence can only to my knowledge have really bad consequences if others have suffered such really bad consequences before. . . . And unless men have been bringing about evils of a certain kind deliberately recently, there have to be many recent naturally occurring evils if men are currently to have sure knowledge of how to bring about or prevent such evils. (pp. 204–207)

Swinburne's argument, then, comes to this. Men cannot make serious and effective choices between good and evil unless they know which of their actions will result in good and which in evil. But they can know the consequences of their actions only by more or less direct induction from past experience; and the closer to their own experience their actions are, the surer their knowledge about the consequences will be. Now men can have experience of the evil consequences of actions in two ways. Either they can see such evil consequences resulting from other human actions (including their own past actions), or they can learn of the evil consequences by seeing them occur naturally, as a result of accident or natural disaster, for example. According to Swinburne, however, there must be a first occasion for any given kind of deliberately committed human evil. And the agent committing the evil on that first occasion can learn about the evil consequences of *his* intended action only by observing some natural evil, not by observing other men deliberately doing the same sort of action. So, in the last analysis, "there must be naturally occurring evils . . . if men are to know how to cause evils themselves or are to prevent evil occurring" (p. 207).

To illustrate his point, Swinburne gives several examples, of which these are representative:

(1) Thus we know that rabies causes a terrible death. With this knowledge we have the possibility of preventing such death . . . , or of negligently allowing it to occur or even of deliberately causing it. . . . But for us to gain knowledge of the effects of rabies it is necessary that others die of rabies (when the rabies was not preventable by man), and be seen to have done so. (p. 207)

(2) How are men to have the opportunity to stop future generations catching asbestosis, except through knowledge of what causes asbestosis, and
how is that to be obtained except through records which show that persons
in contact with blue asbestos many years ago have died from asbestosis
thirty years later? (p. 208)

(3) Or suppose that men are to have the choice of building cities along
earthquake belts, and so risking the destruction of whole cities and their
populations hundreds of years later, or of avoiding doing so. How can such
a choice be available to them unless they know where earthquakes are likely
to occur and what their probable consequences are? And how are they to
come to know this, unless earthquakes have happened due to natural and
unpredicted causes, like the Lisbon Earthquake of 1755? (p. 208)

The account I have presented here constitutes the core of Swinburne's
justification of natural evil. It can be extended easily to cover cases of deliberately caused human evil as well. Swinburne's summarizing remarks,
in fact, cover not only cases of natural evil but also cases of intentionally
produced evil; and so his solution, if it succeeds, is a solution to the entire
problem of evil. He summarizes his position in this way:

> the fewer natural evils a God provides, the less opportunity he provides for
> man to exercise responsibility. For the less natural evil, the less knowledge
> he gives to man of how to produce or avoid suffering and disaster, the less
> opportunity for his exercise of the higher virtues, and the less experience of
> the harsh possibilities of existence; and the less he allows to men the op-
> portunity to bring about large scale horrors, the less the freedom and re-
> sponsibility which he gives to them. What in effect the objection [to God's
> allowing evil in the world] is asking is that a God should make a toyworld,
> a world where things matter, but not very much; where we can choose and
> our choices can make a small difference, but the real choices remain God's.
> For he simply would not allow us the choice of doing real harm, or through
> our negligence allowing real harm to occur. (pp. 219–220)

In this way, Swinburne thinks he has shown that God is justified in allowing "Hiroshima, Belsen, the Lisbon Earthquake, or the Black Death"
(p. 219).

THE ACCEPTABILITY OF SWINBURNE'S SOLUTION

For a number of reasons, it seems to me that Swinburne's solution to the
problem of evil is not acceptable.

To begin with, one of the crucial premises of Swinburne's argument is, I think, not true. It is false that men can have knowledge of the consequences of their actions only by induction on the basis of past experience. To start with the most obvious counter-example, God himself might provide his creatures with this knowledge; and if God himself provided knowledge about the consequences of men's actions, instances of natural evil would no longer be necessary for educational purposes.

Swinburne recognizes this is an objection to his account, but he dismisses it because he thinks of God's providing such knowledge is incompatible with a higher-order good involving man's freedom. Swinburne conceives of God's providing the knowledge in question as God's "saying out loud" what the consequences of certain actions will be: "if you walk near the cliff, you will fall over, or if you want to kill your neighbor, cyanide is very effective" (p. 211). The drawback in this route to knowledge, Swinburne argues, is that it would entail that all men know of the existence of God. Furthermore, men would know God directly and so would know him also to be good and worthy of worship. Thus, according to Swinburne, self-interest and reason both would dictate conformity to God's will; consequently, men would have little temptation to do evil, and hence little choice of destiny. Therefore, in order to protect the higher-order good of men's choice of destiny, God cannot provide men with knowledge of the consequences of their actions.

I think Swinburne's argument would be cogent if the only way in which God could provide knowledge were by talking out loud and meeting man face-to-face. But surely talking face-to-face with man is not the only way an omniscient, omnipotent deity can provide knowledge. To take just one possibility, God could provide information in dreams. He could, for instance, give the president of the relevant labor union a violently vivid dream in which he appears to see in grisly detail workers exposed to asbestos subsequently suffering with the symptoms of asbestosis, being all the while convinced in his dream that the use of protective masks would have prevented his men's suffering. If the emotional force of such a dream were not enough to prompt precautions with asbestos, the veracity of the dream's message could be tested—by animal experiments, for example.[5] If men regularly had such vivid, message-laden dreams and if their dreams were regularly shown true (by subsequent scientific testing, for example), men would be inclined to accept the dreams' messages as true, or at least to conduct the tests necessary to discover whether or not a dream's message was true. But such dreams, even if regularly shown true, would no more compel belief in God than would cases of precognition if they could be shown to occur regularly. In this way, then, God could provide information to men without the enormous quantity of terrible suffering brought about by natural evils and yet without incurring any of the infelicitous results of speaking with men face to face. And this is by no means the only way for God to provide information without speaking to men face-to-face. The Old Testament abounds in examples: certain individuals (the prophets) have special, divinely bestowed insight into the consequences of men's actions and serve as a source of knowledge for the rest of the community[6]; men have veridical, message-laden visions[7]; inanimate objects accurately predict the future[8]; and animals speak[9].

So it seems to me that a crucial premiss of Swinburne's argument is false. We do not need induction from experience of natural evils to have knowledge about the consequences of our actions. God could provide such knowledge, and he could do so without infringing on our freedom.

For at least some natural evils, we do not even need to postulate supernatural cases to provide counter-examples to Swinburne's claim that natural evil is necessary for the knowledge in question. Take the case of asbestosis again. Surely neither many cases of death and disease from asbestos nor supernaturally induced knowledge is necessary for men to know that exposure to asbestos is dangerous to human health. We can learn about the effects of exposure to asbestos in altogether natural ways, without relying on evidence from natural evils, by conducting scientific tests. Swinburne might argue here that we would realize the need to conduct tests of the effects of chemicals on human health only after a number of men had suffered from exposure to them. Such a contention seems to me in fact false. Scientific understanding of biology, which has advanced in tandem with the technology that makes such diseases as asbestosis a real problem, is sufficient to warrant caution about any significant alteration of an animal's biological or chemical environment. We do not need naturally produced deaths from microwave sickness in order to realize the possible dangers of exposure to microwaves, for example; and we can test the results of such exposure and take precautions against its effects *before* anyone dies of it. But even if Swinburne were right that we need natural evils to call our attention to the dangerous effects of biological and chemical pollution, such a claim justifies natural evil only until the time men recognize the danger and the need to test in advance for harmful effects. Once that recognition has been achieved, and we know we need to be cautious about altering an individual's biological or chemical environment, there is no need for knowledge which hinders God from preventing, for example, all cases of accidental lead poisoning (that is, cases in which the victim's suffering is not a result of his choice or negligence regarding exposure to lead).

In addressing this sort of objection, Swinburne tends to talk about "victims of the system." For men to have knowledge of the consequences of their actions, the laws of nature must operate regularly; and if they do, there will be victims of the system (p. 210). That is, the pain caused by fire, which is good on Swinburne's account because it causes men to try to escape from fire, must still occur even if it is not possible for the victim to attempt to escape (because the victim is an infant or completely paralyzed). Otherwise natural laws will not operate regularly. But, we might feel, God is neither a system nor a machine; he is a very powerful person. And the need for the regular operation of natural laws no more prevents his rescuing the helpless victims of fire than it prevents any human person from doing so. Swinburne, however, seems to think that if God regularly rescued the helpless from disaster, humans would fall into the habit of leaving rescue to God (pp. 210–211). It is not clear to me that an inclination on the part of humans to try to rescue victims of natural evils is worth the sufferings of all the victims who are not rescued; but I will assume for the sake of argument that it is. We have then simply restricted the cases in which it is good for God himself to do the rescuing to those in which humans *cannot* effect a rescue, either because they are not present or because although present they lack the necessary means or for some other reason. Hence, even if we give Swinburne everything he wants, countless injuries and deaths are still unjustified on his account, namely, all those which men could not have prevented and whose occurrence is not necessary to produce or stimulate new knowledge.

So it seems to me that natural evil is not justified by the value of knowledge necessary for serious exercise of free will, as Swinburne claims. God could provide men with such knowledge himself, thus obviating the need for natural evils. Or, at least in some cases, men can acquire knowledge of the consequences of their actions by scientific means, without either supernaturally induced knowledge or naturally occurring evils, or at any rate without anything like as many natural evils as do presently occur.

Against this attack on his crucial claim that men need inductive evidence from natural evils for the knowledge necessary for freedom, Swinburne has one last defense:

> When men are contemplating any serious action, we feel that they should be *fully* alert to the consequences of that action. However well they think that they can imagine it, their imagination needs to be pulled into line by

seeing how things really are. Reports given in language will necessarily fail to capture the detail and bring home the feel of those consequences, even if they were reports given by God. . . . That full alertness to consequences can be gained only from the experience of similar consequences. . . . Even if God could give verbal knowledge of the consequences of our actions without impairing our choice of destiny, that knowledge would be less adequate than the knowledge obtained by induction from experience. It is a very deep philosophical truth that by and large all knowledge comes from experience, and that proximity to experience gives surer knowledge." (pp. 213–214)

"So proximity to experience gives more certain knowledge. It is notorious that people are much more inclined to take precautions against disaster if they have suffered before themselves or if a similar disaster has happened to those close to them than if they are warned of the need for precaution by some impersonal distant authority. (pp. 205–206)

Swinburne's line, then, is that even if it were not *necessary* for men to acquire the knowledge at issue from naturally occurring evils, it is nonetheless *better* if they do so, because the knowledge so acquired is surer knowledge than knowledge acquired in some other way, such as knowledge obtained from verbal warnings issued by God. He believes that knowledge gained from natural evils is surer knowledge at least in part because he thinks that people are inclined to take precautions against disaster in direct proportion to their nearness to experience of such disasters. But this is, I think, to confuse knowledge with the inclination to act on that knowledge. It is also notorious that students are more inclined to take precautions against academic disaster as the term is drawing to a close, but this does not mean that they gain increasingly surer knowledge about the consequences of their actions as the term progresses. It means only that as the end of the term approaches, students are more inclined to act on the knowledge they have had from the beginning of the term, namely, that they will be tested on their term's work at the end of the term. Similarly, we may be much more inclined to give up smoking after seeing a friend who is a heavy smoker develop lung cancer; but it is not the case that our knowledge has become surer, only that we are motivated by our friend's disaster to act on knowledge we already have, namely, that there is a strong link between smoking and cancer. And, in general, what is produced by proximity to experience of natural evils which cannot be produced by verbal warnings even from God seems to me increased motivation to act, not increased certainty of knowledge.

Swinburne might reply that even if this objection is correct, it does not have much force against his argument, because whether we describe what proximity to natural evil produces as surer knowledge or as increased motivation to act on knowledge, either way the end product of such proximity is a good thing, something important for man to have, which justifies the occurrence of natural evils.

But here it must be remembered that in effect the point of Swinburne's arguments is to justify God's actions. Now suppose I know that the rocks at the edge of the river where you are intending to walk probably cannot support a person of your weight. I can warn you of that fact and point out to you the unpleasantness of a bruising, chilly, wet fall into the river, and I know that you will not doubt the truth of what I say. But I also know that you are a happy-go-lucky sort of person and that you will probably walk at the edge of the river anyway, in spite of my warning—until, that is, you do tumble into the river; after that, I know, you will be more careful about where you walk. Should I in these circumstances warn you? After all, I know that the knowledge you gain from my warning will be considerably less efficacious (either because the knowledge is less sure or because it produces less motivation) in altering your behavior than knowledge gained from proximity to the experience of a fall would be. But if I warn you and you walk at the river's edge anyway and do fall in, your falling in is *your* fault. I did what I could; I warned you. On the other hand, if I do not warn you and you fall in, your falling in is partly my responsibility. I knew, as you did not, that you were in danger of falling in, and I said nothing. Furthermore, even though the knowledge gained from my warning is less sure or less efficacious than the knowledge gained from experience of a fall, nonetheless that less efficacious knowledge is more advantageous to you. If I warn you, you *may* heed my warning and so avoid a fall; but without my warning, you are far less likely to avoid this first fall. On the other hand, if you do not heed my warning, you simply incur the same risk of a tumble that you would have incurred without my warning. Nothing is lost, then, and something is gained by my warning you. Hence the less sure or less efficacious knowledge gained from my warning is in fact better for you, more in your interest, than the more efficacious knowledge gained from a fall.

Both morality and prudence, then, dictate that I warn you, even if the knowledge gained by my warning is less efficacious than that gained by your experience; and the same sort of reasoning applies to God with regard to natural evils. The knowledge which a warning from God could supply might be less effective in getting men to take precautions than knowledge gained from experience of natural evils would be. But if men suffer because they do not heed God's warning, that is their fault. If they suffer because God failed to warn them (and when they could not have known unless God had warned them), then their suffering is God's fault. Similarly, it is in man's interests for God to warn men; with his warning there is a chance of avoiding some suffering which would otherwise be unavoidable. Hence, I think, Swinburne's claim—that even if it is not *necessary* that knowledge of the consequences of our actions be gained only from natural evils, it is nonetheless *better* if it is gained that way—is false.

One further point remains to be made about Swinburne's solution to the problem of evil. Suppose for the sake of argument that Swinburne is right after all, that experience of natural evils is either necessary or better for producing knowledge of the consequences of our actions. The value of this knowledge is what is supposed to justify God's causing or permitting natural evils to occur. But why should we value this knowledge? Swinburne's examples of natural evils and what he says about them suggest two plausible answers. In the first place, knowledge about the consequences of our actions in building cities on earthquake fault lines, for example, is valuable because it enables us to avoid building cities there. Knowledge of the death caused by rabies is valuable because it enables us to attempt to prevent or avoid the disease. And, in general, knowledge of this sort is valuable because it enables us to avoid or escape suffering. But there is something frustratingly circular in such an explanation. God is good to allow natural evils, because they are good in virtue of the fact that they produce knowledge of a certain sort; and this knowledge is good because it enables us to avoid natural evils. But the knowledge of how to avoid rabies is useless unless there is rabies in the world. If God had not allowed rabies in the world—or earthquakes or hurricanes or congenital malformations of infants, and so on—there would be no point in having knowledge of such things. If you conceal traps in my front yard, then my repeated attempts to get from my front door to my car parked at the curb will produce in me knowledge about the consequences of my movements. And this knowledge will be useful to me, if I live long enough to acquire it, because it will enable me to avoid traps in the future. So this knowledge is good, it is gained from experience of the evil which you have introduced into my yard, and without this knowledge I could not avoid the evils of the traps. But *you* are not morally justified in setting traps in my front yard—no matter how good and useful the knowledge about the consequences of my actions may be and no matter how dependent that knowledge is on my experiencing the jaws of the trap.

The other plausible reason for valuing the knowledge in question has to do with the value of man's free will. Swinburne sometimes writes as if he thinks the knowledge gained from natural evils is to be valued not so much because it allows us to escape or prevent suffering but because it presents us with serious choices—to try to prevent rabies, to allow rabies to occur through negligence, or even to cause rabies deliberately (cf. p. 207). And he suggests that if God were to prevent major evils such as the Lisbon earthquake, men would no longer have a serious choice of destiny; men's choices would matter "but not very much" (p. 219), because God could be counted on to prevent the worst of disasters. It is not clear whether Swinburne with this argument intends to address the problem of natural evils only or of all evils, including those deliberately caused by men. Either way, his argument seems to me to leave natural evils unjustified. As an argument defending only God's failure to prevent natural evils, it seems to me clearly unacceptable. Belsen was entirely the work of man's hand, and evils of that magnitude with the serious choices they entail are still possible even if God were to prevent all hurricanes, earthquakes, mental retardation, birth defects, and so on. As an argument defending God's failure to prevent all major evils, it seems to me to have some force. But God could fail to prevent all major evils, thus leaving man serious choices and a serious choice of destiny, simply by failing to prevent all major man-made evils, those for which man rather than God is responsible. And so it is not necessary for God to allow natural evils to occur in order to give man serious choices.

Consequently, I think the value of the knowledge gained from natural evils cannot be used as a justification of God's actions in allowing natural evils to occur. Such knowledge is not necessary for serious choices, and its value as a means of escaping suffering would vanish if God had not allowed natural evils in the first place.

Hence it seems to me that Swinburne's solution to the problem of evil fails. Neither the need for knowledge or the value of it, on the one hand, nor the importance of serious choice, on the other, justifies God's allowing all of the evil he does allow.

NOTES

1. Oxford, Clarendon Press, 1979. Further references to this book will be given by page number in the text.

2. In recent literature, most notably H. J. McCloskey, "God and Evil," *Philosophical Quarterly* 10 (1960) 97–114; and J. L. Mackie, "Evil and Omnipotence," *Mind* 64 (1955) 200–212.

3. Cf. Chapter 5 in his *God and Other Minds* (Ithaca, New York: Cornell University Press, 1967) and Chapter 9 of his *The Nature of Necessity* (Oxford: Clarendon Press, 1974).

4. Before he turns to his own solution, Swinburne considers and sets aside certain other traditional attempts at a solution. For example, he considers the view that the evil which God allows man to suffer is simply punishment for his sins. This he rejects out of hand because it cannot account for the suffering of infants and animals. He also discusses the suggestion that natural evil is the result of free choices by fallen angels. This suggestion he also rejects, on the grounds that the hypothesis of the existence and evil actions of fallen angels is blatantly *ad hoc*; there is no independent evidence for the hypothesis, and it seems to have been brought in just to handle this otherwise intractable problem. Many, perhaps most, theists would agree with Swinburne's rejection of the first solution, and with his reasons for it. (Moses Maimonides seems to be a notable exception; cf., e.g., *The Guide of the Perplexed*, tr. Shlomo Pines [Chicago: The University of Chicago Press, 1963], pp. 469–470, and his discussion of the story of Job in Bk. III, Chapters 22 and 23.) It is perhaps worth noticing in this connection that taking human suffering as just punishment for sins also has some consequences which are incompatible both with ordinary moral sense and with some of the ethical exhortations of the major monotheisms. If suffering is punishment for sins, then if Smith can safely help his neighbor Jones escape from a burning house and does not try to help him, Jones's subsequent suffering will be just punishment for his sins. So Smith has done no wrong in leaving Jones to burn. An account of suffering with such implications is clearly morally repugnant and is incompatible with such religious exhortations to altruism as the Golden Rule. Many theists might feel more hesitation about agreeing with Swinburne's attitude towards the hypothesis of fallen angels. But regardless of one's view of that hypothesis, it seems clear that it does not so much solve the problem of evil (even of natural evil) as transfer it. If earthquakes in densely populated areas, for example, are the result of free choices by fallen angels, the problem of why God allows such earthquakes is not solved. It is simply shifted to the problem of why God allows fallen angels to be successful in bringing about the evil they have willed.

5. Such tests might necessarily involve pain or death for laboratory animals. I am not considering the problem of the suffering of animals in my discussion of Swinburne on evil; but for present purposes perhaps it is enough to suggest that if such tests do necessarily involve animal suffering, we can nonetheless argue with some force that a world in which some laboratory animals are deliberately made to suffer but there are no natural evils is a better world than one with natural evils and no animal suffering in scientific tests.

6. E.g., Jeremiah 42:1–16: "Then . . . all the people from the least even unto the greatest came near and said unto Jeremiah the prophet . . . pray for us unto the Lord thy God . . . that the Lord thy God may show us the way wherein we may walk and the thing that we may do. . . . And it came to pass after ten

days that the word of the Lord came unto Jeremiah. Then he called . . . all the people . . . , and said unto them, Thus saith the Lord, the God of Israel . . . If ye will still abide in this land, then will I build you, and not pull you down. . . . But if ye say, We will go into the land of Egypt, . . . then it shall come to pass that the sword, which ye feared, shall overtake you there in the land of Egypt; and the famine, of which ye were afraid, shall follow close after you there in Egypt; and there ye shall die."

    7. E.g., the visions of the prophet Daniel, esp. Daniel 8–10.

    8. E.g., David's use of the ephod, I Sam. 23:9–11 and 30:7–8.

    9. See the well-known example of Balaam's donkey alerting him to the presence of an angel with a warning from God about what Balaam must say to the princes of Balak; Numbers 22:22–35.

Why Plantinga Must Move from Defense to Theodicy

JERRY L. WALLS

In his numerous writings on the "Free Will Defense" Alvin Plantinga has taken pains to emphasize that he is not engaged in theodicy. In *God, Freedom, and Evil,* for instance, Plantinga wrote as follows: "Quite distinct from a Free Will Theodicy is what I shall call a Free Will Defense. Here the aim is not to say what God's reason *is* [for permitting evil], but at most what God's reason *might possibly be.*"[1] The Free Will Defense proposes then, that it is *possible* that God could not create a world containing moral good without creating one with moral evil as well. This possibility hinges, of course, on the further notion that moral good can be produced only by persons who are free in the libertarian sense. It is libertarian freedom which raises the possibility that God might not be able to create a world with moral good, but without moral evil.

Now the question I want to pursue is whether Plantinga must be committed to libertarian freedom, given his view of God's goodness. It is not altogether clear whether or not Plantinga himself thinks he is required to accept libertarian freedom. He is quite clear, however, that he need not believe the proposition he suggests to save theism from the charge of contradiction, namely, that God could not have created a world containing moral good, but no moral evil. In order to save theism from contradiction, one needs only to identify some proposition which is compatible with the claim that God is omnipotent, omniscient, and wholly good, and which entails that there is evil in the world. The proposition one identifies need

From *Philosophy and Phenomenological Research,* vol. 51, 2 (1991): 375–78. Used by permission of the editor.

not be true or even plausible. Indeed, the proposition can do the job even if we know it is false.[2]

Given the fact that libertarian freedom is a key assumption in Plantinga's proposal that possibly God could not have created a world containing moral good but no evil, I shall take Plantinga to mean that he need not, qua free will defender, believe in libertarian freedom. So the issue is not whether Plantinga actually believes in libertarian freedom. It is clear from his writings as a whole that he does. But I take him to be saying that, in his role as free will defender, for all he knows we are actually not free in the libertarian sense. Perhaps all our actions are determined and we are free only in the compatibilist sense.[3]

This is what I want to dispute. If God is necessarily perfectly good, as well as essentially omnipotent and omniscient, then it is not even possible that we are free only in the compatibilist sense, given the evil in our world. Rather, it follows from God's necessary goodness that we are free in the libertarian sense. This can be shown as follows.

1. If God is necessarily perfectly good, He eliminates all evil He can properly eliminate in all possible worlds.[4]

2. In all worlds in which persons are not free or are free only in the compatibilist sense, God could properly eliminate all moral evil.[5]

3. Therefore, there are no possible worlds in which persons are free only in the compatibilist sense, and in which there is moral evil.

4. Our world contains much moral evil.

5. Therefore, in our world persons are free in the libertarian sense.

Or to turn the argument around, we can show that if we are not free in the libertarian sense, then God is not necessarily perfectly good.

2. In all worlds in which persons are not free or are free only in the compatibilist sense, God could properly eliminate all moral evil.

4. Our world contains much moral evil.

5. It is possible that we are free only in the compatibilist sense.

7. It is possible that God could properly eliminate all moral evil, but has chosen not to do so.

8. Therefore, it is possible that God is not perfectly good.

Now it might be objected against this argument that there may be some reason why God could not eliminate all moral evil, even if we are not free in the libertarian sense. Premise 2, in other words, could be disputed.

However, I do not think there is much prospect for coming up with such a reason. For moral evil is the product of human choices, and if freedom and determinism are compatible, then God could determine all persons to make only good moral choices.

This conclusion could be resisted, however, in the following manner. One could argue that God's full glory would not be displayed unless He exercises His justice. And for His justice to be exercised, there must be moral evil which God consequently punishes. Thus, God must determine some to do evil so He can punish them. Otherwise, there would be the great injustice that God would not receive the full glory which is due Him.

Arguments like this have in fact been advanced by those who hold that God predestines some persons for damnation. The question now is whether such an argument could be used as a possible account for why God could not create a world with moral good but without moral evil. Even if one did not think it was true, or even plausible, could he not use it as a possible defense of his belief that our world was created by a God who is omnipotent, omniscient, and perfectly good?

The answer to this question depends upon whether such an account is consistent with the claim that God is perfectly good. If it is consistent, it will do the same job as the Free Will Defense. Otherwise, it will not. It is clear to me, however, that such an account, far from being consistent with the claim that God is perfectly good, is a total distortion of anything resembling perfect goodness. Therefore it cannot serve as a possible explanation of why our world contains moral evil.

I conclude then that there is no other possible explanation of the moral evil in our world apart from our free will. Unless one is willing to deny that God is necessarily perfectly good, or thinks the account I just rejected is consistent with perfect goodness, he must be committed to the belief that we are free in the libertarian sense.

This conclusion has significant implications for Plantinga's fundamental approach to the problem of evil. It means that he must hold that we are in fact free in the libertarian sense. And if we are so free, then it naturally follows that God must think that freedom and its related goods outweigh the evil in our world. And with this commitment in hand, Plantinga must move out of the relatively modest realm of defense into the bolder arena of theodicy.[6]

NOTES

1. *God, Freedom, and Evil* (Grand Rapids: Eerdmans, 1977), p. 28.

2. See *God, Freedom, and Evil*, p. 28. *The Nature of Necessity* (Oxford: The Clarendon Press, 1974), p. 165; 192–93. *Alvin Plantinga*, ed. by James Tomberlin and Peter van Inwagen (Dordrecht: D. Reidel, 1985), p. 43.

3. In *God, Freedom, and Evil*, Plantinga writes: "And what does the Free Will Defender mean when he says that people are *or may be* free?" (p. 29, my emphasis). The emphasized words would not be appropriate if Plantinga thought the free will defender was committed to the actuality of libertarian freedom.

4. Plantinga affirms this as a condition for perfect goodness in *God, Freedom, and Evil*, pp. 20–22. God can properly eliminate an evil according to Plantinga if He can eliminate it without either eliminating an outweighing good or bringing about a greater evil.

5. For the sake of simplicity, I limit my discussion to moral evil caused by human beings. I leave aside moral and natural evil which may be caused by fallen angels or other nonhuman beings. I also leave aside the question of whether some natural evil is necessary if free agents are to acquire the knowledge they need to make significant moral choices. Richard Swinburne argues for the necessity of such natural evil in *The Existence of God* (Oxford: The Clarendon Press, 1979), pp. 202–214.

6. I am grateful to Alvin Plantinga, Thomas Flint, and Michael Peterson for helpful comments on an earlier version of this paper.

Ad Walls

ALVIN PLANTINGA

Professor Walls asks whether "Plantinga must be committed to libertarian freedom, given his view of God's goodness."[1] Here 'libertarian freedom' has approximately the following meaning: a person has libertarian freedom with respect to a given action if and only if he is free with respect to that action, and furthermore it is not possible both that he is free with respect to that action and that all of his actions are determined. (To assert that someone has libertarian freedom with respect to some action, therefore, is to deny compatibilism.) And the question at issue is not whether Walls presents a good argument for the conclusion that human beings have libertarian freedom, but whether I am committed to the view that they do. More exactly, the question is whether my view that God is essentially or necessarily good, together with what I have said about the free will defense, commits me to the view that human beings have libertarian freedom.

Walls proposes an argument for the conclusion that I *am* so committed; a central premise of his argument is

(2) In every possible world in which persons are not free or are free only in the compatibilist sense, God could properly eliminate all moral evil.

(Here 'properly eliminate' is as in Walls' paper; and moral evil is evil due to the free activity of significantly free creatures.) But if the conclusion of Walls' argument is that I am committed to human beings having libertarian freedom, then what his argument really seems to require is not just the *truth* of (2) but the proposition that *I am committed to* (2).

There is an initial difficulty here: I am inclined to think the notion of moral evil implies the notion of libertarian freedom; that is, it is nec-

From *Philosophy and Phenomenological Research*, vol 54, 3 (1991): 621–24. Used by permission of the editor.

essary, I think, that anyone who commits moral evil, has or has had libertarian freedom with respect to at least one action. If that is so, then (2) is vacuously true: there *aren't* any possible worlds in which persons are not free or are free only in the compatibilist sense, and in which there is moral evil. For purposes of argument, however, suppose we ignore this caveat and consider it possible that there be moral evil even if there is no (creaturely) libertarian freedom.

Now I have never, so far as I know, affirmed (2)—for the reason that I am not at all sure it is true. But then how could it be that I am committed to it? Under what conditions is someone who has never affirmed a given proposition, nevertheless *committed* to it? This is a question of considerable interest and great delicacy.[2] It isn't enough, of course, that (2) be true, or even necessarily true. Realism with respect to universals is (I believe) necessarily true; it doesn't follow that nominalists are committed to realism about universals. (And if I am wrong and it is nominalism that is necessarily true, it doesn't follow that realists are committed to nominalism.) Still, it is clear that you *can* be committed to a proposition to which you have never assented. Suppose, for example, I propose the theory that there are two uniquely tallest men. You point out that according to my theory, there is more than one uniquely tallest man; I demur, replying that on my theory, it is not true that two is greater than one. What I have said nonetheless commits me, I think, to the proposition that there is more than one uniquely tallest human being.

So you can be committed to a proposition p even if you never assert it; and you can be committed to a proposition q that follows from what you explicitly say only with the help of another premiss r, even if you do not assert r and indeed reject it. Perhaps it is sufficient that r be utterly obvious to every normal human being, in the way in which it is utterly obvious to every normal human being that two is greater than one.

But of course Walls' (2) is not like that: it isn't utterly obvious to any normal human being who thinks about it. At least it isn't utterly obvious to me. For all I can see, (2) might be true; but also, for all I can see, it might be false. According to (2) it is necessarily true that if human beings do not have libertarian freedom, then God could properly eliminate every case of moral evil; so necessarily, if God is necessarily good and human beings do not have libertarian freedom, there is no moral evil. Equivalently, the claim is that there is no possible world a good God would actualize in which there is moral evil but no libertarian freedom. (So if God is necessarily good, it follows that there are no possible worlds at all in which there is moral evil but no libertarian freedom.) But is this really obvious? Maybe a certain amount of evil is necessary to every really good possible world. Perhaps among the really good possible worlds, there are some in which there is no creaturely freedom, but there are creatures capable of knowledge. Perhaps it is a good thing that those creatures be able to appreciate the great value of the world in question; but perhaps they couldn't appreciate its great value unless there were some evil with respect to which to contrast that value; and perhaps that evil could be of several kinds, including evil due to the free (in the compatibilist sense) activity of creatures. If all this is so, and for all I know, it *is* so, then (2) would be false.

Accordingly, I am not committed to (2). Furthermore, in arguing that the existence of a wholly good, omniscient and omnipotent God is compatible with evil *simpliciter,* I am not committed to our actually having libertarian freedom, although, of course, I do believe that we do.

When it comes to some of the terrible evils that in fact disfigure our world, however, things are different. It might be plausible to hold that *some* evil is necessary for creatures properly to appreciate good; it isn't plausible, however, to think that the appalling evils we do in fact find are necessary for us to appreciate the world's good, and it isn't clear that those evils wouldn't in any event be too heavy a price to pay for the value involved in creatures' being able to appreciate that good. Perhaps *some* evil is organically required by some great goods; but it is certainly hard to see what goods might organically require some of the horrifying evils the world in fact displays. With respect to those appalling evils, therefore, I am inclined to agree with Walls (more exactly, I think it likely that the analogues of (2) involving reference to those horrifying evils are true). The only reasons God could have for *those* evils, one is inclined to think, must involve creaturely freedom of one sort or another.

To put this in terms of the free will defense: the free will defender argues that

(1) God is omnipotent, omniscient and wholly good

is compatible with the existence of evil (where, following the tradition, we think of evil as including pain and suffering). He does this by finding some proposition *r* that is compatible with (1) and together with (1) entails that there is evil. Where the effort is just to argue that (1) is compatible with the existence of evil *simpliciter* (nevermind how much or of what kinds) then it seems to me that a large variety of *r*'s can plausibly play this role. But the free will defender may also try to rebut the claim that the *quantity* of evil (however one tries to specify it) the world displays is inconsistent with (1), by arguing that the quantity of evil we find is in fact consistent with (1). And he may also try to argue for the consistency of (1) with a proposition specifying that there is some special *kind* of evil: natural evil, for example, or suffering on the part of children, or the sort of evil involved in particularly vicious examples of human cruelty. And with respect to some of the evils of this kind, the only plausible *r*'s I can think of involve creaturely freedom. Some of the evils the world displays are such that I can't see how God could have any reason for permitting them, that did not involve the sort of goods that depend upon there being libertarian creaturely freedom. And if in fact you *asserted* both that (1) is compatible with the existence of these evils, *and* that the only propositions that can plausibly play the role of *r* with respect to these evils involve libertarian creaturely freedom, then perhaps you would be committed to libertarian creaturely freedom.

As for me, however, I'm only *inclined* to think that the only plausible *r*'s involve libertarian creaturely freedom. I can't see any other kind of reason God could have for permitting some of the appalling evils we do in fact find; but there is a big difference between failing to see that something is possible and seeing that it is impossible. So even here I resist being committed to the relevant versions of (2), and (*qua* free will defender) to libertarian creaturely freedom.

NOTES

1. Jerry L. Walls, "Why Plantinga Must Move from Defense to Theodicy," *Philosophy and Phenomenological Research* 51 (June, 1991), p. 375.

2. See my "Two Concepts of Modality: Modal Realism and Modal Reductionism" in *Philosophical Perspectives I, Metaphysics, 1987* ed. by James Tomberlin (Atascadero, CA: Ridgeview Publishing Co., 1987), pp. 221 ff.

Taking Suffering Seriously

KENNETH SURIN

The principle that the self-revelation of God on the cross of Christ is the self-justification of God is integral to the 'practical' approach to the theodicy-problem. In the face of this divine self-justification the attempt by the *human* thinker to justify God vis-à-vis the fact of evil (which of course is what theodicy essentially is) becomes superfluous. The Christian who takes the atonement seriously has no real need for theodicy. ('Theodicy' in this context refers specifically to the 'theoretical' aspect of the theodicy-question.) Theodicy, we are suggesting, has to wait on what God reveals to humankind about the pain and suffering that exist in his creation. In this way theodicy (thus conceived) becomes a "speaking-out" of the event of revelation, a revelation with a texture to be articulated in terms of a *theologia crucis*. What God reveals is that divinity itself, through the cross of the Son, endures the sufferings that afflict us. Divinity is "accessible," without being "knowable," to humankind by this action of God on the cross. [1]

(It is highly contentious theological issue whether the "involvement" of God with suffering creatures must involve suffering on the part of the Godhead. We have seen that the exponents of the "practical" approach to theodicy—Soelle, Moltmann and Forsyth—waive the "axiom of *apatheia*" in the course of affirming this intimate divine involvement with the pain of his creation. Herbert McCabe has challenged this view in a recent essay titled "The Involvement of God." [2] Invoking the classical teaching of Augustine and Aquinas, McCabe argues that it is not in the nature of God to be an "object" in history, a being alongside other beings, and so God cannot depend on his creatures in any way. It follows from this that God can-

From *Theology and the Problem of Evil* (Oxford: Basil Blackwell, 1986), pp. 142–153. Used by permission of the publisher.

not suffer, though he does have the "most intimate possible involvement with the sufferings of his creatures." It would be impossible to do justice to McCabe's fascinating essay in a short digression like this, but it is not entirely clear how God can have the capacity to be *concerned* about the travails of his creatures if he does not have some kind of "attitude" towards them, and the possession of this "attitude" would seem willy-nilly to imply that God is more than just notionally related to those who are the object of his concern. Whether the having of this concern requires us to say that God *is* a co-sufferer is of course another matter altogether. I am inclined to think that it does not.)[3]

The revelation that constitutes the core of "theodicy" is (if it is genuine) only secondarily, and not primarily, an impartation of knowledge, a "gnosis"; primarily it is, and can only be, God's action to bring salvation to humankind in and through the life, death and resurrection of Jesus Christ. The Christian "answer" to the "problem of evil" is the hesitant, stammering bringing of this reconciling action to speech. This, one hopes, is the only approach to the "problem of evil" that can even aspire to reflect the true dimensions of the epistemological crises, and the spiritual predicaments, of the Ivan Karamazovs of this world. Of course for the person in a different situation and with a correspondingly different intellectual horizon (say, the professor motivated by apologetic considerations who, in the tranquillity of her study, seeks to present a theoretical justification of God in the face of the fact of evil), the primary question when reflecting on the "problem of evil" may well be the issue of the intelligibility of theism.[4] In chapter 1 it was suggested that theodicy is a signifying practice, and the theodicist a producer of a system of signification. In the context of a *theologia crucis,* the putatively objective basis of such signification is supplied by the texts which contain the narratives of the passion of Jesus Christ and of the passion of all victims. This *theologia* emerges from the theologian's confrontation with, and interrogation by, the events of the passion of the Son of God and of the passion of all innocent victims. The manner of the theodicist's confrontation with these narratives, and with the *events* presented for representation in these narratives, depends in part on what theological problems, issues or questions she identifies as important. Or to put it in the parlance of the philosophy of social science: her "theologizing" (which in this context will take the form of the creation of a narrative) is always "interest-relative." It is vital, therefore, that we attend to the "grammar" of such "interest-relative" narrative formations before we proceed to consider the specific "grammar" of the atonement, that is, the material form of the "practical" approach to theodicy.

THE INTEREST-RELATIVITY OF THEODICY

Alan Garfinkel (1945–) has drawn attention to the "interest-relativity" of explanation and argues that a "why-question" (for example, the question 'Why does God allow evil to exist?') always presupposes a "space" of relevant alternatives. Garfinkel makes this point by referring to the famous (or perhaps one should say infamous) American bank robber Willie Sutton, who is supposed to have been asked the question "Why do you rob banks?" by a clergyman anxious to reform him. Sutton's reply was: "Well, that's where the money is." Garfinkel argues that two conceivable "spaces" surround the question asked by the clergyman: (1) the space which surrounds the clergyman's *own* asking of the question, whereby the question really means: "why do you rob at all?"; and (2) the space which surrounds the question to which Sutton's answer would have been the appropriate answer; that is, a question like "Why do you rob banks, as opposed to, say, jeweller's shops?" That is to say, where the *clergyman's* question is concerned, the object of explanation (or narrative rendition) and its surrounding alternatives are

$$
\text{Sutton} \left\{ \begin{array}{c} \text{does not rob} \\ \text{robs} \end{array} \right\} \text{banks,}
$$

whereas *Sutton's* object of explanation is

$$
\text{Sutton robs} \left\{ \begin{array}{l} \text{jeweller's shops.} \\ \text{petrol kiosks.} \\ \text{banks.} \end{array} \right\}
$$

Applied to theodicy, Garfinkel's argument reminds us that the explanations provided by the theodicist are always "interest-relative," and that we must therefore ask ourselves the question, "What 'space' is being presupposed by our asking of the questions that fall under the rubric of theodicy?"[5] Where the "theoretical" theodicist is concerned, the object of explanation (or narrativization) and its surrounding alternatives are

$$
\text{Evil exists because} \left\{ \begin{array}{l} \text{the world is a "vale of soul-making."} \\ \text{we are free beings.} \\ \text{good is impossible without the} \\ \text{possibility of evil.} \end{array} \right\}
$$

whereas for the victim of such evil (and hence for the "praxis-oriented" theodicist) the object of explanation and its surrounding spaces are more likely to be

$$\text{Evil exists because} \left\{ \begin{array}{l} \textit{I} \text{ am imprisoned } \textit{here.} \\ \textit{We} \text{ are being tortured } \textit{now.} \\ \textit{You} \text{ are indifferent to } \textit{our} \text{ hunger.} \\ \textit{God} \text{ is an indifferent spectator.} \end{array} \right\}$$

The "praxis-oriented" theodicist, unlike her theoretically-minded counter-part, will locate the "problem of evil" in the "space" occupied by victims, and will invariably discuss it with a quite different context of narrative construction in mind. The presuppositions that underlie the expla-nations advanced by the two approaches are radically different.[6] In the case of the "theoretical" approach, the implicit or explicit question being answered is

Given that there is evil (*in general*), why does evil (*in general*) exist?

whereas for the victim-oriented theodicy, the implicit or explicit question being asked is

Why is *this* (specific evil) being done to *me/us*, by *you/them*, here and *now?*[7]

Given that this is the "logical" or "explanatory space" occupied by the victims of evil, the proponent of the principle that "the only 'acceptable' theodicy is an adequate atonement" must ask herself the question: can the "syntax" and "vocabulary" of an "incarnate salvation" be inserted into this "explanatory space"? Or is this space fundamentally such that no nar-rative of salvation and atonement can be grounded in it? This question must be addressed before the "grammar" of an "incarnate salvation" can be delineated in substantive terms. There are doubtless many who will say that *all* theological speech in the dark places of this world is inherently mystifying, even the words "And the Word became flesh, and dwelt amongst us." For those of this persuasion, even the stammeringly uttered and deeply felt truth that God himself keeps company with those who are oppressed, excluded and finally eliminated will almost certainly be an ut-terance which is ideologically tainted.[8]

Central to this application of the principle of the "interest-relativity" of explanation is the notion that the only theological discourse *about* Auschwitz which can be permitted is a discourse which could have been enunciated *in* Auschwitz by its inmates. As Metz says, there can be prayer after Auschwitz because there was prayer in Auschwitz. But, and this is now the crucial question, was there "theodicy" in Auschwitz? *Could* there have been "theodicy" in Auschwitz? Does the "language" of Auschwitz contain the "grammatical" resources for undertaking "theodicy"? In try-ing to resolve these questions we come up against an immediate problem, one posed by the very nature of the "language" of Auschwitz itself. Elie Wiesel has said that

> the language of night was not human, it was primitive, almost animal— hoarse shouting, screams, muffled moaning, savage howling, the sound of beating . . . This is the concentration camp language. It negated all other language and took its place.[9]

There can be no possibility of rational speech in such conditions. This is virtually a truism (except, of course, for the metaphysical theodicist). The person who is not already convinced that this is the case needs to dwell on an absolutely unspeakable episode which took place in Auschwitz in the summer of 1944. This episode was recounted in the testimony of S. Szmaglewska, a Polish guard, to the Nuremberg War Crimes Tribunal:

> *Witness* . . . women carrying children were [always] sent with them to the crematorium. [Children were of no labour value so they were killed. The mothers were sent along, too, because separation might lead to panic and hysteria, which might slow up the destruction process, and this could not be afforded. It was simpler to condemn the mothers too and keep things quiet and smooth.] The children were then torn from their parents outside the crematorium and sent to the gas chambers separately. [At that point, crowding more people into the gas chambers became the most urgent consideration. Separating meant that more children could be packed in separately, or they could be thrown in over the heads of adults once the chambers were packed.] When the extermination of the Jews in the gas chambers was at its height, orders were issued that children were to be thrown straight into the crematorium furnaces, or into a pit near the crematorium, without being gassed first.
>
> *Smirnov (Russian prosecutor)* How am I to understand this? Did they throw them into the fire alive, or did they kill them first?
>
> *Witness* They threw them in alive. Their screams could be heard at the camp. It is difficult to say how many children were killed in this way.
>
> *Smirnov* Why did they do this?
>
> *Witness* It's very difficult to say. We don't know whether they wanted to economize on gas, or if it was because there was not enough room in the gas chambers.[10]

Greenberg proposes that this episode should serve as an "orienting event" or litmus-test for post-Auschwitz theological formulation: "No statement, theological or otherwise, should be made that would not be credible in the presence of the burning children."[11] No attempted justification of God on the part of human beings can aspire to meet this test; indeed, the very thought that it is possible for someone to say, with the sufferings of these children in mind, that God is justified, is a blasphemy. This episode can only prompt penance and conversion; it cannot motivate a theodicy, even one which takes the form of an atonement. In saying that this episode cannot ground the narrative of such an atonement it is not being implied that there cannot, in principle, be a collision or engagement between such a narrative of faith and the narratives generated by Auschwitz. Indeed, Wiesel himself allows for a similar possibility in *The Gates of the Forest,* when Gregor, whose faith had been destroyed by the holocaust, has a passionate exchange with the Hasidic rebbe:

> Gregor was angry. "After what happened to us, how can you believe in God?"
>
> With an understanding smile on his lips the Rebbe answered, "How can you *not* believe in God after what has happened?"[12]

The narrative of faith collides with the narrative of its negation, but neither achieves an ascendancy over the other. At the level of belief, Auschwitz gives one reason *both* to believe and to disbelieve: the testimony of its witnesses speaks for both these seemingly irreconcilable moments, moments which must nevertheless be simultaneously affirmed. At the level of cognition, the affirmation of the one moment at the expense of its counterpart testimony of negation, and vice versa.[13] To safeguard the possibility of truth it is necessary to hold the one moment as the necessary dialectical negation or counterpoise of the other. The testimony of affirmation needs to be "ruptured" by its counterpart testimony of negation, and vice versa.[13] The acknowledgement of the inescapable need for such a linguistic "rupture," however, can only take place at the level of (mere) cognition. But is it enough for us, when confronted with the brute reality of Auschwitz, to be content with a purely cognitional grasp of the implications of the testimony of its victims? Or does this testimony point us beyond the dialectic of belief and unbelief? The Hasidic Rebbe in *The Gates of the Forest* indicates that this dialectic is doomed to be unresolved if it is confined to the realm of cognition. In his words, God "has become the ally of evil, of death, of murder, but the problem is still not solved. I ask you a question and dare you to answer: "What is there left for us to do?"[14] If this dialectic is to be overcome, the Rebbe avers, it must be transposed from the sphere of cognition to the field of *action*.[15] Or in terms of our discussion, there must be a transposition from the realm of a theological (or more specifically, soteriological) discourse to that of a discourse which facilitates a messianic praxis. This praxis-facilitating discourse will perhaps be the only one which is capable of being grounded in the "explanatory space" occupied by victims. The irreducibly *theological* affirmation of an "incarnate salvation" can only be made from within the circle of faith, and we have seen that it is hard to dispute the suggestion that it would be blasphemous to assume that there is going to be room for this "circle" (and its accompanying theological affirmations) in the utterly unique "explanatory space" inhabited by the citizens of *l'univers concentrationnaire*.

"THEODICY" AS SECOND-ORDER THEOLOGICAL DISCOURSE

Our discussion has gravitated towards the insight that theodicy is best conceived as a second-order theological discourse ranging over a first-order praxis-generating discourse. This discourse has to confess its inability to address the "problem of evil" from a cosmic perspective which enables us to justify God. Reflection on the testimonies and testaments of those who were inhabitants of the kingdoms of night indicates that the person who wishes to speak theologically in response to these narratives must acknowledge that the God who disengages himself from the afflictions of victims cannot be justified, either by human beings or himself. The God who is a mere onlooker when confronted with gratuitous suffering is a demon and not a God. For those who suffer, however, the utterance of this truth, no matter how deeply it is felt by those who utter it, can only be half a consolation.

The most pressing question for any person interested in the possibility of a (first-order) praxis-facilitating discourse is bound to be: what is the conceivable structure and content of such a discourse? Susan Shapiro has pointed out that three pervasive experiences underpin the "rupture" of language brought about by the holocaust. It seems to me that our first-order language (which will almost certainly *not* be a specifically theological discourse) must, at the very least, seek to articulate these experiences; only in this way will it be possible for our theological languages to be "chastised" by narratives of pain and godforsakeness, thereby allowing themselves to be broken into by the reality which is "spoken" by these narratives. According to Shapiro, the first of these linguistically normative experiences is the almost universal experience of having been abandoned by God. She quotes Wiesel's words in *Night:* "Theirs was the kingdom of night. Forgotten by God, forsaken by Him, they lived alone, suffered alone, fought alone."[16] The second experience is the concerted and relentless endeavour of the Nazis to dehumanize their victims prior to eliminating them.[17] The third experience was the world's almost total indifference to the fate of the Jews. Again, Shapiro cites Wiesel: "Alone. That is the key word, the haunting theme . . . The world knew and kept silent . . . Mankind let them suffer and agonise and perish alone. And yet, and yet, they did not die alone, for something in all of us died with them."[18] The first-order language that we need to allow for would be a language that promoted solidarity with those who were forced to undergo these experiences. It would be a language premised upon Wiesel's own injunction to allow the stories of the victims to be communicated:

> Let us tell tales. Let us tell tales—all the rest can wait, all the rest can wait. Let us tell tales—that is our primary obligation . . .
>
> Tales of children so wise and so old. Tales of old men mute with fear. Tales of victims welcoming death as an old acquaintance. Tales that bring men close to the abyss and beyond—and others that lift him up to heaven and beyond. Tales of despair, tales of longing. Tales of immense flames reaching out to the sky, tales of night consuming life and hope and eternity.
>
> Let us tell tales so as to remember how vulnerable man is when faced with overwhelming evil. Let us tell tales so as not to allow the executioner to have the last word. The last word belongs to the victim. It is up to the witness to capture it, shape it, transmit it and still keep it as a secret, and then communicate that secret to others.[19]

Our first-order language would therefore be one that registered, formed and communicated the stories of victims. In doing this it would bear in mind Wiesel's stricture that "not all tales can be, should be, communicated in language."[20] In many cases, the first-order discourse would, so to speak, be no more than a set of quotation marks round the narratives of these stories. In the context of the aftermath of the holocaust, it would be a language that aimed (in Metz's words) to further "a kind of coalition of messianic trust between Jews and Christians in opposition to the apotheosis of banality and hatred present in our world."[21] Only by engendering and sustaining the praxis of such a messianic trust will this first-order dis course be able to serve as an instrument of interrogation and critique for all (second-order) theological affirmations. In short, it would rivet the attention of the makers of these essentially theological affirmations on Irving Greenberg's devastating reminder: take burning children seriously.

NOTES

1. In seeking to ground the *theologia crucis* in God's salvific deed of revelation on the cross I am bearing in mind Wolfhart Pannenberg's formula that God is "accessible . . . by his own action." Pannenberg makes this point in *Theology and the Philosophy of Science* (London: Darton, Longman & Todd, 1976), p. 310. Nicholas Lash rightly says that Pannenberg's formula is a necessary condition for the enterprise of critical theology. See his *Theology on Dover Beach* (London: Darton, Longman and Todd, 1979), pp. 16–23. To quote Lash: "unless God is accessible by his own action, Christian faith expresses only man's hope, and theology is rendered incapable of speaking of God" (p. 17).

2. Herbert McCabe, "The Involvement of God," *New Blackfriars*, 66 (1985), pp. 464–76.

3. In my articles "The Impassibility of God and the Problem of Evil," *Scottish Journal of Theology*, 35 (1982), pp. 97–115, and "Theodicy?" *Harvard Theological Review*, 76 (1983), pp. 225–47, I argued against the "axiom of *apatheia*." I am now less certain that the denial of this axiom is a pre-condition of affirming that God is "involved" in the sufferings of his creatures. For a lucid conspectus of recent work on the theme of divine suffering, see Warren McWilliams, "Divine Suffering in Contemporary Theology," *Scottish Journal of Theology*, 33 (1980), pp. 35–53. A more general survey is to be found in Richard Bauckham, " 'Only the suffering God can help': divine passibility in modern theology," *Themelios*, 9 (1984), pp. 6–12.

4. Such a person may even believe that it is possible to have an explanation which makes evil and suffering intelligible. The perspective assumed in this book agrees with the author of *The Brothers Karamazov* that it is not possible—in principle—to provide such an explanation.

5. For Garfinkel's discussion, see *Forms of Explanation: Rethinking the Question in Social Theory* (New Haven: Yale University, 1981), ch. 1. See Hilary Putnam, *Meaning and the Moral Sciences* (London: Routledge & Kegan Paul, 1978), pp. 42–3, for another discussion of the "interest-relativity" of explanation.

6. In characterizing the differences between the two "explanatory spaces" I have borne in mind Lucien Goldmann's injunction that "if we want to study a human phenomenon we must circumscribe the object in a certain way and try to determine the essential questions: Who is the subject? In whose life and practical activities (*praxis*) did the mental structures and categories and the forms of thought and affectivity arise which determined the origin and behaviour of the object studied?" See his "Structure: Human Reality and Methodological Con-

cept," in R. Macksey and E. Donato, eds., *The Languages of Criticism and the Sciences of Man* (Baltimore: Johns Hopkins, 1970), p. 94.

7. In arriving at this formulation I have been guided by J-B Metz's cautionary reminder: "After Auschwitz, every theological 'profundity' which is unrelated to people and their concrete situations must cease to exist. Such a theology would be the very essence of superficiality." See his *The Emergent Church: the Future of Christianity in a Postbourgeois World,* trans. Peter Mann, (London: SCM, 1981), p. 22.

8. J-B Metz asks himself how Christians can come to terms with Auschwitz and says: "We will in any case forgo the temptation to interpret the saving of the Jewish people from our standpoint, in terms of saving history. Under no circumstances is it *our* task to mystify this suffering! *We* encounter in this suffering first of all only the riddle of our own lack of feeling, the mystery of our own apathy, not, however, the traces of God." See *The Emergent Church,* p. 19.

9. Elie Wiesel, "Why I Write," in Alvin H. Rosenfeld and Irving Greenberg, eds., *Confronting the Holocaust: The Impact of Elie Wiesel* (Bloomington: Indiana University, 1978), p. 201. Elsewhere Wiesel says: " . . . Treblinka means death—absolute death—death of language and of the imagination. Its mystery is doomed to remain intact." See his essay "Art and Culture After the Holocaust," in Fleischner, ed., *Auschwitz,* p. 405.

10. Quoted from Irving Greenberg, "Cloud of Smoke, Pillar of Fire: Judaism, Christianity, and Modernity after the Holocaust," in Fleischner, ed., *Auschwitz,* pp. 9–10.

11. Irving Greenberg, "Cloud of Smoke, Pillar of Fire," p. 23.

12. *The Gates of the Forest* (New York: Avon, 1967), p. 192. Wiesel has said in an essay that "this event [the holocaust] could not have been without God, nor could it have been with God." See "Freedom of Conscience—A Jewish Commentary," *Journal of Ecumenical Studies,* 14 (1977), p. 643. See also Wiesel's contribution to the symposium "Jewish Values in the Post-Holocaust Future," *Judaism,* 16 (1967), p. 281: " . . . the Holocaust has terrifying theological implications . . . It can be explained neither with God nor without Him."

13. For accounts of this dialectical hermeneutics of testimony, see Robert McAfee Brown, *Elie Wiesel: Messenger to all Humanity* (Notre Dame: University Press, 1983), pp. 162ff; and Susan Shapiro, "Hearing the Testimony of Radical Negation," in *The Holocaust as Interruption,* p. 9. To quote Irving Greenberg; "The holocaust offers us only dialectical moves and understandings—often moves that stretch our capacity to the limit and torment us with their irresolvable tensions." See his "Cloud of Smoke, Pillar of Fire," p. 22.

14. Wiesel, *The Gates of the Forest,* p. 197.

15. On the Hasidic rebbe's exploration of the question of doing (as opposed to the question of cognition), see Ted L. Estess's informative essay, "Elie Wiesel and the Drama of Interrogation," *The Journal of Religious Studies,* 56 (1976), p. 29.

16. Susan Shapiro, "Hearing the Testimony," *The Holocaust as Interruption*, p. 3.

17. Shapiro, "Hearing the Testimony," p. 3.

18. Shapiro, "Hearing the Testimony," p. 3. Wiesel is quoted from his "The Holocaust as Literary Inspiration" in Lucy Baldwin Smith, ed., *Dimensions of the Holocaust* (Evanston, Ill.: Northwestern University, 1977), p. 7. See also "Art and Culture After the Holocaust" (p. 407), where Wiesel says: "Had they [the inmates in the murder factories] been aware that the outside world knew— and knew everything—many would have wanted to die sooner . . . as several hundred children did after their liberation. They who had managed to resist and survive the wickedness of the executioner, were helpless and desperate when they discovered the truth: the world knew and was indifferent."

19. Wiesel, "Art and Culture After the Holocaust," Fleischner, ed., *Auschwitz*, p. 403.

20. Wiesel, "Art and Culture After the Holocaust," Fleischner, ed., *Auschwitz*.

21. J-B Metz, *The Emergent Church*, p. 32. See also his "Facing the Jews," in *The Holocaust as Interruption*, p. 33.

Can Theodicy be Avoided? The Claim of Unredeemed Evil

JAMES WETZEL

Theodicy begins with the recognition that the world is not obviously under the care of a loving God with limitless power and wisdom. If it were, why would the world be burdened with its considerable amount and variety of evil? Theodicists are those who attempt to answer this question by suggesting a possible rationale for the appearance of evil in a theocentric universe. In the past theodicists have taken up the cause of theodicy in the service of piety, so that God might be defended against libel from humans, particularly the accusation that God's reign lacks justice. Contemporary practitioners, who live in a world where the existence of God can no longer be presumed, tend to favour theodicy as an exercise in securing the rationality of religious belief. Their hope is that one crucial theoretical obstacle to responsible belief in God will have been eliminated, once the idea of God has been reconciled with the reality of evil. What has commonly united theodicists, at least since the Enlightenment, is that they must answer to a non-believing antagonist. Until relatively recently, theodicy has been a debate between apologists for theistic faith and their cultured detractors.

As the debate progresses, however, one cannot help but notice that theodicy often does not sit well with the faithful. Kenneth Surin represents a growing theological backlash when he claims that theodicy can never be responsible theological discourse as long as it remains ahistorical in form and merely theoretical in interest.[1] He calls for a new kind of theological discourse about the problem of evil, one which "facilitates a

From James Wetzel, "Can Theodicy Be Avoided? The Claim of Unredeemed Evil," *Religious Studies* 25 (1989): 1–13. © Cambridge University Press, 1989. Reprinted with the permission of Cambridge University Press.

practice that interrupts the reality which causes victims and torturers to exist and to flourish."[2] He refers to this discourse as *practical* theodicy in contradistinction to the theoretical theodicy currently in fashion. Practical theodicists would focus on specific, historically situated evils, replace philosophy's abstract and impassible God with a God who suffers, concern themselves more with the elimination of evil than with its explanation, and gauge the success of their theodicies by their political and societal consequences.[3]

When the faithful begin to rail against theodicy, we need to reassess why anyone would have chosen to take it up in the first place. Most contemporary theodicists would say that the form of the problem of evil emerges either as the appearance of inconsistency between a God of certain attributes and the mere presence of evil, or as the yawning of an evidential gap between God's existence and the magnitude of evil. The motivation for theodicy would then be to dispel the appearance and close the gap. It may be the case, as Surin suggests, that theodicy's success here is worse than its failure, but any putative replacement for theodicy would have to do better what theodicy attempted to do, or it would have to show that theodicy was never motivated by a real problem. The growing theological discontent with theodicy marshals a moral critique against a perhaps overly complacent theoretical enterprise. In what follows, I want to suggest that even if this critique were successful, theodicy would not be easily avoidable. The vices of theodicy, which I will have occasion to discuss, do not necessarily vitiate the attractiveness of theodicy. As is often the case, vices exert their own form of attraction.

To begin with, it should be said that contemporary theodicists are aware that they are open to accusations of moral insensitivity. They parry these accusations by sharply distinguishing the philosophical activity of theodicy-making from political and moral struggle of the faithful against the world's injustices. Provided that the distinction holds, theodicy need not interfere with nor detract from solutions to the practical problem of evil. John Hick, one of the premier theodicists of the English-speaking world, holds to such a distinction, and he further argues that the theodicist is not committed to the unseemly task of providing rationales for evil. He believes that the purpose of theodicy can be served if the theodicist restricts his or her attention to why a wholly good and sovereign God would permit evil to infiltrate creation.[4] Although Hick never explains how a justification for God's permission of evil fails to be a rationalization of evil, it is fairly clear what he must have in mind. When theodicists ponder evil as an abstract and general phenomenon in human experience, they do not purport to explain why individuals are moved to perpetuate the world's ills. Individuated evils, evils identified in reference to particular victims and victimizers, lose none of their power for torment and despair at the hands of the theodicist, whose theoretical ambitions fail to extend to individual cases. Theodicy does not justify evils taken singly, only evil taken abstractly.

Alvin Plantinga, another notable theodicist of sorts, prefaces his own philosophical work on the problem of evil with the caution that insofar as the problem of evil precipitates a crisis of faith, it must move out of the hands of the philosopher and into the hands of the pastor.[5] Plantinga has modest ambitions for what a theoretical reconciliation of God's existence with the presence of evil might accomplish. Certainly it brings no peace to the troubled soul. At best the carpings of the non-believer against the rationality of belief in God are fended off, and perhaps the faithful enjoy a mild illumination in knowing that God possibly has good reason for permitting evil to exist.

It is ironic that Surin would choose to impale contemporary theodicy upon the practical/theoretical distinction, the very distinction most philosophers use to purge theodicy of the taint of moral insensitivity. Of course, when Surin refers to practical theodicy, he is still talking about a preeminently theoretical activity, only it is a theoretical activity that no longer disavows or distances itself from human struggle against the encroachment of evil in the world. By refusing to countenance theodicy's practical innocence, Surin challenges theodicists to make their own practical commitments explicit. The ones who purport to restrict the problem of evil to abstract philosophical space are liable to find themselves in tacit complicity with the status quo of evil. Such complicity rides on the assumption that there is some connection—a practical connection—between justification of evil in the abstract and tolerance for evil in the concrete. Purely theoretical theodicy will thereby come to represent a moral failing as much as an intellectual mistake, and theodicists will be unable to escape the charge that they serve as apologists for the evil that they would, as a matter of practice, deplore.

The moral undermining of theodicy boils down, then, to kind of reverse *ad hominem* argument. If a person indulges in theodicy, then that person is morally corrupt. If a person is not morally corrupt, then he or she will not be indulging in theodicy.[6] When thus stigmatized, theodicy is defeated indirectly, since it can no longer be discussed by reasonable, morally sensitive people. Notice, however, that the merits and motivations of theodical arguments are not squarely addressed by a moral critique. They are bypassed by taking the high moral ground from theodicy's theorists.

Without a highly detailed and convincing account of how the philosophical activity of theodicy contributes to the continued existence of evil, advocates of theoretical theodicy are likely to dismiss the moral critique of theodicy as relying on an arbitrary or overly simplistic picture of how theory mediates practice. Certainly they would be right if the account were supposed to remove traditional theodicy from theological discourse without having first discredited the motivation behind the impulse to theodicize. But, short of this, there are good reasons to believe that a wholesale exclusion of practical interests from theodicy can actually compromise the theoretical interest of the investigation. I wish now to indicate briefly how practical and theoretical vices can sometimes implicate one another in a single vice that partakes of each—much in the way, say, that a failure of moral imagination partakes of truncated sensibilities and narrowed perceptions.

I. MINIMALIST THEODICY

In the philosophical literature, there are two sorts of theoretical resolution to the problem of evil, both of which invoke human freedom as the crucial source of restriction upon God's creative activity. Theodicists unite in claiming that God could not have created and maintained a universe free of evil if God also desired to have genuinely free human beings inhabit that universe. They differ, however, on the matter of whether the appeal to human freedom in the context of the problem of evil need commit the theodicist to a substantive claim about what God's intentions actually were in creating the universe. Alvin Plantinga is the greatest living representative of a minimalist theodicy.[7] He will suggest a reason for why God has permitted evil only insofar as the hypothetical truth of this reason frees the believer from the stigma of having inconsistent beliefs. He does not concern himself with whether the reason he suggests is actually true. As a problem for the philosophy of religion, Plantinga restricts the problem of evil to a strict matter of logic, namely to whether theistic beliefs end in contradiction when their implications are explored. Other theodicists, such as John Hick and Richard Swinburne, believe that the philosophical task of theodicy goes beyond the formal question of consistency and must also concern itself with the plausibility of the reason God might have for permitting evil.[8] Neither Swinburne nor Hick thinks that theodicy can evade the attempt to speculate why God would want a world with the considerable amount of evil that our world has. They accomplish this task by setting forth concrete goals and designs that God would have in mind in creating the world. It is important to keep minimalist and speculative theodicy apart, since their respective successes embody the vices of different limitations.

Plantinga, it should be said, prefers not to be called a theodicist. He associates theodicy exclusively with speculation about God's actual reason for permitting evil. But his rejection of the name obscures his own prominent place among contemporary theodicists, and I see no harm in referring to him as a theodicist, albeit one with minimal ambitions.[9] The basic strategy of Plantinga's minimalist theodicy is to extend problematic beliefs about God with beliefs which, when entertained as true, generate a total set of beliefs free of any suspicion of contradiction. The traditional problem of evil counterposes propositions affirming God's omniscience, omnipotence, and benevolence with the proposition that evil exists. Plantinga extends this set with two additional assumptions. One is that human beings are significantly free; that is, they are self-determining with respect to most of their actions. The other is that human beings are essentially depraved, by which Plantinga means that significantly free people will inevitably fail to be moral in regard to at least one of their actions.[10]

Neither the depravity nor the freedom of human beings is obviously inconsistent with the creative activity of the omniscient, omnipotent, and benevolent God, and both freedom and depravity are clearly compatible with evil's existence. In fact, their conjunction carries the inevitability of some moral evil in the world. Under the supposition, then, that we as creatures are corrupt yet self-determining, our creator can in the face of evil continue to remain the God of classical theism.

Minimalist theodicy draws the logically possible limits to omnipotence in order to make room for evil. Plantinga's decision to invoke freedom and depravity to suggest the relevant limits is not uncontroversial, since he must also invoke highly contested notions of necessity, essence, and self-determination. Nevertheless, were we to stipulate that his efforts are successful, the results would still hardly be encouraging for those who seek a philosophical resolution of the problem of evil rather than merely a logical one. It is true, of course, that considerations of logic sometimes legitimately carry the principal interest of a philosophical investigation. But when it comes to dealing with the collision between theological commitments and the recalcitrance of an unjust and painful world, a demonstration of theism's logical consistency with evil barely begins to contain the damage that evil could potentially wreak upon the intelligibility of faith.

If with Plantinga we were to restrict our attention to the logically possible limits of omnipotence, then any world short of a wholly evil one would be logically admissible within those limits. As long as the appeal to the significant freedom and essential depravity of rational agents were coherent, freedom and depravity could serve as the logically possible sources of whatever amount of evil the world should contain, past, present or future.[11] Only a world of total, unrelieved evil would formally rule out God's existence, since it is quite impossible that a benevolent God would for any reason create a world wholly devoid of redeeming features. Such a generous admission of evil into a theocentric universe should be far from comforting to the theist. If God's existence is compatible with vast amounts of evil, it becomes very unclear why this God is worthy of attention, let alone devotion and respect. Omnipotence, omniscience, and benevolence, the honorific titles favoured by God's court philosophers, could lose all religious interest in the face of substantial evil, however consistent these attributes might be shown to be with evil's existence.[12] But more to the point, once we allow logical possibility to negotiate God's relationship to evil, we obscure why anyone should be moved to worry about the problem of evil except as the occasion for an interesting exercise in logic. The vice of Plantinga's minimalist theodicy lies precisely in its minimalism. No issues of substantive religious import are engaged. For a philosopher of *religion,* this lack of engagement is rather damning.

I recognize that some philosophers might find in Plantinga's mimimalism a laudable division of labour between the philosopher, who has only philosophical worries to address, and the pastor, who has broader concerns with the care of souls. But I think it is questionable, certainly, whether philosophers of religion can afford to overlook what makes religious beliefs compelling and interesting for believers, any more than pastors can afford to ignore the intellectual and rational content of faith. If truth is a legitimate philosophical interest, then pastors and philosophers, believers and sceptics, theists and atheists all share a common problem of evil—the need for insight into the mystery of human iniquity and tragedy. Theodicy promises to supply this insight from the wisdom of religious faith, a source of insight that is presumably lacking to those on the outside. Non-believers should nevertheless be able to learn and profit from these insights, should they be forthcoming.

Plantinga would have theodicists narrow their vision to the question of theism's compatibility with evil, thereby reducing theodicy to a protective strategy promising little in the way of insight. Rather than explore the truth of theistic traditions, theodicists are to formulate theism's basic beliefs about God, render them consistent with the fact of evil and, insofar as rationality requires consistency, secure their claim to reason. The only sort of antagonist this should satisfy is the one who was contentious enough to raise the problem of evil merely to discredit religious belief. A demonstration of consistency would be beside the point, however, for all those who wonder whether religious traditions can responsibly use the language theodicy to express the hope of theistic faith in the presence of evil. This hope, in order to be credible, would have to be rooted in an understanding of evil superior to what could be offered without recourse to faith. Logic alone will fail to satisfy here.

II. SPECULATIVE THEODICY

Minimalist theodicy is in fact a minority position among theodicists. It is more common, as in the seminal work of John Hick and Richard Swinburne, to want to advance a plausible rationale for God's permission of evil's existence. The basic strategy of speculative theodicy, which Hick and Swinburne represent, is to incorporate evil within the economy of providential history, so that evil's presence serves the end of perfecting or completing creation in accord with God's good design. This end can be described in various ways. Swinburne emphasizes God's desire to foster a world in which human beings are allowed to grow in virtue and moral sensitivity, assume significant responsibility for one another, and increase in their religious, aesthetic and scientific knowledge. Hick's scheme, being more sharply focused on the eschatological redemption of creation, portrays the world with all its evil as the "vale of soul-making," wherein humans are afforded the occasion and opportunity to develop freely a loving communion with God.

Human freedom is a constitutive element of either end, for without it the evolution of human creatures into moral and spiritual awareness would be a sham, a prearranged fabrication of a deity too mean-spirited to trust humanity with autonomy. Yet while freedom contributes to the acquisition of complex goods, it also introduces the possibility of grievous evils, such as the variety of moral evils all too common in our experience. It is incumbent upon the theodicist to advance the claim that the costs are worth the benefits.

The ingenuity theodicists have shown in balancing the ledger of costs and benefits has been considerable. Swinburne, for example, secures a place for natural evils in creation by arguing that they are byproducts of the regular operation of natural laws. He argues that we cannot have a world without natural calamities, such as fires, earthquakes, famines, plagues, and poisonings, and still have a world run with predictable and lawlike regularity. This regularity supplies us with our best access to the knowledge of what causes and what prevents physical harm, and this inductive knowledge of the world remains crucial for human moral development. Without it we would never be able to assess responsibly the consequences of our actions and decisions. Nor would we, without natural disasters, have a whole host of occasions for exercising our capacity for virtue and responsibility toward others. Needless to say, there will be, as Swinburne puts it, "victims of the system," but the overall benefit to human development is supposed to have established a wide margin of acceptable loss. [13] As long as the variety and amount of evil can be plausibly related to a worthy end, the theodicist will have established an economy for evil.

There is something enormously unsettling about this sort of calculus, insofar as it seems to rule out that some evils are unconditionally evil, regardless of what might happen in conjunction with their occurrence. On the other hand, it is often difficult to discern what speculative theodicists would want to say about the status of evils that are supposedly outweighed by a greater good. Hick vehemently denies that his appeal to divine design should be taken to diminish or deny the gravity of evil. With Nazi atrocities specifically in mind, he remarks that

> These events were utterly evil, wicked, devilish and, so far as the human mind can reach, unforgivable; they are wrongs that can never be righted, horrors which will disfigure the universe to the end of time, and in relation to which no condemnation can be strong enough, no revulsion adequate. It would have been better—much, much better—if they had never happened. Most certainly God did not want those who committed these fearful crimes against humanity to act as they did. His purpose for the world was retarded by them and the power of evil within it increased. [14]

For all these protestations, Hick will go on to claim that when viewed retrospectively from God's eschatological completion of creation, the legacy of evil will be seen to have served the triumphant purpose of the divine creator. Evil, for Hick, may be real and threatening, but it is also inevitably defeated and "made to serve God's good purposes." [15] And if evils even as grave as genocide can find their way into the scheme of human redemption, it is hard to see how theodicy manages to avoid trivializing human tragedy at the very moment it attempts to go beyond it.

The vice of speculative theodicy is that it cannot accept the possibility of irredeemable evil. Many theologians of course may not see this as a vice at all, but as the hopeful conclusion of religious faith. As believers we would be expected to place our trust in the hands of a God who controls creation with wisdom, however the situation may look from the ground up. Nevertheless, theodicy will express an obscene hope if it moves facilely from the acknowledgement of real suffering to the perspective of the big picture. In some way the impulse to theodicy must be reconciled with the tragic recognition that in the balance of history there are some losses which can never be recouped. Otherwise speculative theodicy will continually need to beg the indulgence of the victims of the system for its success.

The prospects for reconciliation are not promising. Karl Jaspers, the great German existentialist philosopher, stated baldly that Christian tragedy is impossible because Christian redemption undercuts any serious acknowledgement of tragic loss.[16] Jaspers may have overstated his point, but he does have a point. The possibility of tragedy rests on the possibility that human suffering overreaches what can be accounted for in terms of just retribution for human moral failure or short-sightedness. We sometimes use tragedy in an extended sense to mean serious misfortune of any sort. Its more revealing sense, however, preserves the connection between the faltering and fallible but essentially worthy human pursuit of ideals, and the powers, divine or otherwise, which conspire against the success of that pursuit. Tragedy relates catastrophe to what humans will for themselves, but it also indicts the order that is ultimately responsible for the exploitation of human vulnerability.[17] It is hard to see, when God is the one in control of the created order, how the acknowledgement of tragedy could fail to carry with it an indictment of divine justice. Ricoeur is quite right when he notes that tragic theology would challenge the holiness and innocence of God and leave the religious consciousness in tatters.[18]

The traditional Christian evasion of tragedy has been to magnify the scope and gravity of sin in order to cover all possible cases of suffering as instances of punishment. For those cases where human beings do not even seem capable of moral perversity, as with infants, there has always been the expedient of original sin, a fault that needs no direct personal involvement on the part of the condemned. Today few of us have the taste for the *ad hoc* cynicism such an evasion would require. The more appealing evasion by far is theodicy's recourse to the economy of redemption, the temptation to claim that as black as it may look now, it is all working out for the best.

We should be clear why this is a temptation. Speculative theodicy exploits the idea that what is utterly evil in its inception and commission may nevertheless, under a different description, have served some useful purpose. One person's intentional act of cruelty, for example, may be re-scribed in the perspective of theodicy as another person's opportunity for compassion for the victim, for courageous resistance against the victim-izer, or for self-examination aimed at the elimination of one's own cruel tendencies. The cruel intentional act, when redescribed in terms of its un-intended good consequence, can find some place in the economy of re-demption. A God who had control over the ultimate consequences of every human action could design the created order in such a way that intentional perpetrations of evil served worthy ends that were quite unintended or un-foreseen by the perpetrators, who would remain fully responsible for the evil they intended. The theodicist, in accepting such a view, would not be committing God to the cynical deployment of evil to achieve good ends. The intended evil still remains a matter of human design, and as a product of human freedom, it falls outside how a benevolent deity would choose to exercise freedom. God never intends evil, but only that the consequences of human autonomy serve in some way the realization of human goodness.

It is somewhat less plausible to extend this strategy to cases of nat-ural evils, since the lines of responsibility from these evils to God's design are not interrupted by the intervention of human intentions. The evil of natural suffering traces its rationale directly back to the purposes of the benevolent creator, thereby raising the prospect that God creates evil to effect good—a compromising posture, certainly, for an innocent God to be in. But if natural occasions of human suffering can be redescribed as the necessary accompaniments of humanity's providential education, their "evil" character may be restricted to the finite and imperfect point of view of the creature. Were we to view the natural causes of death and devasta-tion from God's vantage, we would see that ultimately they are not evils at all, but moments in both the collective and the individual development of the human spirit. By contrast, the view from eternity would preserve the evil character of moral evil. As long as evil may be traced to human intention, the superimposition of a beneficent divine intention does not abrogate the evil quality of the human intentional act. It merely redirects its consequences to serve a divine end.

In principle, the redescription of evil in terms of a good end need be no more offensive an idea than our perfectly acceptable inclination to allow God to arrange the best outcome for regrettable instances of human suffering and perversity. It becomes offensive only when the scale of evil involved is considerable and our ambitions for recovery are excessive. Speculative theodicists indulge ambitions of considerable scope. They claim that the recovery from evil under divine auspices will be great enough to compensate for the cost of the original evil, or at least it will when humanity's potential for ethical and spiritual development has reached its full realization. The sources of this optimism reside in a commitment to the traditional understanding of God as sovereign over the course of human history and a commendable desire not to want evil to have the last word. But although theodicy seems to follow naturally from the drift of theological reflection, it still seems too Panglossian a resolution to the challenge of evil, one which may tend to deaden us to the harsher realities of our world.

The source of dissatisfaction here is not, of course, that theodicists have no *right* to revise our ethical sensibilities and refuse to discount the possibility that any evil can become part of a redemptive economy. It is rather that they do not work through the countervailing sensibility before they set it aside. Speculative theodicy gives every indication of being committed at the outset to the teleological redescription of evil, where even the blackest of sins finds association (and it may be quite indirect) with the promotion of the end of creation. Whether this kind of redescription is suited to all cases of evil is not conceived as relevant to the task of speculative theodicy, which proceeds as the articulation of the global economy of evil, not as the local determination of evil's possible redescription in the light of divine purposes.

Theodicists may sense, quite rightly, that the redescription of local instances of evil in the language of providence could hardly avoid the appearance of being an apologetic for evil. It is not easy to fathom, however, why strong reservations against the rationalization of evil at the local level should dissipate and disappear once a proper level of abstraction has been assumed. The global rationalization of evil should, in point of fact, carry with it the onus of all the reservations we would have in individual cases. If it does not, it is because speculative theodicy has banked on truncating our sensibilities against the rationalization of evil. In other words, the possibility that our apparent perceptions of irretrievable loss and senseless suffering might be veridical in some way would have to remain a question begged in favour of a seamless moral universe. But the price of such begging is that theodicy never relevantly addresses the very phenomenon it purports to explicate. Evil resists too ethereal an abstraction.

III. PRACTICAL THEODICY

Unfortunately, it is not clear how speculative theodicy can be avoided without giving tragedy too much scope within a theocentric universe. Those who would reject too quickly the theoretical pretensions of traditional theodicy to explicate evil can easily succumb to a complementary blindness, wherein questions of meaning and significance no longer are seen to stand out from a backdrop of practical, emancipatory concerns. But evil's challenge to faith's intelligibility fails to respect the contested border between the practical and the theoretical point of view, and exponents of neither side can avoid coming to terms with the possibility of irredeemable suffering. When presented with this kind of evil, practical theodicists are no less evasive than their theoretical counterparts.

To take one example, we might look to the work of Dorothee Soelle, whom Surin describes as a leading exponent of practical theodicy. In her book, *Suffering,* Soelle is primarily concerned to dismantle theological ideologies which justify or glorify human suffering and thereby discourage efforts to change the societal conditions under which people suffer. She would certainly include speculative theodicy as just such an ideology. But can her own approach, which is more self-consciously aimed at the elimination of suffering, deal with the possibility or irredeemable evil? Soelle admits that even after the good fight has been fought, we will still encounter "boundaries that cannot be crossed." She identifies these impasses as the irreversible losses brought on by death, brutality, and insensitivity. Yet in a very puzzling line, she qualifies her observation with a prescription for how the impasses might be passed. "The only way these boundaries can be crossed," she says, "is by sharing the pain of the sufferers with them, not leaving them alone and making their cry louder."[19]

There are, I think, two ways of interpreting this. Either Soelle means for us to identify with those who suffer so that we might find motivation within ourselves to help relieve their suffering, in which case Soelle really has not admitted the possibility of irredeemable evil. Or she is counselling sympathy as the only available response to tragedy. And if she is willing to admit tragedy and permanent loss within the economy of redemption, she should also be prepared to face evil as a theological problem and acknowledge the temptation of theodicy.

Practical theodicists, such as Soelle and Surin, will be hard pressed to eliminate traditional theodicy, if that is indeed their intention. It is one thing to "interrupt" theological discourse to prevent its usurpation by apologists for evil, quite another to suggest that theology owns no voice to address the evil that has passed beyond the powers of humans to prevent or undo. Practical theodicy could not enjoin theology's perpetual silence in the face of evil without beginning to assume the nonbeliever's distance from the resources of faith. I would therefore rather cast practical theodicy in the role of the tradition's loyal opposition than see it as the indignant rejection of theodicy's attempt to make sense of evil.

It is the great virtue of practical theodicy to remind theodicists of all stripes that they cannot stray far from the material encounters of individuals with evil without evacuating the troublesome reality of evil of its content—a strategy guaranteed to deprive theodicy of its integrity. Nor can they refuse to probe the truth of their own religious traditions, unless they would propose to deny themselves the very resources they need to address the reality of evil with religious insight. It is also salutary to remember that theory has its season, and for even the most conscientious theodicist, silence is sometimes appropriate. None of the caveats of practical theodicy, however, will displace the deepest motivation for the problem of evil: our desire to determine the source and limits of a moral universe. For however long evil remains part of our experience, we will be driven to find a meaning for it, even as we seek to eradicate its continued presence from our midst. The question posed to theists, both from their loyal and their not-so-loyal opposition, is whether this meaning can ever be arrived at honestly from the perspective of providence.

Christian thought in particular experiences the continual tug of war between the acknowledgment of tragedy and the impulse to theodicy, since Christianity has always insisted on hanging redemption upon a cross. Nevertheless the problem of credibility on the matter of evil emerges acutely for anyone who would choose to acknowledge the sovereignty of a good God over history. Neither the poles of theodicy nor tragedy seem to be acceptable standards for God's sovereignty, but the alternatives, if there are any, await articulation. No one has yet managed to explain how divine designs for human destiny can respect the claim unredeemed evil makes upon our moral understanding of ourselves and our world. Until that time, theodicy will be difficult to avoid.[20]

NOTES

1. Kenneth Surin, *Theology and the Problem of Evil, Signposts in Theology* (Oxford: Basil Blackwell, 1986). See especially chapters 1–3, where he advances a very powerful critique of contemporary theodicy in light of its enlightenment heritage.

2. Surin, *Theology,* p. 52.

3. Surin identifies Dorothee Soelle, Jürgen Moltmann, and P. T. Forsyth as guides for this sort of theodicy.

4. Hick, *Evil and the God of Love,* rev. ed. (San Francisco: Harper and Row, 1978), pp. 8–9.

5. Alvin Plantinga, *God, Freedom, and Evil* (Grand Rapids: William B. Eerdmans, 1974), pp. 28–29.

6. For this kind of argumentative ploy, see the response of D. Z. Phillips to Richard Swinburne's theodicy in the context of a Royal Institute of Philosophy symposium, printed in *Reason and Religion,* ed. Stuart C. Brown (Ithaca and London: Cornell University Press, 1977), pp. 115–18. Surin *Theology,* pp. 83–85, echoes Phillip's sentiments.

7. Plantinga's most detailed treatment of the problem of evil appears in *The Nature of Necessity* (Oxford: Clarendon Press, 1974), pp. 164–65.

8. The best statement of Hick's theodicy is the revised edition of *Evil and the God of Love,* especially Part IV. Swinburne's theodicy is well expressed in his *The Existence of God* (Oxford: Clarendon Press, 1979), pp. 180–224.

9. I follow Surin in *Theology,* p. 74, in casting Plantinga as a theodicist even in light of the important distinction Plantinga draws between a defence of theism's consistency and a full-blown theodicy.

10. See Plantinga, *Nature,* pp. 184–89, for his formal definition and discussion of transworld depravity.

11. In order to stretch depravity and freedom to cover all the evil of the world, it would be necessary to reduce natural evil to species of moral evil. Plantinga, *Nature,* pp. 191–93, is quite prepared to make such a reduction. He submits that it is logically possible that natural evil is always the malicious influence of nonhuman moral agents, such as fallen angels.

12. Cf. Marilyn McCord Adams, "Redemptive Suffering: A Christian Solution to the Problem of Evil," in *Rationality, Religious Belief, and Moral Commitment,* ed. Robert Audi and William J. Wainwright (Ithaca: Cornell University Press, 1986), pp. 250–51. Adams presses a similar criticism against Plantinga's overly restricted treatment of the philosophical problem of evil.

13. See Swinburne, *Existence,* pp. 200–214, for a fuller account of the connection between natural laws and theodicy.

14. Hick, *Evil,* p. 361.

15. Hick, *Evil,* p. 364.

16. Karl Jaspers, *Tragedy is not Enough,* trans. Harald Reiche, Harry Moore, and Karl Deutsch (Boston: Beacon Press, 1952), pp. 32–39.

17. I have been much edified by the discerning discussion of tragedy in John D. Barbour, *Tragedy as a Critique of Virtue: The Novel and Ethical Reflection* (Chico: Scholars Press, 1984).

18. Paul Ricoeur, *The Symbolism of Evil,* trans. Emerson Buchanan (Boston: Beacon Press, 1967), p. 226. I would venture here, however, a meagre qualification of Ricoeur's observation, which may nevertheless suggest why Jaspers overstates his point against the possibility of tragedy in the Christian scheme of redemption. As long as hell, the place of eternal damnation, remains a part of a religious tradition's spiritual geography (as still may be the case in Christianity), that tradition *ipso facto* acknowledges some evil to have fallen beyond redemption. The eternal suffering of the damned in hell seems to outrun whatever could be accounted for in terms of the just punishment for sins, and the resulting gap between desert and damnation opens theology to tragedy. Whether the evils of hell have anything ultimately to do with the acknowledgment of tragedy depends, of course, on what one wants to make of hell. Not many contemporary theologians or philosophers, least of all the theodicists among them, have found the subject of hell worthy of much discussion. I cannot help but think, though, that we are sometimes too ready to outgrow tradition, as if, in the case of hell, its hold on the Western moral imagination has been due solely to the habits of superstition and mean-spiritedness.

19. Dorothee Soelle, *Suffering,* trans. Everett R. Kalin (Philadelphia: Fortress Press, 1975), p. 178.

20. A shorter version of this paper was read before the Mid-Atlantic Meeting of the American Academy of Religion. I would like to thank the Program Director, Prof. Peter H. Van Ness of Union Theological Seminary, for the opportunity to address a critical audience in a congenial atmosphere.

Bibliography

Ackerman, Robert. "An Alternative Free Will Defense." *Religious Studies* 18 (1982): 365–372.

Adams, Marilyn McCord. "Duns Scotus on the Goodness of God." *Faith and Philosophy* 4 (1987): 486–505.

———. "Hell and the Justice of God." *Religious Studies* 11 (1975): 433–447.

———. "Horrendous Evils and the Goodness of God." *The Aristotelian Society: Supplementary Volume* 63 (1989): 297–310.

———. "Problems of Evil: More Advice to Christian Philosophers." *Faith and Philosophy* 5 (1988): 121–143.

———. "Sin as Uncleanness." *Philosophical Perspectives* 5 (1991): 1–27.

———. "Theodicy without Blame." *Philosophical Topics* 16 (Fall 1988): 215–245.

Adams, Robert M. "Existence, Self-Interest, and the Problem of Evil." *Nous* 13 (1979): 53–65.

———. "Middle Knowledge and the Problem of Evil." *American Philosophical Quarterly* 14 (1977): 109–117.

———. "Plantinga on the Problem of Evil." In *Alvin Plantinga*, edited by James Tomberlin and Peter van Inwagen, 225–255. Dordrecht: Reidel, 1985.

Ahern, M. B. *The Problem of Evil.* London and New York: Routledge and Kegan Paul, and Schocken Books, 1971.

Aiken, Henry David. "God and Evil: A Study of Some Relations Between Faith and Morals." *Ethics* 68 (1958): 77–97.

Allen, Diogenes. "Natural Evil and the Love of God." *Religious Studies* 16 (1980): 439–456.

———. "Theodicies: Rebuttals to a Challenge." In *The Reasonableness of Faith: A Philosophical Essay on The Grounds for Religious Beliefs.* Washington, D.C.: Corpus Books, 1968.

Alston, William. "The Inductive Argument from Evil and the Human Cognitive Condition." *Philosophical Perspectives* 5 (1991): 29–67.

Andre, Shane. "The Problem of Evil and the Paradox of Friendly Atheism." *International Journal for Philosophy of Religion* 17 (1985): 209–216.

Anglin, Bill. "Evil Is Privation." *International Journal for Philosophy of Religion* 13 (1982): 3–12.

Appleby, Peter C. "Reformed Epistemology, Rationality and Belief in God." *International Journal for Philosophy of Religion* 24 (1988): 129–141.

Aspenson, Steven S. "Reply to O'Connor's 'A Variation of the Free Will Defense'." *Faith and Philosophy* 6 (1989): 95–98.

Ayers, Robert H. "A Viable Theodicy for Christian Apologetics." *Modern Schoolman* 52 (1975): 391–403.

Baldwin, Dalton D. "Evil and Persuasive Power: A Response To Hare and Madden." *Process Studies* 3 (1973): 259–272.

Banning, Andrew. "Professor Brightman's Theory of a Limited God: A Criticism." *Harvard Theological Review* 27 (1934): 145–168.

Barnhart, J. E. "An Ontology of Inevitable Moral Evil." *Personalist* 47 (1966): 102–111.

———. "Persuasive and Coercive Power in Process Metaphysics." *Process Studies* 13 (1977): 439–453.

———. "Theodicy and the Free Will Defense: Response to Plantinga and Flew." *Religious Studies* 13 (1977): 439–453.

Basinger, David. "Christian Theism and the Free Will Defense." *Sophia* (Australia) 19 (July 1980): 20–33.

———. "Determinism and Evil: Some Clarifications." *Australasian Journal of Philosophy* 60 (1982): 163–164.

———. "Divine Omniscience and the Best of All Possible Worlds." *Journal of Value Inquiry* 16 (1982): 143–148.

———. "Divine Power: Do Process Theists Have a Better Idea?" In *Process Theology*, edited by Ronald Nash, 197–213. Grand Rapids, Mich.: Baker Book, 1987.

———. "Evil and a Finite God: A Response to McGrath's 'Evil and the Existence of a Finite God'." *Philosophy Research Archives* 13 (1987–88): 285–287.

———. "Evil as Evidence against the Existence of God: A Response." *Philosophy Research Archives* 4 (1978): no. 1275.

———. "Human Freedom and Divine Omnipotence: Some New Thoughts on an Old Problem." *Religious Studies* 15 (1979): 491–510.

———. "In What Sense Must God Do His Best? A Response to Hasker." *International Journal for Philosophy of Religion* 18 (1985): 161–164.

———. "Must God Create the Best Possible World? A Response." *International Philosophical Quarterly* 20 (1980): 339–342.

———. "Plantinga's 'Free-Will Defense' As a Challenge to Orthodox Theism." *American Journal of Theology and Philosophy* 3 (1982): 35–41.

Basinger, Randall, and David Basinger. "Divine Determinateness and the Free Will Defense." *Philosophy Research Archives* 8 (1982): no. 1517.

———. "Divine Omnipotence: Plantinga vs. Griffin." *Process Studies* 11 (1981): 11–24.

Bauckham, Richard. " 'Only the Suffering God Can Help': Divine Impassibility in Modern Theology." *Themelios* 9 (1984): 6–12.

———. "Theodicy from Ivan Karamazov to Moltmann." *Modern Theology* 4 (1987): 83–97.

Beaty, Michael D. "The Problem of Evil: The Unanswered Questions Argument." *Southwest Philosophy Review* 4 (1988): 57–64.

Becker, Ernest. *The Structure of Evil: An Essay on the Unification of the Science of Man.* New York: Free Press, 1976.

Benditt, Theodore. "A Problem for Theodicists." *Philosophy* 50 (1975): 470–474.

Bennett, Philip W. "Evil, God and the Free Will Defense." *Australasian Journal of Philosophy* 51 (1973): 39–50.

Bertocci, Peter A. "Idealistic Temporalistic Personalism and Good-and-Evil." *Proceedings of the American Catholic Philosophical Association* 51 (1977): 56–65.

Betty, L. Stafford. "Making Sense of Animal Pain: An Environmental Theodicy." *Faith and Philosophy* 9 (1992): 65–82.

Beversluis, John. "Grief." In *C. S. Lewis and the Search for Rational Religion.* Grand Rapids, Mich.: Eerdmans, 1985.

Boer, Steven. "The Irrelevance of the Free Will Defense." *Analysis* 38 (1978): 110–112.

Bowker, John. *Problems of Suffering in Religions of the World.* Cambridge: Cambridge University Press, 1970.

Brecher, Robert. "Knowledge, Belief, and the Sophisticated Theodicist." *Heythrop Journal* 17 (1976): 178–183.

Brightman, Edgar Sheffield. *The Problem of God.* New York: Abingdon, 1930.

Brown, Patterson. "Religious Morality." *Mind* 72 (1963): 235–244.

Brown, Robert McAfee. *Elie Wiesel: Messenger to All Humanity.* Notre Dame, Ind.: University of Notre Dame Press, 1983.

Buber, Martin. *Good and Evil.* New York: Charles Scribner's Sons, 1952.

Buckham, John Wright. "Creating Creators: A Christian Theodicy." *Personalist* 24 (1943): 190–199.

Burch, Robert. "Plantinga and Leibniz's Lapse." *Analysis* 39 (1979): 24–29.

Burgess-Jackson, Keith. "Free Will, Omnipotence, and the Problem of Evil." *American Journal of Theology and Philosophy* 9 (1988): 175–185.

Burke, Michael B. "Theodicy with a God of Limited Power: A Reply to McGrath's 'Atheism or Agnosticism'." *Analysis* 47 (1987): 57–58.

Burkle, Howard. *God, Suffering, and Belief.* Nashville, Tenn.: Abingdon, 1977.

Burns, J. Patout. "Augustine on the Origin and Progress of Evil." *Journal of Religious Ethics* 16 (1988): 9–27.

Burrell, David. "Maimonides, Aquinas and Gersonides on Providence and Evil." *Religious Studies* 20 (1984): 335–352.

Burt, Donald X. "The Powerlessness of God or of Man." *Proceedings of the American Catholic Philosophical Association* 46 (1972): 142–148.

Buttrick, George A. *God, Pain and Evil.* Nashville, Tenn.: Abingdon, 1966.

Cahill, Lisa Sowie. "Consent in Time of Affliction: The Ethics of A Circumspect Theist." *Journal of Religious Ethics* 13 (1985): 22–36.

Cahn, Steven M. "Cacodaemony." *Analysis* 37 (1977): 69–73.

Calvert, Brian. "Descartes and the Problem of Evil." *Canadian Journal of Philosophy* 2 (1972): 117–126.

——— . "Dualism and the Problem of Evil." *Sophia* (Australia) 22 (Oct. 1983): 15–28.

Campbell, Keith. "Patterson Brown on God and Evil." *Mind* 74 (1965): 582–584.

Campbell, Richmond. "God, Evil and Humanity." *Sophia* (Australia) 23 (July 1984): 21–35.

Capitan, William H. "Part X of Hume's Dialogues." *American Philosophical Quarterly* 3 (1966): 82–86.

Carson, D. A. *How Long, O Lord?* Grand Rapids, Mich.: Baker Book House, 1991.

Cartwright, Nancy. "Comments on Wesley Salmon's 'Science and Religion'." *Philosophical Studies* 33 (Fall 1978): 177–183.

Chaves, Eduardo O. C. "Logical and Semantical Aspects of the Problem of Evil." *Critica* 10 (1978): 3–42.

Chernoff, Fred. "The Obstinance of Evil." *Mind* 89 (1980): 269–273.

Chisholm, Roderick M. "The Defeat of Good and Evil." *Proceedings and Addresses of the American Philosophical Association* 42 (1968–69): 21–38.

Christlieb, Terry. "Which Theisms Face an Evidential Problem of Evil?" *Faith and Philosophy* 9 (1992): 45–64.

Chryssides, George D. "Evil and the Problem of God." *Religious Studies* 23 (1987): 467–475.

Chrzan, Keith. "Hudson on 'Too Much' Evil: Response to Hudson's 'Is There Too Much Evil in the World'." *International Philosophical Quarterly* 27 (1987): 203–206.

——— . "Linear Programming and Utilitarian Theodicy." *International Journal for Philosophy of Religion* 20 (1986): 147–157.

——— . "Plantinga on Atheistic Induction." *Sophia* (Australia) 27 (July 1988): 10–14.

——— . "The Irrelevance of the No Best Possible World Defense." *Philosophia* (Israel) 17 (1987): 161–167.

——— . "When Is a Gratuitous Evil Really Gratuitous?" *International Journal for Philosophy of Religion* 24 (1988): 87–91.

Clark, Kelly James. "Evil and Christian Belief." *International Philosophical Quarterly* 29 (1989): 175–189.

Clark, Stephen R. L. "God, Good and Evil." *Proceedings of the Aristotelian Society* 77 (1976–77): 247–264.

Cobb, John B. *God and the World*. Philadelphia: Westminster Press, 1969.

――――. "The Problem of Evil and the Task of Ministry." In *Encountering Evil*, edited by Stephen T. Davis, 167–180. Atlanta, Ga.: Knox Press, 1981.

Collins, Joan. "Josiah Royce: Evil in the Absolute." *Idealistic Studies* 13 (1983): 147–165.

Collins, John. "C. A. Campbell and the Problem of Suffering." *Religious Studies* 16 (1980): 307–316.

Connellan, Colm. *Why Does Evil Exist: A Philosophical Study of the Contemporary Presentation of the Question*. Hicksville, N.Y.: Exposition Press, 1974.

Conway, David A. "The Philosophical Problem of Evil." *International Journal for Philosophy of Religion* 24 (1988): 35–66.

Cooper, K. J. "Here We Go Again: Pike vs. Plantinga on the Problem of Evil." *International Journal for Philosophy of Religion* 14 (1983): 107–116.

Copp, David. "Leibniz's Theory That Not All Possible Worlds Are Compossible." *Studia Leibnitiana* 5 (1973): 26–42.

Coughlan, Michael J. "In Defense of Free Will Theodicy." *Religious Studies* 23 (1987): 543–554.

――――. "Moral Evil without Consequences?" *Analysis* 39 (1979): 58–60.

――――. "The Free Will Defense and Natural Evil." *International Journal for Philosophy of Religion* 20 (1986): 93–108.

Crenshaw, James. *Theodicy in the Old Testament*. Philadelphia: Fortress Press, 1983.

Crisp, Roger. "The Avoidance of the Problem of Evil: A Reply to McGrath." *Analysis* 46 (1986): 160.

Curylo-Gonzales, Irena. "Historiosophic Theodicy of August Cieszkowski" (in Polish). *Etyka* (1978): 147–161.

――――. "Theodicy, Naturodicy, Historiodicy" (in Polish). *Etyka* (1977): 31–54.

Dalton, Peter C. "Death and Evil." *Philosophical Forum* 11 (1979): 193–211.

Davies, Martin. "Determinism and Evil: Some Clarifications." *Australasian Journal of Philosophy* 58 (June 1980): 116–127.

Davis, Douglas P. "The Privation Account of Evil: H. J. McCloskey and Francisco Suarez." *Proceedings of the American Catholic Philosophical Association* 61 (1987): 199–208.

Davis, John W. "Going out the Window: A Comment on Tweyman's 'Hume's Dialogues on Evil'." *Hume Studies* 13 (1987): 86–97.

Davis, Stephen T. "A Defense of the Free Will Defense." *Religious Studies* 8 (1972): 335–343.

――――. "Assurance of Victory." *Pulpit Digest* 41 (May–June 1981): 65–69.

――――. "God the Mad Scientist: Process Theology on God and Evil." *Themelios* 5 (1979): 18–23.

————— . "The Problem of Evil in Recent Philosophy." *Review and Expositor* 82 (1985): 535–548.

————— . "Why Did This Happen to Me?—The Patient as a Philosopher." *Princeton Seminary Bulletin* 65 (1972): 61–67.

————— ., ed. *Encountering Evil: Live Options in Theodicy*. Atlanta, Ga.: Knox Press, 1981.

De Beausobre, Julia. "Creative Suffering." *Theoria to Theory* 12 (1978): 111–121.

Dedek, John F. "Intrinsically Evil Acts: An Historical Study of the Mind of St. Thomas." *Thomist* 43 (1979): 385–413.

Dilley, Frank B. "A Modified Flew Attack on the Free Will Defense." *Southern Journal of Philosophy* 20 (1982): 25–34.

————— . "Is the Free Will Defense Irrelevant?" *Religious Studies* 18 (1982): 355–364.

Doob, Leonard. *Panorama of Evil: Insights from the Behavioral Sciences*. Westport, Conn.: Greenwood Press, 1972.

Dore, Clement. "Does Suffering Serve Valuable Ends?" In *Theism*. Dordrecht: D. Reidel, 1984.

————— . "Do Theists Need to Solve the Problem of Evil." *Religious Studies* 12 (1976): 383–390.

————— . "Do Theodicists Mean What They Say?" *Philosophy* 48 (1974): 357–374.

————— . "Ethical Supernaturalism and the Problem of Evil." *Religious Studies* 8 (1972): 97–113.

————— . "Plantinga on the Free Will Defense." *Review of Metaphysics* 24 (1971): 690–706.

Dragona-Monachou, Myrto. "Providence and Fate in Stoicism and Prae-Neoplatonism: Calcidius as an Authority on Cleanthes' Theodicy." *Philosophia* (Athens) 3 (1973): 262–306.

————— . "The Problem of Evil in Phil of Alexandria" (in Greek). *Philosophia* (Athens) 5 (1975–76): 306–352.

Draper, Paul. "Evil and the Proper Basicality of Belief in God." *Faith and Philosophy* 8 (1991): 135–147.

Dupré, Louis. "Evil—A Religious Mystery." *Faith and Philosophy* 7 (1990): 261–280.

Ehman, Robert R. "On Evil and God." *Monist* 47 (1963): 478–487.

Evans, G. R. *Augustine on Evil*. Cambridge: Cambridge University Press, 1982.

Evans, J. N. "LaFollete on Plantinga's Free Will Defense." *International Journal for Philosophy of Religion* 14 (1983): 117–122.

Fackenheim, Emil L. "The Holocaust and Philosophy." *Journal of Philosophy* 82 (1985): 505–514.

Fales, Evan. "Antediluvian Theodicy: Stump on the Fall." *Faith and Philosophy* 6 (1989): 320–329.

———— . "Should God Not Have Created Adam?" *Faith and Philosophy* 9 (1992): 192–208.

———— . "Evil and Omnipotence." *Australasian Journal of Philosophy* 36 (1958): 216–221.

Farmer, H. H. *The World and God.* New York: Harper and Brothers, 1935.

Farrell, P. M. "Evil and Omnipotence." *Mind* 67 (1958): 399–403.

Farrer, Austin. *Love Almighty and Ills Unlimited.* London: Collins, 1962.

Feinberg, John S. *Theologies and Evil.* Washington, D.C.: University Press of America, 1979.

Felt, James W. "God's Choice: Reflections on Evil in a Created World." *Faith and Philosophy* 1 (1984): 370–377.

Ferré, Frederick. "Theodicy and the Status of Animals." *American Philosophical Quarterly* 23 (1986): 23–34.

Ferré, Nels. *Evil and the Christian Faith.* New York: Harper, 1947 (Reprint New York: Books for Libraries Press, 1971).

Fisher, Peter F. "Milton's Theodicy." *Journal of the History of Ideas* 17 (1956): 28–53.

Fitzpatrick, F. J. "The Onus of Proof in Arguments about the Problem of Evil." *Religious Studies* 17 (1981): 19–38.

Flemming, Arthur. "Omnibenevolence and Evil." *Ethics* 96 (1986): 261–281.

Flew, Antony. "Are Ninian Smart's Temptations Irresistible?" *Philosophy* 37 (1962): 57–60.

———— . "Compatibilism, Freewill, and God." *Philosophy* 48 (1973): 231–244.

———— . "Divine Omnipotence and Human Freedom." *Hibbert Journal* 53 (Jan. 1955): 135–144.

———— . "The 'Religious Morality' of Mr. Patterson Brown." *Mind* 74 (1965): 578–581.

Flint, Thomas P. "Divine Sovereignty and the Free Will Defense." *Sophia* (Australia) 23 (July 1984): 41–52.

Forrest, Peter. "The Problem of Evil: Two Neglected Defenses." *Sophia* (Australia) 20 (April 1981): 49–54.

Forsyth, P. T. *The Justification of God: Lectures for War-Time in a Christian Theodicy.* London: Duckworth, 1916.

Frankenberry, Nancy. "Some Problems in Process Theodicy." *Religious Studies* 17 (1981): 179–197.

Friedman, R. Z. "Evil and Moral Agency." *International Journal for Philosophy of Religion* 24 (1988): 3–20.

Fulmer, Gilbert. "Evil and Analogy." *Personalist* 58 (1977): 333–343.

———— . "John Hick's Soul-Making Theodicy." *Southwest Philosophical Studies* 7 (1982): 170–179.

Galligan, Michael. *God and Evil.* New York: Paulist Press, 1976.

Gan, Barry L. "Plantinga's Transworld Depravity: It's Got Possibilities." *International Journal for Philosophy of Religion* 13 (1982): 169–177.

Garcia, J. L. A. "Goods and Evils." *Philosophy and Phenomenological Research* 47 (1987): 385–412.

Garcia, Laura L. "A Response to the Modal Problem of Evil." *Faith and Philosophy* 1 (1984): 378–388.

Geach, Peter. *Providence and Evil*. Cambridge: Cambridge University Press, 1977.

Geach, Peter, and Brian Fulmer. "An Exchange between Peter Geach and Gilbert Fulmer." *Southwestern Journal of Philosophy* 11 (1980): 165–170.

Gellman, Jerome I. "A New Look at the Problem of Evil." *Faith and Philosophy* 9 (1992): 209–215.

Gelven, Michael. "The Meanings of Evil." *Philosophy Today* 27 (1983): 200–221.

Gibson, A. Boyce. *The Religion of Dostoevsky*. London: SCM Press, 1973.

Glatzer, Nahum, ed. *Dimensions of Job: A Study and Selected Readings*. New York: Schocken Books, 1969.

Goldstein, Melvin. "Spenser and Dante, Two Pictorial Representatives of Evil." *Journal of Aesthetic Education* 2 (1968): 121–130.

Gordis, Robert. *The Book of God and Man: A Study of Job*. Chicago and London: University of Chicago Press, 1978.

Gordon, David. "Is the Argument from Evil Decisive?" *Religious Studies* 19 (1983): 407–410.

Gordon, Jeffrey. "The Dilemma of Theodicy." *Sophia* (Australia) 23 (Oct. 1984): 22–34.

Gracia, Jorge. "Good and Evil." In *Handbook of Metaphysics/Ontology*, edited by H. Burkhardt and B. Smith. Munchen, Hamden, Wien: Philosophia Verlag, 1991.

Gracia, Jorge, and Douglas Davis. *The Metaphysics of Good and Evil According to Suarez: Metaphysical Disputations X and XI and Selected Passages from Disputation XXIII and Other Works*. Translation with Introduction, Notes, and Glossary. Analytica Series. Munchen, Hamden, Wien: Philosophica Verlag, 1989.

Grave, S. A. "On Evil and Omnipotence." *Mind* 65 (April 1956): 259–262.

Gregory, Peter N. "The Problem of Theodicy in the *Awakening of Faith*." *Religious Studies* 22 (1986): 63–78.

Griffin, David R. "Actuality, Possibility, and Theodicy: A Response to Nelson Pike's 'Process Theodicy and the Concept of Power'." *Process Studies* 12 (1982): 168–179.

———. "Creation out of Chaos and the Problem of Evil." In *Encountering Evil*, edited by Stephen T. Davis, 101–136. Atlanta, Ga.: Knox Press, 1981.

———. "Divine Causality, Evil, and Philosophical Theology: A Critique of James Ross." *International Journal for Philosophy of Religion* 4 (1973): 168–186.

———. *Evil Revisited: Responses and Reconsiderations*. Albany, N.Y.: SUNY Press, 1991.

———. *God, Power, and Evil: A Process Theodicy.* Philadelphia: Westminster Press, 1976.

———. "Philosophical Theology and the Pastoral Ministry." *Encounter* 33 (1972): 230–244.

———. "Values, Evil, and Liberation Theology." *Encounter* 40 (Winter 1979): 1–15.

Grigg, Richard. "Theism and Proper Basicality: A Response to Plantinga." *International Journal for Philosophy of Religion* 14 (1983): 123–127.

Grünbaum, Adolf. "God and the Holocaust." *Free Inquiry* 8 (Winter 1987–88): 23.

Guirdham, Arthur. "Evil and Disease." *Systematics* 11 (1974): 267–276.

Halberstam, Joshua. "Philosophy and the Holocaust." *Metaphilosophy* 12 (1981): 277–283.

Hall, Thor. "Theodicy As a Test of the Reasonableness of Theology." *Religion in Life* 43 (1974): 204–217.

Hare, Peter. "Review of David Ray Griffin, *God, Power, and Evil.*" *Process Studies* 7 (1977): 44–51.

———. "Review of George Schlesinger, *Religion and Scientific Method.*" *Metaphilosophy* 11 (1980): 292–295.

Hare, Peter, and Edward Madden. "Evil and Inconclusiveness." *Sophia* (Australia) 11 (Jan.–June 1972): 8–12.

———. "Why Hare Must Hound the Gods." *Philosophy and Phenomenological Research* 29 (1969): 456–459.

Harrison, Peter. "Theodicy and Animal Pain." *Philosophy* 64 (1989): 79–92.

Hartshorne, Charles. "A New Look at the Problem of Evil." In *Current Philosophical Issues: Essays in Honor of Curt John Ducasse,* edited by F. C. Dommeyer, 201–212. Springfield, Ill.: Charles C. Thomas, 1966.

———. "The Dipolar Conception of Deity." *Review of Metaphysics* 21 (1967): 273–289.

Hasker, William. "Must God Do His Best?" *International Journal for Philosophy of Religion* 16 (1984): 213–224.

———. "The Necessity of Gratuitous Evil." *Faith and Philosophy* 9 (1992): 23–44.

———. "Suffering, Soul-Making, and Salvation." *International Philosophical Quarterly* 28 (1988): 3–19.

Hatcher, William S. "A Logical Solution to the Problem of Evil." *Zygon* 10 (1974): 245–255.

———. "The Relative Conception of Good and Evil." *Zygon* 10 (1975): 446–448.

Hauerwas, Stanley. "God, Medicine, and the Problem of Evil." *Reformed Journal* 38 (April 1988): 16–22.

———. *Naming the Silences: God, Medicine, and the Problem of Suffering.* Grand Rapids, Mich.: Eerdmans.

———. *Suffering Presence: Theological Reflections on Medicine, the Mentally Handicapped, and the Church.* Notre Dame, Ind.: University of Notre Dame Press, 1985.

Hebblethwaite, Brian. *Evil, Suffering, and Religion.* New York: Hawthorne Books, 1976.

Hedentius, Ingemar. "Disproofs of God's Existence?" *Personalist* 52 (1971): 23–43.

Herman, A. L. "God, Evil and Annie Besant." *Philosophica* (India) 11–14 (1982–85): 80–95.

———. "Indian Theodicy: Samkara and Ramanuja on Brahma Sutra II." *Philosophy East and West* 21 (1971): 266–281.

———. *The Problem of Evil in Indian Thought.* Delhi: Motlial Banarsidass, 1976.

Hershbell, Jackson P. "Berkeley and the Problem of Evil." *Journal of the History of Ideas* 31 (1970): 543–554.

Hick, John. "Coherence and the God of Love Again." *Journal of Theological Studies* 24, Part 2 (1973): 522–528.

———. "Evil and Incarnation." *Incarnation and Myth: The Debate Continued.* Michael Gouldner, ed. London: SCM, 1979.

———. *Evil and the God of Love.* 2d ed. New York: Harper & Row, 1978.

———. "Freedom and the Irenaean Theodicy Again." *Journal of Theological Studies* 21, Part 2 (1970): 419–422.

———. "God, Evil and Mystery." *Religious Studies* 3 (1968): 539–546.

———. "God, Evil and Mystery." In *God and the Universe of Faiths*, edited by John Hick. London and New York: Macmillan and St. Martin's Press, 1973.

———. "Remarks." In *Reason and Religion*, edited by Stuart Brown. Ithaca, N.Y.: Cornell University Press, 1977.

———. "Review of E. H. Madden and P. H. Hare, *Evil and the Concept of God.* *Philosophy* 44 (1969): 160–161.

———. "The Problem of Evil." In *The Encyclopedia of Philosophy*, 136–141. New York: Macmillan and Free Press, 1967.

———. "The Problem of Evil in the First and Last Things." *Journal of Theological Studies* 19, Part 2 (1968): 591–602.

Hicks, David C. "Moral Evil As Apparent Disvalue." *Religious Studies* 13 (1977): 1–16.

Higgins, David. "Evil in Maritain and Lonergan." In *Jacques Maritain*, edited by J. Knasas, 235–242. Notre Dame, Ind.: University of Notre Dame Press, 1988.

Hitterdale, Larry. "The Problem of Evil and the Subjectivity of Values Are Incompatible." *International Philosophical Quarterly* 18 (1978): 467–469.

Hoffman, Joshua. "Mavrodes on Defining Omnipotence." *Philosophical Studies* 35 (1979): 311–313.

Hoitenga, Dewey. "Logic and the Problem of Evil." *American Philosophical Quarterly* 4 (1967): 114–126.

Holmes, Arthur F. "Why God Cannot Act." In *Process Theology*, edited by Ronald Nash. Grand Rapids, Mich.: Baker Books, 1987.

Horbury, William, and Brian MacNeil, eds. *Suffering and Martyrdom in the New Testament.* Cambridge: Cambridge University Press, 1981.

Howe, Leroy T. "Leibniz on Evil." *Sophia* (Australia) 10 (Oct. 1971): 8–17.

Hsu, Sung-peng. "Lao Tzu's Conception of Evil." *Philosophy East and West* 26 (1976): 301–316.

Hudson, Yeager. "Is There Too Much Evil in the World?" *International Philosophical Quarterly* 25 (1985): 343–348.

———. "Response to Chrzan's 'Hudson on "Too Much" Evil'." *International Philosophical Quarterly* 27 (1987): 207–210.

Jooharigian, Robert Badrik. *God and Natural Evil.* Bristol: Wyndham Hall Press, 1985.

Journet, Charles. *The Meaning of Evil.* New York: P. J. Kennedy, 1963.

Kahn, Sholom J. "The Problem of Evil in Literature." *Journal of Aesthetics and Art Criticism* 12 (1953): 98–110.

Kane, G. Stanley. "Evil and Privation." *International Journal for Philosophy of Religion* 11 (1980): 43–58.

———. "Soul-Making Theodicy and Eschatology." *Sophia* (Australia) 14 (July 1975): 24–31.

———. "The Concept of Divine Goodness and the Problem of Evil." *Religious Studies* 11 (1975): 49–71.

———. "The Failure of Soul-Making Theodicy." *International Journal for Philosophy of Religion* 6 (1975): 1–22.

———. "The Free-Will Defense Defended." *New Scholasticism* 50 (1976): 435–446.

———. "Theism and Evil." *Sophia* (Australia) 9 (March 1970): 14–21.

Kaufman, Gordon D. "Evidentialism: A Theologian's Response." *Faith and Philosophy* 6 (1989): 35–46.

———. "God and Evil." In *God The Problem*. Cambridge, Mass.: Harvard University Press, 1972.

Kekes, John. "The Problem of Good." *Journal of Value Inquiry* 18 (1984): 99–112.

———. "Understanding Evil." *American Philosophical Quarterly* 25 (1988): 13–24.

Kielkopf, Charles F. "Emotivism As the Solution to the Problem of Evil." *Sophia* (Australia) 9 (July 1970): 34–38.

King, James T. "The Meta-Ethical Dimension of the Problem of Evil." *Journal of Value Inquiry* 5 (1971): 174–184.

———. "The Problem of Evil and the Meaning of Good." *Proceedings of the American Catholic Philosophical Association* 44 (1970): 185–194.

King-Farlow, John. "Cacodaemony and Devilish Isomorphism." *Analysis* 38 (1978): 59–61.

———. "Evil: On Multiple Placings in Time and Space." *Sophia* (Australia) 25 (Oct. 1986): 44–46.

———. "Must Gods Madden Madden?" *Philosophy and Phenomenological Research* 29 (1969): 451–455.

———. "Through a Glass Darkly: God and Evil." In *Reason and Religion*. London: Darton, Longman, and Todd, 1969.

Kitamori, Kazoh. *Theology of the Pain of God*. Richmond, Va.: John Knox Press, 1965.

Kivy, Peter. "Voltaire, Hume, and the Problem of Evil." *Philosophy and Literature* 1 (1977): 211–224.

Kohák, Erazim. "The Person in a Personal World: An Inquiry into the Metaphysical Significance of the Tragic Sense of Life." *Independent Journal of Philosophy* 1 (1977): 51–64.

Kohn, Jacob. "God and the Reality of Evil." *Personalist* 33 (1952): 117–130.

Kondoleon, Theodore J. "Moral Evil and the Existence of God: A Reply." *New Scholasticism* 47 (1973): 366–374.

———. "More on the Free Will Defense." *Thomist* 47 (1983): 1–42.

Korsmeyer, Carolyn. "Is Pangloss Leibniz?" *Philosophy and Literature* 1 (1977): 201–208.

Kraemer, Eric, and Hardy Jones. "Freedom and the Problems of Evil." *Philosophical Topics* 13 (Fall 1985): 33–49.

Kretzmann, Norman. "God among the Causes of Moral Evil: The Hardening of Hearts and Spiritual Blinding." *Philosophical Topics* 16 (Fall 1988): 189–214.

———. "Omniscience and Immutability." *Journal of Philosophy* 63 (1966): 409–421.

Kroon, Frederick W. "Plantinga on God, Freedom, and Evil." *International Journal for Philosophy of Religion* 12 (1981): 75–96.

Kropf, Richard W. *Evil and Evolution: A Theodicy*. Cranbury: Associated University Press, 1984.

LaCroix, Richard R. "Unjustified Evil and God's Choice." *Sophia* (Australia) 13 (April 1974): 20–28.

LaFollette, Hugh. "Plantinga on the Free Will Defense." *International Journal for Philosophy of Religion* 11 (1980): 123–132.

Langton, Douglas. "The Argument from Evil: Reply to Professor Richman." *Religious Studies* 16 (1980): 103–113.

Langtry, Bruce. "God, Evil and Probability." *Sophia* (Australia), 28 (April 1989): 32–40.

Larue, Gerald A. "The Book of Job on the Futility of Theological Discussion." *Personalist* 45 (1964): 72–79.

Legenhausen, G. "Notes toward an Ash'arite Theodicy." *Religious Studies* 24 (1988): 257–266.

Lewis, C. S. *A Grief Observed*. New York: Bantam Books, 1961.

———. *The Problem of Pain*. New York: Macmillan, 1962.

Lewis, Delmas. "The Problem with the Problem of Evil." *Sophia* (Australia) 22 (April 1983): 26–36.

Lomasky, Loren E. "Are Compatibilism and the Free Will Defense Compatible?" *Personalist* 56 (1975): 385–388.

Londis, James J. "God, Probability and John Hick." *Religious Studies* 16 (1980): 457–463.

Lotter, H. P. P. "Hick, Evolution and the Problem of Evil" (in Dutch). *South African Journal of Philosophy* 6 (1987): 140–148.

Lovin, Keith. "Plantinga's Puddle." *Southwestern Philosophical Studies* 4 (April 1979): 103–108.

Lugenbehl, Dale. "Can the Argument from Evil Be Decisive after All?" *Religious Studies* 18 (1982): 29–35.

Mackie, J. L. "Review of Hick's *Evil and the God of Love*." *Philosophical Books* 3 (1966): 17.

———. "Theism and Utopia." *Philosophy* 37 (1962): 153–158.

———. "The Problem of Evil." In *The Miracle of Theism*. Oxford: Clarendon Press, 1982.

MacKinnon, Donald. "Evil and the Vulnerability of God." *Philosophy* 62 (1987): 102.

MacLeish, Archibald. *J. B.* Boston: Houghton-Mifflin, 1956.

McCabe, Herbert. "God: Evil." *New Blackfriars* 62 (1981): 4–17.

McCloskey, H. J. "Evil and the Problem of Evil." *Sophia* (Australia) 5 (1966): 14–19.

———. "God and Evil." *Philosophical Quarterly* 10 (1960): 97–114.

———. *God and Evil*. The Hague: Martinus Nijhoff, 1974.

———. "The Problem of Evil." *Journal of Bible and Religion* 30 (1962): 187–197.

McCullough, H. B. "Theodicy and Mary Baker Eddy." *Sophia* (Australia) 14 (March 1975): 12–18.

McGill, Arthur. *Suffering: A Test of Theological Method*. Philadelphia: Geneva Press, 1968.

McGrath, P. J. "Evil and the Existence of a Finite God." *Analysis* 46 (1986): 63–64.

———. "Is There a Problem of Evil?" *Philosophical Quarterly* 39 (1989): 91–94.

McHarry, John D. "A Theodicy." *Analysis* 38 (1978): 132–134.

McKenzie, David. "A Kantian Theodicy." *Faith and Philosophy* 1 (1984): 236–248.

McKim, Robert. "Worlds without Evil." *International Journal for Philosophy of Religion* 15 (1984): 161–170.

McMahon, William E. "The Problem of Evil and the Possibility of a Better World." *Journal of Value Inquiry* 3 (1969): 81–90.

McWilliams, Warren. "Divine Suffering in Contemporary Theology." *Scottish Journal of Theology* 33 (1980): 35–53.

Madden, Edward, and Peter Hare. "Evil and Inconclusiveness." *Sophia* (Australia) 11 (Jan.–June 1972): 8–12.

———. *Evil and the Concept of God*. Springfield, Ill.: Charles C. Thomas, 1968.

Maker, William A. "Augustine on Evil: The Dilemma of the Philosophers." *International Journal for Philosophy of Religion* 15 (1984): 149–160.

Maritain, Jacques. *God and the Permission of Evil*. Milwaukee: Bruce, 1966.

———. *St. Thomas and the Problem of Evil*. Milwaukee: Marquette University Press, 1942.

Martin, Michael. "A Theistic Inductive Argument from Evil?" *International Journal for Philosophy of Religion* 22 (1987): 81–87.

———. "Corrections to 'The Formalities of Evil and a Finite God'." *Critica* 9 (1977): 89–92.

———. "God, Satan and Natural Evil." *Sophia* (Australia) 22 (Oct. 1983): 43–45.

———. "Reichenbach on Natural Evil." *Religious Studies* 24 (1988): 91–99.

———. "The Coherence of the Hypothesis of an Omnipotent, Omniscient, Free and Perfectly Evil Being." *International Journal for Philosophy of Religion* 17 (1985): 185–191.

———. "The Formalities of Evil and a Finite God: Corregenda." *Critica* 10 (1978): 133–135.

Mavrodes, George. "Keith Yandell and the Problem of Evil." *International Journal for Philosophy of Religion* 20 (1986): 45–48.

———. "Some Recent Philosophical Theology." *Review of Metaphysics* 24 (1970): 82–111.

———. "The Problem of Evil." In *Belief in God: A Study in the Epistemology of Religion*, chap. 4. New York: Random House, 1970.

Mesle, C. Robert. "Does God Hide from Us? John Hick and Process Theology on Faith, Freedom and Theodicy." *International Journal for Philosophy of Religion* 24 (1988): 93–111.

Mijuskovic, Ben. "Camus and the Problem of Evil. *Sophia* (Australia) 15 (March 1976): 11–19.

Miller, Ed. "The Problem of Evil." In *God and Reason*. New York: Macmillan, 1972.

Miller, Randolph Crump. "Process, Evil and God." *American Journal of Theology and Philosophy* 1 (1980): 60–70.

Moore, Harold F. "Evidence, Evil and Religious Belief." *International Journal for Philosophy of Religion* 9 (1978): 241–245.

――――― ."Evidence—Once More: Reply to E. Wierenga's Reply to H. Moore's 'Evidence, Evil and Religious Belief'." *International Journal for Philosophy of Religion* 9 (1978): 252–253.

Mora, Freya. "Thank God for Evil?" *Philosophy* 58 (1983): 399–401.

Morris, Thomas V. "A Response to the Problems of Evil." *Philosophia* (Israel) 14 (1984): 173–186.

Morriston, Wesley. "Gladness, Regret, God, and Evil." *Southern Journal of Philosophy* 20 (1982): 401–407.

――――― . "Is God 'Significantly Free'?" *Faith and Philosophy* 2 (1985): 257–264.

――――― . "Is Plantinga's God Omnipotent?" *Sophia* (Australia) 23 (Oct. 1984): 45–57.

Morrow, Lance. "Evil." *Time* (June 10, 1991): 48–53.

Moser, Paul K. "Natural Evil and the Free Will Defense." *International Journal for Philosophy of Religion* 15 (1984): 49–56.

Moulder, James. "Philosophy, Religion and Theodicy." *South African Journal of Philosophy* 3 (1984): 147–150.

Murphree, Wallace. "Can Theism Survive without the Devil?" *Religious Studies* 21 (1985): 231–244.

Myers, C. Mason. "Free Will and the Problem of Evil." *Religious Studies* 23 (1987): 289–294.

Nash, Ronald. "The Problem of Evil." In *Faith and Reason*, Part 4. Grand Rapids, Mich.: Zondervan, 1988.

Nelson, Mark. "Naturalistic Ethics and the Argument from Evil." *Faith and Philosophy* 8 (1991): 368–379.

Nerny, Gayne. "Aristotle and Aquinas on Indignation: From Nemesis to Theodicy." *Faith and Philosophy* 8 (1991): 81–95.

Nordgulen, George. "New Spokesmen in an Old Dialogue." *New Scholasticism* 47 (1973): 324–338.

Novak, Joseph A. "Comments on Calvert's 'Dualism and the Problem of Evil'." *Sophia* (Australia) 26 (March 1987): 42–49.

Oakes, Robert A. "Actualities, Possibilities, and Free-Will Theodicy." *New Scholasticism* 46 (1972): 191–201.

――――― . "God, Evil, and Professor Ross." *Philosophy and Phenomenological Research* 35 (1974): 261–267.

――――― . "God, Suffering, and Conclusive Evidence." *Sophia* (Australia) 14 (July 1975): 16–20.

――――― . "The Problem with the 'Problem of Evil'." *Personalist* 55 (1974): 106–114.

Oates, David. "Social Darwinism and Natural Theodicy." *Zygon* 23 (1988): 439–454.

O'Connor, David. "A Variation on the Free Will Defense." *Faith and Philosophy* 4 (1987): 160–167.

———— . "In Defense of Theoretical Theodicy." *Modern Theology* 5 (1988): 61–74.

———— . "On Natural Evil's Being Necessary for Free Will." *Sophia* (Australia) 24 (July 1985): 36–44.

———— . "On the Problem of Evil's Not Being What It Seems." *Philosophical Quarterly* 37 (1987): 441–447.

———— . "Swinburne on Natural Evil." *Religious Studies* 19 (1983): 65–74.

———— . "Theism, Evil and the Onus of Proof—Reply to F. J. Fitzpatrick." *Religious Studies* 19 (1983): 241–247.

Owens, Joseph. "Theodicy, Natural Theology, and Metaphysics." *Modern Schoolman* 28 (1951): 126–137.

Paluch, Stanley. "A Cosmomorphic Utopia." *Personalist* 54 (1973): 89–91.

Pargetter, Robert. "Evil As Evidence." *Sophia* (Australia) 21 (July 1982): 11–15.

———— . "Evil As Evidence against the Existence of God." *Mind* 85 (1976): 242–245.

Paulsen, David L. "Divine Determinateness and the Free Will Defense." *Analysis* 41 (1981): 150–153.

Penelhum, Terence. "Divine Goodness and the Problem of Evil." *Religious Studies* 2 (1966): 95–107.

Pentz, Rebecca D. "Rules and Values and the Problem of Evil." *Sophia* (Australia) 21 (July 1982): 23–29.

Perkins, R. K., Jr. "McHarry's Theodicy: A Reply." *Analysis* 40 (1980): 168–171.

Peterson, Michael. "Evil and Inconsistency." *Sophia* (Australia) 18 (July 1979): 20–27.

———— . *Evil and the Christian God.* Grand Rapids, Mich.: Baker Book House, 1982.

———— . "Evil as Evidence for the Existence of God." In *Kerygma and Praxis: Essays in Honor of Stanley R. Magill,* edited by W. Vanderhoof and D. Basinger, 115–131. Rochester, N.Y.: Roberts Wesleyan College Press, 1984.

———— . "God and Evil in Process Theology." In *Process Theology,* edited by Ronald Nash, 117–139. Grand Rapids, Mich.: Baker Book, 1987.

———— . "God and Evil: Problems of Consistency and Gratuity." *Journal of Value Inquiry* 13 (1979): 305–313.

———— . "Recent Work on the Problem of Evil." *American Philosophical Quarterly* 20 (1983): 321–339.

———— . "The Problem of Evil: The Case Against God's Existence." In *Reason and Religious Belief: An Introduction to the Philosophy of Religion,* edited by Peterson et al., 92–116. New York: Oxford University Press, 1991.

Petit, François. *The Problem of Evil.* New York: Hawthorn Books, 1959.

Petrie, Asenath. *Individuality in Pain and Suffering.* Chicago: University of Chicago Press, 1978.

Phifer, Kenneth. "Why Me; Why Now?" *Religious Humanism* 19 (1985): 40–45.

———. "Postscript." In *Reason and Religion,* edited by Stuart Brown, 134–139. Ithaca, N.Y.: Cornell University Press, 1977.

Phillips, D. Z. "The Problem of Evil." In *Reason and Religion,* edited by Stuart Brown, 103–121. Ithaca, N.Y.: Cornell University Press, 1977.

Pielki, Robert G. "Recent Science Fiction and the Problem of Evil." *Philosophy in Context* 11 (1981): 41–50.

Pike, Nelson. "Divine Omniscience and Voluntary Action." *Philosophical Review* 74 (1965): 27–46.

———. "God and Evil: A Reconsideration." *Ethics* 68 (1958): 116–124.

———. "Hume on Evil." *Philosophical Review* 72 (1963): 180–197.

———. "Of God and Freedom." *Philosophical Review* 75 (1966): 369–379.

———. "Over-Power and God's Responsibility for Sin." In *The Existence and Nature of God,* edited by Alfred Freddoso, 11–36. Notre Dame, Ind.: University of Notre Dame Press, 1983.

———. "Plantinga on Free Will and Evil." *Religious Studies* 15 (1979): 449–473.

———. "Plantinga on the Free Will Defense: A Reply." *Journal of Philosophy* 63 (1966): 93–104.

———. "Process Theodicy and the Concept of Power." *Process Studies* 12 (1982): 148–167.

Plantinga, Alvin. "Existence, Necessity, and God." *New Scholasticism* 50 (1976): 61–72.

———. *God and other Minds: A Study of the Rational Justification of Belief in God.* Ithaca, N.Y.: Cornell University Press, 1967.

———. *God, Freedom, and Evil.* Grand Rapids, Mich.: Eerdmans, 1977.

———. "Is Theism Really a Miracle?" *Faith and Philosophy* 3 (1986): 122–123.

———. "Pike and Possible Persons." *Journal of Philosophy* 63 (1966): 104–108.

———. "Replies to Articles." In *Alvin Plantinga,* edited by James Tomberlin and Peter van Inwagen, 313–396. Dordrecht: Reidel, 1985.

———. "Reply to the Basingers on Divine Omnipotence." *Process Studies* 11 (1981): 25–29.

———. "Self-Profile." In *Alvin Plantinga,* edited by James Tomberlin and Peter van Inwagen, esp. 36–55. Dordrecht: Reidel, 1985.

———. "The Free Will Defense." In *Philosophy in America,* edited by Max Black. London: George Allen and Unwin, 1965.

———. *The Nature of Necessity.* Oxford: Clarendon Press, 1974.

———. "The Probabilistic Argument from Evil." *Philosophical Studies* 35 (1979): 1–53.

———. "Tooley and Evil: A Reply." *Australasian Journal of Philosophy* 60 (1982): 66–75.

———. "Which Worlds Could God Have Created?" *Journal of Philosophy* 70 (1973): 539–552.

Plantinga, Theodore. *Learning to Live with Evil*. Grand Rapids, Mich.: Eerdmans, 1982.

Platt, David. "God, Goodness and a Morally Perfect World." *Personalist* 46 (1965): 320–326.

Pontifex, Mark. "The Question of Evil." In *Prospect for Metaphysics*, edited by Ian Ramsey. London: George Allen and Unwin, 1961.

Pradhan, Sudhir Chandra. "The Problem of Evil and Human Freedom." *Indian Philosophical Quarterly* 13 (1986): 15–24.

Puccetti, Roland. "The Concept of God." *Philosophical Quarterly* 14 (1964): 237–245.

Purtill, Richard. "Walton on Power and Evil." *International Journal for Philosophy of Religion* 6 (1975): 163–166.

Quinn, John M. "Triune Self-Giving: One Key to the Problem of Suffering." *Thomist* 44 (1980): 173–218.

Quinn, Michael. "Mustn't God Create the Best?" *Journal of Critical Analysis* 5 (1973): 2–8.

Quinn, Philip L. "A Pseudosolution to the Problem of Evil." *Zygon* 10 (1975): 444–446.

———. "Original Sin, Radical Evil and Moral Identity." *Faith and Philosophy* 1 (1984): 188–202.

Rader, Melvin. "Shelley's Theory of Evil." In *Shelley: A Collection of Critical Essays*, edited by George M. Ridenour. Englewood Cliffs, N.J.: Prentice-Hall, 1965.

Ramberan, Osmond G. "Evil and Theism." *Sophia* (Australia) 17 (April 1978): 28–36.

———. "Evil, Falsification and Religious Language." *Indian Philosophy and Culture* 8 (1981): 227–246.

———. "God, Evil and the Idea of a Perfect World." *Modern Schoolman* 53 (1976): 379–392.

Reichenbach, Bruce. *Evil and a Good God*. New York: Fordham University Press, 1982.

———. "Evil and a Reformed View of God." *International Journal for Philosophy of Religion* 24 (1988): 67–85.

———. "Natural Evils and Natural Law: A Theodicy for Natural Evils." *International Philosophical Quarterly* 16 (1976): 179–196.

———. "The Deductive Argument from Evil." *Sophia* (Australia) 20 (April 1981): 25–42.

———. "The Inductive Argument from Evil." *American Philosophical Quarterly* 17 (1980): 221–227.

Resnick, Lawrence. "Evidence, Utility and God." *Analysis* 31 (1971): 87–90.

Richards, Norvin. "Gods and Viruses." *Analysis* 35 (1975): 102–104.

Richman, Robert J. "Plantinga, God, and (Yet) Other Minds." *Australasian Journal of Philosophy* 50 (1972): 40–54.

————— . "The Argument from Evil." *Religious Studies* 4 (1969): 203–211.

Rist, John. "Coherence and the Love of God." *Journal of Theological Studies* 22 (1972): 95–105.

Rohatyn, D. A. "Augustine, Freedom, Evil, and the Contemporary Predicament in Philosophy." *Aitia* 4–5 (1976–77): 74–80.

Rosenberg, Alan, and Gerald Myers, eds. *Echoes from the Holocaust: Philosophical Reflections on a Dark Time.* Philadelphia: Temple University Press, 1988.

Rosenberg, Jay F. "The Problem of Evil Revisited." *Journal of Value Inquiry* 4 (1970): 212–218.

Rosenthal, Abigail L. *A Good Look at Evil.* Philadelphia: Temple University Press, 1987.

Ross, James. "Evil." In *Introduction to the Philosophy of Religion,* 113–148. New York: Macmillan, 1969.

————— . " 'God is Good' and the Problem of Evil." In *Philosophical Theology,* 222–278. Indianapolis and New York: Bobbs-Merrill, 1969.

Roth, John K. *A Consuming Fire: Encounters with Elie Wiesel and the Holocaust.* Atlanta: Knox Press, 1979.

————— . "A Theodicy of Protest." In *Encountering Evil: Live Options in Theodicy,* edited by Stephen T. Davis, 7–37. Atlanta, Ga.: John Knox Press, 1981.

————— . "The Silence of God." *Faith and Philosophy* 1 (1984): 407–420.

————— . "William James and Contemporary Religious Thought: The Problem of Evil." In *The Philosophy of William James,* edited by W. R. Corti. Hamburg: Felix Meiner, 1976.

Rowe, William L. "Evil and the Theistic Hypothesis: A Response to S. J. Wykstra." *International Journal for Philosophy of Religion* 16 (1984): 95–100.

————— . "Evil and Theodicy." *Philosophical Topics* 16 (Fall 1988): 119–132.

————— . "God and Other Minds." *Nous* 3 (1969): 259–284.

————— . "Plantinga on Possible Worlds and Evil." *Journal of Philosophy* 70 (1973): 554–555.

————— . "Ruminations about Evil." *Philosophical Perspectives* 5 (1991): 69–88.

————— . "The Empirical Argument from Evil." In *Rationality, Religious Belief, and Moral Commitment,* edited by Robert Audi and William Wainwright. Ithaca, N.Y.: Cornell University Press, 1986.

————— . "The Problem of Evil." In *Philosophy of Religion: An Introduction.* Encino and Belmont, Calif.: Dickenson, 1978.

————— . "The Problem of Evil and Some Varieties of Atheism." *American Philosophical Quarterly* 16 (1979): 335–341.

Royce, Josiah. *Studies in Good and Evil.* Hamden: Archon Books, 1964.

Runzo, Joseph. "Omniscience and Freedom for Evil." *International Journal for Philosophy of Religion* 12 (1981): 131–148.

Russell, Bruce. "The Persistent Problem of Evil." *Faith and Philosophy* 6 (1989): 121–139.

Russell, Bruce, and Stephen Wykstra. "The 'Inductive' Argument from Evil: A Dialogue." *Philosophical Topics* 16 (Fall 1988): 133–160.

Russell, Jeffrey Burton. "The Experience of Evil." *Listening* 9 (1974): 71–83.

———. *The Prince of Darkness: Radical Evil and the Power of Good in History.* London: Thames Hudson, 1989.

Russell, Robert John. "Entropy and Evil." *Zygon* 19 (1984): 449–468.

Sainsbury, R. M. "Benevolence and Evil." *Australasian Journal of Philosophy* 58 (1980): 128–134.

Salmon, Wesley. "Religion and Science: A New Look at Hume's *Dialogues.*" *Philosophical Studies* 33 (1978): 143–176.

Sanders, Paul. *Twentieth Century Interpretations of the Book of Job.* Englewood Cliffs, N.J.: Prentice-Hall, 1968.

Saunders, John T. "Of God and Freedom." *Philosophical Review* 75 (1966): 219–225.

Schilling, Paul. *God and Human Anguish.* Nashville, Tenn.: Abingdon, 1977.

Schlesinger, George. "On the Possibility of the Best of All Possible Worlds." *Journal of Value Inquiry* 4 (1970): 229–232.

———. *Religion and Scientific Method.* Dordrecht: D. Reidel, 1977. Part I.

———. "The Moral Value of the Universe." *Journal of Value Inquiry* 22 (1988): 319–325.

———. "The Problem of Evil and the Problem of Suffering." *American Philosophical Quarterly* 1 (1964): 244–247.

———. "The Theological Implications of the Holocaust." *Philosophical Forum* (Boston) 16 (1984): 110–120.

Schloegl, Irmgard. "Suffering in Zen Buddhism." *Theoria to Theory* 11 (1977): 217–227.

Schrader, David E. "Evil and the Best of Possible Worlds." *Sophia* (Australia) 27 (July 1988): 24–37.

Schwartz, Richard B. *Samuel Johnson and the Problem of Evil.* Madison: University of Wisconsin Press, 1975.

Seeskin, Kenneth. "Job and the Problem of Evil." *Philosophy and Literature* 11 (1987): 226–241.

Segal, Robert A. "A Jungian View of Evil." *Zygon* 20 (1985): 83–89.

Sennett, James F. "The Free Will Defense and Determinism." *Faith and Philosophy* (forthcoming 1991).

Settle, T. "A Prolegomenon to Intellectually Honest Theology." *Philosophical Form* (Boston) 1 (1968): 136–170.

Sharma, R. P. "The Problem of Evil in Buddhism." *Journal of Dharma* 2 (1977): 307–311.

Shaw, Russell B. *Beyond the New Morality: The Responsibilities of Freedom.* Notre Dame, Ind.: University of Notre Dame Press, 1974.

Shea, Winslow W. "God, Evil, and Professor Schlesinger." *Journal of Value Inquiry* 4 (1970): 219–228.

Siebert, R. J. "Theodicy: Compassionate Solidarity" (in Yugoslavian). *Filozof Istraz* 28 (1989): 143–157.

Silverstein, Harry S. "The Evil of Death." *Journal of Philosophy* 77 (1980): 401–423.

Siwek, Paul. *The Philosophy of Evil*. New York: Ronald Press, 1951.

Smart, Ninian. "Omnipotence, Evil and Supermen." *Philosophy* 36 (1961): 188–195.

———. "Probably" (Response to Flew). *Philosophy* 37 (1962): 60.

Smith, Michael. "What's So Good about Feeling Bad?" *Faith and Philosophy* 2 (1985): 424–429.

Smith, Quentin. "The Anthropic Principle and Many-Worlds Cosmologies." *Australasian Journal of Philosophy* 63 (1985): 336–348.

Soelle, Dorothee. *Suffering*. London: Darton, Longman, & Todd, 1975.

Solon, T. P. M. and S. K. Wertz. "Hume's Argument from Evil." *Personalist* 50 (1969): 383–392.

Sontag, Frederick. "God and Evil." *Religion in Life* 34 (1965): 215–223.

———. *God, Why Did You Do That?* Philadelphia: Westminster Press, 1970.

———. "Technology and Theodicy." *Nature and System* 1 (1979): 265–275.

———. *The God of Evil: An Argument from the Existence of the Devil*. New York: Harper & Row, 1970.

Springsted, Eric O. "Is There a Problem with the Problem of Evil?" *International Philosophical Quarterly* 24 (1984): 303–332.

Stahl, Roland. "Professor Brightman's Theory of the Given." *Religion in Life* 23 (1954): 537–548.

Stark, Judith C. "The Problem of Evil: Augustine and Ricoeur." *Augustinian Studies* (1982): 111–122.

Steuer, Axel D. "Once More on the Free Will Defense." *Religious Studies* 10 (1974): 301–311.

Stewart, Melville. "*O Felix Culpa*, Redemption, and the Greater Good Defense." *Sophia* (Australia) 25 (Oct. 1986): 18–31.

Stump, Eleonore. "Dante's Hell, Aquinas' Moral Theory, and the Love of God." *Canadian Journal of Philosophy* 16 (June 1986): 181–198.

———. "Suffering for Redemption: Reply to Smith's 'What's So Good about Feeling Bad'." *Faith and Philosophy* 2 (1985): 430–435.

———. "The Problem of Evil." *Faith and Philosophy* 2 (1985): 392–423.

Surin, Kenneth. "The Impassibility of God and the Problem of Evil." *Scottish Journal of Theology* 35 (1982): 97–115.

———. "Theodicy?" *Harvard Theological Review* 76 (1983): 225–247.

Sutherland, Stewart. *Atheism and the Rejection of God: Contemporary Philosophy and "The Brothers Karamozov"*. Oxford: Basil Blackwell, 1977.

———. "Horrendous Evils and the Goodness of God." *Aristotelian Society: Supplementary Volume* 63 (1989): 311–323.

Suttle, Bruce B. "On God Tolerating Evil." *Sophia* (Australia) 26 (Oct. 1987):
    53–54.
Swinburne, Richard. "A Theodicy of Heaven and Hell." In *The Existence and Na-
    ture of God,* edited by Alfred Freddoso, Notre Dame, Ind.: University of
    Notre Dame Press, 1983. 37–54.
————. "Does Theism Need a Theodicy?" *Canadian Journal of Philosophy* 18
    (1988): 287–311.
————. "Knowledge from Experience, and the Problem of Evil." In *The Ra-
    tionality of Religious Belief: Essays in Honor of Basil Mitchell,* edited by Wm.
    Abraham and S. Holtzer. Oxford: Clarendon Press, 1987.
————. "Postscript." In *Reason and Religion,* edited by Stuart Brown, 129–133.
    Ithaca, N.Y.: Cornell University Press, 1977.
————. "The Problem of Evil." In *Reason and Religion,* edited by Stuart Brown,
    81–102. Ithaca, N.Y.: Cornell University Press, 1977.
————. "The Problem of Evil." In *The Existence of God.* Oxford: Clarendon
    Press, 1979.
Talbott, Thomas. "Providence, Freedom, and Human Destiny." *Religious Studies*
    26 (1990): 227–245.
————. "The Doctrine of Everlasting Punishment." *Faith and Philosophy* 7
    (1990): 19–42.
Tangwa, Godfrey. "God and the Problem of Evil." *Thought and Practice* 4 (1982):
    79–85.
Thelakat, Paul. "Process and Privation: Aquinas and Whitehead on Evil." *Inter-
    national Philosophical Quarterly* 26 (1986): 287–296.
Theobald, John. "Blake's Ideas of Good and Evil." *Personalist* 37 (1956): 264–
    273.
Thompson, David. "The Godly and the Good Life: The Relationship between
    Character and Circumstance." *Asbury Seminarian* 34 (April 1979): 26–48.
————. "The Godly and the Good Life in Biblical Thought." *Christian Scholar's
    Review,* forthcoming.
Tomberlin, James, and Frank McGuinness. "Good, Evil, and the Free Will De-
    fense." *Religious Studies* 13 (1977): 455–475.
Tooley, Michael. "Alvin Plantinga and the Argument from Evil." *Australasian
    Journal of Philosophy* 58 (1980): 360–376.
————. "The Argument from Evil." *Philosophical Perspectives* 5 (1991): 89–134.
Trau, Jane Mary. "Fallacies in the Argument from Gratuitous Suffering." *New
    Scholasticism* 60 (1986): 585–589.
————. "The Positive Value of Evil." *International Journal for Philosophy of Re-
    ligion* 24 (1988): 21–33.
Trethowan, Dom Illtyd. "Dr. Hick and the Problem of Evil." *Journal of Theological
    Studies* 18 (1967): 407–416.
Tripathi, R. K. "Two Approaches to the Problems of Evil." *Journal of Dharma* 2
    (1977): 312–317.

Tsai, Denis Hsin-An. "God and the Problems of Evil in Berkeley." *Philosophical Review* (Taiwan) 6 (1983): 125–136.

Tsanoff, R. A. *The Nature of Evil*. New York: Macmillan, 1931.

Tweymen, Stanley. "Hume's Dialogues on Evil." *Hume Studies* 13 (1987): 74–85.

Van Der Hoeven, J. "The Problem of Evil—Crucible for the Authenticity and Modesty of Philosophizing: In Discussion with Paul Ricoeur." *South African Journal of Philosophy* 5 (1986): 44–52.

Van Der Walt, J. "Hegel's Theodicy—A Philosophy of Equanimity" (in Dutch). *South African Journal of Philosophy* 6 (1987): 58–67.

Van Inwagen, Peter. "The Magnitude, Duration, and Distribution of Evil: A Theodicy." *Philosophical Topics* 16 (Fall 1988): 161–187.

———. "The Problem of Evil, the Problem of Air, and the Problem of Science." *Philosophical Perspectives* 5 (1991): 135–165.

Varma, Ved Prakash. "Monotheism and the Problem of Evil." *Indian Philosophical Quarterly* 2 (1975): 341–352.

Vertin, Michael. "Philosophy-of-God, Theology, and the Problems of Evil." *Laval Theologique et Philosophique* 37 (1981): 15–32.

Vicchio, Stephen J. *The Voice from the Whirlwind: The Problem of Evil and the Modern World*. Westminster, Md.: Christian Classics, 1989.

Vitali, Theodore R. "The Importance of the A Priori in Whiteheadian Theodicy." *Modern Schoolman* 62 (1985): 277–291.

Wachterhauser, Brice R. "The Problem of Evil and Moral Skepticism." *International Journal for Philosophy of Religion* 17 (1985): 167–174.

Wadia, A. R. "Philosophical Implications of the Doctrine of Karma." *Philosophy East and West* 15 (1965): 145–152.

Wainwright, William. "Christian Theism and the Free Will Defense." *International Journal for Philosophy of Religion* 6 (1975): 243–250.

———. "Freedom and Omnipotence." *Nous* 2 (1968): 293–301.

———. "God and the Necessity of Physical Evil." *Sophia* (Australia) 11 (July 1972): 16–19.

———. "The Presence of Evil and the Falsification of Theistic Assertions." *Religious Studies* 4 (1969): 213–216.

Wall, George. "A New Solution to an Old Problem." *Religious Studies* 15 (1979): 511–530.

———. "Heaven and a Wholly Good God." *Personalist* 58 (1977): 352–357.

———. "Other Worlds and the Comparison of Values." *Sophia* (Australia) 18 (July 1979): 10–19.

Wallace, Gerald. "The Problems of Moral and Physical Evil." *Philosophy* 46 (1971): 349–351.

Walls, Jerry. *Hell: The Logic of Damnation*. Notre Dame, Ind.: University of Notre Dame Press, 1992.

———. "Hume on Divine Amorality." *Religious Studies* 26 (1990): 257–266

————— . "The Free Will Defense, Calvinism, Wesley, and the Goodness of God." *Christian Scholar's Review* 13 (1983): 19–33.

Walter, Edward. "Are Actualities Prior to Possibilities?" *New Scholasticism* 46 (1972): 202–209.

Walton, Douglas. "Language, God and Evil." *International Journal for Philosophy of Religion* 6 (1975): 154–162.

————— . "Modalities in the Free Will Defense." *Religious Studies* 10 (1974): 325–331.

————— . "Purtill on Power and Evil." *International Journal for Philosophy of Religion* 8 (1977): 263–267.

————— . "The Formalities of Evil." *Critica* 8 (1976): 3–9.

Ward, Keith. "Freedom and the Iranaean Theodicy." *Journal of Theological Studies* 20 (1969): 249–254.

Wei, Tan Tai. "The Question of a Cosmomorphic Utopia." *Personalist* 55 (1974): 401–406.

Weinstock, Jerome A. "What Theodicies Must But Do Not Do." *Philosophia* (Israel) 4 (1974): 449–467.

Wennberg, Robert. "Animal Suffering and the Problem of Evil." *Christian Scholar's Review* 21 (1991): 120–140.

Whale, J. S. *The Christian Answer to the Problem of Evil.* London: SCM Press, 1957.

Wharton, Robert V. "Evil in an Earthly Paradise: Dostoevsky's Theodicy." *Thomist* 41 (1977): 567–584.

White, David. "The Problem of Evil." *Second Order* 4 (1975): 14–24.

Whitney, Barry L. *Evil and the Process God.* New York: Mellen Press, 1985.

————— . "Hartshorne and Theodicy." In *Hartshorne, Process Philosophy, and Theology,* edited by Robert Kane, 53–69. Albany, N.Y.: Suny Press, 1989.

————— . "Process Theism: Does a Persuasive God Coerce?" *Southern Journal of Philosophy* 17 (1979): 133–143.

Wierenga, Edward. "Reply to Harold Moore's 'Evidence, Evil and Religious Belief'." *International Journal for Philosophy of Religion* 9 (1978): 246–251.

Wilcox, John T. *The Bitterness of Job: A Philosophical Reading.* Ann Arbor, Mich.: University of Michigan Press, 1989.

Windt, P. Y. "Plantinga's Unfortunate God." *Philosophical Studies* 24 (1973): 335–342.

Wisdom, John. "God and Evil." *Mind* 44 (1935): 1–20.

Wolterstorff, Nicholas. *Lament for a Son.* Grand Rapids, Mich.: Eerdmans, 1987.

Wood, Forrest, Jr. "Some Whiteheadian Insights into the Problem of Evil." *Southwestern Journal of Philosophy* 10 (1979): 147–155.

Wykstra, Stephen J. "The Humean Obstacle to Evidential Arguments from Suffering: On Avoiding the Evils of 'Appearance'." *International Journal for Philosophy of Religion* 16 (1984): 73–94.

Yandell, Keith E. "A Premature Farewell to Theism (A Reply to Roland Puccetti)." *Religious Studies* 5 (1969): 251–255.

——— . "Ethics, Evils and Theism." *Sophia* (Australia) 8 (July 1969): 18–28.

——— . "Gratuitous Evil and Divine Existence." *Religious Studies* 25 (1989): 15–30.

——— . "The Greater Good Defense." *Sophia* (Australia) 13 (Oct. 1974): 1–16.

——— . "The Problem of Evil." *Basic Issues in the Philosophy of Religion.* Boston: Allyn and Bacon, 1971.

——— . "The Problem of Evil." *Philosophical Topics* 12 (Winter 1981): 7–38.

——— . "The Problem of Evil and the Content of Morality." *International Journal for Philosophy of Religion* 17 (1985): 139–165.

——— . "Theism and Evil: A Reply." *Sophia* (Australia) 11 (Jan.–June 1972): 1–7.

Young Robert. "Omnipotence and Compatibilism." *Philosophia* (Israel) 6 (1976): 49–67.

THE PROBLEM OF EVIL

Library of Religious Philosophy

NUMBER 8